The Western Allies and Soviet Potential in World War II

World War II was the largest and most devastating war in modern history with far-reaching consequences. The single most important campaign was the Soviet–German war, which consumed the lion share of Germany's military resources. In contrast to the tone in German and Anglo-American pre-campaign assessments, the USSR ws able to repulse the invasion after huge losses and turn the table on Germany and her minor Axis allies.

This book examines how the two most important Western Allies in World War II, the United States and the United Kingdom, assessed the economic and military potential of the Soviet Union in 1939–1945. Since the USSR was the single most important military contributor to the Allied victory in Europe, and the main target of Germany's military strength, these assessments are of paramount importance in order to understand how the Anglo-Americans perceived the overall war situation and adjusted their own war effort in accordance with it. Utilising a wide range of documents produced by the Anglo-Americans during and shortly before World War II, this book explores why Soviet strength was underestimated, and how the Soviet economic system, Soviet society and military capabilities were viewed by Western Government observers.

The Western Allies and Soviet Potential in World War II is a fascinating read for those in academia studying economic history, international economics and security studies, especially areas on military and strategic.

Martin Kahn is a Swedish economic historian. He is a docent (associate professor) affiliated with the Department of Economy and Society at the University of Gothenburg, Sweden.

Routledge Explorations in Economic History

Edited by Lars Magnusson, Uppsala University, Sweden

For a full list of titles in this series, please visit www.routledge.com/series/SE0347

The Western Allies and Soviet Potential in World War II

Economy, Society and Military Power

Martin Kahn

Routledge
Taylor & Francis Group

LONDON AND NEW YORK

First published 2017 by Routledge

2 Park Square, Milton Park, Abingdon, Oxfordshire OX14 4RN
52 Vanderbilt Avenue, New York, NY 10017

Routledge is an imprint of the Taylor & Francis Group, an informa business

First issued in paperback 2019

British Library Cataloguing in Publication Data
A catalogue record for this book is available from the British Library

Library of Congress Cataloging in Publication Data
A catalog record for this book has been requested

ISBN: 978-1-138-92737-7 (hbk)
ISBN: 978-0-367-87373-8 (pbk)

Typeset in Times New Roman
by Taylor & Francis Books

Contents

Abbreviations

ABC	America, Britain, Canada
AI	Air Intelligence (British)
BEW	Board of Economic Warfare (US)
CCS	Combined Chiefs of Staff (US and British)
CIA	Central Intelligence Agency
CIC	Combined Intelligence Committee (US and British)
CID	Committee of Imperial Defence (British)
CIGS	Chief of the Imperial General Staff (British)
COI	Coordinator of Information (US)
COS	Chiefs of Staff (British)
DMI	Director of Military Intelligence (British)
FBI	Federal Bureau of Investigation
FO	Foreign Office (British)
FPC	Foreign Policy Committee
G-2	US Army Intelligence (equivalent to MID)
GDP	gross domestic product
GNP	gross national product
IIC	Industrial Intelligence Centre (British)
JCS	Joint Chiefs of Staff (US)
(British) JIC	Joint Intelligence Sub-Committee (of the COS)
(US) JIC	Joint Intelligence Committee
JPS	Joint Planning Staff (US)
MEW	Ministry of Economic Warfare (British)
MI	Military Intelligence (British)
MID	Military Intelligence Division (US)
MIS	Military Intelligence Service (US)
NID	Naval Intelligence Division (British)
NKVD	People's Commissariat of Internal Affairs (Soviet secret police)
OKH	*Oberkommando des heeres* (German Army High Command)
OKW	*Oberkommando der Wehrmacht* (German Armed Forces High Command)
ONI	Office of Naval Intelligence (US)
OSS	Office of Strategic Services (US)

PHP	Post Hostilities Planning Committee (British)
R & A	Research and Analysis Branch, OSS (US)
RAF	Royal Air Force
RG	Record Group
SAF	Soviet Air Force
SD	State Department (US Department of State)
SIS	Secret Intelligence Service (British)
UPA	University Publications of America
USSBS	United States Strategic Bombing Survey
VCIGS	Vice-Chief of the Imperial General Staff (British)
WD	War Department (US)
WO	War Office (British)

1 Introduction

"Perception is also truth because it is an imperative that causes us to act."
Robert Kershaw[1]

1.1 General background

The general subject of this book is the United States and the British government's assessments and perceptions of the Soviet Union during the World War II period, with specific focus on war potential. There has always been interaction between Russia and the West, but World War II (and the subsequent Cold War) made this interaction of greater importance than ever before. World War II was the most destructive and no doubt one of the most important wars in the history of mankind. Nowhere on Earth was this truer than in Eastern Europe. According to V. Mastny, June 1941 – when Nazi Germany and her Axis allies begun their invasion the USSR – can be considered "one of the great turning points in history."[2] The conflict between Germany and the USSR devastated large parts of Eastern and Central Europe, and tens of millions died. The Soviet–German conflict was the single largest military campaign in World War II and the most decisive factor Germany's defeat. Germany committed about four-fifths of her total ground forces on that front and was caused a corresponding proportion of her total military losses there.[3] The campaign was also of paramount importance for the Western Allies for exactly the same reasons.

Most American and British government observers predicted, when Germany attacked the USSR, that the Red Army shortly would suffer a decisive defeat. If the war had developed in accordance with these pessimistic predictions the British, and – in the long run – the US strategic situation would have been worsened very seriously. There would have been no credible enemy, in terms of military strength, opposing Germany on the European continent, and the overall Japanese strategic situation in the Far East would have improved.[4] The final outcome, however, was different. Since the Red Army defeated the bulk of Germany's military might, the United States and Great Britain were able to fight the war with more flexibility and without sustaining the huge losses suffered by the Soviet and German Armed Forces. The major Soviet effort against Germany limited the Anglo-American need to commit large ground forces, as the British was forced to do in World War I. Averell Harriman, an adviser and personal friend to President Roosevelt, believed that the president had it in his mind "that if the great armies of Russia could stand up to the Germans, this might well make it possible for us to limit our participation largely to naval and air power".[5]

The outcome of the war elevated the United States and the USSR to superpower status. In 1945 the Red Army had reached Berlin and Central Europe. The Soviet victory over Germany, and the subsequent establishment of Soviet satellite states in Eastern Europe, can to a large extent explain why the USSR achieved that status. Now the former allies became locked in the Cold War that would dominate international politics for more than 40 years. It is well known that the West and especially the United States tried to assess the economic and military strength of the USSR during the Cold War, but in fact these assessments begun in earnest already during World War II. The core story of this account is about these assessments and their implications.

1.2 War potential and the general purpose of this study

In the history of international great power politics, war, and the capacity to wage war, has always been of paramount importance. It is therefore only natural that the ability to assess the military capabilities of other nations is of interest for most countries. The course of World War II, and other conflicts, has to a certain extent been influenced by the belligerents' mutual assessments of intentions and capabilities. Many of these assessments were erroneous but still greatly influenced events. One obvious example is the Japanese pre-Pearl Harbor-attack expectation in 1941 that the United States would seek a compromise peace with them after their initial military successes. Another, more recent, example is the US Bush administration's allegation that Iraq possessed weapons of mass destruction, which could be a potential danger to the West. History is full of examples like this, and more of them, concerning World War II and the USSR, will be scrutinized below.

That perception of Soviet military strength had some relevance to British and US policy in some specific respects shortly before, and during the war, has already been stated in more general terms by some scholars.[6] The purpose of this study is to show the "missing" aspect of the Anglo-American picture of the USSR during World War II. The study deals with what they knew about military operations and capabilities, but also their assessments of the underlying economic strength, and the ability of Soviet society in general to wage war. By doing this it is not only possible to add another dimension to the reality of Anglo-American perceptions and decision making during the war, but also to gain some additional insight into how the USSR was perceived by the US and British governments on the eve of the Cold War.

However, it can be risky to *directly* connect the assessments with decisions made by the US and British Governments. An approach like this would require documents (of any kind) that could show that a *specific* decision was dependent on (wholly or partly) perceptions of Soviet strength. Even if it had been possible to find such documents the approach would have required extensive investigations of other more politically oriented sources than those included in this study. Besides, in the words of Laqueur: "Intelligence is an essential service, but only a service. It is important in the decision-making process, but only one element; its usefulness depends entirely on how it is used and guided."[7]

On the other hand, this does not exclude that Anglo-American assessments really had some impact on US and British policy in 1939–1945. Earlier research on the connection between intelligence – in this respect meant to include assessments and perceptions – and the decision making process seem to support the notion that the former influenced the later to some extent. Referring to the 1939 situation Herndon claims that the British Prime Minister Chamberlain was "very much influenced" by intelligence assessments. Neilson argues that: "The international position and the perceived military strength of the [USSR ...] were important factors in the British diplomacy."[8] That intelligence really had importance for policy during the 1930s, not only regarding the USSR, has been claimed by many scholars.[9] It is therefore, as stated, possible to add another dimension to the background of Anglo-American decision making during the war, as well as at the beginning of the Cold War.

Extensive mappings of British wartime intelligence, like those of Hinsley and others, have shown how the British reacted on the actions of the Germans on the Soviet-German front, but there must also have been a specific view of the Soviet strength, and the internal situation in the USSR. According to Matloff little was known in Washington about Soviet capabilities in 1941 – "a condition that was to obtain throughout the war".[10] Is this true? This study is an attempt to get behind the superficial picture of the Soviet war effort, painted by large and well known events (e.g. victory at Stalingrad), and investigate how the Western Allies really perceived Soviet military-economic capabilities as a factor in the war. This, in turn, makes room for an in-depth study of the many aspects of Soviet society, as seen from the perspective of the Western Allies. War potential as such is comprised of a large array of economic and military related factors, and the object of the Anglo-American interest was at the time the world's only purely planned economy and communist great power.

Notes

1 Kershaw (2000), 8.
2 Mastny (1979), 307.
3 Ellis (1993), 229, 255.
4 In 1935 armed clashes between the Soviets and the Japanese began, which culminated in 1939 in the Japanese defeat in the battle of Khalkin-Gol. The Soviets also supported the Chinese side in the Sino-Japanese war from 1937, and had

supported anti-Japanese guerrillas in Manchuria already in 1935. A Soviet–Japanese Neutrality Pact was signed in In April 1941, but the countries still had large forces facing each other until 1945. Coox (1990), 94; Coox (1993), 68–69; Coox (2012).

5 Harriman had known Roosevelt since childhood, and he was Roosevelt's special envoy to Great Britain and the USSR during the war. In October 1943 he was appointed US ambassador to Moscow until 1946. Harriman & Abel (1976), vii; Dear & Foot (eds.) (1995), 523–524.

6 See, for example, Matloff (1960) and Neilson (1993).

7 Laqueur (1985), 344.

8 Neilson (1993), 219; Neilson (1983), 309.

9 See, for example, Niedhart (1983), 292–293; Niedhart (1995), 122–123, 131; Niedhart (1987), 22–23; Niedhart (1985).

10 Matloff (1959), 4.

2 The Anglo-American assessments in a wider context

The following sections provide a wider context for understanding the meaning, nature and importance of the Anglo-American assessments. They are in many cases tantamount in nature to the intelligence estimates that, for example, the US Central Intelligence Agency (CIA) made during the Cold War, regarding Soviet intentions and capabilities. However, in this case a much larger array of government organizations has been taken into account; practically all the US and British organizations that made assessments and/or processed information about the USSR. The estimates were of course influenced by what the analysts and government observers believed to be important for understanding the internal situation in the USSR.

2.1 The US and British government organizations responsible for assessing the USSR

Most of the source material used in this study originates from the US and British government institutions responsible for the assessment of internal conditions in other countries 1939–1945. Far from all the information taken into consideration was collected and produced by intelligence agencies in the strict sense (e.g. military intelligence). There is also a lot of information which was produced by, for example, the US Department of State (SD) and the British Foreign Office (FO). Regardless of which institution that produced the intelligence – in the broader sense of the word – it was often widely distributed among various other government organs, and was frequently part of the agenda at different kinds of government meetings. It is of course impossible to take account of all the informal ways that information was distributed among government officials, even though memoirs and biographies can shed some limited light on that issue.

There was also a considerable exchange of information between the British and the Americans during the war, which included the analysis of each other's intelligence assessments, and the production of common intelligence reports. It is apparent that at least the Americans took some interest in the British analysis of the Soviet situation, even before the US war entry. The British and the Americans had already reached provisional agreements on the exchange of intelligence by the spring of 1941. By 1942 the collaboration became more intimate through the establishment of new agreements. Intelligence missions were exchanged between Washington and London by 1941.[1] When the war ended the British and Americans had been through four years of close intelligence cooperation.[2]

2.1.1 British and combined Anglo-American government institutions

Some of the most useful British organizations for the purpose of this study were military-related intelligence agencies, such as the Joint Intelligence Sub-Committee (JIC) and the different Military Intelligence Sections (e.g. the MI3 and the MI14). Material from several other military organizations, such as the Chiefs of Staff (COS), the Naval Intelligence Division (NID) and the intelligence agencies of the Air Ministry have also been useful to a certain extent. The FO and its representatives all around the world, especially those in the USSR, sent assessments back to London on Soviet matters. The most interesting information for the purpose of this study often came from the military attachés, which were a part of the diplomatic legations. When the Soviet–German war started in 1941 the British upgraded its representation in Moscow and sent a special military mission, the 30 Military Mission, which produced many assessments. One of the principal tasks of the Mission was to collect intelligence on the Soviet Union's power and capacity to fight the Germans, in order to help the London intelligence agencies in their evaluations.[3] Several other British Government departments were involved in assessing the USSR, most notably the Ministry of Economic Warfare (MEW).

All of these government institutions exchanged information between themselves to some extent. However, the JIC was the only intelligence agency whose function specifically was to compile intelligence from all the other institutions. The JIC representatives came from several other institutions, especially the military service departments. The FO (the JIC chairman was a FO representative) and the MEW were also represented. The JIC and the military service ministries handled strategic estimates during the war. The JIC was also to receive attention and feedback from the prime minister, or from members of his personal staff.[4] The organization was important in this context, since it also had the task of "ensuring that any Government action which might have to be taken should be based on" the best available information.[5] The COS was also a central organization, but had no direct responsibility for the collection of intelligence. Both organizations were coordinating agencies.[6]

Before the war much information circulated through the COS, which at that time was a sub-committee to the Committee of Imperial Defence (CID). The principal members of the COS were the chief of the general staff and the chief of the air force, in addition to the First Sea Lord. Sometimes the prime minister and the minister of defence attended the meetings. When war broke out in 1939 the CID ceased to exist, and instead the COS became a permanent committee with the responsibility of reporting to the War Cabinet.[7] The War Cabinet consisted of the inner circle of top party leaders.[8]

As already indicated there existed formal bodies for the exchange and evaluation of intelligence between the Anglo-Americans. The British JIC had the role of presenting its views to the US Joint Intelligence Committee (US JIC), and vice versa. In addition it had the role of assisting the US JIC with the preparation of papers that were to be presented to the Combined Chiefs of Staff (CCS).[9] The Combined Intelligence Committee (CIC) was formed in February 1942, by the combination of the US JIC and that part of the British JIC which was stationed in Washington. The task of the CIC was to prepare appreciations for the CCS. Later, at the beginning of March 1942, the Americans established their own JIC department in Whitehall. From August 1942 the US JIC and the British Washington JIC met as the Combined Intelligence Sub-Committee.[10] Intelligence cooperation was not limited to the JIC, but took place during the war between the British Admiralty and the US Naval Department, between the Royal Air Force (RAF) and the US Air Force, and between the British Military Intelligence (MI) and the War Department (WD).[11] In addition to this there were many other arrangements that fostered intelligence exchange between the British and the Americans on many levels in their respective war organizations.[12] The Office of Strategic Services (OSS), for example, had access to some British intelligence (e.g. material from the MEW).[13]

2.1.2 US government institutions

According to Farago the state of US Army intelligence (the Military Intelligence Division or G-2) left a great deal to ask for up to mid-1942. President Roosevelt mistrusted Army military intelligence. Intelligence was, relatively speaking, a low priority area in the US Armed Forces. Roosevelt had not, unlike Churchill, much faith in the usefulness of intelligence. On the other hand, he had great trust in Colonel William J. Donovan, who became the head of the first independent US intelligence organization (see below). Roosevelt summoned Donovan to the White House in January 1942 and allegedly told him that "We have no Intelligence Service!" But the state of US intelligence was not as bad as one might believe from the President's statement, not even before mid-1942.[14]

Just as in the British case many of the organizations useful for this study on the US side were mainly of military origin. These were the Military Intelligence Division (MID or G-2) – from March 1942 the MID became the Military Intelligence Service (MIS) – the JIC and the Joint Chiefs of Staff (JCS). There were also organizations of civilian and mixed military-civilian composition such as the SD and the OSS, and its predecessor the Office of the Coordinator of Information (COI). The intelligence organizations of the Navy, the Office of Naval Intelligence (ONI), and the air force also produced intelligence on the USSR, but to a somewhat lesser extent.

The SD evaluated much of the intelligence and the reports that reached the US administration. Both the secretary of state and the president took part in these evaluations to various extents. The military's agencies for information analysis were more specialized. At the time of Pearl Harbor the cooperation between the MID and the ONI was only sporadic, but their efforts were coordinated by the Joint Army-Navy Board (the predecessor to the JCS), which created[15] the US JIC. Intelligence was also coordinated from July 1941 via Colonel William J. Donovan, who was appointed COI by the President. Donovan's task was to collect and analyse all intelligence related to national security.[16] The COI was to manage the flow of information from other agencies and produce vital syntheses of existing facts. Donovan turned to professional academics from many disciplines.[17] Before the COI the US had no central organization for economic intelligence comparable to the British MEW.[18]

After the outbreak of war Donovan's organization evolved into the OSS.[19] Among other things the OSS compiled reports on a very large number of subjects related to the US war effort. Some of these reports were called Research and Analysis reports ("R & A reports"). The R & A reports were initially prepared by the Office of the COI, subsequently by the Research and Analysis Branch of the OSS, and, from September 1945, by various organizational units of the SD.[20] Most of the people employed in the R & A branch during the war were academics educated at the Ivy League schools.[21]

There was no direct US equivalent to the British 30 Military Mission in Moscow until October 1943, when a Military Mission was established which included all military liaison activities, including Lend-Lease supplies. Before the mission the US had been represented by its ambassador, the military and naval attachés, and by the agency called the US Supply Mission. The new Military Mission absorbed the US Military Attaché Office,[22] and no military attaché or other direct representative of the G-2 was appointed. Attempts were instead made to require information for the G-2 from the British or directly from the Soviets.[23]

A well-informed reader might wonder why the US Lend-Lease authorities are not included in this review of US organizations. On the direction of President Roosevelt the Lend-Lease authorities made no effort to evaluate Soviet needs. There were no attempts to determine the uses of the equipment the Soviets received.[24] Kestner concluded – concerning the Lend-Lease authorities – that: "It is safe to assume that never in history has so much commercial activity produced so little economic knowledge about another country."[25]

2.2 The origins, analysis and dissemination of information

The sources used in this study mostly consist of reports and papers made by the described US and British Government institutions. One of the two most common variants is the comprehensive report/paper, made in the US or in Great Britain by a central intelligence institution or the SD and the FO. These reports were often about the whole spectrum of Soviet war potential, but could also be about a specific subject related to it. The sources used were often varied (e.g. books, official Soviet statistics, interviews, papers or reports produced by another government institution, or diplomatic reports). The second variant is the diplomatic report, which almost always consisted of a paper prepared by an official at the embassy in the USSR or another diplomatic legation inside or sometimes in a country neighbouring the USSR.[26] These reports, or "despatches", could, in turn, be exactly like a report produced by a Government institution in Washington or London. But they were also often made up of interviews with individuals who were supposed to have insight into Soviet affairs. Official Soviet sources were often an important part of many reports. The sources used could also in certain cases be of other origin, just as long as the Anglo-American government officials believed that the source could say something about the Soviet situation. These official US and British sources are complemented by the opinions of some of the most prominent persons involved in US and British diplomacy, politics and intelligence gathering, as presented in biographies and the literature.

For the British the most obvious and extensive sources of information about other countries before the war were the diplomatic legations stationed abroad. One of their foremost tasks was to supply London with information about political, military, and economic developments in the countries where they were stationed. The embassies could obtain information from public publications or statements, observations or personal contacts.[27] During 1941, before the US war entry, the US administration received intelligence from several sources: diplomatic reports (which included reports from military attachés),[28] information from friendly countries, press and media[29], and private persons.[30] Before the war, when the US military attachés tried to obtain information about the military capabilities of the Axis powers, they worked in the same manner as other diplomats, but they also read training manuals, spoke with the officers of their host country, observed troops and military equipment on parades and manoeuvres, visited army bases and naval vessels, while at the same time exchanging information with other military attachés.[31]

During the war the different methods of collecting information changed in some ways. The British and the Americans collected their information from the same types of source. It could be through the "open" channels mentioned above, but also from confiscated documents, by the censorship of mail, interrogations of prisoners of war, espionage, air reconnaissance and signal intelligence, conducted by monitoring ciphered wireless traffic.[32] Obviously some of these methods, which were used against the Axis, could not be used against the Soviets, but some information could be acquired indirectly. According to the British JIC (May 1945), information on the Soviet Armed Forces was often obtained from German and Japanese sources, and after the German attack in 1941 the British were able to receive information on the course of operations on the Soviet-German front from the German Enigma.[33]

During the war American and British personnel often visited the Soviet Union to carry out some specific task. Many of the US experts who visited the USSR during the later stages of the war were interviewed by G-2 on their return.[34] There are also examples of the British doing the same thing.[35] The OSS used an US engineering firm doing Lend-Lease work in the USSR to acquire information about the Soviet defence industry.[36]

There were several specific problems connected with the collection of information about the USSR both before and during the war, since Soviet society to a large extent was closed to foreigners. The regime was not interested in letting foreigners know too much about the country, especially when it came to military matters or information that could be regarded as giving a negative picture of the USSR. The British embassy in Moscow had a complicated task when it came to obtaining information from the Soviet authorities before the war.[37] Furthermore – according to Kestner – since 1937 the Soviet government had enforced an effective blackout on all important economic information, especially statistics.[38] The Germans encountered these problems in their military planning against the Soviet Union. According to Wegner no figures were published in Soviet newspapers and magazines (but this allegation is not entirely true, see note 39),[39] and espionage in the usual sense of the word was almost impossible, and the reports obtained from the few people allowed to visit the USSR were often unreliable and coloured by personal prejudices.[40]

Opportunities to obtain information about Soviet conditions improved somewhat in theory after the start of the Soviet–German war, since the Anglo-American authorities could then receive confidential information from newly established military liaisons.[41] But in practice the outbreak of war hardly improved British access to Soviet sources of information[42], despite the fact that the two countries now were allies. For the British at least the indirect possibility for gaining access to information improved after June 1941, since they could decrypt secret German intelligence traffic (and the Germans now were at full scale war with the Soviets).[43] But the lack of information in general about the Soviets was often stressed in several reports from various British and US government institutions.

Contacts between Anglo-American and Soviet officials during the war were also far from problematic. In his book *Sharing Secrets with Stalin*, B. F. Smith describes the mutual suspicion that was ever present between the Soviets and the Western Allies. The Soviets were very reluctant to hand over information of any kind to the Anglo-Americans, even though more information was passed over to them during certain periods.[44] According to the British NID, which in 1942 issued a written guidance for those who came into contact with personnel from the Soviet Naval Mission, the Soviets suffered from suspicion (towards British imperialism), fear (of their own government), isolation (from foreigners), and lack of a broader education (even if they did not lack technical training). The Soviets were believed to admire and appreciate efficiency on the part of the British, which was also seen as a way to relieve their suspicion.[45] In a January 1945 memorandum addressed to the US Chief of Staff, from the commanding general of the US military mission in Moscow, the problems of collaborations with Soviet personnel were presented: distrust of foreigners;

fear of political implications; lack of confidence in US security; doubts as to the necessity of collaborating up to the present time; desire to remain operationally unhampered by the Allies and a desire to keep their people ignorant of foreign standards.[46] A British embassy official in Moscow commented in August 1945 that the "secretiveness" of the Russians was "deeply ingrained" in their character.[47]

Exchange of information even on a strictly mutual beneficial basis was often very complicated (e.g. regarding German troop dispositions and German intentions). The personnel of the British military 30 Mission, sent to Moscow in late June 1941, were often much troubled and outraged over how difficult it was to acquire intelligence from the Soviets. This often also applied to other British and American personnel who had to cooperate with the Soviets. Sometimes the Soviet authorities allowed Anglo-American personnel to travel around the USSR and inspect various facilities and installations, military as well as civilian. It seems that during the war as a whole, the Soviets were relatively more interested in providing the Americans with information than the British.[48] The Anglo-Americans also had purely administrative problems in their dealings with the Soviets. The Americans experienced problems with language barriers and different administrative practices. Apart from the fact that the Americans considered Soviet administrative practices as inferior, the Soviets also kept fewer records of their own dealings, which caused problems in the eyes of the Americans.[49]

2.3 The assessment's reliability and the selection of reports for this study

We can see that it was difficult for the Anglo-Americans to acquire information about the situation in the USSR, but even the information obtained was not always entirely trusted. Most US and British JIC reports contained paragraphs stating how problematic it was to evaluate information about the Soviet Union. This sentence, from an August 1943 US JIC report – concerning the Soviet situation, capabilities, and intentions – is typical: "It must be borne in mind that present US knowledge of the U.S.S.R. is fragmentary and lacking in precision."[50] The situation was usually considered as better at the end of the war, but still lacking in precision. The following statement from a British JIC report dated 8 May 1945 shows how the JIC valued their own intelligence information: "Our statistical knowledge of the Russian economy is limited but we are satisfied that the broad lines of our appreciation are substantially correct."[51]

Doubts as to the correctness of Soviet statistics (and other information) were sometimes expressed in despatches, papers and reports produced by the different British and US Government institutions. In this particular case meaning that the Anglo-Americans did not trust the information published by the Soviets.[52] This was of course not surprising, considering the nature of Stalin's regime, and the mutual mistrust the prevailed between the Soviets and many Anglo-American officials at the time.

Nevertheless, one must assume that the intention of US and British authorities was to produce intelligence reports and analyses that were as truthful as they could be, with the information they had at their disposal. Of course the problem of limited and unreliable information diminished the "truth value" of British and American intelligence, but what they produced was what they believed to be their best estimates. It is, of course, not impossible that some observers strived to "adjust" their analysis in one direction or another (i.e. producing reports which they did not believe to be completely true themselves) – for example, in order to satisfy some preconceived opinion of the superiors. If this was the case, it is not possible to either confirm or reject (or even identify) such suspicions with the help of the available source material.

However, it is important to be sceptical regarding how intelligence assessments was handled and interpreted by Government officials. Jackson argues that one have to consider the handling of papers within government institutions and to take account of "institutional cultures" and attitudes towards intelligence in these organizations. In addition the wider context of "political and cultural dynamics" in society has to be considered.[53] When an OSS official was interviewed many years after the war about the importance of ideology for personal opinions he stated: "Military judgments went along with ideology."[54] But even if an official for example harboured negative attitudes towards communism and the Soviets, which was common at the time, and it could be argued that this attitude influenced his assessments, it still does not mean that the official in question actually did not believe in his own assessment.

Not all diplomatic and intelligence reports found in the archives have been used in this study, only the ones that have best shown how the Anglo-American intelligence institutions assessed Soviet war potential. For example, when the Anglo-Americans themselves judged a report, from an outside source, to be less credible it has not been included. On the other hand, more or less all the reports produced by the aforementioned institutions (themselves), during the period in question, has been noted by me if they in some way had anything do with the assessments of war potential and related subjects.

2.4 The reality and contemporary perceptions of war potential

The purpose of this section is to present an overview of what war potential was in the World War II era. It is of interest to know this in order to understand what contemporary US and British observers of the USSR focused on. The concept of war potential refers to all the different factors that form the base of military strength in a country. The military force that a nation can project on the battlefield is only a manifestation of the total war potential. War potential is made up of several different factors: demographic, technological, industrial, psychological, etc.[55] It can be argued that intelligence capabilities is a part of war potential, even though this aspect was not present in the Anglo-American analyses of the Soviets at the time.

World War I is often referred to as the first total war in history, forcing all the major belligerents to convert their civilian societies to the needs of the war effort.[56] This war, which before World War II was called the Great War, exerted a heavy influence on the interwar military mentality. The Great War would in practice bring about both a widening and a change in what one can call the war potential of a nation. The industrial societies could support a total war effort on a scale unseen before. The industrialization made mass production of munitions and other necessary supplies possible.[57] In combination with the railways this laid the foundations for armies numbering several million men. Technical progress, greatly facilitated by industrialization, also contributed to the introduction of new and more lethal armaments. World War I resulted in the introduction of the tank, and a use of massed air power, both of which would have importance for the development of interwar military doctrines. In terms of firepower, though, artillery was still the single most important arm.

Relatively these advances greatly increased the combat troop's firepower, but not yet so much mobility. The tanks used from 1916 onwards were not yet sufficiently technically advanced (and also relatively few) to allow for a decisive impact. An aircraft could deliver firepower and thereby facilitate a breakthrough in the enemy front, but it could not hold ground. The dominance of firepower over mobility, and the general experience of the Great War, would affect the military doctrines formulated by the major power during the interwar years.

The fact that industrially manufactured war materials became more and more important was something that many were well aware of when the war raged, even if these realizations became fully apparent only after the initial phase.[58] The size of the armies, modern technology and industrial capacity lessened the importance of the art of war.[59] After the war the concept of industrial mobilization became widespread. Plans to convert the economy and the industry to war production, in the event of a new large-scale war, were made in Europe and the United States.[60]

As for the social and psychological aspect of war potential the war as such also gave examples of how revolutionary moods and the reluctance to fight among the populations of the several of the Great Powers – Russia, Austria-Hungary and even Germany – came to influence the outcome of the war and contribute to these countries suing for peace. It is true that this influence to a certain extent had its beginning in earlier military defeats during the war and the sea blockades (in the case of Germany and Austria-Hungary), which, in turn, partly could be explained by military-industrial shortcomings in comparison to their enemies; but factors like these nevertheless contributed to the outcome of the war.[61] As we will see, the notion of a breakdown in military resistance, based on the idea of a weakness (other than economic deficiencies) of the society upholding the military strength, was also present in World War II.

During the interwar years the military doctrines of the Great Powers took different forms in different countries. Innovative ideas concerning tank warfare were discussed during the interwar years by military thinkers, and some advocated that air power and especially bomber aircraft would be the decisive weapon of the future. The French and the British, the victors of the Great War, shaped their doctrines along defensive World War I lines. German military thinking was more offensive; it emphasized movement, speed, surprise and exploitation as central elements in warfare. The so-called German *Blitzkrieg* doctrine, used so successfully by the German Army during the initial period of World War II, was already embraced in principle by the military theorists by the 1920s. *Blitzkrieg* was in practice an adaptation of these principles to tanks and motorized troops.[62] The doctrine was foremost a tactical and operational instrument for achieving a breakthrough that could be exploited, and it was not a complete concept even after the Polish campaign.[63]

Regardless of preferred doctrine, the increased significance of aircraft and tanks as means of warfare, suggested that future wars would be even more capital intensive than in 1914–18. Major Desmond Morton, director of the British Industrial Intelligence Centre (IIC), an organization created to monitor the military-industrial preparedness of foreign countries, had a vision which he expressed in May 1937: "in the next war of national effort the economic front will be of more importance than the front line, in so far as the latter can only be maintained by a constant stream of highly-mechanized weapons and large quantities of relatively precision-made material."[64]

The concept of war potential was not something unfamiliar to observers outside the circle of government-employed experts. In his book *The Military Strength of the Powers*, written by the end of the 1930s, Max Werner describes what he calls "The elements of war potential". Manpower and economic resources, and the extent to which these resources had been adapted for military needs, are described as decisive for military capabilities. However, large manpower reserves can only be of military value if they are connected with an effective economic system. Werner argued therefore that the basis for war potential is economic potential. But economic war potential is greater than industrial potential since it also includes the availability and supply of raw materials and foodstuffs. Furthermore, economic potential (in combination with the availability of manpower) cannot be regarded as equal to war potential, since the preparedness for war – both material and moral – also plays a part in certain crucial stages of a war. Preparedness for war includes both the development of war industries, the ability to convert all industry to the purpose of war and a "militarization" of the population. This permits a country well prepared for war to defeat another country of similar economic strength, before the other country succeeds in converting its economic strength to military strength.[65]

The concept of war potential was also mentioned in the contemporary press. An example of this is an article from *The Economist* in April 1939, with the title "Russia's war potential". The article put forward several factors of importance for war potential. Military and civil morale were two of these factors, but it was mainly economic factors that were emphasized, such as the capacity of factories to support the armed forces and industrial production.[66]

The increased international tension of the 1930s contributed to a rearmament race.[67] Werner commented on Europe's rearmament: "Compared with 1939

European armaments in 1932 seem almost like a plaything both in quality and quantity. Between 1932 and 1939 lie the biggest revolution in military technique and the most violent armament race the world has ever seen."[68] The kinship between wartime mobilization and governmental programs responding to the economic crisis of the 1930s seems apparent. As all the major industrial nations, one after another, expanded arms manufacture, the pace of improvement in weapons design suddenly accelerated, especially for airplanes and tanks. Superior designs of a given year, once put into production, was obsolete two or three years later.[69]

But tanks and aircraft were far from the only weapons of importance, both in the Soviet–German war as well as in other theatres of war. Between the periods of breakthroughs and quick overland exploits, which often happened during dry weather periods, warfare was still characterized by long and relatively static fronts facing each other over no man land. Artillery still played a very important role.[70] The importance of artillery for land warfare in Europe during World War II is highlighted by Kennedy: "the Second World War in Europe was preeminently a gunner's war and a tank crew's war".[71] All the divisions[72] of the major combatants had, regardless of arm, at least one sub-unit consisting only of artillery. Artillery was also, like the air force, the only arm that had a long striking range on the battlefield.[73] Motorized artillery was also used more frequently as the war progressed. The different military units were also equipped with machine guns, mortars, anti-tank guns, anti-aircraft guns and – for the single infantry man – rifles, sub-machine guns, hand grenades and later in the war hand-held anti-tank weapons. But there is no doubt that it was heavy weapons that were relatively more important for the conduct of warfare.

Infantry and other more lightly armed units still, however, played an important role during the Soviet-German war, and many other fronts. The number of infantry divisions was always in a majority during the war in relation to other more capital-intensive units such as armoured divisions, mechanized divisions, motorized divisions and artillery divisions.[74] And just as there were artillery units in every division there were also infantry units of some kind in almost every German or Soviet division, regardless of arm.[75] Despite its low relative contribution to enemy losses and modest role in mobile offensive operations infantry were nevertheless a basic ingredient of the armies, which had to be supplied with war materiel. It is also important to remember the importance of transport vehicles as an integral part of military units. The core of mobile warfare in World War II was not only provided by aircraft and tanks, but also by trucks.[76]

The trucks were also of great importance for the supply system, of which no army could do without. Measured as tonne-kilometres, most supply (in the Soviet–German war) was carried on the railways, but from the railway head to the troops other means of transport must be available. Apart from trucks and weapons the armed forces also consumed a lot of other industrially manufactured materiel, and a substantial amount of food.[77]

Naval warfare played a very modest role in the Soviet-German war, compared to other theatres in World War II, even if naval units from both sides participated, and the naval aspect was a part of the Anglo-American assessments.

It is possible to make a distinction between contemporary perceptions of war potential and later research on the subject, but there is no great need for this distinction. This has already been shown to a certain extent by the references to contemporary observers above, but it can also be illustrated by reports produced by the very institutions that assessed Soviet capabilities in 1939–1945.[78]

Notes

1 Hinsley (1981), 41.
2 Smith (1992), 50.
3 The office of the DMI was the main "contact point" of the 30 Mission in White-hall. Smith (1992), 51–52.
4 Cradock (2002), 13, 16, 19, 22. The JIC was a sub-committee of the COS. Dear & Foot (eds.) (1995), 1154.
5 In 1941 the Joint Intelligence Staff was created, which was an important drafting sub-committee to the JIC. Herman (1996), 260–261.
6 Smith (1996), 203.
7 CAB 53.
8 Harriman & Abel (1976), 125.
9 16-3-1942, MM(S)(42)10, CAB122/1584.
10 The British JIC in London made their contributions to the combined appreciations through its Washington branch. The British JIC's Washington department also had civilian representatives, from the MEW and the FO. Hinsley (1981), 42–44.
11 Ibid, 47–49.
12 Between the OSS and the British SIS, just to mention one example. Hinsley (1981), 50–58.
13 Smith (1983), 172.
14 Farago (1961), 205–215.
15 The British JIC assisted the Americans to establish a JIC of their own. Hinsley (1981), 41.
16 Kahn (1984), 487–489; According to Kestner Donovan was a man of complex and often contradictory tendencies: "an Irish Catholic who was an Anglophile, a Republican seeking favor from a Democratic Administration, and a decorated war hero who envisioned an intelligence agency embracing professional academics". Kestner (1999), 18.
17 Ibid, 18–19.
18 Hinsley (1981), 46.
19 Kahn (1984), 487–489.
20 M1221, RG59.
21 Smith (1983), 361.
22 Deane (1947), 10–12.
23 Matloff (1959), 290.
24 Gaddis (1972), 82.
25 Kestner (1999), 34. Apart from this the Soviet authorities requested, and received, a large variety of material, covering almost every aspect of warfare and material life. Jones (1969), 114–115, 119.
26 According to Falkehed "human intelligence" was the most important means of available when assessing the military capabilities of other nations at the time. The attaché was in, turn, the most important source of "human intelligence". Falkehed (1994), 83–84.

27 Hinsley (1979), 45–46, 52–53.
28 The diplomatic reports were based on personal observations, newspapers, conversations with officials or private citizens in the host nation, and on exchange of information with other diplomats. Kahn (1984), 479.
29 This category included newspapers, magazines, radio, books and news movies.
30 However, according to Kahn, the United States did not use spies before the outbreak of war, since it was not believed that the extra information that could be obtained from these outweighed the potential damage that such methods could have on relations with other countries. Therefore there were no US agents in foreign countries. Kahn (1984), 479–480.
31 Ibid.
32 At the end of the 1930s the coded wireless traffic was impossible to decipher. Hinsley (1987), 209.
33 8–5-1945, JIC(45)148(0)(Final)(Limited Circulation), CAB81/128; Hinsley (1981), 68. British decrypts of German Enigma traffic proved to be a valuable British source of information on the Soviet Armed Forces after the start of the Soviet-German war. Hinsley (1981), 58.
34 Smith (1996), 176.
35 16–6-1943, "Some [...]", CAB121/465.
36 Smith (1996), 160.
37 Hinsley (1979), 45–46, 52–53.
38 Kestner (1999), 23.
39 Wegner is wrong concerning this specific fact, since many British and American reports before and during the Soviet-German war were partly based on figures derived from Soviet newspapers and magazines. If they really believed these figures is of course another matter.
40 Wegner (1987), 294–295. As a matter of fact, racist delusions still played a part in American assessments concerning Japan at the time of World War II. Kahn (1984), 476–477.
41 A Soviet military delegation sent to London, a British military delegation sent to Moscow and the office of the US military attaché in Moscow. Smith (1996), 33.
42 On 24 July 1941 Stafford Cripps, for example, reported to the FO that "my sources of information are extremely restricted". 24–7-1941, "From [...]", CAB163/2.
43 Hinsley (1981), 67–68.
44 Smith (1996). Hinsley has also described how the British authorities found that they had considerable problems when it came to exchanging intelligence with the Soviets. Hinsley (1981), 58–66.
45 23–8-1942, "N.I.D.04316/42", ADM223/506.
46 22–1-1945, "Memorandum [...]", Part 1: The Soviet Union, Records of the JCS, UPA1981.
47 1–8-1945, N10346/928/38, FO371/47933.
48 Smith (1996).
49 Gaddis (1972), 81.
50 20–8-1943, JIC72dMtg, 625–2(JIC 129) (1st Revision) (20–8-1943), Box-214, RG218.
51 8–5-1945, JIC(45)148(0) (Final) (Limited Circulation), CAB81/128.
52 See for example 22–1-1940, "The [...]", WO208/5171 and 20–7-1939, N3505/18/38, FO371/23677.
53 Jackson (2008), 9.
54 OSS Oral History Project Transcripts, Box-2., RG263.
55 Knorr (1979), 3–4, 40–41.
56 Johansson (1991), 194; Haythornthwaite (1992), 336, 338; Luraghi (2001), 62.
57 Johansson (1991), 82; McNeill (1982), 223–232.
58 Haythornthwaite (1992), 330; Johansson (1991), 189; Knorr (1979), 36–37.

59 Knorr (1979), 32, 37; Samuelson (1999), 30, 34, 42–49.
60 Samuelson (1999), 77–81; Wark (1985), 160–161.
61 Johansson (1991), 194–195, 210, 223–225; Knorr (1979), 92.
62 Johansson (1991), 236–260, 275–286; Dunn (1980), 5.
63 Lord (2001), 66–69.
64 Wark (1985), 160.
65 Werner (1939), 13–16.
66 22-4-1939, "Russia's […]", Box-3133, Entry-77, RG 165.
67 Keegan (ed.) (1989), 30–36; Abelshauser (1998), 123–124, 127, 131; Davies (1998), 51, 59; McNeill (1983), 350.
68 Werner (1939), 13.
69 McNeill (1983), 346, 350.
70 Johansson (1991), 337.
71 Kennedy (1989), 353.
72 The word division is frequently used in literature that deals with militarily related matters. Division is a military unit that comprises a large array of different troops still under a unified command. A German division during the Second World War could, in its theoretical setup, comprise between 10,000 and 17,200 men (depending on which specific arm it belonged to) and, for example, contain infantry, artillery, anti-tank units and engineer units. In some cases, the Soviet Army could call some units which in size corresponded to a division, a corps. The role of a division in the military organization during the war can be described as being the main building blocks of the armies. Ellis (1993), 201, 203–204; Johansson (1991), 353.
73 Ellis (1993), 203–207, 222–223, 305–306.
74 Ziemke (1968), 7–9; Erickson (1975), 98; Salmaggi & Pallavisini (1997), 140–141; Ellis (1993), 117–124, 137–139, 169–170, 223, Table 36 (statistical appendix).
75 Ellis (1993), 203–207, 222–223.
76 Overy (1996), 210.
77 According to a US MID 1942 estimate, a June 1941 Soviet infantry division, apart from weapons, armoured vehicles, and trucks, was equipped with 6000 horses, 1500 wagons, 100 rolling kitchens, 50 motorcycles, 110 tractors, 25 cars, 101 radios, 73 radio-telephones, 702 telephones, 68 switchboards, 1041 km insulated wire, 40 km bare wire, 5 telegraph sets, 58 dogs and 30 pigeons. 1-4-1942, "Russian […]", CCS350.05USSR, Box-212, RG218.
78 See the following sources for more examples concerning contemporary perceptions of war potential: 8–10-1943, "ACASI/250A/43", ADM223/506; 10-11-1943, "Major […]", Box-3100, Entry-77, RG165; USSBS 1945a, ix, 1; USSBS 1945b, iii, 6–11; Knorr (1979), 40–41, Chapter 3, Part II and part III.

3 The Soviet Union and the West

The pre-war experience and international Great Power politics before World War II

The Bolsheviks came to power in late 1917 and shortly after the Russian Civil War Soviet Russia was formally transformed into the USSR. The Bolshevik's agenda was from the very beginning anti-capitalistic and anti-imperialistic, and therefore by implication also anti-Western. Onto this came the Western intervention in the civil war. Even though the events of World War I pushed the political agenda leftwards in the whole of Europe, Communist parties never took lasting control anywhere in Europe outside the USSR. The Soviet Communist party was representing a world order that included the abolishment of capitalism and the Western Power's still existing colonial empires. Even though the attempts to export the revolution westwards was abolished for the moment in the USSR during the 1920s, the Bolsheviks and the USSR was still considered to be a potential threat in the eyes of many Western observers. This threat was accentuated by the fact that domestic Communist parties had been established in the West after the Russian revolution and World War I. Many of these parties were politically loyal to Moscow.

The estrangement between Russia and the West was not only based on the establishment of one party state Communism, but was to a certain extent present long before. There are several aspects that can be mentioned in this context depending on time period and preference. Going as far back as the Middle Ages brings to mind the schism between Western Catholicism and Orthodox Christianity, of which Russia was the foremost proponent of after the fall of the Byzantine/East Roman Empire. During the early modern era Russia became increasingly backwards in comparison to the growing economic power of the West. Although being of vast extent and having a large population at the beginning of 20th century, the Russian empire were still backwards economically, socially and politically in comparison to the West. Even though the West at the time was not yet fully-fledged democracies, by 21st century standards, Russia was looked down upon. Keith Neilson argues that "Tsarist Russia had been generally viewed with distaste in Britain".[1] From the late 19th century the American public opinion became increasingly aware of human rights abuse in Russia, and the shift to a negative image of Russia came before communism.[2]

In World War I, Imperial Russia became a useful ally to the Western Entente Powers in their common struggle against the Central Powers. The backwardness of Tsarist Russia contributed greatly to her ultimate defeat in the war. After the downfall of the Tsarist regime in the early months of 1917 the new provisional Government was soon recognized by the Entente. But the economic and military realities did not change for the better. After eight months of shaky government the regime fell due to a Bolshevik coup, and the so called October revolution was a reality. The Bolshvik's agenda included a separate peace with Germany, in order to help bring Russia out of the ongoing chaos and economic deterioration. This move, and the far leftist politics of the Bolsheviks, made Soviet Russia the enemy of the Entente. The later intervened on the side of the Bolshevik's enemies in the Civil War, but could not stop the Red's ultimate victory.

The negative picture of Russia in general could now – after the October revolution – also be complemented by a Red Scare in the United States.[3] According to Ziegler the "Fear of 'Godless communism' and Soviet expansionism solidified anti-Russian attitudes in America in the twentieth century."[4] Not everybody in the West harboured negative attitudes towards the USSR during the interwar years. With example from Britain Neilson writes that many representatives of the political left "viewed the great socialist experiment as a harbinger of the New Jerusalem". However, just as in the US the establishment of a communist regime had rather worsened the picture of the USSR in Britain from the perspective of the political right, and in terms of diplomatic relations between the UK and the USSR.

There is no doubt that there existed what may be labelled anti-communism and anti-Soviet sentiments among many officials in the US and British governments during the 1920s and the 1930s. Both the US and (especially) the British governments were afraid of the risk that the working class might be affected by Soviet propaganda during the early 1920s. There was a fear of communism in the United States during this period. This fear continued to be both extensive and intense within the leading circles of the United States. American leaders showed both in public and in private their contempt for the Bolsheviks. During the 1920s and the 1930s the US and the British police worked actively against communist groups and individuals. Military officials in both countries tended to be strongly anti-communist, and especially suspicious towards the USSR. The US and the British foreign departments were just as busy as the military during the interwar years with the perceived Soviet threat. The security services in both countries were also occupied with the monitoring of communist activities and trying to detect Soviet agents.[5] According to Smith there were always "anti-Soviet feelings" bubbling beneath the surface in many offices in London.

The USSR was relatively isolated diplomatically and her trade relations with the outside world were very limited, even in comparison with the foreign trade conducted by Tsarist Russia. In principle the Soviet regime of the mid- and late 1920s wanted to uphold the rhetoric of the revolution and the civil war years (exporting the world revolution) to some extent, but in practice the Bolsheviks concentrated on building socialism in one country. The Soviets tried to break the isolation and establish closer cooperation with the West.[6] Generally, though, Soviet-Western relations were far from good during the 1920.[7]

During the First Five Year Plan of the late 1920s and the early 1930s, the Soviets intensified foreign trade with the West, in order to gain capital equipment and know-how from the industrially more advanced West. The First Five Year Plan was very costly in terms of investments and human suffering, but the Bolsheviks made good use of their Western trade relations. Despite the extensive famine in different parts of the southern agricultural regions 1931–1933, the Soviets managed to increase industrial output substantially during the first plan, and even more so during the second plan (1933–1937). There was some knowledge in the West of what was happening in the USSR, but no observer actually knew the whole truth and political opinions coloured perceptions of events. The great depression, breaking out in the West in the early 1930s, brought down the economies of the West in a way not experienced before in modern times. As we have seen the depression contributed to a worsening of the international situation and it worked against democracy in Europe, in more countries than Germany.

The establishment of a Nazi regime in 1933 was very worrying to the Soviets and meant a change in their foreign policy. Instead of working against other – non-communist and non-Moscow loyal – left wing socialist parties in the West, which had been the official policy since the late 1920s, the Soviets now tried to promote cooperation through the so called Popular Fronts.[8] The new policy was officially launched in 1934 and included cooperation with social democrats and socialists against fascists. The realization that Nazi Germany was a potential threat was also manifested through the establishment of a Franco-Soviet defence pact in 1935. This move was not entirely uncontroversial in France. The French foreign minister was forced by his government to sign the treaty, since he believed that a pact with the USSR was neither necessary nor wanted. Due to amendments made by the Foreign Minister the Pact was not what his predecessor (and initiator of the pact) initially intended, and it became far from an effective deterrent. Hitler used the pact as a pretext to remilitarize the Rhineland, an act strictly forbidden according to the Versailles treaty.[9] As we will see this was not the last time the USSR was unwanted by Western politicians, even in security arrangements against Hitler.

Soon after annexing Austria in March 1938 Hitler demanded the Sudetenland from Czechoslovakia. The Western Powers were still interested in coming to terms with Nazi Germany and the British Premier Chamberlain believed that a satisfactory agreement could be struck with Hitler in Munich. The 1938 Munich agreement has been lively debated in the context of what actually caused World War II. This agreement, which effectively handed over a militarily and economic important part of Czechoslovakia to Hitler, can be regarded as the most conspicuous part of the appeasement policy. This policy had been pursued by Britain and France during the 1930s in order not to aggravate Nazi

Germany. In Munich the USSR (and Czechoslovakia) had been kept out of the dealings regarding Czechoslovakia's future. The Soviets had a mutual military assistance treaty with Czechoslovakia, as did the French. Even though the Soviets were excluded from the agreement the USSR could have been a factor in the defence of Czechoslovakia. According to Neilson the British "doubted [the Soviet] intention and [...] capacity to do so."[10]

Notes

1 Neilson (1993), 191.
2 Ziegler (2014), 685–686.
3 Levin (1971), 29.
4 Ziegler (2014), 686.
5 Smith (1996), 3–4, 64, 156.
6 Nekrich (1993).
7 Jabara Carley (2014).
8 Worley (ed.) (2004).
9 Ragsdale (2006).
10 Neilson (1993), 216.

4 From the guarantee to Poland to the Molotov-Ribbentropp pact

Even though the USSR was not involved in the war on a really large scale before 22 June 1941 Anglo-American, and especially British, assessments of Soviet strength were of major significance already from March 1939. These assessments were a factor in the decisions taken by the British during the period immediately before the outbreak of war (on 1 September).

4.1 British anguish: the value of the Soviet Union as an ally and the "gathering storm" in Europe

In his infamous speech, when returning from the September 1938 Munich negotiations with Adolf Hitler, British Prime Minister Neville Chamberlain stated that the agreement meant "peace for our time". However, despite the hopes of Britain and France, Hitler was not content with the Sudetenland. In March 1939 the rest of Czech territory was occupied and Slovakia became a puppet state. By this time German political pressure on Poland begun to increase. This became the last straw for the British and the French; at least as far as open appeasement was concerned.

On 31 March, Chamberlain stated in the House of Commons that the United Kingdom and France guaranteed Polish independence. The guarantee highlighted the possibility of Soviet military support to Poland. The USSR was the only Great Power, apart from Germany, which bordered Poland. Chamberlain, alongside his Secretary of State for Foreign Affairs Lord Halifax, wanted to create a "peace front" against aggression. They wanted to include as many nations as possible in this initiative but were less interested in including the USSR. With hindsight this attitude might seem strange. We know that Imperial Russia had sided with Britain and France in World War I. Russia contained large Central Power forces for more than three years, which of course was well known to most British government officials in 1939.

A more recent event was the large scale Soviet industrialization process, from the end of the 1920s. This industrialization had propelled the USSR into one of the largest industrial nations in the world. Huge investments were made in heavy, engineering and especially defence industries. It is clear from later research that Soviet war potential was greatly augmented by the forced industrialization.[1] This was also a reason for including the Soviets. But from the perspective of contemporary British observers this was not obvious, and there were also different interpretations of Soviet strength prevailing at the time. In the British Parliament references were often made to the size of the Red Army and the Soviet Air Force (SAF), and demands were made for an Anglo-Soviet agreement.[2] Anthony Eden[3] stated in the House of Commons on 19 May, when the negotiations between the Soviets and British was under way: "It seems [...] that the chief problem before us [...] is the question of the negotiations [...] between this country and Soviet Russia, for I agree with several speakers [...] – and I think nobody has dissented [...] – that the outcome of these negotiations may have the gravest significance for the future peace of the world."[4]

However, regardless of views expressed in the Parliament, and by Conservative dissenters such as Eden and Churchill, the leadership over British foreign and defence policy was ultimately residing in the hands of Chamberlain and Lord Halifax.[5] Why were Chamberlain and Halifax reluctant to include the USSR in the peace front, and what did they know about Soviet war potential? Both privately had a very negative attitude towards the USSR[6] and communism, but for the actual assessments of Soviet strength, their nearest formal source of information was different government institutions. From the relatively limited information we have about the immediate pre-1939 assessments made by these institutions (the FO, the Moscow Embassy, the COS, the War Office (WO) and prominent officials associated with these), it is possible to conclude that they held Soviet strength in very low esteem. This low regard extended to military as well as economic strength, even though some positive remarks could be noted regarding certain aspects of Soviet war potential. The Great Terror purges, climaxing in 1937–38, were seen as very damaging for economic and military strength; retarding some of the limited improvements actually accomplished before them. The USSR was not seen as ready for war yet.[7]

4.2 Soviet war potential and the possible inclusion of the USSR in a "peace front"

It is difficult to know exactly how intelligence assessments and information about the internal situation in other countries affects the decision making process, and they can only be regarded as one component among others influencing it.[8] The failure to establish Anglo-Soviet cooperation against Germany in 1939 has probably almost as many causes as there are scholars who have investigated the subject.[9] However, the relative importance and the implications of a possible cooperation with the USSR, at this crucial point in time, involved many high ranking officials. Due to this the discussions – as apart from the concrete assessments – concerning the assessments about the Soviet Union is more richly documented for posterity than after the spring of 1939, even though the volume of concrete assessments would grow immensely after June 1941. The discussion about Soviet war potential and the possible inclusion of the USSR in a common "peace front" against aggression was discussed in the Cabinet, the COS and the Foreign Policy Committee (FPC). The participants sometimes referred directly to intelligence and other reports concerning Soviet war potential.

The discussions among the British decision-makers regarding a possible Anglo-French-Soviet alliance must been seen in a wider context. The involved had all experienced, in one way or another, World War I and the following interwar political landscape, which in turn was heavily influenced by the war. The war had been an extremely taxing and tragic experience for the European nations, even for those on the winning side. Many were prepared to go to great lengths in order to avoid a future war. The war also left a lasting political legacy in Eastern and Central Europe. The war had toppled the region's authoritarian monarchies but also helped to establish Russia's communist regime; a regime seen with great suspicion by many in the West. The ascendancy of the German Nazi dictatorship did not necessarily change this outlook among British conservative politicians, even though Hitler's expansionistic policies had to be dealt with somehow.

Already in the mid-1930s British officials – two prominent examples are Anthony Eden and Robert Vansittart – harboured the idea of moving closer to the USSR due the possibility of a more expansionistic Germany. Their point of view was not shared by all members of the Cabinet. Chamberlain – from 1937 prime minister and the Conservative party leader – and other Cabinet members were anti-Soviet (and anti-Eden) as well as uninterested in cooperating with communists.[10] Whitehall officials were generally suspicious towards the Soviets and they also feared, based on information from intelligence and diplomatic sources, that a Soviet-British rapprochement might bring Japan closer to Germany.[11] The risk of a Soviet–German rapprochement was seen as remote by the opponents of British–Soviet cooperation. They also argued that such cooperation might counteract the possibility of including Germany peacefully in European affairs, and instead alienate her.[12] This outlook was based on the assumption that Germany and Hitler could be appeased.

At the time (1935), Orme Sargent, the assistant undersecretary superintending the FO's Central Department, shared this point of view. He strived for the avoidance of *any* rivalling Great Power alliances, and he did not hold the military strength or political reliability of the USSR in great esteem. The FO shifted gradually in favour of Sargent's outlook in 1935–1936. Some prominent FO officials distrusted the Soviets even more than Germany or Japan, but Manne argues that this was not the chief reason for the reluctance to move closer to the USSR. The main reason was instead, despite the obvious Soviet interest in an Anglo-Soviet rapprochement, (according to Manne) Hitler's anti-Soviet campaign. It was a very important goal of the British Government not to disrupt the chances of coming to terms with Germany. The importance of this was not lessened by the conclusion of the Franco-Soviet pact in 1935. The pact was used by Hitler in order to paint a picture of a Czech-Franco-Soviet encirclement.[13]

At the time of Munich agreement (1938) the French had the same general impression as the British regarding Soviet military strength and political reliability. Some prominent French officials even wanted to distance France from earlier security arrangements with Poland and the USSR. Even those French opposed to such a strategy – such as Chief of Army Staff General Colson – seem not to have put much confidence in the Soviet card, but instead in "Poland's fifty divisions". However, the French officials believing that Eastern Europe was worth defending, or even go to war for, eventually won the argument. If Germany would get free reigns in the region it would only strengthen her in the long run, and cost France potential allies. Therefore Soviet economic, and possibly military, support for the Eastern European countries would be essential, although it was not French perceptions of the USSR that changed, but rather the "need" for Soviet assistance.[14]

After the spring of 1939 the French were very eager to secure Soviet cooperation, but the Soviet inclusion in a Peace Front was a problem from the British point of view, particularly for Chamberlain and Halifax.[15] The proponents in the FO – like Vansittart – of a closer cooperation with the USSR were ignored. Basically the power over British foreign policy rested in the hands of Halifax and especially Chamberlain.[16] However, these two, and other members of the Cabinet, had to take notice of the available British assessments of Soviet war potential.

At the beginning of March 1939 the FO received a memorandum from the Moscow embassy concerning the Soviet regime's stability, analysed from several perspectives: political, military, aviation (military) and economic. This was, judging by the available archive files, the first comprehensive 1939 report on Soviet war potential. It is likely that the report was made in light of the increasing tension in Europe, and the possibility of including the USSR in some kind of security arrangement. The British ambassador, Sir W. Seeds, added some personal comments to the opinions of his staff. It seems that the London FO officials who commented on the memorandum were in general agreement with its conclusions.[17]

The military sections were written by the military and air attachés, Colonel Firebrace and Wing Commander Hallawell. According to them the Red Army[18] had 1.6 million men, 9000 tanks and between 4000 and 5000 first-line aircraft. Firebrace believed that, after the outbreak of war, 100 infantry and 30 cavalry divisions could be mobilized on the Soviet west front (potentially against Germany) within three months. Even though it is not fully obvious from his writing, one must assume that he meant that these troops could be mobilized in addition to the peacetime strength of 110 infantry and 30 cavalry divisions. There were no more mechanized troops available from mobilization in addition to the five mechanized corps already in service, and the wartime strength in the Far East was 32 infantry and 5 cavalry divisions.[19] Later in March Firebrace regarded the information given by the Soviet People's Commissar of Defence, Marshal Voroshilov[20] in a speech, as a "fair indication" of the Red Army's size: in the vicinity of 1.6 to 1.7 million men (i.e. slightly more than in his earlier estimates). Firebrace assessed the potential mobilized war strength to over 4 million men, and the purges of recent years as one of the reasons for the reduced efficiency of the Army.[21]

It is hard to assess the actual impact of the purges on the efficiency of armed forces. However, most contemporary observers believed that the purges had a very negative impact, and it also seems that later academic research support such a conclusion. Proportionally, the purges affected mostly the higher echelons of Soviet society, and not the least the officer corps. It was foremost the higher officers that was executed, imprisoned or sacked. However, if we look at the officer corps as a whole "only" 3.7 to 7.7 per cent was purged in the real sense of the word, most other "purged" officers were only expelled from the communist party.[22] Therefore, assessing the effect of the purges, hinges to a very large extent on what one makes of the fact that the majority of the higher officers (and commissars) was purged. It is easier, though, to comment on quantitative estimates. The Red Army's manpower size was, rather, correctly estimated. On 1 June 1938 the Red Army (i.e. the Army and the Army Air Force) numbered little more than 1.5 million men, but it was only slightly larger on 1 September 1939.[23]

The tank and aircraft strength estimates was probably less accurate. On June 1941 the Soviets had nearly 21,000 military aircraft,[24] and in January 1933 they had 5000.[25] Even though the Soviet military aircraft inventory were regularly upgraded, i.e. older models was replaced by newer, the actual 1939 air strength ought to have been closer to the June 1941 figure than the January 1933 figure.[26] Therefore, the British estimate was probably somewhat too low, even if it only was about the first line strength. It is more certain that the tank estimate was too low. Actual tank strength in June 1941 it was 22,600,[27] and already in January 1933 it was 10,000 tanks and other armoured vehicles.[28] The total tank output during 1933–1939 was approximately 21,700 units.[29]

Even if the British probably underestimated tank and aircraft strength the estimated figures might seem rather impressive anyway, especially if compared to British assessments of the strength of the German *Wehrmacht*. In late July 1939 the WO and the IIC estimated the total size of the German Army in the event of war to between 121 and 130 divisions – that is, more than the actual strength (103 divisions, including 5 armoured divisions) at the outbreak of war in September.[30] However, it was not the size of the Soviet Armed Forces that was considered as their weakness.

When referring to the situation already before the 1937 purges, Firebrace described the Red Army's "tactical doctrines [... as] unsound and its administration suspect". Its offensive value was very low, maybe sufficient for an advance into Poland of some depth, but not more, before inefficient command and especially administrative problems would halt the advance. However, even though it would still suffer from the same problems, he definitively believed that the Red Army would do much better in defence. It would have a greater fighting spirit, be able to use its numerical superiority better, and it could also benefit from the USSR's poor communications, which would work against an invader.[31]

According to Hallawell the practical effectiveness of the SAF would not be counting for much in operations against the Germans. Regarding aircraft quality he believed it to be suicidal to send the 500 obsolete heavy bombers against "a real air defence". Only about 1000 fighters and 420 medium bombers were "reasonably modern".[32] He was most probably correct in his assertion concerning the SAF's quality in comparison the *Luftwaffe*, and the SAF used many outdated aircraft at the time. The SAF's expansion had commenced a few years earlier than the *Luftwaffe* build up, and for that reason alone, considering the fast pace of technical aircraft development during the 1930s, it was stuck with many outdated aircraft.

Ambassdor Seeds argued in the memorandum that: "the Soviet regime is as firmly established as any regime can reasonably expect to be". He wrote that the memorandum (as a whole) covered every aspect of what the press[33] referred to as "Russia's approaching collapse". The internal situation might be problematic in the event of a military offensive or longer war, but compared to Tsarist Russia there were great differences. The new regime possessed "a stronger moral stamina", despite the fact that there existed "a certain inborn inefficiency". The regime's ruthlessness and total control over the population contributed to it being more stable than the Tsarist regime. But he also spotted some enthusiasm for the new regime and better general education, which in turn made people more recipient to propaganda. F. H. R. Maclean, who had prepared the memorandum's political section, did not anticipate any "political upheaval" in the country, apart from in the event of war or economic collapse. The population's passivity, the Government's totalitarian style, the lack of alternatives and the population's ignorance of the outside world were reasons for this. He claimed to represent the embassy as a whole on this opinion.[34]

In April Ian Fleming (the creator of the fictional James Bond character) commented on a memorandum written by a recent visitor to the USSR. In the spring Fleming was himself officially visiting the USSR on behalf of *The Times* and unofficially for the FO. He sent the (other visitors) memorandum to the FO, and it painted a rather bright picture of the Red Army's strength, morale and efficiency, compared to other British accounts. The ability of the civilian society to withstand the strain of war was considered as good, but the ability of industry to supply the armed forces with war material in the event of a large and prolonged conflict was not. Fleming believed that the memorandum was too optimistic with respect to the probability of internal revolution in the event of war. There was "considerable latent unrest" in the USSR. The political direction of the Red Army could result in the murder of political commissars in wartime, which in turn could spark internal trouble on a grand scale.[35]

Firebrace outlined his views on the Red Army's readiness for war in another later March memorandum, which was commented by FO and WO officials. The description of the Red Army's numerical strength was the same as in the previous report, with some minor alterations (9800 tanks and 35 cavalry divisions instead). There was enough trained manpower reserves for a further expansion of the Army, but available arms and equipment were lacking. Additional infantry and cavalry units could be mobilized in the event of war, but he wrote nothing about any additional armoured or mechanized units. The assessment regarding the Red Army's pre-Purge qualitative state was repeated, and he added that the Army's discipline had been weakened since the purges. The Red Army's was loyal to the Soviet leadership, but problems might arise in the long run during a war. In war the civilian population was seen as likely to suffer rather than the Army. The Red Army's defensive value was considered as much greater in the defence of Soviet territory. But even so it was "doubtful" if the USSR "could stand up long to the strain of a war".[36]

The WO, commenting on Firebrace's memorandum on the request by a secretary of state,[37] agreed in general and described it as "a reasonable appreciation of the present value of the Red Army". They added that the Red Army's Far Eastern troops probably were better trained, more disciplined, and had a higher morale than the rest of the Army, partly as a result of being less affected by the purges. Since the Far Eastern troops had less contact with the population than troops in the country's Western parts, they had also been less influenced by the discontent prevailing among the workers and peasants there. As a final comment it was added that if there were any error in Firebrace's estimate, it was on the low side.[38]

Naval power has historically never had been one of Russia's hallmarks as a Great Power, but the Navy was given attention in a few reports. According to a March report from the Admiralty's Intelligence Division to Sir Laurence Collier (the Head of the FO's Northern Department)[39] based on information from the Moscow Naval Attaché, H. Clanchy, and originally requested by Lord Halifax, the purges had affected the Navy very adversely, due to the massive liquidation of high-ranking officers. Since there only were junior commanders on active service in the submarine force and the "Naval Air Wing", the efficiency had largely been retained in these services. However, the efficiency of the Navy was improving, from the low points of the purge and political control. Several concrete problems were identified: young inexperienced personnel, lack of comradeship, lack of coordination, poor staff work, low morale and discipline, and a low level of organization. But Clanchy saw hope for the Navy if the political control could be ended. The individual ship efficiency was good in general and the submarine service was numerically strong, as well as of a relatively high standard. The Navy had 3 battleships, 6 cruisers (one light), 7 flotilla leaders, 26 destroyers, and 195 submarines (a minimum), in addition to many smaller vessels. With the exception of the submarines, many of the larger warships were of World War I or even of pre-War design.[40] The actual size of the Navy at the time was close to his estimate.[41]

Soviet air power was of course potentially more useful for defending Poland than naval strength. According to a March FO memorandum, containing an Air Ministry reply to a Secretary of State request for an evaluation of Soviet armed strength, the Red Army had 4281 aircraft; about two-thirds being various bomber types and most of the rest fighters. In contrast to the fighters, believed to be relatively modern, the bombers were obsolete. Air force training, maintenance (of materiel), and expected efficiency in the event of war were not being up to adequate standards. Organization in general, and the low quality of personnel, was expected to contribute further to the Air Force continuing to be less efficient for a considerable time. But despite this, and additional problems in the form of inadequate supply, it was stated that it "may still be regarded as a strong deterrent to any country contemplating aggression."[42]

The assessments presented so far points in the direction that the Soviet Armed Forces was suffering from low efficiency, especially in comparison with the Western Power's Armed Forces. This state of affairs was of course to a certain extent explained by the purges, even though it seems that this factor alone cannot explain the picture of low efficiency harboured by the British. The fact that war might result in internal instability was stated the observers. Some also mentioned several positive features possessed by the Soviet Armed Forces, and although they thought very little of its offensive capabilities, they at least described its defensive strength as much better (especially within Soviet territory). But as we will see the foremost problem with Soviet war potential, from the British perspective, was not military efficiency in the narrow sense of the word.

Today the economic size of a country is often discussed in terms of gross domestic product (GDP) or similar measuring units, often expressed in per capita. We know that methods to measure national income existed a few centuries before the 1930s, but the modern concept of GDP was still in its infancy then. However, it does not seem that the Anglo-Americans used any aggregate concrete measures (in numbers) of national income when discussing the Soviet economy, but only commented more specifically (in terms of numbers) on certain industries and branches. The Moscow embassy's comprehensive March memorandum contained an economic section, written by the Commercial Secretary Frank H. Todd. He believed that it was unlikely that the economic apparatus could be expanded to meet the demands of war, due to an ongoing lowering of labour productivity, lack of technical skills, poor planning, and the all too frequent changes of personnel in higher factory management. The purges had hurt industry. Industrial output was increasing, but the overall situation was unsatisfactory since the plans were not being fulfilled. The defence industry was receiving the best available labour and had priority in the allocation of raw materials, but the transport sector would not cope with the strain of war, and more skilled labour could not be obtained easily. He stated that "defence industry is no doubt working to full capacity already, and it is difficult to see how production can still be further speeded up in view of the lack of skilled personnel". The replacement of worn out equipment was very difficult under wartime conditions, and the already high proportion of defective goods produced would certainly increase. As for the living standard of the population even the present levels of defence commitment made the population live "on a bare subsistence level".[43]

Even though their part of the memorandum was about military matters Firebrace and Hallawell also regarded that the strain of war would be too much for the country in general. Hallawell believed that the danger to the SAF would come as much from the rear as from any opposition in the air. He doubted that the transport system could provide the SAF with supplies in a war.[44]

According to the FO memorandum intended for a Secretary of State, the war industry would not be able to replace wartime aircraft losses.[45] In his March memorandum on the Red Army's readiness for war Firebrace also pointed out the weakening of industry as an effect of the purges, which would in turn affect its ability to provide the army and the population with their needs.[46] In the Clanchy report the shipbuilding programme was described as suffering from "steadily deteriorating" industrial conditions since early 1937.[47] Later that month he stated that the industry was less potent than the official picture, both regarding its capacity to manufacture warship armour and the general experience of industry's work force. Both machinery and personnel would have to be imported from abroad in order to make it possible to manufacture battleships.[48]

On the strategic level the British COS, at the time a sub-committee of the CID, believed that the USSR could be useful to a certain extent, in the event of a future confrontation with Germany (and other potential enemies). In a report dated 18 March (based on minutes from a meeting), and a report from April, they believed that the USSR had a value as a deterrent to Germany and Japan. The Red Army could be of help to Romania and Poland, and the COS recommended diplomatic action to achieve this result, even though the USSR military was an "uncertain quantity". The situation would be more advantageous with the Soviets on the side of the British, with Poland as a neutral, than the other way around. That preference of the USSR over Poland was probably due to COS's assertion that Poland's military situation was precarious, and that the Poles would be unable to withstand large German forces for any longer duration of time. The Polish would fight "stoutly" and the USSR would not take any military action outside her borders, but defend her own territory.[49]

Soviet participation on the British side would also be disadvantageous to Germany. Their situation in the Baltic areas would be more "difficult" and the Swedish supply of iron ore to Germany could be disrupted. The Soviets could contain "considerable" German naval forces and also provide naval bases for the British. The SAF could also be useful since it could pose a limited threat to Germany if based outside the USSR, have some value in containing German air defence forces and add some positive assistance to Poland's air defences. The COS also added that the "fighting value" of the Soviets had improved lately. However, despite these advantages the USSR could not "afford material support to Poland" or "maintain in Romania or in Turkey any Military effort of a size which would have a material effect on the situation". Help to Romania could be delivered, but the communications from the USSR into Romania was so poor that it would prevent any large scale military operations. The best thing that was said about the Army was that it "would contain substantial German forces [...] in the event of Poland and Roumania being overrun".[50]

Polish neutrality would prevent effective Soviet air operations against Germany and use of Red Army manpower outside the USSR. Despite the fact that the USSR was preferred over Poland, the former was unable to deliver any significant military strength outside her borders, and due to this the COS could not recommend the British Government, from a "purely military aspect", to "challenge" Germany regarding Romania. A Soviet intervention in the Mediterranean area was not believed to make any difference. A possible effect of a Soviet intervention in the Far East would be to delay Japanese aggression, or at best deter them from going to war with Britain.[51]

The COS also stated that a war against Germany, Japan and Italy simultaneously was too much for present and future British military strength, even if Britain would be allied to France and the USSR. This conclusion was based on earlier assumptions from 1938, which the COS still held as true.[52] The inclusion of the USSR in an alliance was not regarded as sufficient even in 1939 to create a credible military opposition to Germany in Eastern Europe. The paper version of the report from the meeting never reached the Cabinet[53] but other papers based on the same reasoning was reaching the Cabinet in April. The service departments' leading proponents attended the 18 March meeting, as did the Cabinet member Lord Chatfield, the minister for co-ordination of defence.[54] A conclusion like this was, of course, not bright for the prospects of defeating the fascist powers if hostiles would commence.

However, it would seem better, as the COS also argued in principle over the question of Poland versus the USSR, to have the Soviets on their side than not. Nonetheless, the prime minister and Lord Halifax stated many times that they did not want to include, especially openly, the Soviets in the peace front: they were afraid of alienating potential allies (who disliked communism and the USSR) and provoke Germany with such a move. An Anglo-French-Soviet triple alliance could also help to weaken the assumed internal German opposition to Hitler. During most of the government meetings about this issue their point of view was iterated, and the pros and cons of Soviet military support was discussed at the same time. Chamberlains arguments can be summarized: the Soviets were so politically unreliable and the USSR so militarily weak that her inclusion in a peace front would cost more than it would bring. Some top officials also seemed to prefer Poland, a political antagonist to the Soviets, as an ally instead of the USSR, and some of these arguments were based on the assumption that Poland actually might be militarily stronger than the USSR. Halifax, General Ironside, the chief inspector of the British Armed Forces, and Lord Chatfield, all argued along these lines; even though the latter at least stated that the Germans might probably regard the USSR as a greater deterrent than Poland.[55] With one exception[56] no one participating in the discussions deviated from the notion that Soviet military strength, especially regarding offensive capabilities, was very poor.

A 27 March FPC meeting made it clear that the inclusion of the USSR was unwanted, since it would alienate a large part of other potential allies in Europe and overseas, including the assumed next victims of German aggression – Poland and Romania. Chamberlain and Halifax, supporting and promoting this position, were not arguing against including the USSR in some kind of understanding to defend Poland and Romania, but only if such an agreement could be reached in secret (and indirectly) between the British government and the Soviets. Chamberlain proposed a verbal gentleman's agreement with the USSR, when being asked by other attendants how to keep an agreement secret.[57]

The prime minister and Halifax also hoped that Germany still could be contained peacefully, and that Germany's potential allies Italy and Japan could be distanced from her. An open association with the USSR would counteract these hopes. In contrast to the conclusions reached by the COS at their meeting on 18 March, Halifax preferred Poland as an ally over the USSR. He also referred to French Foreign Minister Bonnet's opinions of the USSR and concluded that Bonnet regarded her as "deceitful and unreliable" and that in the case of an emergency she would not give much, if any, effective help. Chatfield agreed with Halifax regarding the relative military value of Poland vis-à-vis the USSR, but at the same time he stated that the Germans would be more deterred by an alliance with the USSR. As a comment on Chatfield Halifax referred to the reports produced by the Moscow embassy earlier in March, and repeated a summarized version of them. The only thing that actually could be called "good" about the Soviet Armed Forces was the so called "defensive qualities" of the Army. Poland's 50 divisions, on the other hand, he argued, were expected to make a "useful contribution". Chatfield thought that Romania was worth defending and the country was worth something from a military point of view, and he also believed that care should be taken so closer cooperation with the USSR would not antagonize Japan.[58]

From the meetings held in March it is clear that different opinion prevailed among the British government's leading figures, but they were also more or less unanimous in their very low esteem of Soviet military strength. This perception was, as we have seen, backed up by (and in most cases probably emanating from) the assessments made by the government institutions responsible for analysing Soviet capabilities. Manne has taken an interest in some of the discussions referred to above and according to his analysis Halifax and Chatfield regarded the USSR as a "militarily almost worthless power". This is perhaps true, especially regarding Halifax's opinions (see below for a further elaboration of Chatfield's view), but some of the other British observers did not go that far. On the other hand Manne believes that the views present in the COS's analysis of 18 March as "relatively sanguine".[59] From what we know today about Soviet strength it is hard to agree with him.

In April the COS analysed Soviet military strength again in the report "Military implications of the new situation in Europe", dated the 19th. They concluded, just like their colleagues in the Moscow embassy, that the Red Army's offensive capabilities were poor, and much for the same reasons: the purge had created a shortage of experienced military leaders, the training of personnel was inferior, and the right of the political commissars to exercise command over the troops had an inhibiting effect on the initiative of the military commanders. But the Red Army nevertheless had some merits, since in the event of war it could engage considerable German ground and air forces, and also contribute to the Romanian war effort if that country should be attacked. The COS envisaged a mobilization scenario for the USSR. In 7 to 14 days after the ordering of mobilization the Red Army would have 5 armoured divisions, 31 cavalry divisions and 86 infantry divisions. After 21 to 31 days the number of divisions would have increased to 35 cavalry and 110 infantry, and the COS assessment was that after 90 days the number of infantry divisions would have increased to 170. The numbers of armoured divisions would never exceed five. According to the COS this was an army of formidable proportions, well equipped with tanks, but with the inherent weaknesses described above.[60]

The SAF had 4387 aircraft: 1324 fighters, 1206 long range bombers, 1656 as either bombers, ground attack or reconnaissance planes, and 201 as flying boats. Most of the bombers were seen as outdated and very slow, even if it was considered that they had some advantages as long range and were usable for night bombing. The fighter planes were described as relatively modern, but not in comparison to British or German fighters. The reserves were about 50 per cent of the first line strength, which would then add up to a total of 7180.[61]

In the report, and in another from the 24th, the COS did not believe that there would be any problem for the USSR to supply and support at least 100 divisions in the field, during the initial stages of a major war. In the event of a total industrial mobilization even larger numbers could be supplied, but the industrial base was not adequate for maintaining these large forces in the field for a long time. One explanation for this deficiency was that the large new factories, which had been built with foreign help, had fallen into disrepair, along with the machinery in them. There was not enough skilled labour to go around in order to increase output above the normal in the event of an emergency. The administration was in a state of hopeless inefficiency, and the situation had not improved since the purges, which instead had affected the defence industry's organization in a negative way, and on top of this were perceived as still being in effect. When commenting on the aircraft industry, they described its internal organization as riven with major flaws, its raw material supply as inefficient, and that any wartime output increase was unlikely.[62]

These industrial problems, in combination with the deficiencies of the railway system, were working against the functioning of a sound economic foundation for the armed forces. The communications were also not adequate for the purpose of transporting large masses of troops. One problem was the constant repair of railway facilities, and another was the lack of an organization for the supply of troops operating beyond the western border. The transportation system was sufficient for the mobilization of the army during the first weeks of a war, but that this would have serious repercussions on the economy. After two to three weeks the Soviet leadership would be forced to cancel the military mobilization, in order to avoid "a complete breakdown in industry and national life." After a few weeks of war the government would find itself in a situation where it could possibly supply its troops along the western border with the supplies needed, but only at the expense of a considerable fall in the production of war materials. As a matter of fact, the COS did not believe that the economy could deliver more war supplies to the western border than would be sufficient to maintain 30 field divisions.[63] This statement is very remarkable in light of the fact that 30 divisions is a relatively small force. Compare this, for example, with the estimated size of the German war establishment (see above) and the fact that even France, with a smaller industrial base than Britain and a population of only circa 40 million, could field 117 divisions in 1940.[64]

In April the Moscow embassy issued an annual economic report on the USSR containing information about economic inefficiency, and an industrial structure still suffering from the purges. The labour productivity was decreasing in industry and it showed unsatisfactory results and experienced a shortage of skilled personnel. The collectivized farmers were expressing discontent, and the living conditions of the workers were one reason given for the decreasing labour productivity.[65]

Hallawell returned to the aircraft situation in April; commenting on a speech by the People's Commissar of the Aircraft Industry, M. M. Kaganovich.[66] Judging by the despatch the aircraft industry used modern industrial equipment to mass-produce aircraft. Kaganovich was aware that improvements could be made to raise efficiency. Hallawell did not state to what extent he really believed in what Kaganovich said, but he acknowledged the earlier expansion of the aircraft industry and the possibility that it could be expanded further. This expansion would demand an increase in the number of specialists, managers and experienced foremen, and he regarded it as an open question if this goal could be meet. The Soviets would benefit from engaging foreign specialists, but he also stated: "Recently, Soviet conceit and spy mania have prevented specialists from justifying their employment."[67]

As evident from the discussion about actual air strength it is clear the FO and the COS estimates was clear underestimations. The same can probably be said about the perceived Soviet capacity to mobilize troops after the ordering of mobilization. Since there was no full-scale mobilization until June 1941, a precise comparison with reality is difficult. The June 1941 mobilization can be used as a proxy, but the actual capacity can of course have been ameliorated since 1939. If actual capabilities increased from 1939 the USSR would be able to mobilize more troops in 1941, everything else being equal. This is true, but the foundation of military-economic strength was already in place in 1939. The gross national product (GNP) and population did increase until June 1941, but mostly due to territorial annexations. In 1939–1940 the population increased by approximately 23 million, potentially adding recruits for the armed forces, but the total population in 1940 was almost 190 million, and in June 1941 even larger. The GNP did increase during 1939–1940 and the first half of 1941. The annexations contributed to increasing GNP, alongside GNP growth inside the pre-1939 borders, from 216.3 billion rubles (1938) to 250.5 billion rubles (1940). The increase was substantial, but dwarfed by the expansion of the Five Year Plans from 1928, when GNP stood at a mere 123.7 billion roubles. Real GNP growth was lower during 1939–1940, excluding the onetime annexation increase, than it had been on average since the end of the 1920s.[68]

As for industry, the most important branch for military-economic strength, annual average growth 1939–1940 was considerably lower than 1928–1938.[69] Not until the first six months of 1941 did industrial output increase at a faster pace again.[70] The lion share of economic and industrial build up took place before 1939, inside the pre-1939 borders. The industrial development level of the in 1939–1940 annexed areas was lower than the USSR's on average, especially regarding military-industrial capacity. The defence industries were established during the Five Year Plans, and the largest increase in munitions output took place during the First and Second Plan (1928–1937). Therefore military-industrial strength was basically already established in 1939. Munitions output continued to increase 1938–1940, but during these years a much larger share of the economy was diverted to munitions.[71]

The actual strength of the Red Army increased from about 1.5 million men in 1938 to nearly 5.4 million in June 1941. At that time the Red Army had 303 divisions and 22 independent brigades.[72] After the outbreak of war the Soviet mobilized a huge amount of troops, far in excess of the British assessments, and was basically able to supply them in the field (see Chapter 13 for more details). This mobilization effort was accomplished at the same time as an enemy invasion was in progress, while large parts of industry alongside millions of civilians were evacuated eastwards, and while at the same time munitions output increased substantially.[73] During this period Western Allied material assistance to the USSR was almost non-existent.[74] It is therefore rather safe to assume that the British estimate regarding the wartime mobilization scenario was a clear underestimation.

Later in April the COS presented more or less the same picture as before regarding military capabilities in the report "Military value of Russia", dated the 24th, made on the commission of the FPC. Another weakness, not mentioned in other reports, affecting the Red Army's offensive capabilities, was the notion that the Soviet leadership would be unwilling to let their forces operate on foreign territory, where the troops would come under "bourgeois influence". This, in combination with the earlier supposed shortcomings of military capabilities, contributed to the picture of the limited value of the Red Army as an ally.[75] They added that the system of political control – the COS almost certainly referred to the political commissars (which had been reintroduced in the Red Army from May 1937) – had resulted in a dual command system. The effect of this was that "The inherent desire of the Russian to shirk responsibility is given full scope [... and] has resulted in [... a formerly good discipline] being now of an indifferent standard."[76]

They repeated that the USSR would have considerable difficulties supplying large forces in the field, due to inadequate reserves and defective communications. In contrast to the earlier report, dated just five days earlier, it was estimated that the USSR would be able to mobilize 100 infantry divisions in the western part of the USSR during the first three months of war, a significantly lower number than that one stated in the earlier report (138 divisions).[77] Red Army equipment was described in the following manner: "The equipment of this army is more noteworthy for its quantity rather than its quality." The opinion of the artillery was that it had low firepower and consisted mostly of old pieces.[78] As for the 9000 tanks these had light armour, even if they were considered to be of high quality in general. But it was also assumed that they had no defence against a modern and efficient anti-tank defence.[79] The Navy was also analysed in this and the previously mentioned report, but nothing new was stated in principle (in comparison to the Clanchy report, see note 80[80] for more details).

The COS reports contained several underestimations of Soviet capabilities, just as the earlier British reports. The notion about the unwillingness of the Soviets to allow their troops to enter foreign territory was of course in practice proven false, due to subsequent events. The idea about the poor supply and communications situation will be commented on in more detail below. A statement like the one about the inherent desire to shirk from responsibility is of course very difficult to compare to "reality", even though the statement as such indicates something about the way the British looked upon the Russians. The commissar system as such was abolished in August 1940, only to be reinstated again in July 1941.

Red Army equipment was of a higher standard than the COS believed. The actual quality of tanks in 1939 was at least higher on average than German tanks.[81] The claim that Soviet tanks lacked efficient anti-tank defence was erroneous, relatively speaking. The Red Army's tank and anti-tank guns had better amour-piercing capabilities on average against German tanks, than the Germans had against Soviet tanks.[82] The COS correctly assessed that artillery had relatively low firepower and consisted mostly of old pieces. Compared to German artillery it is likely that firepower was lower. Soviet artillery was hampered by neglected communications and a shortage of signal assets. According to some most pieces were of older design and they had a comparatively short range.[83] On the other hand, a direct comparison with German divisional pieces reveals that they too often were old (even from World War I). Comparing muzzle velocity, range, rate of fire and weight of the projectile there is not much difference between German and Soviet artillery. Some Soviet models were actually superior in certain respects.[84] If, as the COS believed, Soviet artillery was mostly consisting of older models; then the same can be said about German artillery.

The three weapon systems aircraft, tanks and artillery was the most important for World War II warfare. A comparison of lighter weapons would be of limited value, maybe with the exception of mortars (which in a sense can be regarded as light artillery). There is no indication that Soviet mortars were inferior to German, actually quite the contrary. As for infantry weapons, mainly rifles and machine guns, it can possibly be argued that German equipment was somewhat better; mostly due to the modern MG 34 machine gun. But Soviet infantry units by 1939 had some equipment available that the Germans had not introduced yet, as semi-automatic rifles and very heavy (.50 cal.) machine guns.[85] Considering all the above it seems fair to say that the Red Army did not have inferior ground equipment, at least in comparison to Germany.

On 24 April the FPC returned to the Soviet problem and they discussed the COS report dated the same day ordered by them. Chatfield summarized the report, and believed that the USSR was a "great power", but her military strength was only of "medium rank". In this he apparently dissented somewhat from Halifax's opinion, and stated that militarily the value of Soviet assistance would be "considerable" in war, but on the other hand not "great". As we have seen there were some parliament members (and even members of the Conservative party) who had a higher regard for Soviet military strength than the Cabinet members, and perhaps it was those that Chatfield referred to when he also stated that Soviet military assistance was "not nearly so great as certain quarters represented it to be".[86] Two days later Halifax uttered something similar in the Cabinet, referring to prominent members of the Labour party.[87] On the 24th (in the FPC) the secretary of state for the colonies remarked that it would be better if the Soviets was allied to Britain, instead of being neutral or allied to Germany. Halifax stated that the Government should "play for time" (i.e. not conclude an agreement with the Soviets anytime soon).[88]

4.3 The Soviets propose an alliance

Despite their low regard for Soviets strength and distrust of Soviet intentions, the British hoped that the USSR would deliver supplies to Poland, and in April a slight shift in the attitude towards the USSR was noticeable within the administration. The USSR was asked by the British to assist her Eastern European neighbours if necessary. According to Manne the reason for the change was threefold: in parliament there were some loud supporters for an agreement; the full implications of the consequences of the guarantees to Poland, Romania and Greece were suddenly felt; and there were some warnings about a possible Soviet–German rapprochement. Instead of accepting the limited deal that the British and the French proposed, the Soviet government proposed a full blown military alliance with the Western Powers on 17 April. Under parliamentary and French pressure more and more member of the Cabinet became convinced that an alliance was a sound idea. It was especially the threat of a Soviet–German rapprochement that weakened earlier opposition, but real negotiations did not begin until 25 May, more than a month after the Soviet counterproposal.[89]

In a new report dated 10 May, with the telling title "Balance of strategical value in war as between Spain as an enemy and Russia as an ally", the COS gave further indication on just how weak they believed the USSR to be. A few strategic disadvantages were envisaged in the Mediterranean area for Britain and France, if Spain should become allied with the Axis in a war. Under the condition that the USSR was not a direct ally of the Axis, but instead neutral, an alliance with the Soviets from a purely military perspective would bring less advantage relatively than the disadvantage of open hostility with Spain. But, if the USSR considered becoming a full ally of the Axis, this was perceived as a very dangerous situation, which would call for reconsideration.[90]

On 16 May Chatfield chaired a COS meeting, and the possibility of including the USSR in the peace front was debated. One of the obstacles to an inclusion was worries about Spain's reaction. Even though these events were not specifically discussed at the meeting, General Franco's forces had won the Spanish Civil War less than two months earlier. Franco's government was clearly anti-communist and anti-Soviet. However, the general impression left by the meeting was one of commitment to an inclusion. It was feared that a failure to include the USSR could produce serious repercussion from a diplomatic and military perspective, and that it might end up in a Soviet-German rapprochement. The possibility of Soviet support to Poland and Romania was also stressed, as was worries about a situation where the USSR after hostilities in Europe might end up in a "dominating position".[91]

The next day the situation was discussed again in the Cabinet, and it was now clear that the COS had altered their attitude regarding an alliance. The change in attitude was noted by the Chancellor of the Exchequer, and Chatfield answered his remark about this by referring to an amendment of an earlier COS report. The report in question was the 10 May paper about the relative value of Spain and the USSR. As apparent from that report it was not worth alienating Spain by moving closer to the USSR, and a reconsideration of this position was only warranted if there was a risk that the USSR would become a full ally of the Axis powers.[92]

The amendment, on the other hand, downplayed Spain's importance but did not inflate (in comparison to the earlier report) Soviet capabilities. The content of the amendment was more about political necessities than military capabilities. Actually, it seems that Chatfield was still in doubt regarding the relative importance of Spain versus the USSR. Chamberlain asked him a direct question concerning the actual help the USSR could bring in a conflict, and then Chatfield answered by referred to the original report. He characterized the value of a Soviet participation by the word "appreciable". The Soviet Armed Forces could contain "substantial" hostile forces and provide war material to Britain's Eastern European allies.

However, Chamberlain and Halifax persisted in their belief that the political price might be too high. The later regarded the arguments for a pact as "sound" from a military standpoint, and the former, although dismissing the value of Soviet assistance in a Mediterranean war, expressed that the value of such assistance during a war in Western Europe would be somewhat different. Despite this he insisted that "as against the military advantages of Russian assistance must be weighed the political objections." In his reply Chatfield stated that from a military standpoint there where arguments both for and against a Soviet participation, but from the German point of view a two front war should be avoided, and therefore a inclusion might act as an deterrent for Germany. But he also added: "On the other hand, Russia was not a great military power and her military effort in a European war was more likely to be disappointing than otherwise."[93] When commenting on the value of Russia as an ally, he concluded (based on a COS report) that "this value was not nearly as great as was commonly supposed, more specially from the point of view of the possibility of Russia undertaking offensive operations."[94]

The prime minister was actually "alarmed", as he expressed it, that the COS wanted to increase British liabilities, without adding to British assets. The liability in this case was closer cooperation with the USSR. Despite his obvious doubts regarding Soviet capabilities Chatfield continued to argue for the COS's opinion. He said that the Soviets could be in a "dominant position at the end of hostilities", if she would be neutral in a coming conflict. Coming from Chatfield this statement seems somewhat contradictory, since even a "medium rank" (in his own words) military power would probably have a hard time to defeat a (by war) exhausted first class power. Furthermore, apart from repeating the argument about the Soviets being a potential deterrent to Germany, he said that it could not be excluded that Soviet support to Poland would have some economic and military benefits, in spite of Soviet weakness. During the meeting other people expressed opinions about how to act regarding the situation, and some were concerned about the possibility of the Soviets concluding a deal with Germany.[95] In the COS's opinion it was better for the British to ally with the USSR, despite the anticipated negative reactions from other nations, since an alliance would negate the danger of a Soviet-German rapprochement.[96]

While the top level officials discussed the wise in closer cooperation with the USSR, lower level officials continued to analyse her war potential. A Major Kirkman from the British MI2 gave a lecture at the Imperial Defence College. A written copy of the lecture was sent to the FO on 18 May. Kirkman did not believe that the Red Army's fighting strength and efficiency was much greater than the picture painted in earlier British reports, and much for the same reasons (e.g. the purges). If the Red Army should engage in offensive operations outside the Soviet borders it would not do much better than the Tsarist Army in 1914. But he also described some strong features: "its size [...] its thousands of tanks [...] its air-mindedness [...] its efficient propaganda machine [...] and under certain circumstances, in its enthusiasm." The major weaknesses were its leadership, which were considered to be untried, inexperienced and suffering from a lack of initiative; and disorganization of training, the lowered standard of discipline, as well as the interference of political commissars in the Army leadership. Just like many other observers he recognized the (in his words) "formidable" defensive value of the army, especially in defence of Soviet territory.[97]

He concluded that the purges had affected industry as badly as the armed forces, but he also recognized some advantages of the military-economic position: being almost self-sufficient in raw materials, heavy industries out of range of enemy bombing and the world's largest permanent armament industry. The armament industries could turn out 1500 tanks per year (the Red Army currently had 9000, he believed), and the armament industries had a capacity adequate to turn out equipment to support 30 divisions (unspecified which divisions) during wartime conditions. The quality of the manufactured equipment was "quite good" when first produced, but with a short life. Even though civilian industry was ready for conversion to armaments output in war, he did not believe that the existing armament industries could increase output during war. But the efforts to mobilize industry were just good on paper, and these plans could not be realized to their full extent due to problems of organization, administration, transportation and the "human element". The railways were inefficient and the road net inadequate, as were as the country's truck fleet. A FO official commented that Kirkman's opinions were nothing new to them.[98]

Kirkman's paper also shed some light on internal stability. In this respect the purges of 1936–1938 were seen as a stabilizing factor, and according to "competent observers" Stalin's regime was in a "considerable stronger position" than the Tsarist regime in 1914. Also regarding this, the "ruthless and despotic" nature of the government was an advantage, as was the "permanent organisations" responsible for the preparation and conduct of war. As for the efficiency of the higher administrative and organizational circles of the government his judgement was more ambiguous. The readiness for war was considerably improved over the 1914 situation, but it was nevertheless something of a paper tiger. He wrote: "on the other hand, it [the organization for war] also depends for its working on the human element; and time alone will show whether the Soviet system is really succeeding in eradicating those inherent defects in the Russian character such as irresponsibility, lack of initiative, and an absence of administrative ability. There seems, at present little indication that much progress in this direction has been made, and the purge has probably accentuated rather than cured them."[99]

Based on this, and the other comments regarding internal stability, it is obvious the British did not believe that the regime's stability was in any danger at the moment, but in the event of war the situation would be very different. It is also clear that they, although identifying some advantages compared to the pre-revolutionary situation, did not have much respect for the administrative competence and ability of the government structure. The Kirkmans paper and all the other reports had the same point of view (when discussing it) regarding the possibility of the USSR to increase munitions output during wartime. Soviet industry would be unable to produce sufficient munitions for its troops and not even be able to supply them adequately. This was a grave underestimation (and more will be said about this below).

The USSR was regarded as a potential supplier of armaments to Poland (and Romania).[100] The IIC produced a report on this subject in May, in which they concluded that the USSR in fact had a "relatively large manufacturing capacity", and large stocks of armaments; but that she would need both her stocks and manufacturing capacity for her own armed forces if she was engaged in active large scale operations. The JIC noticed the report and also wondered, on behalf of Lord Chatfield, if actual supplies could really be delivered to Poland due to the inefficiency of the transport system.[101] The inefficient state of transport was also mentioned in connection with a JIC meeting on 18 May, again regarding the Soviet ability to supply Poland with arms in the event of war.[102] The problem of transport was also touched upon in the late August Joint Planning Sub-Committee paper JP 529, where it was described as "one of the principal limiting factors in Russian development and trade".[103] Without doubt the transport sector was inefficient compared to Western standards, but the British underestimated actual capacity (see below).

From the above it seems clear that the British regarded the economy as inefficient and plagued with serious problems. It is hard to know from their reporting what they thought in detail about the official statistics published by the Soviet government. As we have seen the British harboured a general distrust towards the regime and it seems likely that they did not trust the economic statistics, even though some of the British reporting was based upon such data. According to a report from ambassador Seeds in Moscow the defence expenditures for 1939 would be 26 per cent of the total state budget. This figure was derived from public information, which a FO official considered misleading. He believed that there were several concealed items not accounted for in the official figure, which would have inflated the budget if it had been of a "normal type".[104]

Material produced by the Department of Overseas Trade, in January 1939, suggests that the British had a rather accurate picture regarding the volume of output within different sectors of the national economy. The report was made on behalf of the FO, concerning the consequences of a Ukrainian detachment from the USSR; with Ukraine instead becoming a German protectorate. It was distributed among many military and civilian government departments. The figures concerning production revealed that the Department of Overseas Trade overestimated agricultural output, but underestimated minerals and heavy industry output. But the errors in the estimate were rather small in most cases. They also stated that the loss of the Ukraine would be a devastating blow to the economy and the chances of Soviet survival during a war. If the Germany took control over the Ukraine, the Ukraine's economic efficiency would be considerably greater.[105]

The aforementioned annual economic report uncritically listed some physical output figures (see note 106) for some industrial branches, which roughly was in accordance with the actual output level (as we know it from later academic research).[106] In July the commercial secretary Todd expressed disbelief regarding the officially alleged achievements of industry during the first six months of 1939.[107]

On 24 May the Soviet situation was on the Cabinet's agenda again. Halifax had produced a memorandum about the advantages and disadvantages of an Anglo-Soviet pact. The USSR's material contribution was actually placed in the section about disadvantages: "It has also to be considered that the actual material assistance to be expected [...] is not very great. It is true that the Soviet fleet might contain a proportion of German naval forces [...], and that the Soviet air forces might be able to render some assistance. It is, however, unlikely that on land their military effort could be of very much effect, and even in the matter of furnishing munitions and war materials their assistance would be limited by the fact that the Russian transportation system is in an extremely backward state."[108]

The secretary of state for air lent support to Halifax's view and argued that the SAF "may well be the largest [...] in the world, [but] it was unlikely to play a decisive part in a war in the near future". However, he stated that the SAF "would constitute a considerable deterrent to any country contemplating aggression". But he also believed that the aircraft industry, according to "reliable information", failed almost completely to keep pace with foreign developments. Due to these circumstances the industry relied "almost entirely upon American production for the replacing of their fighter and general purposes aircraft and flying boats." With a phrase perhaps borrowed from the COS he also said the following about the Army: "the [Army's] equipment was more noteworthy for quantity than for quality." Just as Chamberlain he argued for a more loosely based understanding, and he expressed the hope "that undue importance would not be attached to the military value of Russia."[109]

At the end of May Seeds transmitted another of Clanchy's reports to the FO. The despatch stated that the USSR was about to embark on a rapid naval expansion, primarily to meet a perceived German threat in the Baltic, but also to strengthen its naval position in the Far East. He seems to have considered it to be an open question whether or not the industry could stand up to the strain of further naval expansion.[110]

As we have seen the British observers mentioned a perceived strain and/or stagnation in industry. It was true that the USSR was experiencing a relative stagnation in industrial growth during this period. The very high growth rate of the Second Five Year Plan had been replaced by considerably lower GDP and industrial growth during the Third Plan (1938–1942). To precisely estimate whether or not labour productivity was falling in the spring of 1939, due to the causes enumerated by the Moscow embassy, is very hard, because of lack of data, and unclear connections between cause and effect. But during the period 1937–1940 it seems that industrial labour productivity increased very marginally.[111] A tendency towards declining labour productivity can be noticed in the iron and steel industry during 1938–1940.[112] The fault of the assessments in this specific respect was not so much the perceived stagnation of industrial labour productivity, but rather that they made too much of this considering the general and future state of the economy.

A possible alliance with the USSR was also discussed in public forums. It seems that in late May many in the British Government, and most people in parliament, was favourably inclined towards an alliance. The public and press support for an alliance was overwhelming. The anti-communist regimes of

Poland and Romania were earlier against closer cooperation with the USSR, but now also they changed their attitudes. In order to avoid a breakdown in the negotiations with the Soviets, Halifax and the Permanent Under Secretary of State Sir Alexander Cadogan also changed their standpoint.[113] Cadogan is notable in this context since he in March had regarded an "association with the Soviet[s] as more of a liability than an asset"; instead preferring to ally with Italy. According to Neilson and Otte, he, just as the COS, changed his mind due to the fear of a Soviet-German rapprochement.[114] Chamberlain was forced to change his attitude on 24 May by the majority of his cabinet colleagues, in spite of a threat from his side to resign. However, he would still not concede to a full blown alliance and he managed to include his reservation about this in the new proposal – and he continued to argue for his original point of view. And although Chamberlain had been forced to abide by the majority of the Cabinet, there were still other prominent government officials not totally convinced that an alliance was the best course of action.[115]

With a vantage point in an analysis of the Anglo-Soviet negotiations from late May Manne assumes that the British changed their perceptions of Soviet military strength. However, the actual assessments do not support this assumption. The actual negotiations were problematic (described as "bazaar haggling" by Chamberlain) and by the end of July several British officials doubted that the Soviets really wanted an alliance. This strengthened the notion that the Soviets were "unreliable".[116]

4.4 Assessments on the eve of the Moscow negotiations

Diplomatically and politically the summer months mattered in the sense that the negotiations between the Anglo-French and the Soviets went on, and only really definitively ended due to the Molotov-Ribbentrop pact. Because of the effort to establish a pact against Hitler and Germany, the British and the French sent military missions to Moscow for negotiations. The members of these relatively low-level and half-hearted missions arrived at Moscow on 11 August, after first travelling to the USSR by slow-boat to Leningrad. The low level of the missions was noticed both by US and British embassy officials.[117] The summer brought very little in the way of new British assessments. However, some comments on British (and French) assessments were made by the Americans.

The US Moscow embassy's military attaché, Major Frank B. Hayne, reported on 3 August – he knew then that the missions were coming – to the US WD about the British and French military attaché's opinions regarding the Red Army and the Soviet Government. Hayne believed that the missions' opinions, and consequently, to a certain extent those of the British and French government's, were based largely upon what they learned from their military attachés. Therefore their assessments deserved attention. The French attaché, General Palasse, was the only attaché who appeared to have a favourable opinion of the Red Army and the Soviet government's capabilities. Not even Palasse's assistant, Major Abraham, had a very high opinion of the Red Army's ability to operate outside the borders of USSR in order to render any great assistance to its allies. The French air attaché, Lieutenant-Colonel Luget, did not have a very high opinion of Soviet aviation in general.[118]

Firebrace's opinion was noted: as already seen he believed that the Red Army could be quite formidable defensively inside the USSR. It could be better supplied under those conditions, the individual soldiers would fight better, and such a war would be decidedly more popular with the population. If the Soviets would fight outside the USSR, the High Command, high-level staff work, and the transport and supply situation would be especially bad. The Red Army would not be able to function effectively, after it had gone beyond 150 kilometres outside the border.[119]

Neither Clanchy, nor Hallawell, believed, respectively, that the Navy or the SAF had any great value. The submarine fleet could at best be a threat to the Germans in the Baltic. The SAF had 6900 planes, of which 4600 was defined as first-line. No SAF aircraft compared favourably with German or Italian planes if in actual combat. According to Hayne, the latest British estimate revealed that the Red Army had 114 (possibly 120) infantry and 35 cavalry divisions, 5 mechanized corps, and 34 tank and mechanized brigades.[120] This assessment was fairly consistent with an 11 August G-2 estimate, based upon a report from Hayne.[121] Judging by Hayne's interpretation of the British assessments it does not seem that they had changed markedly since the spring.

According to Manne the British were sincere in their attempts to establish an alliance, at least from the end of May onwards.[122] Since it actually was Poland's territory that was going to be defended, the Polish position had to be considered. As already stated their regime was hostile in principle towards the USSR, but Britain and France had great influence with the Poles. Apart from being Poland's allies, and from March also the guarantors of her borders from outside threats, the Anglo-French could affect military affairs in Poland. One example is that their diplomatic actions actually delayed Polish mobilization since they convinced Poland to cancel general mobilization, when it first begun on 27 August, in order not to antagonize Hitler. The Poles agreed to delay until 31 August, but the contra order a few days earlier not only delayed general military readiness, but also contributed to creating some degree of disorder in the process. Poland was heavily dependent upon Anglo-French military power for her very survival as an independent nation. The Polish defence plan was based on the fact that Germany initially would commit the bulk of her troops against Poland, and that the Polish forces would hold out, even under very heavy losses, until the Western Powers begun their offensive against Germany. The whole Polish defence effort was hanging on the anticipated Franco-British offensive.[123]

The Red Army was, of course, another option. But the question of letting it pass through Polish (and Romanian) territory was never successfully concluded, of which the Soviet were fully aware. Manne believes that the British never could relinquish their suspicions regarding Soviet intentions and sincerity, and that they never were willing to take any risks in coming to terms with the Soviets. Even if Stalin preferred a pact with Germany over the Western powers, which we really do not know, German documents reveal that he could not be sure of such a pact until August.[124] The Soviet–German commercial agreement, which had been discussed since the spring, was not signed until 19 August and Stalin did not receive guarantees from Germany regarding the secret protocol (dividing Poland) to be included in a proposed pact until the 21st.[125] Kenez argues that the Soviets decided to make a pact with Hitler relatively late, and that they preferred to keep their options open as long as possible.[126] The aforementioned French General Palasse believed on 23 August that the Soviet–German deal was a last resort for the Soviets, and was from the Soviet perspective taking place instead of their desired option – a deal with the Western Powers. Another Frenchman, the former air Minister, stated that the negotiations with the Soviets had been conducted with "incredible clumsiness".[127]

When the Cabinet, despite Chamberlains continued resistance, swung in favour of concluding an alliance in May Halifax made some efforts to press the matter. He admitted that he feared a Soviet-German rapprochement, and the French were pressuring him. In August he even applied a mild form of blackmail against the Poles, to make them accept Soviet assistance. The British military planners were very eager that the Soviets should take an active part in helping the Poles. Even if a direct Soviet military intervention would not take place, they at least wanted Soviet material aid. But Soviet capabilities to deliver aid to the Poles were questioned. In May the IIC concluded that only half, at best, of Poland's material needs could be provided by the Soviets. The CID was not happy with this conclusion and gave the JIC the task of examining the question. The JIC argued that the material facts were not relevant but instead that the Soviets willingness to help the Poles was the important factor. Therefore the final version of IIC report was altered to include this newly established "fact".[128]

Imlay argues that the so called Eastern Front, from the British perspective in August, depended on the Red Army marching into Poland, despite earlier assessments regarding the Soviet inability to conduct offensive operations. He interprets the British attitude change as a sign of desperation, and an adjustment to what was needed, instead of what was possible. This was a march from earlier British reluctance to include the Soviets, and also a sign of Chamberlains decreasing influence. In addition he believes that more could have been done to "win over the Soviets", even though the Soviets themselves were more to blame for the failure.[129]

Although rumours about a Soviet–German rapprochement apparently made the British more eager to establish closer cooperation, it is also true that the FO dismissed these rumours as unrealistic, with the exception of Vansittart, who still was regarded as an alarmist. The WO was more open to the possibility of a Soviet–German pact, but Chamberlain assured the Cabinet as late as 10 July that this was "quite impossible".[130] He was not alone in his belief, and rumours about Soviet–German negotiations were dismissed by some in the FO as Soviet scare tactics. British (and French) officials believed until the very last moment before the Soviet-German pact was signed that the Soviets would prefer isolation to a rapprochement with Germany.[131]

According to Steiner the British wished for a continuation of the negotiations in order to accommodate British opinion. She also argues that it might have been even more important – for the continuation – that Halifax and others believed that a Soviet inclusion was crucial for the credibility of the policy of deterrence. If this was the case, it seems unlikely that it was because of Halifax's appreciation of Soviet strength, but instead probably more due to Chatfield's (and later Halifax's) claim that the Germans might be deterred by an inclusion. However, Chamberlain did not share this belief regarding German perceptions (see below). Many in the Cabinet did not want to pay the price, Steiner argues, and accept the Soviet demands in the negotiations in order to gain the possible deterrent that a Soviet inclusion would bring. Only some in the Cabinet regarded Soviet support as necessary in war.[132] British assessments of Soviet strength add an extra dimension to this suggestion.

Chamberlain and Halifax, in late July, were reluctant to enter into military negotiations with the Soviets, and the former believed that negotiations would break down. If it would had been up to Chamberlain the negotiations would have already been abandoned.[133] According to Andrew, the British had begun the Anglo-Soviet talks without "either enthusiasm or a sense of urgency". In August, with negotiations still ongoing, Chamberlain confessed to the leader of the British Military Mission in Moscow that it was the House of Commons that had pushed him further in the direction of an alliance than he wished to go. The head of the Secret Intelligence Service (SIS), Admiral Sinclair, was just as Chamberlain an ardent anti-Bolshevik, and he held the belief that the USSR was more or less military worthless. Sinclair was directly negative towards engaging in negotiations, and told the head of the Mission going to Moscow that nothing much was to be expected.[134] The personnel composition, the authority and the manner in which they British military mission travelled to Moscow, gave a less than fully sincere impression considering the mission's officially alleged task, which was noted by Stalin.[135]

The hope that Hitler would not dare to start a war might have been a contributing factor in the British reluctance to go all in with the Soviets. At least Cadogan and Guy Liddell, a high-ranking British intelligence officer, expressed such beliefs (regarding the hope) in the very last days of August, based on a large amount of intelligence pointing in that direction.[136] It also seems that Chamberlain and Halifax, at least at the beginning of 1939 and maybe later, fostered hopes of a politically unstable Nazi regime, which might fall in the not too distant future.[137] General war preparations were taking place in Britain, but privately Chamberlain believed that Hitler could be brought to the negotiations table. He was anxious to avoid any action that could provoke the Führer, but he also believed that Hitler concluded that the time was not right for Germany to start a major war.[138] It also seems safe to assume that the British underestimated the cynical attitudes of the European dictators. The later threw all their ideological baggage overboard in order to create the Soviet-German pact; something that Chamberlain and other more democratically inclined persons seemed to have a harder time to do.

Chamberlain was probably sincere in his (officially expressed) opinions concerning the USSR, since he repeated them in private letters to his sisters. For example, if Spain would side with the Axis, the peace front would "lose far more in the West [Spain] than we could ever hope to gain in the East [the USSR]"; or: "I am so skeptical of the value of Russian help that I should not feel that our position was greatly worsened if we had to do without them"; or: "If we do get an agreement [with the USSR], as I rather think we shall, I'm afraid I shall not regard it as a triumph. I put as little value on Russian military capacity as I believe the Germans do." Had it not been for his government colleagues, he had wished to adopt an even firmer attitude towards the Soviets.[139] It is also likely that Chamberlain's assertion that he did not want to upset Hitler with an alliance is true. After all, he did not want to include Churchill in the Cabinet for the very same reason (even though not only for that reason).[140] In addition, we know that Chamberlain valued the opinions and policy advice of the SIS head Sinclair, and the later seems to have shared Chamberlain's low regard for Soviet strength and wished to avoid an Anglo-Soviet pact.[141]

Notes

1   See, for example, the works of Davies et al (eds.) (1994) for a closer examination of these issues.
2   Herndon (1983), 308.
3   Eden had been foreign secretary in Chamberlain's government but resigned in February 1938 partly due to issues related to the appeasement policy. He returned to this post in December 1940 under Churchill's wartime Government. Dutton (1997).
4   Hansard, "International Situation", HC Deb, 19 May, 1939, vol. 347, cc1809–86.
5   Crowson (1995); Self (ed.) (2006), 235.
6   Liddell Hart (1983), 24.
7   It is also hard to know if Neilson and Herndon have considered all available pre-1939 estimates, since they at least partly refer to different assessments. Neilson (1993), 207–216; Herndon (1983).
8   Scott & Jackson (2004), 142–143.
9   See, for example, Hucker (2008); Hucker (2006), 47–84, and Maiolo (2008), for a comment on earlier research.
10 McKercher (2008), 419–420; Manne (1981), 726–751.
11 Ferris (1995), 167.
12 Manne (1981), 726–751.
13 Ibid.
14 Imlay (2003), 37–46, 74, 96.
15 Ibid.
16 Ferris (1995), 161, 167; Steiner (2011), 750–51.
17 6–3-1939, N1292/233/38, FO371/23684 and FO418/85.
18 It is not explicitly clear from the report, and others to follow, that the British distinguished between the different parts of the Soviet Armed Forces when they referred to the "Red Army". Strictly speaking, the Red Army of the time was not

only the Army but also the Army Air Force. The Soviet Navy had a separate air arm. Therefore, when the British commented on the Red Army, these comments might include the Army air force, even though specific comments often were made with respect to the air forces.

19 6–3-1939, N1292/233/38, FO371/23684 and FO418/85.
20 Bialer (ed.) (1984), 639.
21 20–3-1939, N1602/485/38, FO371/23688.
22 Lee (2008), 56.
23 Harrison (1996), 270.
24 Total SAF strength was 20,978 aircraft (including the 1445 aircraft under the control of the Soviet Navy) on the 22 June 1941. Of the 19,533 Red Army planes 3934 were used at school and training facilities. On the other hand, only 16,502 (of the grand total) were serviceable at that date and 13,211 were combat ready. Glantz (1998), 21.
25 Samuelson (1999), 182.
26 Harrison (1985), 250; Whiting (1978), 66.
27 Glantz & House (2000), 306.
28 Samuelson (1999), 182.
29 Harrison (1985), 250.
30 Wark (1985), 111, 244, 248.
31 6–3-1939, N1292/233/38, FO371/23684 and FO418/85.
32 Ibid.
33 Although not specified, one has to assume that Seeds referred to the British press and perhaps other non-Soviet publications.
34 6–3-1939, N1292/233/38, FO371/23684 and FO418/85.
35 18, 19 and 21 April 1939, The memorandum "Russia's Strength" with various supplementary letters, FO371/23688.
36 16–3-1939, N1542/485/38, FO371/23688.
37 Probably the Secretary of State for War.
38 The reason forwarded for Firebrace's "low estimate" was that he had had a "very difficult and depressing year". 16–3-1939, N1542/485/38, FO371/23688.
39 Woodward (1970), 628.
40 17–3-1939, N1860/1012/38, FO371/23696; 21–3-1939, N1603/1012/38, FO371/23696.
41 Rohwer & Monakov (2001).
42 23–3-1939, N1572/1572/38, FO371/23698.
43 6–3-1939, N1292/233/38, FO371/23684 and FO418/85; 7–12–1939, N181/181/38, FO371/24851.
44 Ibid.
45 23–3-1939, N1572/1572/38, FO371/23698.
46 16–3-1939, N1542/485/38, FO371/23688.
47 17–3-1939, N1860/1012/38, FO371/23696; 21–3-1939, N1603/1012/38, FO371/23696.
48 21–3-1939, N1603/1012/38, FO371/23696.
49 18–3-1939, "C.O.S./283rdMtg.", CAB53/10; 21–4-1939, "C.O.S./291stMtg.", CAB53/11; 18–1-1939, "C.O.S./268rd Mtg.", CAB53/10; 24–4-1939, COS887, CAB53/48; 25–4-1939, C.95(39), CAB/24/285.
50 Ibid.
51 Ibid.
52 Ibid.
53 Manne (1981), 86.
54 18–3-1939, "C.O.S./283rdMtg.", CAB53/10; 18–1-1939," C.O.S./268rdMtg.", CAB53/10.

55 Strang (2006), 55; Bond (1983), 199; Niedhart (1983), 292; Liddell Hart (1983), 24, 28–29; 27-3-1939, F.(36)38[th]Mtg., CAB/24/284; April 1939, CP83(39), CAB/24/285; 29-3-1939, Cabinet(15)39, CAB23/98; 5-4-1939, Cabinet 18(39), CAB23/99; 19-5-1939, CP115(39), CAB/24/286; 22-5-1939, CP123(39), CAB/24/287; 17-5-1939, CP116(39), CAB/24/286; 4-9-1939, "War Cabinet 2(39)", CAB/65/1/2; 24-5-1939, Cabinet 30(39), CAB/23/99.

56 Sir Samuel Hoare, the Secretary of State for the Home Department, believed that the USSR was the greatest deterrent against German aggression in the East. Hoare stated that "All experience showed that Russia was undefeatable." 27-3-1939, F. (36)38[t]h Mtg., CAB/24/284. Russian military performance in the Great War was of course of a different kind, which probably was not unknown to other Cabinet members.

57 27-3-1939, "F.(36)38thMtg.", CAB/24/284.

58 27-3-1939, "F.(36)38thMtg.", CAB/24/284.

59 Manne (1981), 86.

60 19-4-1939, COS881(J.), CAB53/48.

61 Ibid.

62 19-4-1939, COS881(J.), CAB53/48; 24-4-1939, COS887, CAB53/48.

63 24-4-1939, COS887, CAB53/48.

64 Frieser (2005), 36.

65 15-4-1939, N2035/2035/38, FO371/23698.

66 4-4-1939, N1869/1572/38, FO371/23698; Harrison (1985), 268.

67 The expansion would be one away from the earlier "gigantomania" factories, into smaller ones. 4-4-1939, N1869/1572/38, FO371/23698.

68 Harrison (1996), 297.

69 Davies et al (eds.) (1994), 302.

70 Harrison (1985), 254.

71 Davies et al (1994), 298–300.

72 Glantz (1998), 9, 24.

73 Harrison (1985), 63–79; Harrison (1996), 180, 190–191.

74 Davies (1998), 61–63.

75 24-4-1939, COS887, CAB53/48; 19-4-1939, COS881(J.), CAB53/48.

76 25-4-1939, C.95(39), CAB/24/285.

77 24-4-1939, COS887, CAB53/48; 19-4-1939, COS881(J.), CAB53/48.

78 The number of artillery pieces in every division was estimated at 36, but it was also noted that this number would increase in the future. 24-4-1939, COS887, CAB53/48.

79 Ibid.

80 The Navy had 3 battleships, 3 cruisers, 9 light cruisers, 32 large destroyers, 48 small destroyers, 190 submarines, and 167 marine aircraft. The numbers are based on COS 887 but complemented with information from COS 881. Despite the fact that there was less than one week between the reports the number of ships stated in the reports are somewhat different, but the difference is marginal. There was also information about several lesser surface vessels, among them 169 motor torpedo boats and a smaller number of other vessels such as minelayers. The COS considered the efficiency of the single ships as satisfactory, but the organization and staff work of the Navy as a whole was below standard. The submarine fleet was seen as the most efficient arm. 19-4-1939, COS881(J.), CAB53/48; 24-4-1939, COS887, CAB53/48.

81 Comparing the following sources: Glantz (1998), 119; McCarthy & Syron (2002), 99; Zaloga & Ness (2003), 69, 157–158; Zaloga & Grandsen (1984), 116, 119, 225; Bishop (2007), 39.

82 Zaloga & Ness (2003), 157–158, 199–200; McCarthy & Syron (2002), 103–105; Bellamy (2007), 169, 172; Ellis (1993), 304.

83   Zaloga & Ness (2003), 3.
84   Hoffschmidt & Tantum (1968), 69–70; Chant (2007), 53, 60; Gander & Chamberlain (1979), 170, 174–186, 198–210, 222–224; Zaloga & Ness (2003), 3, 35; Ellis (1993), 203.
85   Gander & Chamberlain (1979), 49, 86, 300, 306–307; Zaloga (2003), 1, 3, 193–194, 198.
86   Colvin (1971), 205; 24–4-1939, Cabinet 22(39), CAB/23/99.
87   26–4-1939, Cabinet 24(39), CAB23/99.
88   Colvin (1971), 205; 24–4-1939, Cabinet 22(39), CAB/23/99.
89   Manne (1981), 86–90.
90   10–5-1939, COS902, CAB53/49.
91   16–5-1939, "C.O.S./295thMtg.", CAB53/11.
92   17–5-1939, CP116(39), CAB/24/286; 10–5-1939, COS902, CAB53/49.
93   17–5-1939, CP116(39), CAB/24/286.
94   17–5-1939, Cabinet 28(39), CAB/23/99.
95   17–5-1939, CP116(39), CAB/24/286.
96   17–5-1939, Cabinet 28(39), CAB/23/99.
97   18–5-1939, N2572/485/38, FO371/23688.
98   Ibid.
99   Ibid.
100 Neilson (2006), 279, 378; 18–5-1939, JIC99, CAB56/4; 14–5-1939, ICF/1176, CAB56/4; 18–5-1939, JIC 26th Mtg., CAB56/1; 26–8-1939, C12194/281/17, FO371/22925.
101 18–5-1939, JIC99, CAB56/4; 14–5-1939, ICF/1176, CAB56/4.
102 18–5-1939, JIC 26th Mtg., CAB56/1.
103 The JP was a sub-committee to the CID. 26–8-1939, C12194/281/17, FO371/22925.
104 26–5-1939, N2669/2035/38, FO371/23698.
105 16–1-1939, ICF/1153(Ukraine), WO208/1750; Davies et al (ed.) (1994), 285–286, 289, 296.
106 The 1938 output of electricity was estimated to 36.5 billion kilowatt hours (kWh); of petroleum: 30.8 million tonnes; coal: 132.9 million tonnes; pig iron: 15 million tonnes; steel: 18 million tonnes; and of rolled steel: 13.5 million tonnes. The estimated output of lorries and passenger cars was 208,000. 15–4-1939, N2035/2035/38, FO371/23698.
107 20–7-1939, N3505/18/38, FO371/23677.
108 24–5-1939, Cabinet 30(39), CAB/23/99; May 1939, CP124(39), CAB/24/287.
109 24–5-1939, Cabinet 30(39), CAB/23/99.
110 30–5-1939, N2758/1012/38, FO371/23696.
111 Davies et al (eds.) (1994), 280 compared to 321.
112 Harrison (1985), 7.
113 Parker (1993), 216–229, 236–239; Colvin (1971), 215; Neilson (2006), 294; Steiner (2003), 39; Steiner (2011), 887.
114 Neilson & Otte (2009), 243–244.
115 Parker (1993), 216–229, 236–239; Colvin (1971), 215; Steiner (2011), 887.
116 Manne (1981), 92.
117 Haslam (1984), 225–226.
118 3–8-1939, "Military Missions." Box-3119, Entry-77, RG165.
119 Firebrace rated the staff work of the divisions and the junior officers as fairly good. Ibid.
120 Ibid.
121 According to G-2 the Red Army had 113 infantry divisions and 35 cavalry divisions. 11–8-1939, "Location […]", Box-3122, Entry-77, RG165.
122 Manne (1981), 92.

123 Zabecki (1999), 1630, 1633.
124 Manne (1981), 92.
125 Murphy (2005), 23; Fest (2002), 582.
126 Kenez (1999), 131.
127 Duroselle (2004), 398.
128 Imlay (2003), 97–99.
129 Ibid, 99–100.
130 Kahn (2013), 740.
131 Steiner (2011), 893–894; Jackson (2000), 373–374.
132 Steiner (2011), 895–896.
133 Ibid, 901.
134 Kahn (2013), 740.
135 Steiner (2011), 902.
136 Andrew (2009), 213.
137 Steiner (2011), 725; Gillard (2007), 140–41.
138 Steiner (2011), 766, 776, 819.
139 Parker (1993), 216–229, 236–241; Colvin (1971), 215; Self (2006), 18, 414–416.
140 Steiner (2003), 39.
141 Andrew (1987), 23.

5 US pre-Barbarossa assessments

We have already seen above earlier the Americans took interest in British assessments. The importance of US assessments at this stage, before Barbarossa and the US war entry, is more indirect. The US still did not have the same direct influence over European politics as the British. The presentation of US assessments at this stage should instead be looked upon as an explanatory background to the immediate pre-Barbarossa assessments, and as a comparative benchmark for the British perceptions. It is also possible, due to the Anglo-American information exchange already before the US war entry, that US assessments might have had an indirect influence on British perceptions.

The USSR was only recognized diplomatically by the US when the Roosevelt administration decided to do so in 1933. One of the factors that contributed to the recognition was Japanese expansionism in the Far East.[1] The US military attaché to the USSR (from July 1934 to January 1939), Colonel Faymonville, and the US ambassador (from November 1936 to June 1938) Joseph Davies had painted a relatively bright picture of the capabilities of the Soviet Armed Forces during the 1930s. Faymonville was considered as a controversial person in the US Army for his relative lack of criticism of the Soviets.[2] They perceived the effects of the purges of 1937–1938 somewhat differently, and were also convinced that the USSR was militarily much stronger than most of their colleagues in Moscow and Washington during the 1930s. In January 1939, Davies (after his ambassadorship) sent President Roosevelt a letter in which he outlined some of his thoughts about Soviet military strength, which he believed to be much greater than "the reactionaries of Europe concede". The (post-Faymonville-Davies) US diplomatic establishment in Moscow and Riga (Latvia) continued to give the purges some attention in 1939. Judging by their, and G2, reports – partly based on newspaper clippings – before the actual period of this study, it seems that the decimation of the officer corps was the Soviet Armed Forces' greatest problem, and that it would take years to rectify the situation.[3]

5.1 The economy and its military potential

Several specific topics were commented on by the Moscow embassy, relating to everything from production figures to methods of economic planning. The embassy's Chargé d'Affaires *ad interim* Alexander C. Kirk reported in March 1939 that the economy (in general) was planned in an "unscientific manner", and that the 1938 oil output was far behind the original plan, despite heavy investment.[4] Later that month the embassy relied heavily on the opinions of the British Naval Attaché in an attempt to evaluate naval matters relating to industrial capacity. Clanchy more or less repeated what he had already stated in the British embassy reports to the FO.[5] In late March the motor transport system was analysed: the trucks and passenger cars were "extremely badly operated under normal circumstances". During war conditions the extra strain put upon the transport system, and on industry in general, would "seriously jeopardize" the use of motor transport, which was considered to be a secondary, but at the same time important transport sector.[6]

In April Kirk reported about the negative effects of centralization and bureaucracy. The general subject of his report was economic development during the year's first quarter. The economy had failed to live up to the plan goals. Only slight increases, or even stagnating output, were noticed in the steel, iron and coal branches during the first quarter. A large turnover of labour hampered the economy, as well as workers showing up for work but not doing their full time. Despite these conditions any excess labour would not be available during wartime: "The [USSR], under the present economic system, possesses little or no idle productive capacity or unemployed labor on which to draw in time of war and consequently the volume of output at any given time displays practically the maximum productivity of labor and managerial efficiency of the country." However, he argued that the government could increase the working hours in the event of an emergency.[7]

The purges were not described as the main cause for the failure of plan fulfillment. The purges were not ongoing in the first quarter of 1939, compared to the situation in 1937–1938. The economic results were not better during this quarter than during the first quarter of 1938. He admitted that it was too early to draw any definite conclusions regarding the effects of the purges, but the fundamental cause of the failure was blamed on the result of planning. The plans would require, for their proper execution, an administrative ability and technical efficiency beyond the capacity of the ponderous bureaucracy, since it was responsible for the minutest details of all Soviet activity.[8]

Many reports on similar subjects were also made by the US Riga embassy. In March the military attaché in Riga, Major George E. Huthsteiner, presented the G-2 with a review of the military-economic situation. Huthsteiner saw the difficulty of obtaining verifiable information about the USSR as an important problem in the study of its national defence capacities. The Soviets was doing everything in their power to withhold any undesirable information, they were only publishing facts that were in keeping with their aims. Generally, the USSR was a country with potentially tremendous military-economic resources, but the development of these resources was incomplete. Therefore, at the time, it would be wrong to estimate military capabilities too highly. The growth of raw material output was stressed; but the economy had several problems and weaknesses. Even though the USSR had almost all the necessary raw materials for the munitions industries, they were not all accessible on account of technical shortcomings and transportation difficulties. The foremost problem with the labour force was their low level of training.[9]

Some remarks were made about the munitions industries geographical location; which mainly was near Moscow and Leningrad. In the event of war and bombing these plants would be evacuated. Many new plants had been built along the Volga and in the Urals district. The munitions industry was inefficient and suffered from a shortage of skilled workers. The waste was unusually high and due to the lack of trained workers, productivity was lower than in Western and Central European plants. In the case of war the USSR would not only be forced to import raw materials, but also armaments. According to a "well informed foreign source", the munitions industry was capable of meeting the wartime demands of about 50 divisions, provided a smooth functioning of the transport system. The munitions industries were already working at full capacity, so a further output increase in wartime seemed improbable.[10]

In this respect, Hutchsteiner had the same perception in principle as the British COS. The COS's (and Kirkman's) estimate was 30 divisions, but in the context of Soviet (and German) World War II divisional numerical strength the difference can be regarded as small. And even the 50 divisions hinged on well-oiled transportation. The erroneous notion concerning the inability to increase wartime munitions output was also similar to COS and other British estimates.

Concerning the food situation, Hutchsteiner stated, in spite of their poor nutrition, that the Russians were capable of hard work. The state and collectivized agriculture was an advantage in the long run since the government now only had to deal with a few production centres, instead of a large number of individuals. However, some problems were foreseen, since the "centuries old hunger of the Russian peasant for more land" was not satisfied by this kind of agricultural organization. This "hunger", if not satisfied, was the economy's weakest spot, and in the case of war, as happened in the Great War, the peasants might leave the front at some critical stage to distribute the land themselves. Hutchstenier estimated that 83 per cent of the total population was employed in agriculture.[11] If the figure 83 per cent was not a printing error, it reveals that he had an outdated notion about the labour force distribution. In 1939 only about 55 per cent were employed within agriculture.

Despite some advantages with centralized agriculture, he believed, the system of state planning, and socialism in general, was not advantageous. The impact of the planning system, and the resulting lack of private competition, due to centralization and bureaucratic methods, had also caused an adverse general influence on production. Planning mistakes were having serious after-effects over the years. The transportation system was the most outstanding example of this, as the failure to plan for increased freight had caused, "as is well known [...] an almost complete collapse of the transportation system". The situation was not helped by country's great geographical distances.[12]

In May Lieutenant-Colonel Sumner Waite, the US assistant military attaché in Paris, citied a prominent French military expert, who stated that the Soviet 1938 military budget was 30 per cent of the general budget. G-2 commented on the defence burden in a short report from July. The increase in military outlays from 1938 to 1939 was see as tremendous, because the estimated total appropriation for the People's Commissariat of Defence and Navy combined grew from 18.7 per cent (1938) to 26.3 per cent (1939). Armaments and war materials stood for 55 or 60 per cent of the later sum.[13] Also counting outlays for the Commissariat of the Interior (the NKVD) as defence outlays, which the Soviets apparently did themselves, total defence outlays were considered by Hutchsteiner (later in July) to be somewhat less than 30 per cent.[14]

The only concrete US figures for munitions output during this period was delivered in a May G-2 memorandum, intended for the assistant secretary of war. The annual 1938 aircraft output was 2150 units, of which 400 were civil. The aviation industry was "handicapped" due to "the mediocrity of its personnel".[15] In Waite's report (see above) it was noted that, although the French expert believed that the abundance of human and natural resources worked to the Soviet advantage in a war, industry would not be capable of increasing production during wartime.[16]

In August the Moscow embassy issued a second quarter economic review, to a large extent about the growth of some important heavy and other industry branches. The development of these branches was sub-standard, at least since 1936. With regards to the coal industry the explanation was labour discipline problems, the high turnover of the workforce and a failure to extend development work satisfactorily. The quality of the steel industry's output was very low and defective. Based on data in Soviet publications, progress in the non-ferrous metallurgical industry was not seen as impressive, since this branch suffered from an inadequate raw material base. The food industry had managed to fulfil the plan, and improvements were also noted for the textile and some other light industries, but there still existed an acute shortage of some food and light industry products in many large industrial areas, in Moscow and other large cities.[17] Problems were also identified in branches not mentioned above and much for the same reasons, even though some exceptions on the positive side were noted. However, on balance the general impression was that industrial expansion since 1936 had been a failure. The expansion had generally not managed to increase the output level, with the exception of some defence industries. This failure meant, in turn, that the national plan had failed, and, moreover, that the goals of enhancing labour productivity and lowering production costs also had failed.[18]

5.2 The size and efficiency of the armed forces

Most US reports during this period in this category was about the SAF. Much of the information used by the US Moscow embassy originated from

Anglo-French sources. The opinions of the aforementioned British air attaché Hallawell were commented on by the military attaché Hayne. Hallawell was regarded as well informed and the same was said about other foreign attachés. Hayne regarded these attachés in practice as the only available source on Soviet military aviation. It is not possible to know if Hayne had seen the exact same reports the British had compiled during the spring, but the information that Hayne took part of seemed to be approximately the same as in these reports.[19] This information, and other reports written by and commented on by US observers during the spring, confirmed the British picture of a relatively inefficient SAF with a strength of about 4000 to 6000 first-line aircraft. Some sources also stated that there existed a considerable number of aircraft in reserve. A large number of these aircraft, especially the non-first line, were seen as obsolescent.[20]

In March, G-2 noted a report from the US military attaché in Belgrade (Yugoslavia), Lieutenant-Colonel E. Villaret, and the attention he paid to the community of "White-Russians" (Russian ex-patriots) there. They had a school which took great interest in the former home country. One of the staff members was a Colonel Pronin, formerly of the Imperial Russian Army, who devoted his full time to collecting information about the Red Army. Villaret regarded Pronin as worthy of attention. Pronin relied upon many sources and according to two sources of German origin the Red Army had 12,600 guns and 6000 tanks, or 10,000 tanks, depending on the source. Villaret also referred to a careful study of "dependable" Soviet source material, which indicated that the strength amounted to 1000 modern tanks, 5500 old tanks, and 6000 tank-ettes (small tanks with machine-gun main armament). Other cited estimates for Red Army manpower strength were 1.8 and 1.3 million men, respectively, organized into around 130 divisions. Regardless of the numerical strength, Villaret saw the Red Army as unfit for war, due to several reasons: the purges; the influence of political commissars and poor battle performance against the Japanese during 1938.[21]

5.3 Internal stability

Villaret also enumerated other reasons for the Red Army's unpreparedness for war; falling more into the category internal stability. He argued that the population detested the communists and the Soviet government. Fugitives from the USSR reported that acts of sabotage by workers in the armament factories were becoming increasingly numerous. He even believed that the population hoped impatiently for war, because war seemed to be the only sure way to shake off the yoke of communism. When millions of men obtained weapons in the event of mobilization, these weapons would soon be turned against the government. For this reason the government, who knew this full well, feared a general mobilization.[22] Earlier in 1939, G-2 had interviewed a Soviet general in exile, "Krivitski", who expressed opinions that resembled Villaret's in principle.[23]

Notes

1 US State Department official website: U.S. Department of State, Office of the Historian, Milestones: 1921–1936; (https://history.state.gov/milestones/1921-1936/ussr); accessed 2015-09-02.
2 Herndon & Baylen (1975), 483–505.
3 5–2-1939, "After […]", Box-3126, Entry-77, RG165; 23–1-1939, Riga, Box-3125, Entry-77, RG165; Appendix 11, Roll-19, M1443, RG165; Herndon & Baylen (1975), 483–505; Davies (1943), 1, 367, 377–378.
4 15–3-1939, Despatch No. 2180, Roll-34, T1249, RG59; 3–3-1939, Despatch No. 2152, Roll-34, T1249, RG59.
5 22–3-1939, Despatch No. 2192, Roll-26, T1249, RG59.
6 24–3-1939, 21–4-1939, Despatch No. 2194, Roll-72, T1249, RG59.
7 26–4-1939, Despatch No. 2282, Roll-34, T1249, RG59; 26–4-1939, "Brief […]", Box-3100, Entry-77, RG165.
8 Ibid.
9 24–3-1939, 2655-D-550, Roll-10, M1443, RG165.
10 Ibid.
11 Ibid.
12 Ibid.
13 1–7-1939, "Annual […]", Box-3127, Entry-77, RG165.
14 6–7-1939, "War […]", Box-3127, Entry-77, RG165.
15 9–5-1939, G-2/2090–383, Roll-23, M1443, RG165.
16 16–5-1939, "Subject: […]", Box-3122, Entry-77, RG165.
17 14–8-1939, "Review […]", Box-3100, Entry-77, RG165; 14–9-1939, "Review […]", Roll-34, T1249, RG59.
18 14–8-1939, "Review […]", Box-3100, Entry-77, RG165.
19 15–3-1939, 4–4-1939, Despatch No. 2182, Roll-26, T1249, RG59; 27–3-1939, Report No. 1474, Roll-20, M1443, RG165.
20 1–4-1939, "Supplementary […]", Box-3154, Entry-77, RG165; 23–3-1939, 2037–1833, Reel-15, M1443, RG165; 4–5-1939, Report No. 10399, Roll-20, M1443, RG165; 9–5-1939, G-2/2090–383, Roll-23, M1443, RG165.
21 23–3-1939, 2037–1833, Reel-15, M1443, RG165.
22 Ibid.
23 17–1-1939, "Historical, […]", Box-3206, Entry-77, RG165.

6 The Molotov-Ribbentrop pact and its consequences

Despite the Anglo-French efforts, or, as we have seen, perhaps partly due to the lack thereof, the Soviets struck a deal with Germany. As apparent from the British discussion during the spring and the summer this was regarded as a very threatening event, and on 23 August this situation became a reality. Hinsley claims that the British had no reliable information regarding the Soviet–German negotiations during the summer.[1] In contrast to the impression that Soviet diplomats tried to create, the pact was more than just a non-aggression treaty, since it included a secret protocol about dividing Eastern Europe. Germany attacked Poland on 1 September 1939, the Soviets waited until the 17th. The Soviet attack can almost be compared to a mopping-up operation, since the Poles by that time were more or less defeated by the Germans.

The Soviet–German deal created both confusion and consternation in London and Paris.[2] It is apparent that they now calculated on the USSR as being a potential enemy. The COS, now directly subordinate to the British War Cabinet, used formulations such as "the intervention of Russia on the side of Germany." The COS believed that the general goal of Soviet foreign policy was to spread world revolution, and that she wished to conquer the areas once held by Tsarist Russia in the West. It seem like the FO shared these opinions in principle.[3]

6.1 The Polish campaign

The campaign in Poland provided the British with an opportunity to make an assessment of the Red Army's capabilities based on its conduct in action. It appears that the campaign did not provide them with any reason to really change earlier perceptions. In October infantry and cavalry were described in a COS report as an undisciplined mob, while the armoured troops gave a satisfactory impression. The equipment of the regular divisions was also satisfactory, but the equipment status of the reserve divisions was significantly worse. The COS assumed that the Soviet Army's fuel supply had broken down during the advance into Poland.[4]

In late September COS estimated the numerical strength of the forces operating in Poland to 30 infantry divisions, 12 cavalry divisions and 10 mechanized brigades.[5] In mid-September the Red Army's estimated total strength were about 4 million men, with 1.5 million stationed on or close to the Polish–Soviet border.[6] This was an appreciable increase in the number of troops compared with the spring estimates, and probably prompted by the perceived effects of the mobilization in connection to the war. A few days earlier Firebrace estimated Red Army strength to two million, soon to increase to 2.5 million and ultimately approaching 3 million men. The recent mobilization effort was estimated to 1.5 million and the annual intake of conscripts to 0.86 million.[7]

The US attaché Hayne also commented on the invasion and it seems probable that he received information from the British, or at least from the same source as the British. He expressed very similar opinions regarding the numerical strength of the troops in Poland, their appearance during operations, their problems with discipline and the Army's perceived fuel supply breakdown.[8] Hayne and the US Moscow Ambassador Laurence Steinhardt sent information to Washington in September and October stating that the regular Army before the mobilization mustered 2 million men, but in early October Hayne stated that the strength had increased to around 4 million. Steinhardt believed that Red Army strength could surpass 4 million before the end of 1939. A late November report from Hutchsteiner estimated regular Army strength to approximately 2 million.[9]

6.2 The USSR as a potential military adversary

During the autumn, in the light of the Molotov-Ribbentrop pact and the Polish campaign, the British analysed Soviet capabilities from the perspective of the USSR as a military adversary. An Admiralty's Intelligence Division report about naval strength was contemplated in late September by some FO officials. This estimate did not differ much from similar assessments written during the spring, except from an increase in the number of submarines (now 202 to 216 vessels). In the case that these submarines were efficient, stated one of the FO officials, their numbers "suggest very unpleasant possibilities".[10] In October Seeds and Clanchy of the Moscow embassy believed that more than 70 subs could operate in the North Sea, but Clanchy regarded the impact of these as nothing more than a "nuisance". Seeds was of another opinion, and, under the condition that the vessels were under German guidance, he thought that they would be "a formidable addition" to the German arsenal. As for the Soviet Navy, in general, Clanchy regarded it as unfit for offensive warfare, and he expressed a low opinion about its administration and Higher Command.

Firebrace and Hallawell still regarded the Red Army unfit for offensive war. The former repeated his opinions about "the inefficiency of the Higher Command, administrative inefficiency and the general effect of the 'purge' on all ranks." He added that the general impact of an offensive war upon the USSR would likely be the most important factor to persuade Stalin not to engage in it. Firebrace also regarded it as unlikely that Soviet ground forces could participate in a war against Britain (in the West), based on the perceived policy not only of the USSR but also of Germany. As for the SAF Hallawell perceived practical problems concerning its possible operation alongside Germany in the West, and added that SAF training was sub-standard compared to the training of the Western Power's air forces.[11]

In October COS delivered much critique regarding Red Army equipment and overall military efficiency, and they believed the Germans were of the same opinion. However, reports existed about eyewitness being impressed by the great number and effectiveness of Soviet tanks.[12] Somewhat in contrast to the embassy staff, the COS acknowledges that the Red Army could be operating alongside Germany against Anglo-French forces in the West, but it was not likely at the moment. The potential danger of subs was also recognized; even though their efficiency was lower than their German counterparts. However, large scale and direct cooperation between the Red Army and the *Wehrmacht* was unlikely. If large German forces, up to 100 divisions, committed to the West, could not bring certain victory, then some additional Red Army troops would not matter much. Germany was already superior to the Anglo-French in terms of aircraft, and the Soviet aircraft models were anyway obsolete in general. On the other hand, they believed that the USSR could contribute indirectly to the efforts of the *Wehrmacht* by threatening and attacking British interests in Asia, such as India, Afghanistan, Iran and Iraq.[13]

6.3 The Red Army enter Estonia

The basically negative impression painted in the September and October reports, concerning the Red Army's efficiency in Poland, was confirmed in the COS's 10 November weekly war résumé.[14] In late November the FO noticed a widely distributed MI2(b) report, based on intelligence collected in the Baltic States and Poland. On 28 September the Estonian government agreed to Soviet demands concerning the establishment of military bases. When Soviet troops moved in (from 18 October) eyewitness accounts could be collected from Estonians. Even though the MI2 report noted that accounts of Polish and Estonian origin could be negatively biased towards the Soviets – exaggerating weakness – they were not seen as completely untrue. In addition, the Estonian/Polish accounts supported the information gathered over the longer and preceding peace time period, showing Red Army weakness. Even though its numbers and "a considerable quantity of good equipment" were regarded as strong feature, its weaknesses were salient enough to render it the epithet "amorphous mass". It could, however, sustain hard blows from an enemy, but it was in no way capable of deliver the same against large scale organized opposition. The administrative apparatus and the leadership suffered from very serious weaknesses, and the main weakness of the lower ranks and soldiers were "lack of initiative" and "apathy". The overall impression gained from the report was that its capability for conducting war was low, but that its defensive capabilities were considerably better.[15] This impression mirrored to a large extent earlier British assessments.

An FO official commented the report and believed the Polish/Estonian perceptions as prejudiced. He preferred rather to notice the observations delivered by the Swedish and British military attachés in Estonia. They had been "quite favourably impressed" by the garrisons sent to Estonia. Nevertheless, the report confirmed to him the general impression already gained in the FO (i.e. that the Red Army was incapable of offensive action against any European Great Power, but that it could have "a devastating effect against most small powers – especially its neighbors in Central Asia"). Another FO official reviewed the report on 5 December – five days after the Soviet attack on Finland – and to him recent events in Finland seemed to confirm the "unfavourable" picture conveyed by observers in contact with the Red Army.[16]

It seems that Huthsteiner, probably due to his position as the US military attaché in neighbouring Latvia, personally had seen Soviet troops march into Estonia in October, and he reported about it to the MID. His observations included many vehicle breakdowns and he regarded the quality of military equipment as poor. He claimed that other "competent observers" confirmed his views by their observations.[17] His negative take on the Red Army continued in a late November report, in which he stated that "The morale of the numerous peasants called to the colors in case of war is a very uncertain factor and may easily prove catastrophic to the Soviet régime."[18]

6.4 Assessments regarding the economy during the autumn

The Western observers also perceived negative implications for the economy as a result of the mobilization in connection to the Polish campaign. Hayne saw it as likely that the mobilization effort had affected the balance of the economy negatively, and that even under normal circumstance the transportation system barely functioned effectively. Steinhardt was more or less of the same opinion.[19] A late September US Moscow embassy dispatch continued familiar information about the problems in some important heavy industry branches: failure to improve results, raw material shortages, defective output, inefficient operations and "constant breakdown in machinery". Industry, in general, and the transport sector had been disrupted somewhat due to the operations and mobilization of the Polish campaign. The men that had been mobilized were replaced by untrained women labour, and therefore the already existing problems with labour shortages and untrained personnel were going to increase.[20]

The same was stated in principle in the embassy's third quarter economic review from November. An even larger percentage of defective output was expected, as well as a more rapid deterioration of the condition of machinery, and a labour productivity decline. The authorities had failed to improve the conditions during the quarter and the September mobilization would affect the economy adversely. Many enterprises were operating at less than full capacity due fuel shortages. From an economic perspective the USSR was weak, lacking the strength of a Great Power, since "there are still too many weak points in the economic structure". The shortage of essential raw materials and the overburdened transport system were two of the most important weaknesses.[21] Later in November the embassy returned to the economic problems in general and the problems incurred by the September mobilization, already described in principle above. They added that the economic situation was so weak that it would have implications for the regime's foreign policy; the Soviets would be extremely cautious which in turn would affect the possibilities of further territorial expansion.[22] The MID returned to the September mobilization as late as January 1940: the call up of around 1 million workers had brought "considerable confusion" in the industry and transport sector. Untrained women were replacing the men and at the same time it had been necessary for workers to manage at least one or two more machines than before.[23]

In a November report containing information concerning the raw material situation, Steinhardt believed that the shortages made the Soviets resort to raw material substitution in the machine building industry. This solution worked against product quality, and the shortage of non-ferrous metals and rubber was serious, with implications for Anglo-Soviet relations: the British could "seriously cripple Soviet industry" since many of the essential materials were imported from the British Empire.[24] Later that month the Riga legation also produced a report related to the raw material situation, and the Soviets dealings with Germany. The author doubted that the USSR could make any difference to the German raw material situation, without at same time laying extra burdens upon its own population.[25] However, in a later part two of the dispatch it was argued that Germany could receive some raw materials in "appreciable quantities", without damage to Soviet economy.[26] In December the Moscow embassy tried to assess the problems that the USSR would encounter when building up a modern large-scale navy. The German Naval attaché in Moscow, Captain von Baumbach, was supplying information in the strictest confidence. Baumbach envisaged a scenario of Soviet industrial weakness for years to come. Therefore, the USSR would not be a threat to Germany even if Germany helped the Soviets to build a large navy – and the Germans were prepared to do that according to the captain. Regarding the Soviet ability to threaten Germany, Steinhardt was of the same opinion as Baumbach, and the former also believed that economic cooperation would be beneficial for both countries.[27]

The British also touched upon the economic implications of Soviet–German cooperation. A British press clip from November, about Soviet setbacks in the output of pig iron, steel and rolled steel, was given some attention by FO officials. If the USSR was unable to supply her own industries with raw material, then she would be even less able to supply Germany. One of the officials commented the news as "encouraging".[28] In the 20 October Moscow embassy memorandum (see above) Clanchy concluded: "Any form of active [Soviet] warfare prosecuted on land, in the air or at sea would bring about a breakdown in the internal economy of the country: the transport system alone would be unable to supply the fuel and stores required."[29]

In October and November the COS commented on the economy in their reports. They assessed the unsatisfactory industrial conditions, and the need for German assistance in order to avoid a long run deterioration of industrial efficiency.[30] The transport sector was inept to handle the military situation.[31] In their reporting to the War Cabinet they returned to effects of the partial mobilization; stating it had caused disorganization in the railway traffic during October. This situation had created great difficulties in the process of equipping the reserve divisions, and furnishing clothes to the regular divisions. They assumed that the Soviet problems of supplying its troops in Poland were common knowledge, and they connected the problematic food situation in the USSR to the mobilization. The COS concluded: "The weight of evidence tends, therefore, to confirm previous estimates that Russia could not at present fight a serious offensive war."[32]

Some aspects of Soviet military and economic resources was analysed in a December WO report; as it seems, solely based on the opinions of one person stationed in China: "Lack of organizing ability is as apparent in the Army as in the industrial and commercial life of the country." Furthermore the source stated that the USSR could not hope to survive a prolonged war against "a first-class power".[33]

6.5 Soviet air strength – autumn assessments

Assessments regarding aircraft were the only estimates available regarding the numerical strength of armaments at this time, and they also included an evaluation of aircraft production. An October report prepared by G-2, relying on different estimates, showed that the Soviets had significantly fewer aircraft than Germany. The figures originated from the Moscow and Riga legations, and revealed that the numerical strength had increased significantly, compared to earlier assessments. The SAF had 8210 (Moscow embassy) and 10,450 (Riga) planes respectively, of which 5370 and 5730, respectively, were stationed in combat units. This only represented 58 and 62 per cent of the estimated German combat aircraft, and significantly less than Britain's 7724 units. Total British and German aircraft strength was 11,278 and 15,336 units, respectively. This made Germany, the UK and the USSR the three largest air powers, followed in (total) strength by Italy, the US, Japan and France.[34]

The above Soviet aircraft totals were tantamount to figures sent to Washington by Huthsteiner and Hayne by the turn of the month August/September. They believed as before that many of the aircraft was obsolescent and the first line strength was 6400 and 5050, respectively. The ongoing aircraft output was relatively outdated. However, Hayne believed that Moscow aimed to substitute all obsolete planes in combat units for newer models before the end of 1939. He predicted that the 1939 military aircraft output would be 4000.[35] Hayne was critical of aviation industry efficiency. Although the authorities were very eager to obtain the latest foreign production technology, the lack of skilled workers to install and operate the machinery inhibited technical progress. He blamed the purges for robbing the industry of some good aircraft designers.[36]

In October Hallawell stated that the factories were working at nearly full capacity to produce outdated planes, to provide the SAF, which had a first-line strength of 4500 units, with more obsolete aircraft.[37] Later in the month the 4500 figure was confirmed in a FO report (British Minister of Supply Leslie Burgin had the same estimate), where it also was stated that British military aircraft were "greatly superior" to Soviet.[38]

6.6 Assessments connected to the Soviet–Japanese conflict

It seems that the British were not fully aware of the circumstances pertaining to the Soviet–Japanese border battles during 1939.[39] The Soviets had defeated the Japanese Army in regular pitched battles, reaching a climax in August. The Japanese experience of the Red Army was probably a contributory factor in the decision to expand southwards by the end of 1941, instead of attacking the USSR alongside Germany.[40] Few Western observers, if any, had reliable information on these events.[41] The very poor Red Army performance against the Japanese during the Lake Khasan battles in 1938 received, in contrast to the 1939 victories, a great deal of attention by Western press.[42] In late July Hayne reported to G-2 about the fighting, based on information from Soviet press sources. Needless to say, the Soviets portrayed the performance of their own troops in a positive light, but it seems that Hayne at least believed that the information contained a grain of truth.[43] Information in a January 1940 MID bulletin indicated a poor performance by Soviet tanks against Japanese forces at Nomonhan in 1939.[44]

According to Herndon the pre-1939 Soviet–Japanese border battles strengthened negative British perceptions of Red Army capabilities, especially if considering that the Far Eastern troops were seen as somewhat better on average.[45] The Soviet–Japanese situation received attention in many British 1939 reports, but they did not include the successful Soviet effort against Japan from May to September.[46] However, it was stated in a November MI2 (b) report: "It is interesting to note that the Japanese reverse this summer was the result of, not of offensive action in the first place by Red Army troops, but of the inability of the Japanese to stand up to the mechanized forces with which the Russians were able to meet the Japanese attack."[47]

6.7 Anglo-French plans to interdict the Soviet oil supply

The Western Powers contemplated the possibility of blocking German iron ore imports from Sweden, but the Soviet–German rapprochement opened up a new perspective – to deny Germany oil from the Caucasus. The Caucasus, especially Baku, was the by far most important Soviet oil-producing region.

The Soviet–German pact included economic cooperation, which among other things meant an annual export of several hundred thousand tonnes of oil to Germany. The French planned for attacks on German tankers in the Black Sea, and the Western Powers also wished to bomb Soviet industrial centres and oil fields in the Caucasus, in addition to spark a Moslem revolt in the region.[48]

In October the COS investigated the desirability of planning for attacking the Caucasus oil resources. The result, titled "Russia: vulnerability of oil supplies", was presented to the War Cabinet 2 December. The matter had been investigated on the initiative of Leslie Burgin who had proposed it in a letter to Lord Halifax.[49] Halifax sent a letter in response to Burgin on 8 November 1939. He believed that the destruction of the Baku fields was one of the most important goals in the event of a war with the USSR.[50] Burgin pointed to the high priority that oil reserves had for the bombing fleets of most countries, and that only a few important Soviet centres of oil production existed (Baku, Grozny and Maikop). Burgin also pointed out another supposed weakness, namely the risk of internal anti-communist revolts. This could happen, according to him, if a large city was conquered or destroyed. For some reason Leningrad was considered as the best target. But it was first and foremost oil as a target that prompted a closer investigation. The JIC was instructed to investigate the facts that were mentioned in Burgin's letter to Halifax.[51]

The JIC commented on the oil situation in three reports.[52] They also concluded that there was no evidence supporting Burgin's theory; that the destruction of a major city would result in anti-communist revolts. The great importance of Baku and other centres were stressed. They estimated, in this instance relatively realistically, that out of the total Soviet 1938 output, 75 per cent originated from Baku, and most of the rest from Grozny and Maikop. They mentioned the increasing importance of oil for the increasingly more mechanized agriculture. The prospects for a successful air attack against the oil wells, and the oil refineries there, were regarded as good.[53] In their 2 December report the COS stated that an aerial attack (on oil) would be an important factor in a possible attempt to exert pressure on the Soviets.[54]

The British seemingly regarded Soviet oil dependence as quite crucial and also believed oil to be in relatively short supply. A November AI2(b) report described present output as barely sufficient for economic needs and the armed forces. In addition, the requirements were increasing much faster than output. The MEW corroborated the later conclusion the same month, and also stated that famine would result from a failure to supply agriculture with sufficient petroleum.[55] In January 1940 the WO reported in the same spirit and stressed the agricultural dependence on oil due to the widespread mechanization. The horses were too few in order to compensate for a possible oil induced mechanized breakdown. A ruined oil industry could lead to disturbances, which in turn could expedite the outbreak of local revolts.[56]

The British figures regarding oil output were relatively realistic. During the autumn the JIC and the Moscow embassy estimated 1938 output to around 30 million tonnes, and nearly 33 million tonnes (in 1939), respectively.[57]

According to later research actual oil output during 1938–1940 was 30.2, 30.3 and 31.1 million tonnes, respectively.[58]

In December the US assistant military attaché in Paris (see above) estimated 1938 output to 28.9 million tonnes. He tried to analyse the Soviet capacity to supply Germany with oil, and in this context he used the words "Slav incompetence". He believed that an increase of output above the 1938 level was unlikely, and if it did increase it would be due to the help of German technicians and organization.[59]

The intervention plans, which eventually also included the Finnish war (see below), in all likelihood fuelled the mutual suspicions between the Soviets and the Anglo-French. The British plans to bomb the oil industry were far reaching and also entertained in 1940.[60] The plans to take military action against the Soviets in the Caucasus had reached Stalin in the form of rumours and documents (confirming the rumours).[61] As we have seen, these plans were in part based on an assumption of military weakness. The plans, in combination with Churchill's ill-concealed anti-Soviet and anti-communist sentiments and some facts concerning British diplomatic activity, made Stalin disbelieve Churchill when he tried to warn the former about the impending German attack upon the USSR in the spring of 1941.[62]

Notes

1 Hinsley (1979), 46.
2 Raack (1995), 29.
3 9–10–1939, COS(39)69, CAB80/3; 28-10-1939, COS(39)171, CAB80/6.
4 6–10–1939, COS(39)66, CAB80/3.
5 28-9-1939, COS(39)52, CAB80/3.
6 13-9-1939, COS(39)32, CAB80/2.
7 11–9-1939, N4458/4030/38, FO371/23699; 14–9-1939, N4406/4030/38, FO371/23699.
8 Hayne stated that his information was obtained from sources regarded as reliable, including foreign intelligence reports and the reports of civilian eyewitnesses. 25-10-1939, "Military [...]", Roll-18, M1443, RG165.
9 13–9-1939, No. 538, Comments (on the current situation), Mar. 1 1939–Mar.1 1941, Box-3172, Entry-77, # RG165; 6–10–1939, "Mobilization – General." Roll-14, M1443, RG165; 28-11-1939, "M/A [...]", Box-3119, Entry-77, RG165.
10 29–9-1939, N4949/1012/38, FO371/23696.
11 20-10-1939, N5778/57/38, FO418/85.
12 27-10-1939, COS(39)103, CAB80/4.
13 9–10–1939, COS(39)69, CAB80/3. The reports 10-10-1939, COS39(71) and 12-10-1939, COS39(76), both in CAB80/4, NAKL, have, in a more compressed form, the same principal content as COS(39)69.
14 10-11-1939, COS(39)119, CAB80/5.
15 27-11-1939, N6630/485/38, FO371/23688.
16 Ibid.
17 Falkehed (1994), 107–109, 122.
18 28-11-1939, "M/A Riga 10549", Box-3119, Entry-77, RG165.
19 13–9-1939, No. 538, Comments (on the current situation), Mar. 1 1939-Mar.1 1941, Box-3172, Entry-77, # RG165; 6–10–1939, "Mobilization – General." Roll-14, M1443, RG165; 28-11-1939.

20 1–11–1939, "Summary [...]", Roll-34, T1249, RG59.
21 1–11–1939, "Brief [...]", Box-3100, Entry-77, RG165.
22 9–11–1939, "The internal [...]", Box-3099, Entry-77, RG165.
23 Some general problems of the previous three years were also described in the
    report, including the inability to properly exploit raw material resources, and the
    general lack of balance in the national economy, due to a neglect of the civilian
    side of the economy and poor conditions for workers. 10–1-1940, "Special [...]",
    Box-3145, Entry-77, RG165.
24 17-11-1939, Despatch No. 155, Roll-34, T1249, RG59.
25 24-11-1939, "The Soviet [...]", Box-3099, Entry-77, RG165.
26 28-12-1939, "Summary [...]", Roll-34, T1249, RG59.
27 13-11-1939, Despatch No. 147, Roll-26, T1249, RG59.
28 18-11-1939, N6922/2035/38, FO371/23698.
29 20-10-1939, N5778/57/38, FO418/85.
30 6–10–1939, COS(39)66, CAB80/3.
31 9–10–1939, COS(39)69, CAB80/3; 20-10-1939, COS(39)92, CAB80/4.
32 4–11–1939, COS(39)112, CAB80/4.
33 22-12-1939, "Russia [...]", WO208/1751.
34 Military aircraft includes army, air force and navy planes. Combat aircraft includes
    bomber, attack and fighter planes. Non-combat includes observation, patrol, train-
    ing and miscellaneous planes. 6–10–1939 (prepared), "Military [...]", Box-3152,
    Entry-77, RG165.
35 1–9-1939, Report No. 10492, Roll-21, M1443, RG165; 31–8-1939, Report No.
    1562, Roll-21, M1443, RG165.
36 31–8-1939, Report No. 1562, Roll-21, M1443, RG165.
37 20-10-1939, N5778/57/38, FO418/85.
38 31-10-1939, N5894/290/38, FO371/23697.
39 Beaumont argues that it was perceptions of Red Army performance in Poland and
    Estonia that dominated British thinking by this time, and not Soviet-Japanese
    fighting in Manchuria. Beaumont (1980), 25.
40 During the 1930s Japan had transformed Manchuria into a puppet state (Manchucko)
    and invaded China in 1937. Erickson (1984), 410; Johansson (1991), 267–268; Willmott
    (1992), 28; Coox (1985), xii.
41 Coox (1985), xi.
42 Habeck (2002), 98–101.
43 26–7-1939, Report No. 1548, Reel-24, T1249, RG59.
44 10–1-1940, "MID, [...]", Box-3145, Entry-77, RG165.
45 Herndon (1983), 297–307.
46 Hardly anyone even in the German military leadership took notice of the battles in
    Manchuria 1939, when the planning of Operation *Barbarossa* was conducted, with
    the exception of the German military attaché in Moscow, General Köstring.
    Wegner (1987), 294.
47 27-11-1939, N6630/485/38, FO371/23688.
48 Erickson (1984), 411–412; Ericson III (1999), 56–61, 198, 201; Kenez (1999), 133;
    Raack (1995), 43; Raack (2002), 52.
49 2–12–1939, COS(39)142, WO193/646; Cantwell (1993), 3, 145.
50 2–12–1939, COS(39)142, WO193/646.
51 6–11–1939, COS(39)113, CAB80/4; 6–11–1939, JIC(39)26, CAB81/95.
52 8–11–1939, JIC(39)27; 15-11-1939, JIC(39)28, and 21-11-1939, JIC(39)29, all in
    CAB81/95.
53 8–11–1939, JIC(39)27, CAB81/95; 21-11-1939, JIC(39)29, CAB81/95.
54 2–12–1939, COS(39)142, WO193/646.
55 7–11–1939, "Enclose B.", CAB104/259; 7–11–1939, "Enclosure C.", CAB104/259.
56 January 1940 (12A), WO193/646.

57 25–9-1939, N4868/1290/38, FO371/23697; 21-11-1939, JIC(39)29, CAB81/95.
58 Harrison (1985), 253.
59 5–12–1939, 2655-D-553, Roll-10, M1443, RG165.
60 Osborn (2000), Chapters 6 and 9.
61 Glantz (1998), 234.
62 Ibid.

7   The Soviet–Finnish Winter War

So far the only ground campaign of importance in the war had been the Polish campaign. This campaign had shown that Germany easily could crush Poland, without risking any major attacks from the Western Powers. The ensuing lull in the West would be known as the "Phoney war", or *der Sitzkrieg* to the Germans. This situation would continue until the German offensive in May 1940. In the East the Soviets wanted to neutralize a perceived potential threat to their north-western border. Finland, which generally was regarded as a Western-style country, had belonged to the Russian Empire before the 1917 Revolution. According to the Molotov-Ribbentrop pact's secret protocol Finland fell into the Soviet sphere of influence. The USSR could therefore forward demands on, and in the end attack Finland on 30 November, without the risk of significant German interference. However, the Western Powers seriously contemplated to interfere militarily against the Soviets. The planned action against the USSR would include a landing of troops near Petsamo in the Arctic, in order to help Finland, a naval blockade against Murmansk and diversionary manoeuvres in the Black Sea.[1] These plans became public in the French press in January 1940, and it seems that they worried Moscow.[2]

The Russo–Finnish war had roused Churchill's old anti-Soviet rhetoric from his younger years. In a 20 January radio broadcast he spoke of Finland's fight for freedom and "the military incapacity of the Red Army and of the Red Air Force [and] how Communism rots the soul of nations, how it makes it hungry and abject in peace, and proves it base and abominable in war."[3] By that time it seems the tough Finnish opposition surprised Stalin.[4] The Red Army suffered severe setbacks in the field, and became the object of international ridicule.[5]

The scale and intensity of the fighting in Finland, although dwarfed in comparison to the Soviet–German war, was something else than the easy Soviet Polish campaign. The Soviets, counting on little opposition, were in for a nasty surprise. The Soviet–Finnish border region was long but with very little infrastructure and heavy forests. Only the southern part of the front had proper railway lines running from the USSR into Finland. This part, the Karelian Isthmus, was relatively narrow, intersected by many lakes and well-fortified. The Soviets had a crushing numerical superiority over the Finns in men, aircraft, heavy armaments and mechanized forces, but the value of these troops was limited by the logistical realities, the terrain and (especially in the case of motorized troops and air power) by the winter weather. Since the Finnish opposition was much more determined than the Soviets expected, hard fighting ensued.

7.1 The Red Army's performance

From the very beginning Red Army operations against Finland confirmed earlier Anglo-American assessments. The COS's weekly reporting to the War Cabinet in December and January contained some information concerning the campaign. Despite only having nine divisions the Finns was believed to have a good chance of holding back the numerically superior Red Army, although not forever. Soviet air superiority was considered as even greater than on the ground. The relatively good prospects for Finnish resistance was seen as depending to some extent on the poor weather and the terrain, which meant logistical problems for the Soviets and improved Finnish defensive position. Apart from this Soviet inefficiency was seen as a factor working to the Finnish advantage.[6] Additional COS, FO and reports from other British institutions, from December and January, repeated earlier notions already expressed in principle, concerning the state and weakness of military capabilities (in the air, on the ground and even on the sea).[7]

It seems that the British at the time also were worried about the Soviets moving against smaller nations in the Middle East (e.g. Afghanistan or Iran), which in contrast to a Western Power were believed to be easy opponents for the Red Army. In this context Lord Halifax distributed a memorandum at a December War Cabinet meeting containing the statement that "the Red Army would almost certainly be no match for the armed forces of a great European Power".[8] In January an FO official, contemplated different aspects of Soviet–German cooperation, stated that Red Army troops, if supporting the Germans in the West, would be "more of a liability than an asset".[9]

As seen the COS at least noted some mitigating circumstances (the weather and the terrain) that could explain the setbacks. In mid-January the COS noted that the Red Army's weaknesses might have been exaggerated. The reverses in Finland were accredited primarily to poor leadership, and also to that Soviet military equipment were not right for the specific local conditions. They concluded that the divisions were organized and equipped according to modern standards, and that the army relied upon motor transport to a larger extent than expected. The terrain of the northern parts of the front was not suitable for the full utilization of modern equipment and motor transport.[10] At the beginning of February it did seem to the COS that the Soviets had learned something from their earlier disasters in the field, and from now on were conducting their operations along sounder guidelines.[11] This line of argument was repeated in the COS 9 February weekly report to the War Cabinet, since by then a slight improvement in the handling of troops on the battlefield was noticed.[12]

COS reports from January and February pointed that the war was unpopular among Red Army personnel. In late January they did not regard Army morale as high, and the attitude of the large mass of soldiers was something like fatalistic apathy.[13] In early February they had received information concerning troops stationed in Poland and Estonia, showing that the war was not popular.[14] Earlier reports had also shown that the Army had problems with troops of Muslim origin in Turkmenistan and elsewhere.[15] They had indications that the Red Army had been forced to acquire recruits for the Finnish war from units already formed all over the European parts of the USSR. It was believed that the regime opted for this since they wanted to avoid mobilizing more troops, due to the serious troubles during the mobilization against Poland.[16] In late February they reported that the morale and discipline among troops in the USSR were low.[17]

At the end of January MI2 prepared a widely distributed evaluation of the Red Army's fighting strength and value for war, which made direct reference to Kirkman's paper from May 1939. In general, the conclusions were the same, even though the report drew information from the experiences in Poland and Finland. The Red Army's poor performance there was stressed, but also to some extent excused. The special circumstances of the Finnish campaign, extreme weather and rough terrain, were not suited for the Red Army's large standardized masses, while the Finns, on the other hand, were considered as accustomed to these conditions. But even though its poor performance was partly excused, the efficiency of the Red Army was nevertheless somewhat downgraded in comparison with the Kirkman paper, since it's earlier assumed "air mindedness" was "somewhat superficial", and it's "propaganda machine" was "less efficient". FO officials commented the report in February and they seemed to have agreed with the main lines.[18]

American perceptions regarding the effort in Finland differed little from British assessments. They relied on British and Finnish sources and eye witnesses. Hayne reported in mid-December that the COS's perception was that Red Army tactics were crude: relying upon frontal assaults, resulting in abnormal losses in men and materiel. But the Finnish General Headquarter had noted two distinct classes of troops. More than half of them (according to Hayne the recently trained reserves) had been of inferior quality and poorly equipped. Other troops, used in more important attacks, were showing a greater tactical efficiency. Judging by the state of prisoners of war, Soviet soldiers were in bad shape, and, according to eyewitnesses, had frozen feet, suffering from undernourishment and exposure. But Hayne did not believe that lack of food, clothing and shelter would bring about any large-scale or organized mutinies, at least for some time to come, since Soviet troops could stand much more hardship than those of any other European country.[19]

He estimated the number of troops operating against the Finns to between 660,000 and 1.25 million men. The total strength of the armed forces was between 4 and 4.5 million men, and no more than 5 million men could be maintained and equipped, due to lack of supplies, limited transportation and the generally strained economic condition of the country. In a supplementary report Hayne commented briefly upon the economic aspect of the Finnish war. The duration of the war would decide the importance of economic factors, and since no economic breakdown was foreseen in the immediate future, he limited his estimate to military factors, despite the fact that the war was an additional strain upon transportation.[20]

Hayne found it very difficult to analyse current Red Army morale, but he concluded the following regarding the mentality of Soviet soldiers: "ox-like docility", little individual initiative and a greater fear of their own government than of the Finns. Propaganda had made the already simple-minded soldier almost fanatical. Ignorance of the outside world was almost as great among the officers as among the men. The system of all-embracing espionage, and the regime's ruthless methods, assured that no revolts against the Soviet order could be successful. In addition the Red Army's combat efficiency could be seriously affected by the adverse supply and weather conditions, but that the men would continue to obey their superiors, and problems at the front would not inspire revolt in the home country.[21]

Reports written by the MID and by Huthsteiner (now transferred to Finland to cover the war)[22] in January pointed to several deficiencies in military capabilities: unable to conduct effective air operations in Finland, substandard aircraft, untrained pilots, poor tanks, high tank causalities due to material defects and faulty employment, dual command system (political commissars), young inexperienced officers (due to the purges), inefficient officers, unsound tactics, wishful thinking, and, connected to the last point, the basing of information for operations in Finland on political intelligence. Huthsteiner's report did, however, contain two positive statements: the soldiers were "good fighters" and their guns and rifles were "fairly good".[23] In early February the Riga embassy reported that Huthsteiner believed that the Finns could hold out for six months in the light of prevailing conditions, or even substantially longer if effective material and manpower assistance could be sent to Finland.[24]

In early February the US military attaché in Istanbul recounted information received from Firebrace. The US attaché learned that the Soviets had assumed the Finns would not fight the Red Army, and therefore the initial mobilization along the Finnish border could be considered as something of a bluff. This would, in turn, explain why the Red Army was so badly prepared for the campaign. Otherwise Firebrace largely repeated some explanations for the poor Soviet performance: lack of planning, inadequate transport, inferior equipment, too much reliance on badly used and mechanically inferior tanks, "the characteristic Russian herd instinct", and the interference of political commissars.[25]

Fewer assessments were made from the second half of February. It is impossible to say if this in some way was connected to the changing course of the war, but in reality a more systematic – primarily concentrated against the Karelian Isthmus – Soviet military effort was going on from January which yielded real results around mid-February. By the first week of March the Red

Army was approaching Viipuri, Finland's second largest city. The Finnish defensive effort was succumbing under the overwhelming pressure, and an Anglo-French relief force would not arrive in the immediate future. From the Soviet perspective the whole campaign had been an embarrassment, damaging the Soviet Union's international reputation in several ways. There was also a risk of an Anglo-French intervention eventually and the spring thaw was coming soon, which would worsen the conditions for troop movements and supplies even more than the winter weather. Since the Soviets at the moment were sitting on a strong hand they could demand even more concessions from Finland than stipulated by their pre-war demands. A peace treaty was signed in Moscow on 12 March that went into effect the day after.

7.2 The economy and the internal situation

As we have seen, Hayne did not believe, in December, that the Red Army's setbacks in the war would result in any unrest at the home front. It seems that many British observes were of a different opinion. In late 1939 and early 1940 several FO reports were about internal problems connected to the Finnish war. "Uneasiness", "unrest", "danger of revolt", "disorganization of railroad traffic", "food shortage", "breakdown in distribution" and "fuel shortage" were some of the words and phrases used to describe the general situation.[26]

In early January the COS stated that the war had caused discontent in the army and among the civil population of Moscow and Leningrad, due to the military losses and the hardships of the war.[27] Later in January a FO report, largely based on a letter from the Moscow embassy's Laurence Collier, concluded that the failure in Finland had revealed many weaknesses, of which the foremost were food shortages and the danger of revolt. Parallels were drawn with the Russian situation in 1905 and 1917, when revolutions had broken out, even though no such dire consequences were imminent at present. The continuation of the war was having disorganizing and disquieting effects (especially in Leningrad and Moscow).[28] A few days later the COS reported that the war was causing a commotion in the country, affecting both civilian and military activities, and that the situation in Leningrad was getting worse and worse.[29] At the end of the month they wrote about a serious shortage of food in these cities, and of unrest prevailing to some extent in other parts of the country, even though no signs of serious trouble were detected due to the unrest. On the other hand, the civilian population was not getting much news about the military setbacks, and there were no indications pointing to a general decline in morale.[30]

Around the turn of January/February, British concrete plans were made concerning an attack on Soviet targets and an intervention in Finland. The MI2 took part in the work and described four Soviet weak spots: industry, transport, the vulnerability of oil supplies, and internal discontent.[31] The conclusions reached concerning the last spot were in line with earlier assumptions, but were if possible even more emphasized now: discontent was very widespread both among the military and the civilian population, but major revolts was not likely, since these had been suppressed with great ruthlessness in earlier attempts. Nevertheless, many signs were noticed to the effect that popular discontent was spreading, which was why the chances for an insurrection as a result of an armed intervention were gradually improving.[32] In early February, Ironside presented a memorandum that stressed the weaknesses already mentioned above.[33] A few days later the implications of a possible conflict with the USSR were discussed by a COS sub-committee. Germany was the principal enemy, while the Soviet threat against allied interests was played down, which is not surprising considering the following statement: "The more commitments Russia undertakes the quicker she is likely to collapse."[34]

An insight into American considerations regarding these issues can be obtained from a January MID special bulletin, in which the morale of civilians in Leningrad was considered to be "at a low ebb" due to the general effects of the war in Finland. But there were no real indications that the authorities had lost control, and there was no revolutionary mood among the population.[35] According to a January telegram from Steinhardt, he had seen reports about a riot in a hospital at Kaluga by wounded Russians due to lack of sufficient food.[36] However, also considering Hayne's earlier opinions, it seems from the available evidence that the British had a more negative attitude regarding Soviet internal stability at the time. Why this was so can probably never be completely clear, but it is not wholly unrealistic that the stronger British negativity can be connected to a portion of wishful thinking, in connection to their intervention plans.

As for the purely economic reporting, the Anglo-Americans continued to stress what they considered as the fundamental weaknesses of the economy, and they definitively believed that the Finnish war had worsened the situation in many respects. Several reports were written during the winter about the organizational inadequacies of the railway system, the shortage of skilled labour, low labour productivity, the problem of the authorities to control the workers, food shortages, increasing food prices, lagging plan goals, the faulty organization of Soviet industry and a general deterioration of economic conditions. In one instance, Steinhardt took particular interest in the aluminium industry – of special importance for aircraft production – and its "unsatisfactory" state, among other things due to obsolete factory equipment and a shortage of electric power. He also noted that the later problem had implications for the development of other industries.[37]

However, judging by the US Moscow embassy's fourth quarter (1939) report, from early February, the embassy's position was not that a collapse was imminent: "The weakness of the Soviet Union from an economic point of view continues and gives signs of becoming more acute"; and "There is little thus far to indicate [...] that the creaky structure threatens to collapse or that it will not continue to function after a fashion, as it has done in the past, barring contingencies which it is by no means possible to predict."[38] Even though all observers continued their usual USSR bashing during this period, there were also some on the British side that wanted to moderate the critique a little. In February the FO official Loy Henderson could not yet identify any revolutionary movement inside the USSR that could overthrow Stalin. Even if Stalin fell, that would not necessarily mean a relaxation in the regime's central control.[39]

During the early part of March the FO had come across a report by three US oil engineers, who had left the USSR in January. The FO was interested since the report said something about the air defences at Baku and the pipelines there, but they were also interested in the so-called bad labour conditions and general disorganization in the USSR. Deputy Under-Secretary of State Orme Sargent commented that although general conditions certainly were bad, and the war had worsened them, it would not be wise to totally write off the USSR as a military and economic force in European affairs. Other FO officials were also of the opinion that the report somewhat overstated the economic difficulties.[40]

In November, Captain Ivan D. Yeaton became the new US military attaché in Moscow. He spoke Russian and had studied Russian history and communism, and had been a part of the US expeditionary force in Siberia 1919–20. In his memories he titled himself as a "communist expert",[41] and he is generally seen as having a negative disposition towards the USSR. In January he argued that military mobilization was felt generally in industry, and that this, in combination with the recall of many US engineers (assisting Soviet factory management), had a particularly negative effect on the aviation and the oil industry.[42] He estimated monthly aircraft output to about 500, and it would not be possible to increase output during wartime; it was rather more likely that output would decrease.[43] According to another embassy report (from early February), based on information from a US engineer, the functioning of aluminium production was far from satisfactory. At the time he was helping with the erection of a rolling mill, to be used in the production of aircraft parts. The Soviets' "carelessness and inefficiency" would make it hard for them to run the mill properly after his departure. It was stated in the report that this was the "usual comment" of US engineers employed on Soviet industrial projects.[44] The engineer was engaged at the Stupino aircraft plant number 150. A few days later Yeaton commented on operations at that plant. The new production methods used in the manufacture of aluminium sheets, if true, could "easily revolutionize airplane body and wing construction".[45]

The idea that closer cooperation with Germany could improve economic performance was repeated during the winter, and, as inferred by F. H. R. Maclean of the FO in mid-January, made more acute for the Soviets due their recent experiences in Finland. However, even if this would occur, Maclean did not consider it as certain that the Germans would be able to increase output in the short run, especially as transportation would have to be reorganized before any possible benefits from industry could be realized.[46] The same opinion, in principle, was expressed in an early February FO memorandum stating that if the Soviets accepted German help it would be long before the German techni-cians could produce any remarkable results, since they would encounter obstruction at a local level and incompetence.[47] On 8 March the COS, in cooperation with the MEW, returned to Soviet–German cooperation and the economy's perceived usual weak spots were emphasized. Some advantages with the Soviet position were also enumerated relating to the size of the country. The size made it in principle self-supporting in natural resources, which in turn made it immune to external economic pressure, and size also contributed to making the industrial areas less vulnerable to air attack. However, further military operations, on a larger scale than those in Finland, would bring extreme pressure on the transport system and industry.[48]

Notes

1 The USSR was expelled from the League of Nations in December as a result of the attack on Finland. Erickson (1984), 411–412; Ericson III (1999), 56–61, 198, 201; Kenez (1999), 133; Raack (1995), 43; Watson (2002), 52.
2 Erickson (1984), 412. The British assumed that the Soviet leadership feared hostilities with the Western Powers because they tried to strengthen their military defence at Murmansk and along the Black Sea coast. 19-1-1940, COS(40)206, CAB80/7.
3 Carlton (2000), 72.
4 Before the attack, Soviet propaganda tried to promote a picture of an oppressed Finnish people, which had to be liberated from their own government, a supposed "marionette" of the British and French "imperialists" and "war mongers". Raack (1995), 43.
5 Ibid.
6 8–12–1939, COS(39)157, CAB80/6. Of course, the Finns received a lot of material help from other countries during the conflict. According to US military intelligence, the material help merely from the Anglo-French up to 1 March was 405 aircraft, 916 artillery pieces, 150 anti-tank guns, in addition to many small arms. 18-3-1940, "War [...]", Box-3145, Entry-77, RG165.
7 8–12–1939, COS(39)157, CAB80/6; 12–1-1940, COS(40)195, CAB80/7; 22-12-1939, COS(39)169, CAB80/6; 29-12-1939, COS(39)180, CAB80/6; 14-12-1939, N7372/1572/38, FO371/23698; 6–12–1939, WP(39)150, CAB66/3; 25-12-1939, N7857/485/38, FO371/23688; 15-12-1939, COS(39)165, CAB80/6; 29-12-1939, COS(39)180, CAB80/6; 5–1-1940, COS(40)187, CAB80/7; 31-12-1939, "Extract [...]", AIR40/2106; 12–1-1940, COS(40)195, CAB80/7; 19–1-1940, COS(40)206, CAB80/7; 5–1-1940, COS(40)187, CAB80/7; 15–1-1940, N1123/132/38, FO371/24850.
8 6–12–1939, WP(39)150, CAB66/3.
9 17-1-1940, N1147/283/38, FO418/86.
10 19–1-1940, COS(40)206, CAB80/7.
11 2–2-1940, COS(40)228, CAB80/8.
12 9–2-1940, COS(40)233, CAB80/8.
13 26–1-1940, COS(40)219, CAB80/7.
14 2–2-1940, COS(40)228, CAB80/8.
15 Ideas existed among certain military representatives that the assumed discontent of the Moslem population in the USSR could be used for starting a propaganda offensive against the USSR, that included the whole Moslem world. 12–1-1940, COS, "Extracts [...]", WO193/646. According to a memorandum from the FO, the British received their information from Turkey – among others. There apparently existed a certain mutual interest between the British and the Turks regarding cooperation to promote a revolt among the Moslem population. The Turks

believed that they would have a good chance to achieve just that in the Caucasus if war broke out with the Soviets. 5–5-1940, JIC(40)53, CAB81/96. The British also discussed this issue with the French and their joint conclusion was that it was not worth the effort to promote Moslem discontent, if it was not attempted in connection with military actions or under other exceptional circumstances. 16–5-1940, JIC(40)69, CAB81/96.

16 In January the COS contemplated that the Finns could inflict a defeat on the Red Army that was worse than the defeat at Suomussalmi, which in turn could force the Soviet government to cease hostilities. 12-1-1940, COS(40)195, CAB80/7. Later in January the COS commented on reports they had received concerning the Soviet troops stationed in Estonia. According to the COS most Estonians held the Red Army in low regard, which among other things was due to the low discipline of Soviet troops. 19–1-1940, COS(40)206, CAB80/7.

17 23-2-1940, COS(40)262, CAB80/8.

18 8–2-1940, N1556/1056/38, FO371/24854; 18–5-1939, N2572/485/38, FO371/23688.

19 17-12-1939, 2037–2100, Roll-18, M1443, RG165.

20 17-12-1939, 2037–2100, Roll-18, M1443, RG165; 20-12-1939, 2037–2100, Roll-18, M1443, RG165.

21 Ibid.

22 Falkehed (1994), 83.

23 20–1-1940, 2037–2100, Roll-18, M1443, RG165; 10–1-1940, "Special [...]", Box-3145, Entry-77, RG165.

24 6–2-1940, "American [...]", Box-3146, Entry-77, RG165.

25 1–2-1940, "Turkey, [...]", Box-3146, Entry-77, RG165.

26 9–1-1940, N337/132/38, FO371/24850; 15–1-1940, N1123/132/38, FO371/24850; 29–1-1940, N1537/132/38, FO371/24850; 5–2-1940, N1919/132/38, FO371/24850; 5–2-1940, N1920/132/38, FO371/24850; 2–3-1940, N3271/132/38, FO371/24850.

27 5–1-1940, COS(40)187, CAB80/7.

28 15–1-1940, N1123/132/38, FO371/24850.

29 One perceived problem was inadequate resources for medical care. 19–1-1940, COS(40)206, CAB80/7.

30 26–1-1940, COS(40)219, CAB80/7.

31 January 1940 (12A), WO193/646; Cantwell (1993), 178.

32 The chances of a revolt against the Soviet regime in the Caucasus were connected with a military intervention in the Black Sea region. It was believed that these revolts could spread to the Ukraine if an intervention was also undertaken in the Crimea. Ibid. The MI2 had also written an annex to the mentioned report that went deeper into the question of which specific ethnical groups in the Caucasus that opposed Soviet rule. Georgia, Armenia and Azerbaijan were mentioned, and the Georgians were considered as being the most discontented. It seemed to the MI2 that the Armenians had become reconciled with the regime while the population of Azerbaijan were regarded as relatively less discontented than the Georgians, but nevertheless not happy with the situation. January 1940 (12A), "Annex", WO193/646.

33 Ironside's conclusion was that an effort against the Caucasus would be the most effective offensive action that could be undertaken against the USSR. 6–2-1940, "Action [...]", WO193/646; 2–2-1940, COS(40)227, WO193/646.

34 8–2-1940, COS(40)230, WO193/646.

35 10–1-1940, "Special [...]", Box-3145, Entry-77, RG165.

36 25–1-1940, "Tel # 106", Roll-23, T1250, RG59.

37 7–12–1939, N181/181/38, FO371/24851; 16-12-1939, "Contemplated [...]", Box-3084, Entry-77, RG165; 27-12-1939, No. 232, Roll-34, T1249, RG59; 10–1-1940, "Special [...]", Box-3145, Entry-77, RG165; 10–1-1940 (49), 12–1-1940 (55), 15–1-1940 (58), 24–1-1940 (98), 25–1-1940 (Tel # 106), Roll-23, T1250, RG59; 19–1-1940, COS(40)206, CAB80/7; # January 1940 (12A), WO193/646; 9–2-1940, COS(40)233, CAB80/8;

2–2-1940, 11–3-1940, Despatch No. 292, Roll-22, T1250, RG59; 7–3-1940, 19–4-1940, Despatch No. 357, Roll-22, T1250, RG59; 19-12-1940, "Soviet […]", Box-3109, Entry-77, RG165; 7–2-1940, "Subject: […]", Box-3108, Entry-77, RG165.

38 2–2-1940, 11–3-1940, Despatch No. 292, Roll-22, T1250, RG59.
39 27–2-1940, N2971/132/38, FO371/24850.
40 12–3-1940, N3145/32/38, FO371/24850; Woodward (1970), 637.
41 Yeaton (1976).
42 8–1-1940, "Subject: […]", Box-3155, Entry-77, RG165; 8–1-1940, Report No. 1673a, Roll-20, M1443, RG165; Appendix 11, Roll-19, M1443, RG165.
43 8–1-1940, "Subject: […]", Box-3155, Entry-77, RG165.
44 5–2-1940, 8–3-1940, Despatch No. 298, Roll-8, T1250, RG59.
45 5–2-1940, 8–3-1940, Despatch No. 298, Roll-8, T1250, RG59; 16–2-1940, Report No. 1666, Roll-20, M1443, RG165.
46 17–1-1940, N1147/283/38, FO418/86.
47 A purely military cooperation was regarded as more probable. 2–2-1940, COS(40) 227, Annex, WO193/646.
48 8–3-1940, COS(40)252, WO193/646.

8   Assessments running up to Barbarossa

All in all, it seems fair to conclude that the Winter War had further lowered the standing of the USSR in the eyes of the Anglo-American observers. There were without doubt mitigating circumstances in the form of the weather and the terrain, which also was noted by the Anglo-Americans, but it must also be remembered that Finland was a very small nation, and poorly armed compared to the Red Army. The large and disproportionate losses suffered by the Red Army were not Western propaganda, but a painful and embarrassing reality to the Soviets, which they under the circumstances could not hide.

In the period after the Finnish war, up to Barbarossa, the general tone of the assessments was pretty much the same as before, even though some reports are worth attention. The focus of the European war now shifted to Western Europe, beginning with Germany's swift occupation of Denmark and the invasion of Norway from 9 April onwards. The Western Powers were prepared to counter Hitler's move in Scandinavia, but much to their misfortune, Germany's main strike for the spring would be delivered against France and the Benelux countries on 10 May. The German campaign was a first class disaster for the Western Powers since it resulted in the capitulation of France (and the Benelux nations). What Germany had failed to do for over four years in World War I was now accomplished in just 1.5 months, by the application of the new *Blitzkrieg* concept. Despite the fact that most of the British troops on the continent managed to get back to Britain, and that the British air defences proved sufficient to thwart the ensuing German air offensive in the summer and early autumn, the British long-term strategic situation was now very precarious.

At the moment the British Isles were safe, but the current naval supremacy of the Royal Navy could be seriously challenged by Germany. Air power was now as important as ships for naval warfare, if not more, and Germany's industrial potential was significantly larger than Britain's, especially considering that Germany now controlled much of the industrial resources of Western and Central Europe. In addition, Germany had almost twice the population of the UK. If the war would continue to play out only between Germany and Britain, the British could easily have lost in the long run. Already by 1940 the British could feel the pressure from the U-boats, a pressure that was increasing in

1941 despite the German attack on the USSR. Germany had the long run option to produce more air and naval military assets than they actually did, and as the subsequent developments of the war proved, it was possible to successfully make large-scale seaborne invasions even against relatively well-fortified opponents. If Germany's military resources could have been concentrated only against Britain, and not for the most part against the USSR, as actually was the case from June 1941 onwards (or even before that time if the build-up for Barbarossa is counted), it seems likely that the war as a whole in the West would have turned out much worse than it actually did.

This dark scenario was, of course, not extraneous to the British leadership, and it made the Soviet situation even more interesting from a strategic perspective. Now, after the fall of France, the only large army left on the continent, apart from Germany's, was the Red Army. Even though, as we have seen, the British did not give much for Soviet war potential, the USSR was at least a potential enemy of Nazi Germany, and one of considerable geographical size and population. Hitler was also aware of the implications this had for the British position. When he met with his highest military leaders in July 1940 to discuss the future, after their recent astonishing victory in the West, Britain were still considered as the primary target for the war effort. A possible invasion of the British Isles was still in the cards, but it is uncertain if Hitler would have tried such a gamble already in 1940, even if the *Luftwaffe* had done much better against the RAF than they actually did. He did not only consider the United States as a potential future military ally of the UK, but also the USSR. The decision to attack the USSR, which was made in July, was not only dependent on ideological and economic considerations, but also on the assumption that Britain counted on the USSR as a potential future ally.

The decision, according to Hitler's plans, made it necessary to raise a further 40 divisions, increasing the total strength of the Army to 180 divisions. As a result, more manpower for service in the ground forces had to be trained, and therefore the Navy and *Luftwaffe* had to make do with less. On 28 May Hitler had informed his commander-in-chief of the Army, Colonel-General von Brauchitsch, that the Army should be decreased in size to between 72 and 76 divisions when Britain was neutralized, thus releasing manpower for industry, the Navy and the Air Force.[1] The Barbarossa plan countermanded this decision. But even if the build-up for, and the subsequent attack on the USSR, created a breathing space for the British, an eventual defeat of the Red Army would make it possible for Germany to concentrate all its resources against Britain again. Since the quick (only a few months) defeat of the USSR was anticipated in 1941 by Hitler and his planners, Germany could resume its main effort against the British after that, now strengthened with the economic resources of the former European USSR. The British observed the German threat to the USSR already when France fell, and tried repeatedly to warn the Soviets (as did the Americans) up to the beginning of Operation Barbarossa.[2]

However, in 1940 the USSR was still not completely disregarded as a threat to British interests. By the end of July the JIC presented some conclusions about Soviet foreign policy to the War Cabinet, which, among other things, argued that it was focused on expansion and that the Soviets were very anxious to avoid a confrontation with Germany. It was feared that the USSR would try to expand in the direction of the Middle East, and in the process threaten British interests.[3] During the autumn of 1940 and winter of 1941, when the risk of a German invasion (at least for now) had receded, speculations regarding a possible Soviet–German war in 1941 continued in Whitehall. The British MI still believed by the winter of 1940–1941 that Germany would first try to conquer Britain before starting a war with the USSR.[4] In April Churchill received credible information showing that Germany really intended to invade the USSR (although some Whitehall authorities were still in doubt), and tried once again to warn the Soviets, just as the Americans had already done in March.[5] During May and June, before the German attack, the JIC was preoccupied with guessing whether or not a Soviet–German war would break out. Several reports were prepared with consideration to this possibility.[6]

After the Finnish war the USSR was not involved in any major military engagements until June 1941. Due to the Molotov-Ribbentrop agreement, Soviet forces could occupy the Baltic States, Bessarabia and Northern Bukovina, during the summer of 1940.[7] All the areas occupied in 1939–1940 were incorporated into the USSR. Germany's quick and relatively easy defeat of France was very worrying for the Soviet leadership. They were, of course, aware of the character of warfare in World War I, and the 1940 campaign was the first major outright campaign between two European great powers since 1918. That Poland was to succumb quickly to German arms was perhaps not that surprising, but the whole French Army, despite being backed up by the powerful Maginot line and a British expeditionary force, was, of course, another matter.

The Soviet military and military-industrial build up continued and the embarrassment in Finland prompted reforms in the Red Army. The reforms aimed at improving its operational and tactical capabilities. When the Germans attacked in June 1941 these reforms were not completed.

8.1 The economy and internal stability

As we have seen the British believed that Germany could have some influence over internal Soviet economic affairs. Another indication of increasing German influence could be found in a March COS weekly report to the War Cabinet, where it was stated that there existed information of a Soviet purchase of German BMW aircraft engines, and the establishment of a Moscow factory to produce these engines under German supervision.[8] The fact that the British apparently contemplated that it was possible for Germany to use the economic resources of the USSR to some extent was probably worrying. One important factor that contributed to the German defeat in World War I was the Western Power's economic blockade. The German victory over Russia in that war came too late to have any significant importance on Germany's economic situation in 1918. But now the so called competent Germans could trade with and seemingly to some extent exploit the resources of Russia. Regardless of what the British thought about Soviet incompetence, and other internal problems, it was clear to all at the time that the USSR was richly endowed with raw materials. And, of course, "regular" Soviet–German trade agreements were already in effect, providing Germany with some badly needed resources.

The conclusion of the Winter War did not alter earlier perceptions regarding the economic situation. In the COS weekly report from 18 March, the impression of a slowly deteriorating and very strained economy was described, a process that was regarded as accelerated by the war. Failures to increase output, dislocated transport, food queues, under-nourishment and disease were some of conditions described as prevailing in the USSR. But it was also added that "The Russians cannot, however, be judged by European standards and seem able to produce some results out of apparent chaos."[9] Additional British analyses and reports during the spring revealed not much new in principle.[10]

From the middle of March 1940 to the middle of June 1941 Yeaton produced nearly 90 reports related in some way to military matters.[11] During the spring and summer 1940 he also reported about various problems in the economy and society regarding the production of inferior gods, rumours of food shortages and food queues.[12]

In May the US Moscow embassy's Charge d'Affaires Walter Thurston described the Soviet authorities as suspicious, indifferent, incompetent, and as having a defective organisation. The report also contained excerpts of interviews, conducted during recent months at the embassy, with several US engineers employed by Soviet enterprises. The engineers assumed that the Soviets would be unable to operate US equipment efficiently, when they themselves were gone. At best the Soviets would be able to operate the machinery at "greatly reduced efficiency". Soviet technicians were overconfident and very hard to cooperate with. The factory managers lacked organizational ability, a lack of incentive existed among workers and a "paralysing fear of the political authorities" prevailed since the purges. A scarcity of consumer goods existed. According to one engineer it was meaningless to use foreign experts in the factory he had been working at, before the factory manager, the head of city Soviet, and the head of the secret police, were exchanged for other people, who had a different outlook on their duties.[13]

A similar story was told to the US embassy in Ankara by two engineers (reported in May), but this time regarding the Grozny oil industry. Authority interference impaired efficiency, as did the inability of Soviet technicians to handle the equipment, resulting in damaged machinery. One engineer stated that the output of the Grozny fields was only a fraction of its potential.[14] Yeaton also reported (in April) that petroleum production was suffering from "poor organisation, lack of material, general inexperience and bad technical leadership". Despite this output was sufficient to cover the needs of both

Germany and the USSR during 1940. Petroleum output was 33 million tonnes in 1940, and it was expected that it could be increased to 44 million tonnes in 1942, with the help of German organization.[15] In November the Moscow embassy returned to the oil industry and its fundamental importance for Soviet economic development. In contrast to Yeaton's estimate this report predicted decreasing output. The 1939 output was 28.5 million tonnes, an almost 6 per cent decrease from 1938, and 1940 output would be even lower.[16] Actual 1940 output was 31.1 million tonnes.[17]

The continued military build-up was noted by the Anglo-Americans in April and May. They had little else than official sources to study for establishing the defence budget, but those figures were indicating very large increases in defence spending. The US embassy noted that the increased spending was diverting attention from agriculture and civilian industry, even though the end of the Finnish war had provided some relief. The previously perceived shortages, deficiencies and problems were largely repeated, and even thought to be getting worse. The authorities' measures to counter the negative tendencies were only decreasing the standard of living even more.[18] In August the embassy reported, considering the further intensification of defence preparations, that the whole economic structure was for all practical purposes mobilized for war. Extraordinary measures had been taken by the authorities to increase productivity and "tighten labor discipline". However, all the efforts were increasing, rather than decreasing, the fundamental weaknesses of the economic organisation.[19]

Major Joseph A. Michela, the US assistant military attaché in Moscow, commented in January 1941 on the total funds used for defence spending in 1940. Smith describes Michela, who in 1941 would become the military attaché after Yeaton, as being only a little less hostile to the Soviets than Yeaton. Michela was a cavalry officer who had studied Russian in the 1930s.[20] He estimated that the total appropriations for national defence in 1940 to 25.4 per cent of the budget, compared to 20.7 per cent in 1939. These figures did not only include expenditure on the armed forces, but also the defence industry, internal affairs, civil aviation, physical culture, "Osoaviakhim" and reserve labour.[21] In March he complemented the estimate with a report based on Soviet sources; forecasting further increases in defence spending for 1941.[22]

In July the FO had obtained a report on statements made by Steinhardt about conditions in the USSR. He reported about "utter chaos in Russia" (and a difficult transport situation).[23] In August a memorandum (written by Clanchy), connecting internal stability to the living standard, was send to London from the British embassy. The preparations for war and the high defence preparedness had already put a high pressure on the welfare of ordinary people, and that the situation could be unbearable if the USSR were engaged in anything but a short war. However, the situation could be somewhat better in one year's time.[24] Three additional FO reports from the latter half of 1940 painted a picture of an economic policy that was straining the living standard in order to facilitate the military build-up.[25] Sometimes food shortages were mentioned without any explicitly stated connection to military spending. At the beginning of May the COS weekly report to the War Cabinet stated that the USSR was suffering from a severe food shortage.[26] In August the embassy official J.W. Russell sent a memorandum to the FO, in which he wrote about an acute food shortage in the areas surrounding Moscow.[27]

During the fall some assessments were made concerning the industry and the transport sector. Yeaton reported to the WD in September about the very poor state of the railways and the military implications of this: "the maximum time the present railroad system could supply the present army in time of war against a first-class power is six months." It was not possible that the railways could support armed forces larger than the present – 4.5 to 5 million men – which in turn made him conclude that there would probably not be any appreciable wartime increase of the army.[28] The US embassy's third quarter economic review emphasized the preparations for war and was about the usual industrial problems, also adding that industrial output was falling behind plan. The total volume of output was not much higher than during the corresponding quarter of 1939. The agricultural situation was somewhat better. The grain harvest would be the biggest since 1937.[29] The next quarterly review, issued in February 1941, told a similar story regarding the military build-up and the pressure it exerted on the working population. However, the previously so criticized economic legalisation, applied by the regime to increase economic efficiency, had an effect in speeding up the industrial tempo during the last months of 1940.[30]

By the turn of the year the German military build-up for the attack on the USSR had been going on for several months. Plans were made and troops and was being moved eastwards. The British would of course benefit from a Soviet–German war. In January 1941 some MI2(b) representatives analysed Soviet-German relations. Based on political and military circumstances, they concluded that the Soviets would not even resist German aggression. Therefore Stalin would not hinder an attempt by Germany to move into the Ukraine. The explanation for this was that the Red Army was weak, that it had not yet concluded its reorganization, or procured enough new equipment, and that Stalin desired to stay in power. The last notion probably implicitly meant that Stalin knew that defeat would follow armed resistance against the Germans, and that defeat could result in an overthrow of his regime. Not only would Stalin let the Germans take the Ukraine, but a mere threat of a resumed German advance in the Caucasus direction would be enough for him to give them further economic concessions.[31] Another document of MI2 origin expressed the same conclusion in principle regarding the Soviet will to resist German aggression. It was seen as *possible* that the Soviets would resist a German entry into the Ukraine.[32] Yet another MI2 document described the Red Army as "mortally afraid" of the German Army, and Stalin would fight Germany only if it was patent to all that Hitler was doomed, in which case the MI2 counted on Stalin to use opportunist tactics.[33] However, not all British observers shared these notions. Stafford Cripps, the new British ambassador in Moscow, was of a different opinion, since he noted in his diary on 12 April that he believed that the Soviets would fight in the event of a German attack.[34] Cripps, a Parliament Member with Marxist sympathies, had been appointed (1940) by Churchill in the belief that Cripps could negotiate with Stalin.

American military intelligence also took notice of information pointing in the direction that the Soviets would not fight the Germans. In April G-2's New York office had interviewed a man by the name of John Poushine, described as the personal representative of the Tsarist pretender Grand Duke Vladimir. Poushine regarded the USSR as so militarily weak that the Soviets would not stop the Germans from occupy the Ukraine or even Baku. A Red Army defeat would be assured in the event of war with Germany, and the defeat would lead to the immediate collapse of the regime. G-2 regarded Poushine as a reliable source.[35]

In the US embassy's first quarter review (from April) the national budget was analysed. Almost two-thirds of the budget was used to finance the expansion of heavy industry and the armed forces. For once the quarter under review had been a good one for heavy industry and the consumer industry, except for heavy machine tools. Food production as well as the spring sowing in agriculture went well. On the other hand the industrial rationalisation process was not especially successful, and the program for capital construction was lagging behind. Several other branches were also behind the plan. The state budget was analysed in an early April special memorandum. The budget was more than ever a military budget, and the people's needs were largely neglected.[36]

In a May MEW memorandum some of the notions regarding a possible German influence over the Soviet economy were repeated. German experts were necessary in order to improve the efficiency of industry and transport. This would allow for an output increase, which in turn would allow for higher exports to Germany. Given a choice between this and a German invasion (with a following defeat), Stalin would choose the former. Exports to Germany did not represent a true surplus but were taken directly from internal demand. Somewhat surprising, considering the context of the memorandum and British reporting in general, the MEW believed that Soviet technology in metallurgical mining and in oil production in general was ahead of similar German technology.[37]

Less than a week (16 June) before the launching of Operation Barbarossa Michela sent a report to the US assistant chief of staff (G-2). He seemingly summarized some of his thoughts about Soviet strength in the following sentence: "It is difficult to picture an efficient Red Army growing out of a country which is still practically illiterate and mechanically backward. The general inefficiency encountered in all spheres of economic life leads to the conclusions of this estimate. It is not based entirely on first-hand knowledge of the army." He also commented on the possible internal problems that the Soviets might experience in the event of war: "Although in the event of an attack by Germany some German influences in the Baltics, combined with separatist movements in the Ukraine, will have some adverse effect. The Moslem influences in the

Caucasus would also have to be reckoned with in the event of hostile action against the middle-eastern states." Yeaton shared the opinions expressed in the report.[38]

8.2 The production and quality of munitions

The aircraft industry and the SAF received relatively much attention from G-2 and the US military attachés during this period. In January 1940 Yeaton estimated monthly aircraft output to 500 and in August to 437, or maybe somewhat higher. In one August G-2 report monthly output was estimated to 287, and in another it was stated that it would be "unwise" to estimate output to less than 500 to 600 military aircraft. In December Yeaton stated that annual output would be around 5,000 and monthly output 600, even though he also included civilian aircraft in these figures. In January 1941 he confirmed the annual (1940) figure to the MID. One of the August G-2 reports also contained information about industrial personnel and production processes. It took a labour force of 79,300 to achieve the output (287 aircraft) in question, in addition to 62,100 in the engine industry. The aircraft and engine factories were being "well equipped" with foreign machinery and tools. The problem with labour in combination with modern machinery were described in the following manner: "Automatic machinery is largely used, primarily because of the difficulties in obtaining skilled labor, and for the same reason, lack of skilled labour, the machinery itself has been difficult to maintain." In addition, the aircraft industry was suffering from a few raw material deficiencies, but shortages in general were more due to poor organisation of subsidiary production programmes, or to a lack of coordination in the transportation system. The purges, and the resulting loss of trained and experienced personnel, were perceived as one of the reasons explaining the industry's various problems.[39]

The US military attaché in London had access to the British Air Ministry's opinions concerning the aircraft industry, and in October he informed the WD about these. The Air Ministry noted that the Soviets tried to improve and expand the industry. However, the improvements were in some respects counterproductive, since no one working in the factories would dare to assume responsibility for the products that would be released from the factories. No one would dare due to the assertion that the government had issued a decree, stressing that defective material was not to be released. This situation was made worse by the "lack of mechanical sense" of "insufficiently trained operatives". The harsh system instigated to maintain discipline was another factor that created unfortunate working conditions, since the workers could receive very severe sentences for minor transgressions.[40]

In January 1941 Yeaton wrote a report that shone some light on the nature of the aircraft industry's perceived deficiencies. He stated: "[it is] believed that with present plant facilities and under United States working conditions the Soviet Union could turn out 10,000 or more planes a year. Because of the peculiar conditions within the Union […] it is […] estimated by the best observers that the greater part of Soviet industry at present operates at between forty and sixty per cent of capacity." Despite this assessment Yeaton believed that the aircraft and aircraft motor industry were "one of the most highly developed and most carefully nartured [*sic*] in the Soviet Union". He also pointed out that the industry had not "yet" reached a 50 per cent "efficiency standard" that could be supported for a longer period. Since he apparently believed that the aircraft industry was a prioritized sector, this statement implicitly also says much about his perceptions regarding industrial conditions in general.[41]

Furthermore, during the Winter War monthly aircraft output had been as low as 300 units, or even lower, due to the war's "disrupting" influence. But when the war ended output had increased again, due to "the freeing of transportation", new labour laws, and other circumstances, and monthly output might have been as high as 600 for a short period during the fall of 1940. A production curve was not possible to draw, due to the irregular production pattern of many factories – "a factory may produce a peak quantity in one month and close down the next month for lack of spare machinery, parts or materials".[42]

In another January dispatch he repeated the notion regarding the annual output of circa 5000 aircraft, but now also specified it to 2800 fighters, 1680 bombers, about 500 heavy bombers, and other types. The figure of 5000 was verified from "entirely different sources".[43] He more or less confirmed these figures in February; stating that the bulk of production "seems" to be located in seven factories producing 4480 planes during 1940.[44] In April he noted that some older models were being phased out, while production instead was concentrated on the fighter I-18, which he considered to be more or less a copy of the US P-40. He repeated the notion about 40–60 per cent efficiency in the factories, and also commented on the production process in the facility called Factory number 1. Thirty per cent of the output in that factory was "being condemned and turned back as defective".[45]

Judging by a March 1940 report to the War Cabinet the COS believed that the Germans indirectly contributed to aircraft production, since the report contained information about Soviet air-force technicians working in German factories to gain experience.[46] In June the COS commented on the quality of the latest aircraft prototypes, which had a good performance, although below the standard of the best Anglo-French aircraft.[47] In November the COS wondered if it was possible for Germany to secure aircraft and engine supplies from Soviet facilities, even though it was not believed that there was much room for this. Any improvements in Soviet conditions to make this possible would in turn require the help of German technicians and instructors.[48]

In October 1940 and in June 1941 the MID and Michela, respectively, commented on military equipment besides aircraft. With respect to infantry equipment the MID assessed that the Red Army was "satisfactorily uniformed and equipped" in an Eastern European context. At the same time the Red Army used obsolescent and obsolete materiel, but most of the materiel used during the Winter War was "satisfactory", and some of it even modern. The modern weapons were based on foreign prototypes, produced under more inefficient conditions, which in turn resulted in the manufacture of materiel less well constructed than the originals.[49]

Michela was perhaps even more critical: "In short, the greatest weakness of the Soviet Army lies in the lack of modern equipment, armament and technique. It needs quality and quantity in modern planes, guns and motor vehicles." The statement referred to all the Red Army's heavy equipment (including artillery). He also stated that: "The tank troops [...] lack sufficient heavy modern tanks. The medium tanks have insufficient armament and all are not dependable mechanically. There is a decided shortage of good mechanics and repair facilities." And: "The air force has few long-range bombers and but one type that can bomb at night (DB-3). It does have a good fast fighter and a new fast bomber recently developed but they are too few in number, and production is slow. The greater portion of planes is [...] obsolescent or obsolete." Yeaton concurred in this estimate.[50]

The Anglo-Americans still underestimated the quality of military equipment. They correctly noted that the Soviets were modernizing their aircraft inventory, but they underestimated the pace and as it seems also the quality of the new aircraft. This was of course associated with the underestimation of aircraft output – if estimated output was lower than the actual rate of output it took longer time to replace outdated aircraft with newer models. In reality, the output pace increased continuously, and many of the latest models were just becoming available for the military units in the spring of 1941. Many of the earlier models, designed already during the late 1920s and early 1930s (like the Polikarpov I-16), were being replaced by more capable models. The huge size of the SAF, the real size of which in 1939–1941 was unknown to Western observers, was made up of models such as the I-16, which at the time of their original design was very capable models. However, the pace of aircraft design was very high in the 1930s and it only took two to three years before a model was outdated. Actual military aircraft output in 1939 was 10,382, increasing to 10,565 in 1940 and the pace continued to accelerate during the first six months of 1941.[51]

As for tanks Michela was probably correct in his assessments that the Red Army suffered from a relative lack of mechanics and repair facilities, otherwise his statement about tanks was unrealistic. Obviously it was hard for him, or the other observes, to know about the new T-34 and KV tanks recently deployed to units, but these tanks were actually the best in the world at the time. The medium heavy T-34's armour was as good as or probably better than any of the best German tanks, was faster than the German medium tanks and had a more powerful gun. The armour of the T-34 was impenetrable for most German anti-tank weapons. The KV-1 was a heavy tank and had a weight of about double contemporary German tanks. The KV-1's armour plates were much stronger than the T-34's, and it was about as fast a German medium tank and had the same gun as a T-34. These tanks were still in the minority in tank units but output was increasingly shifting towards the mass producing of these vehicles. Due to the tactical deficiencies of the Red Army, German air superiority and the general chaos caused by the initial shock of the German invasion, these tanks could not be used properly. Despite this the appearance of these tanks was a very nasty surprise to the Germans and the German tank program was influenced by these models. As a matter of fact one German design idea, which in the end evolved into the Panther tank, was to simply copy the T-34.

8.3 Military efficiency and the size of the armed forces

The Winter War had clearly demonstrated to the observers that their pre-war assessments basically were correct, and the war even worsened their perception of Soviet military capabilities in certain respects. Assessments produced after the war was less frequent. The Red Army was not involved in any major campaign until the June 1941 and the "phoney war" in the West was ending in the spring of 1940.

One way of indirectly estimating military efficiency is to take toll of manpower losses in the field. It was well known at the time that the Red Army suffered several times the losses sustained by the Finns in the Winter War. Actual Soviet irrecoverable losses, which included personnel killed in action, those who died during casualty evacuation, or in the hospital of wounds, disease, and also personnel missing in action, amounted to nearly 127,000. In addition to these almost 265,000 was wounded or became sick (but not dying) during the campaign. This means that total losses were close to 392,000.[52] Information exists about considerable higher losses, but the source for the figures given above is the most detailed account at hand, and this source is, in turn, also based on access to the post-Soviet archives. Finnish losses were 24,923 dead and 43,557 wounded.[53]

Huthsteiner sent a few reports concerning losses to the WD and G-2. By early February Huthsteiner had received information from the Finnish Army General Staff, which stated that Soviet losses were 60,000 killed and just as many wounded; nearly seven times as much as the Finns themselves.[54] In a report to G-2, dated 20 March, total losses up to 1 March were set at 200,000 killed and severely wounded, in addition to 7000 prisoners. Material losses were stated to be 588 airplanes (brought down on Finnish territory) and 1200 tanks.[55] According to the Finnish General Staff these losses were about eight or nine times as great as the corresponding Finnish losses.[56] In an April special bulletin concerning the Winter War the MID repeated the losses given in the G-2 report for manpower and tanks, but they seem not to have trusted the sources for this information entirely, since they also stated that the figures probably were exaggerated.[57] According to an April FO report from the British Helsinki ambassador, which originated from a Finnish minister, Soviet losses during the war were 900–1000 aircraft, 1600 tanks, and about 200,000 killed in combat.[58]

The same month the US assistant military attaché in London reported to the WD about 964 lost military aircraft, based on information from a Finnish army general staff officer.[59] In another report from London dated 1 May, this time from the acting military attaché and based on Finnish and British Government sources, aircraft losses had been 809. In a comparative summary Soviet losses were estimated to 32 per cent of all the planes committed in the war, and Finnish losses to 21 per cent. The estimated number of Soviet aircraft committed was about nine times the number of committed Finnish aircraft.[60] There seems to be no reliable estimates of actual Soviet material losses during the Finnish war, but there is no doubt they were heavy. However, if the manpower losses are to be taken as an indicator, it seems safe to say that the material losses probably were overestimated. Some of the information available to the Anglo-Americans seems to be clear exaggerations. An MI2 document dated in January 1941 revealed that one British source considered total Soviet dead during the war to be at least 0.5 million, or possibly as many as 0.75 million.[61] John Poushine, the G-2's "reliable" source, was of the opinion in April that the Finnish campaign had cost the Soviets between 750,000 and 1 million men in killed, wounded and prisoners.[62]

Despite the Red Army's poor performance, it seems that the actual improvement of operations later in the war made an impression on some observers. Huthsteiner reported in late March to G-2 about the bombing raids over Finland. The Soviets showed an "exceptional improvement" in their bombing during the latter part of the war.[63] In April the US naval attaché in Brussels conveyed a similar message to the Navy Department's intelligence division. According to his "well-informed observer", the Red Army did not have the qualities of either the French or the German armies, but it was "far from [...] a negligible one". The difference in performance between the troops committed early and later in the war was "great". He also reported that the High Command had improved, that heavy guns, tanks and planes were of good quality, and that the pilots were well trained.[64] This report can therefore be regarded as unusual in the sense that it actually portrayed the Red Army in a relatively favourable light, even though, of course, not up the standards of Western forces. It should also be remembered, however, that the US naval attaché in Brussels was not the usual information source regarding the USSR.

In a MID report from September, with a somewhat unclear origin, the Red Army was once again described in a more positive light. The defensive value of the army was praised and the source concluded that "the last six weeks of the Finnish campaign had given evidence to disinterested observers – as distinguished from wishful thinkers – that the Russian army and air force were well trained and well equipped and that neither its striking power nor its defensive qualities should be underestimated."[65] In an October special bulletin the MID commented on the maintenance of equipment, which was satisfactory, even if not up to US standard.[66]

In January 1941 the British MI2 was of the opinion that the lessons from the Finnish war had been well absorbed by the Soviet Armed Forces, and that every effort was being made to raise the standard of efficiency.[67] In reality, the Finnish debacle did produce a reorganization of the Armed Forces. The Communist party addressed the problems that the war had revealed and several changes were initiated. The changes affected tactical shortcomings and deficiencies at higher level command structures, as well as logistics and frontline communications. The reforms also resulted in a more pronounced emphasis on and a wider introduction of some weapon systems.[68] It can be argued that these reforms, although not completed in June 1941, at least mitigated some of the very grave problems that the Red Army encountered in face of the German onslaught.

Shortly before the end of the Finnish war the idea that the Germans' help would improve Soviet (this time military) efficiency was hatched by the COS. The help would at first be in the form of a military delegation which possibly might improve military operations. The Soviets might also agree to the Germans sending ground and air forces to operate side by side with the Red Army. Once again the COS stated that the Soviets were unable to carry out large-scale operations efficiently.[69] Later in March the COS reported to the War Cabinet that German instructors were teaching Soviet pilots in Soviet Poland.[70]

According to an April FO report the Soviets had used German officers to improve military efficiency after the first week in February. The British Helsinki ambassador sent a statement by a Finnish minister to London: Field Marshal Gustaf Mannerheim, the Finnish commander in chief, was convinced that the use of German officers in the field was responsible for Soviet military successes in February. Russian tactics and operational coordination had improved by then, and the appointment of a new Commander-in-Chief, General Shaposhnikoff, was not a sufficient explanation. According to the report several other factors indicated the presence of German assistance.[71] Actually, no direct military collaboration of this kind ever took place between Germany and the USSR during World War II. The economic collaboration was almost exclusively limited to trade.

Earlier in March the WO sent a report to the FO concerning the Red Army's military capabilities. Its content was mostly a repetition of earlier assessments. The report did, however, mention the word "courage", but was otherwise about "grave shortcomings" (concerning leadership, staff work, training and administration) and "very weak" air-cooperation. The aircraft employed were seen as "obsolescent".[72] The presumed substandard air capabilities were also commented on the next month by the American military attaché in London: according to an officer of the Finnish Army General Staff, Field Marshal Mannerheim had stated that "if the Finns had approximately 100 fighter (pursuit) airplanes with ample ammunition, they could have destroyed practically every plane the Russians put into the air." According to the same report the Finns had only 96 military airplanes of various sorts, all obsolete or obsolescent, while the Soviets used at least 2500 aircraft during the war.[73]

The SAF's performance in the Finnish war also inspired an August WD report, with information provided by the military attaché in Helsinki, ultimately expressing the opinions of a US Air Corps major. The SAF was "very large", with 10,000 to 12,000 first line aircraft, but it would still not be a real match for *Luftwaffe*. The SAF was not capable of sustaining operations against another air force of equal numerical strength. The SAF's personnel were see as "brave", but this was not enough, since they suffered from a "lack of broad mentality", poor leadership and poor logistics.[74]

The British low regard for the SAF's efficiency seems to have continued right up until the beginning of Barbarossa, judging by a COS report dated 19 June 1941. This report was more or less based on the SAF's Finnish experiences. The COS also considered most aircraft outdated, although they recognized that the I-18 fighter was comparable to the British Hurricane fighter.[75]

In the aforementioned August 1940 WO report it was recognized that the Red Army was lavishly equipped with mostly good-quality weapons, and that it "probably" possessed 10,000 to 11,000 tanks. All in all, the defensive value of the army was repeated, even though it now seemed that it was not likely to the WO that the Red Army could stand up to an attack by a first class power for very long. The report's last sentence was almost something of a prophecy, stating that the Red Army would be "particularly vulnerable to the effects of surprise, owing to the rigidity of its doctrines and to its inherent inability to provide against the unexpected".[76] The tank strength estimate was higher than earlier Anglo-American estimates, although still without doubt an under-estimation. The WO was, however, much closer to the truth than a WD report from the same month, in which the tank strength was between 4000 and 5000.[77]

In two June reports Yeaton wrote about the armed forces' low morale and discipline. He specifically described why these conditions existed in the Navy: "a backwards society trying to adapt itself to a modern technique", constant NKVD supervision, the dual command system, the population's "deplorable living conditions", "the widespread lack of discipline and supervision during adolescence" and "the lack of unhampered and skilled leaders". He emphasized that high morale and discipline in the Navy could not be achieved before the living conditions in the USSR were greatly improved. Conditions in the Red Army were not better, and the recommended remedy was the same.[78]

In July Yeaton argued that several military observes in Moscow believed that there was no demobilization under way. The size of the Armed Forces was over 4 million men.[79] In September he changed the estimate to between 4.5 and 5 million, with an annual draft of around 1.5 million. His report to the WD also stated that more than half of the drafted had received the "Osoaviakhim" badge "Ready for Labor and Defense".[80] The "Osoaviakhim" was an abbreviation for the Soviet paramilitary organization (often spelled OSOAVIA-KhIM) which translated from Russian stood for Union of Societies of Assistance to Defence and Aviation-Chemical Construction of the USSR. The organization was intended to provide the populations with some pre-military training. In January 1940 the organization mustered nearly 12.9 million members. When the war begun in 1941 more than 7 million of them were immediately transferred to the Red Army and partisan groups.[81]

Michela reported about the OSOAVIAKhIM in December and from what he wrote it seems that he had a fairly accurate understanding of the organization: a "voluntary society composed of 13,000,000 members of both sexes and various ages who devote their spare time to its activities. Its general mission is to create a reserve of partially trained personnel for all military forces". He identified several advantages. Among other things, it saved time for the armed forces since they did not have to start military training of conscripts from scratch, it provided a testing ground for the selection of personnel for various military branches, and it was self-supporting (i.e. outside the regular military budget). The OSOAVIAKhIM was part of the militarization of society.[82] In February 1941 he reported again about pre-military training; commenting on a wide variety of organizations that provided this for mostly younger citizens – "Octoberists", "Pioneers", "Komsomols", trade unions and schools. Even if he believed that these organisations only provided basic military training, they at least fulfilled an accumulative role in preparing younger citizen for regular military training, thus saving time and money for the armed forces.[83] Even though it is hard to exactly assess the effectiveness of the Soviet pre-conscript training, Rottman asserts that "it did help the mobilisation effort and provided some degree of preparation".[84]

In January 1940 Yeaton reported that the SAF had 4500 to 5000 aircraft in service, and an additional 2500 obsolete planes in reserve. It seems that this estimate also allowed for an additional number of 1,500 training and reconnaissance aircraft. The total number would then be 8,500 to 9,000 aircraft.[85] During the second half of 1940 several US assessments were made regarding the SAF's numerical strength. In August Yeaton stated that it was 4839 by 1 May.[86] However, an August MID report, with information originating from Yeaton, estimated total strength on 1 July to 6100. Yeaton added that the preceding report was closer to the truth with regard to effective strength.[87] In October Huthsteiner (now lieutenant-colonel and the military attaché in Helsinki)[88] reported to the MID that estimated strength was 10,700.[89] The next month he reported that it was 7500 combat planes and around 2000 training aircraft. His "reliable source" also informed him about the ongoing modernization of fighters and dive bombers.[90] In two January 1941 MID reports, combat aircraft strength was estimated to somewhat above 7700. According to one of the reports, 3500 of these were obsolescent, and, in addition to the combat aircraft, there were about 3000 other aircraft (including civilian).[91]

In January 1941 Yeaton (now promoted to major) sent at least four reports regarding the SAF's numerical strength to the MID. First he referred to several different sources regarding 1940: an effective fighting strength of 4500 and a total strength of 6100, 7500 or 8500 planes.[92] Later in the month the figure was 6000, many outdated or in need of major repairs. In two later reports he was more specific and stated that total strength was 10,756 planes, divided between 4256 "standard" (of which nearly half was fighters), 3500 "obsolescent" and 3000 "others including civil".[93] In March he returned to the subject with information from other sources, and then stated that total strength was 5732 aircraft (probably referring to first line aircraft) on 1 January.[94]

At the end of March he also reported to the MID about the strength of the Navy, estimated to approximately the same size as in earlier Anglo-American reports, with the exception of the submarine fleet, now having 253 vessels.[95]

During the first six months of 1941 some assessments were made concerning the size of the armed forces. In January Michela believed that the size was nearly 4.3 million men, of which almost 4.1 was in the Army.[96] The ONI reported similar figures in March, referring to a January report from Yeaton. According to the ONI the Red Army's had nearly 4.1 million men, also adding that the "air corps" had 150,000 men and the NKVD 550,000. The number of trained reserves, including pre-conscripts of 16 to 17 years of age, with rudimentary military training, was about 20.5 million.[97]

On 14 June the British JIC estimated the size of the Armed Forces while at the same time evaluating the possible effects of a Soviet-German War. The British knew by now that a German attack might be near. The Armed Forces was large: with 3.5 million men, 18,000 tanks and nearly 6500 aircraft. However, its value for war was still low and its equipment obsolete. The main characteristics of the Army and Air Force, regarding efficiency, were more or less the same as in the Finnish war,[98] although some progress was noticed. The difficulties of divided control between commanders and political commissars were largely eliminated, and there was no doubt that steps had been taken to rectify many of the problems revealed by the war. The Red Army's morale was high, but they doubted that it would last in the face of German mechanized warfare and the *Luftwaffe*. Despite the Red Army's size it would not be able to offer substantial resistance in open warfare, to an army so highly mechanized or ably led as the German.[99]

In the 16 June report to G-2 Michela stated: "Comparable to the high-powered, efficient, modern armies now formed and being formed in the world, the combat efficiency of the Red Army at this time is relatively low." He continued: "Leadership is composed of practical but uneducated and even ignorant men. The purge of 1938 removed the capable army leaders and the present [...] leadership lacks quality. [...] the individual man makes a good and brave soldier but a not too intelligent or resourceful one. However, efforts have been made to raise the educational level of all conscripts with some degree of success." In general, the morale of the army was good, as well as its loyalty.[100] He stated the same regarding morale one week earlier, and added that if the USSR was attacked this would continue to be the case, except in the event that the armed forces were be used on foreign soil.[101]

In the 16 June report he described the infantry troops as reliable in the sense that it would carry out given orders, but they would not do this particularly well. He added: "It is neither well led nor trained. Combat training has suffered due to climatic conditions and to the fact that so many garrisons are in the heart of cities and towns. Firepower in the division is too low and the infantry division itself is too large and cumbersome." However, he had some praise for the cavalry, the artillery ("excellent firing technique") and the tank troops ("excellent"). The overall mobility was commented on in the following way: "The army cannot move much faster than it could thirty years ago." The supposedly outdated Red Army equipment made him conclude: "These deficiencies reduce its air power, fire power and mobility. It could not hold up against a hard-hitting, fast moving army with modern equipment and armament. The supply of manpower would not be a problem. Yeaton fully concurred in Michela's assessments.[102]

On 19 June, three days before the start of Barbarossa, Acting Assistant Chief of Staff (G-2) Colonel C. H. Mason submitted a memorandum to the US chief of staff on the Soviet–German situation. He stated that Red Army strength in Europe was 2.75 million men, a figure that could quickly be raised to 3.25 million. The soldiers had courage and their discipline and training was seen as "fair". The SAF's European strength was 4250 aircraft, some being "fairly modern" and others outdated. The tank troops were rather modern, with many good tanks. The Red Army's weakest element was its officers of higher and middle rank. The Finnish war had confirmed "this historic Russian deficiency". The inefficiency of the railways and communications was a "major factor" in the Red Army's assumed inability to launch successful offensive and defensive operations. In a comparative assessment of military strength, taking into account the size, equipment, training standards, and leadership of the Soviet and German armies, Mason predicted that Germany could "rapidly" defeat the USSR, "overthrow the Stalin regime, and seize [the USSR's] western provinces". The total destruction of the army was a possibility in 1941, which would open up Siberia to the Germans, all the way to Lake Baikal. Mason concluded his memorandum by stating that a German attack on the USSR was a "sound military operation, if launched prior to July 1 [...] with reasonable chances of a full success prior to winter's setting in".[103]

Notes

1 Bellamy (2007), 120.
2 Hinsley (1979), 188, 430–432; Clarke (2002), 186–187.
3 27–7-1940, JIC(40)179, CAB81/97.
4 Hinsley (1979), 431–433, 438–441.
5 Smith (1996), 11; Hinsley (1979), 453–454, 456–476.
6 23–5-1941, JIC(41)218(Final), CAB81/102; 5–6-1941, JIC(41)218(Complement), CAB81/102; 10–6-1941, JIC(41)247, CAB81/102; 13–6-1941, JIC(41)251(Final), CAB81/103; 14–6-1941, JIC(41)234(Revise), CAB81/102.
7 Roberts (1995), 120–121.
8 15–3-1940, COS(40)262, CAB80/8.
9 18–3-1940, COS(40)262, CAB80/8.
10 In April the COS returned to the problematic internal situation and in a May WO report the transport problem was scrutinized again. The WO tried to evaluate how much troops the Soviets could transport on the railways. They did not believe that the transport problem, as compared to the situation shortly before World War I, primarily was a question of inadequate capacity. The supposed

fundamental weakness of the centralization of oil production to vulnerable areas in the Caucasus was considered again in a March FO draft memorandum distributed to the War Cabinet and elsewhere. This weakness could in time, if the oil supply was interrupted, "paralyse the Soviet military machine and disorganise Soviet national life."9–5-1940, Report No. 3903, WO208/1750; 19–4-1940, COS (40)301, CAB80/10; 25–3-1940, "Special [...]", CAB104/259.

11 "Eastern European documents, volume IV to V", "Report, Armament trends since 1937", Box-3181, Entry-77, RG165.
12 14–3-1940, "Comments [...]", Box-3172, Entry-77, RG165; 7–5-1940, "Comments [...]", Box-3172, Entry-77, RG165; 1–8-1940, "Comments [...]", Box-3172, Entry-77, RG165.
13 10–5-1940, "Subject: [...]", Box-3108, Entry-77, RG165.
14 23–5-1940, Despatch No. 1460, Roll-27, T1250, RG59.
15 8–4-1940, 2655-D-555, Roll-10, M1443, RG165.
16 14-11-1940, Despatch No. 928, Roll-27, T 1250, RG59.
17 Harrison (2002), Table 4.2.
18 6 May, 4 June, Despatch No. 451, Roll-22, T1250, RG59; 19–4-1940, N5254/132/38, FO371/24850; 3 May, 5 June, Despatch No. 449, Roll-24, T1250, RG59; 6 May, 4 June, Despatch No. 451, Roll-22, T1250, RG59; May 1940, "Economic [...]", Department of Commerce, Box-3100, Entry-77, RG165.
19 22–8-1940, Despatch No. 705, Roll-22, T1250, RG59.
20 Smith (1996) 33; 17–1-1942, No. 561, "Michela, Joseph A.", Box-1, MECF1941–42, RG84.
21 6–1-1941, 2037–2068, M1443, Roll-18, RG165.
22 6–3-1941, "Summarized [...]", Roll-18, M1443, RG165.
23 19–7-1940, N6128/132/38, FO371/24850.
24 24–8-1940, N6422/4111/38, FO371/24859.
25 24–8-1940, N6422/4111/38, FO371/24859; 3–11–1940, N7156/4111/38, FO371/24859; 9–12–1940, N523/42/38, FO371/24859.
26 3–5-1940, COS(40)314, CAB80/10.
27 16–8-1940, N6421/4111/38, FO418/86.
28 10–9-1940, 2037–1769, Roll-14, M1443, RG165.
29 21-10-1940, 16-12-1940, Despatch No. 868, Roll-22, T1250, RG59.
30 1–1-1941, Despatch No. 1110, Roll-22, T1250, RG59.
31 6–1-1941, "M.I.2 Colonel", WO208/1758.
32 12–1-1940, "Records [...]", WO208/1750.
33 8–1-1941, "Will [...]", WO208/1758.
34 Clarke (2002), 217.
35 3–4-1941, "Current Events", Box-3090, Entry-77, RG165.
36 29–4-1941, Despatch No. 1304, Roll-22, T1250, RG59; 1–4-1941, 13–5-1941, Despatch No. 1247, Roll-24, T1250, RG59.
37 Woodward (1970), 617–618.
38 16–6-1941, "Army [...]", Box-3120, Entry-77, RG165.
39 1–8-1940, "Estimated [...]", Box-3155, Entry-77, RG165; 1–8-1940, "9505 – Digest", Box-3155, Entry-77, RG165; 1–8-1940, "Subject: [...]", Box-3155, Entry-77, RG165; 6–12–1940, "Subject: [...]", Box-3155, Entry-77, RG165; 25–1-1941, "Domestic [...]", Box-3155, Entry-77, RG165; 8–1-1940, Report No. 1634, Roll-20, M1443, RG165; 8–1-1940, "Subject: [...]", Box-3155, Entry-77, RG165; 8–1-1940, Report No. 1673a, Roll-20, M1443, RG165; Appendix 11, Roll-19, M1443, RG165. This perception of the state of affairs in the aircraft industry was pretty much supported by another report, which in practice was a May article from the *Journal of the Royal Service Institution*. "Journal of the Royal Service Institution, May 1940", Box-3154, Entry-77, RG165.
40 18-10-1940, "Subject: [...]", Box-3155, Entry-77, RG165.

41 3–1-1940, Report No. 1831, Roll-21, M1443, RG165.
42 Ibid.
43 25–1-1941, Report No. 1847, Roll-21, M1443, RG165.
44 6–2-1941, Report No. 1853, Roll-20, M1443, RG165.
45 4–4-1941, Report No. 1897, Roll-20, M1443, RG165.
46 22–3-1940, COS(40)272, CAB80/9.
47 7–6-1940, COS(40)435, CAB80/12.
48 14-11-1940, COS(40)942, CAB80/22.
49 29-10-1940, "Special [...]", Box-2152, Entry-79, RG165.
50 16–6-1941, "Army [...]", Box-3120, Entry-77, RG165.
51 Kennedy (1989), 324, 354; Harrison (2002), Table 4.2.
52 Krivosheev (1997), 77, 290.
53 Lunde (2011), 19.
54 6–2-1940, "American [...]", Box-3146, Entry-77, RG165.
55 20–3-1940, 2037–2100, Roll-18, M1443, RG165.
56 19–3-1940, "Grankulla [...]", Box-3147, Entry-77, RG165.
57 1–4-1940, "Special [...]", Box-2152, Entry-79, RG165.
58 8–4-1940, N4094/1/56, FO371/24795.
59 20–4-1940, "Subject: [...]", Box-3158, Entry-77, RG165.
60 The Finnish and British government sources were the Finnish minister in London and Air Ministry officials. 1–5-1940, Report No. 41115, Roll-23, M1443, RG165.
61 12–1-1940, "Records [...]", WO208/1750.
62 3–4-1941, "Current [...]", Box-3090, Entry-77, RG165.
63 28–3-1940, "Subject: [...]", Roll-23, M1443, RG165.
64 9–4-1940, A-6-b, 16382–0, Box-242, Entry-98A, RG38.
65 12–9-1940, "State [...]", Box-3119, Entry-77, RG165.
66 29-10-1940, "Special [...]", Box-2152, Entry-79, RG165.
67 8–1-1941, "Will [...]", WO208/1758.
68 Reece (2008), 831, 851, 847; Glantz (1998), 88, 94, 16.
69 8–3-1940, COS(40)252, WO193/646. A summarized version of the report was given to the French High Command. 25–3-1940, M.R.(J)(40)30, WO193/646.
70 22–3-1940, COS(40)272, CAB80/9.
71 8–4-1940, N4094/1/56, FO371/24795.
72 7–3-1940, N2965/1056/38, FO371/24854.
73 20–4-1940, "Subject: [...]", Box-3158, Entry-77, RG165; Dear & Foot (eds.) (1995), 716.
74 Furthermore, the report expressed the opinion that the *Wehrmacht* could deliver a knock-out blow to the USSR that would enforce a capitulation – under favourable conditions – in two to three months. 28–8-1940, "Estimate [...]", Box-3152, Entry-77, RG165.
75 19–6-1941, COS(41)385, CAB80/28.
76 7–3-1940, N2965/1056/38, FO371/24854.
77 28–8-1940, "Estimate [...]", Box-3152, Entry-77, RG165.
78 18–6-1940, Report No. 1734 and 1735, Roll-6, T1250, RG59.
79 24–7-1940, "To: [...]", Box-3133, Entry-77, RG165. According to the article noted by US military intelligence in the *Journal of the Royal Service Institution*, the total strength of the SAF might be quite large, ranging from 10,000 to 15,000 planes, including reserves and those planes stationed in Asia. But the first-line strength in Europe was considered to be around 5000 to 6000 planes. "Journal of the Royal Service Institution, May 1940", Box-3154, Entry-77, RG165.
80 10–9-1940, 2037–1769, Roll-14, M1443, RG165.
81 Siddiqi (2010), 305.
82 11-12-1940, "Subject: [...]", Box-3154, Entry-77, RG165.

83 4-2-1941, "Pre-Military Training", Box-3136, Entry-77, RG165.
84 Rottman (2007), 10.
85 8-1-1940, Report No. 1634, Roll-20, M1443, RG165; 8-1-1940, "Subject: [...]",
    Box-3155, Entry-77, RG165; 8-1-1940, Report No. 1673a, Roll-20, M1443,
    RG165; Appendix 11, Roll-19, M1443, RG165.
86 10-8-1940, Report No. 1754, Roll-20, M1443, RG165.
87 22-8-1940, Report No. 1761, Roll-20, M1443, RG165.
88 The Americans had to abandon their diplomatic representation in Riga in
    August as a result of the Baltic States being annexed by the USSR. Falkehed
    (1994), 116.
89 31-10-1940, "Subject: [...]", Roll-21, M1443, RG165.
90 12-11-1940, "Subject: [...]", Box-3154, Entry-77, RG165.
91 24-1-1941, "Airplane [...]", Box-3154, Entry-77, RG165; 25-1-1941, Box-3154,
    Entry-77, RG165.
92 3-1-1940, Report No. 1831, Roll-21, M1443, RG165.
93 7-1-1941, Report No. 1836, Roll-20, M1443, RG165; 14-1-1941, Report No.
    1839, Roll-20, M1443, RG165; 24-1-1941, Report No. 1845, Roll-20, M1443,
    RG165.
94 14-3-1941, Report No. 1880, Roll-20, M1443, RG165.
95 28-3-1941, Report No. 1893, Roll-19, M1443, RG165.
96 6-1-1941, 2037-2068, M1443, Roll-18, RG165.
97 18-3-1941, A-6-b, 16382-0, Box-242, Entry-98A, RG38.
98 The JIC stressed the Red Army's lack of initiative; rigid leadership; rigid
    doctrines; failure to coordinate; bad supply arrangements; and lack of training.
    Even though some mitigating circumstances were considered, the Navy was held
    in equally low esteem, with the exception of the large submarine fleet; regarded
    as better than the rest of the Navy. 14-6-1941, JIC(41)234(Revise), CAB81/102.
    According to Woodward the JIC produced a report with a similar content as the
    JIC(41)234(Revise) on the 9th. Woodward (1970), 619.
99 14-6-1941, JIC(41)234(Revise), CAB81/102.
100 16-6-1941, "Army [...]", Box-3120, Entry-77, RG165.
101 9-6-1941, "Morale [...]", Box-3126, Entry-77, RG165.
102 16-6-1941, "Army [...]", Box-3120, Entry-77, RG165.
103 19-6-1941, "Subject: [...]", 370.2USSR Thru 3-9-42, Box-1045, Entry-47,
    RG319.

9 The nature of the assessments, and the "reality"

Without doubt, the Anglo-Americans perceived the USSR as relatively weak before Barbarossa. Dmitrii Fedotoff-White, a former Tsarist naval officer and Russian emigrant, stated already during the war in his *The Growth of the Red Army* (1944): "One of the plausible explanations of the low estimate of the power of resistance of the Red army which existed in some military circles, both in this country [the US] and in Great Britain, at the time of [Barbarossa …], is that it may have had roots in the lack of knowledge on the part of some of the military leaders of these countries of the outstanding facts as to the production of Soviet heavy industry and in their lack of faith in the information reaching them regarding the productivity of the military industry of the U.S.S.R."[1] Was he right, or were there also additional factors involved that could help explain the perceived weakness of Soviet war potential in June 1941?

Most sectors of the Soviet economy and society was seen as weak and inadequate for a war of any significant size and duration. The only thing that the USSR had going for her was size and numbers, and perhaps a general defence preparedness, even though these advantages was not enough (and was underestimated). Even though the observers were wrong in more ways than one, it is hard to blame them considering the circumstances. First of all, they were not alone in their faulty assessments. Other contemporary Western intelligence and state agencies – for example, in Germany, France and Sweden – also held Soviet strength in low regard.[2] It is not unlikely that the observers from the different countries reinforced each other's perceptions. Some of these observers, or more specifically the Germans, also worked under a regime that officially promoted a racist agenda. This agenda portrayed the inhabitant of the Eastern European nations as racially "inferior". The Anglo-American's societies were parliamentary democracies, and the US and UK governments did not promote racist ideas. However, it is well known that racist ideas existed in some quarters, in the US and the UK during the 1930s, even among some prominent representatives of society.

In this case, regarding their perceptions of the Slavs and Russians, it would be wrong to accuse the Anglo-American observers of racism. On the other hand we know that some of the observers seemed to use notions such as "Slav incompetence", "the Russian character" and similar descriptions. This was definitively not a common phenomenon in the reporting, and never occurred in reports produced on higher levels. But this does not exclude that some observers, on the individual level, harboured ideas that perhaps can be compared to a mild form of racism. We know that some contemporary US officials had a racist outlook concerning the Japanese in certain respects, and some British FO officials described the Germans as an "efficient race". Other examples of similar thinking exist, also for example in France.[3] It is therefore not too far-fetched to believe that some of the underlying ideas, that guided Anglo-Americans perceptions, could have been influenced by thinking of this kind.

A more obvious, and probably more important aspect, is the factual circumstances surrounding the USSR and the conduct of its regime. This category includes the view of Russia being backwards, which of course in a strict socioeconomic sense was not wrong, but obviously the great improvement in the economic and military-industrial realm, achieved during the 1930s, was not fully understood. We can also assume that most, if not all, producing and analysing the assessments had little respect for or liking of Communism, the very ideology that Moscow represented. Some actions taken by the Soviets themselves served to strengthen perceptions of weakness. The late 1930s Great Terror purges gave signals to the outside world that was interpreted as weakness, both in general and with respect to the armed forces in particular. This was, as we have seen, a very important part of the assessments, regardless of the actual impact on Soviet strength. Associated with this kind of repressive society is government control of information. The Soviets were not revealing much concrete information to the outside world regarding its military-economic capabilities, other than propaganda and rehearsed manoeuvres. Therefore, military output, and to an even greater extent the actual reserve capacity for such output imbedded in the industrial structure, was not known by anyone outside the closed circle in Kremlin. In the words of Neilson: "The self-imposed Soviet political isolation from the rest of the world reinforced the long-standing belief that Russia was exotic and extra-European."[4]

Taking the historical track record into account, it must be assumed that most observers had a rather good, or at least a basic, understanding of this record. Only looking at the 20th century, Russia had not done particularly well during the Russo-Japanese war, World War I and the war against Poland in 1920. The performance against the Japanese in 1938 and in 1939, before the counteroffensive in August, reinforced this notion. As a matter of fact the only real success of Russian arms so far was the Red Army's victory in the Civil War, a war mainly fought against other Russians and Slavs. The poor track record continued in the Winter War of 1939–1940, and was perceived to continue in the Polish campaign before that.

Was there a marked difference between US and British assessments, and was there no revaluation during the latter part of the period? Some differences existed, but they were not great. It seems that the British were slightly more pessimistic about the capacity of the economy to stand the test of war. They emphasized many of the same factors, and it is hard to find any differences of a systematic character. Fedotoff-White argued that at the beginning of World War II, the Red Army had a reasonably good reputation among many foreign observers, but that the Finnish campaign destroyed it.[5] Actually, the reputation was already destroyed before that, and it was probably the purges that made the worst damage as far as the observers were concerned.

Regarding the revaluations it can be said that it seems that the Finnish war can be seen as a low point, at least concerning military capabilities. But there were also indications that the performance during the latter part of the war was improving. It also seems that some observers believed that the Red Army really learned from the Finnish experience, but generally speaking the critique of the Armed Forces was the same in the spring of 1941 as earlier. There were some revaluations, but only minor ones. Regarding the economic estimates, it is also hard to see that there was any marked difference in the assessments during the period. Many of the same problems were repeated. It can possibly be said that the economy's poor efficiency was more strongly emphasized during 1939 than in 1940–1941. But the only actual improvement in the economic situation noticed by some observers was that industrial output took off in late 1940, from an earlier period of stagnation.

As for the reality of the assessments it has already been concluded that they were underestimations.[6] The greatest underestimation was of course the general idea that the Soviet regime and the system would collapse when confronted with a first class military power. This idea was underpinned by several other underestimations. Obviously the transport sector and the whole of industry did not collapse, and the Red Army did fight the foreign invader. No large-scale popular revolts took place. Many of these phenomena's is difficult to measure in numbers, but the concrete production figures was measured by the observers and it is rather easy to compare these with later research.

Official Soviet figures showed that the two first Five Year Plans had produced spectacular industrial growth (especially concerning capital goods) and that national income increased several times.[7] Regardless to which extent the official figures are misleading, it is clear from later research that economic growth, especially during the Second Plan (1933–1937), was impressive.[8] From the investigated sources it does not seem that the Anglo-Americans at this stage in the war paid any attention to aggregate figures of this kind. They did, however, comment on the performance of different branches. It seems that they basically derived their figures from official Soviet sources, and they seldom explicitly expressed any doubt as to the reliability of these figures. Later research on the subject basically confirm that the official figures for basic industry output was correct, as was output expressed in physical figures (e.g. units, tonnes, etc.). Therefore the Anglo-American estimates regarding these figures generally was correct.[9] The same can be said about the relatively few estimates regarding total defence spending. The estimate from most observers for 1939 was close to 30 per cent. According to Nove (1992) the expenditure on defence as part of the budget amounted to 25.6 per cent in 1939 and 32.6 per cent in 1940.[10]

This was, on the other hand, not the case with physical figures concerning defence output. Since such figures were not published, all observers really had to make an estimate in the more complicated sense of the word. As already seen from the assessments regarding aircraft all observers underestimated output to a considerable extent. In 1939 one British observer believed that the annual tank output was 1500. In reality the 1939 tank (and tankette) output was 2950.[11] Concrete estimates concerning the output of other kinds of military equipment were not made during this period, except for aircraft. Actual aircraft output in 1939 was 10,382, increasing to 10,565 in 1940 and the pace continued to accelerate during the first six months of 1941.[12]

They did comment on the quality of military equipment and in this respect they were often wrong, with the exception of aircraft. Glantz considers that as many as 80 per cent of the available military aircraft in June 1941 were older models, and that compared to German aircraft the SAF's planes were markedly inferior in quality, and that: "In terms of aircraft performance characteristics and firepower, the German machines far outstripped the bulk of their Soviet counterparts."[13] Other authors arrive at the same conclusion in principle.[14] The aircraft matching German designs were not being produced until the very last years before Barbarossa. The newer aircraft models (the Mig-3, Yak-1, Lagg-3, Pe-2 and the Il-2) came into series production by 1940 and were not received by combat units until early in 1941.[15]

So while most observers were fairly correct regarding the quality of aircraft, they were not right concerning the quality of tanks (see sections 4.2 and 8.2). On the other hand, at least some British observers stated already as early as 1939 that the tank arm was fairly good. Generally speaking, though, it seems that the tank force was somewhat underestimated. They certainly underestimated the available numbers of tanks and aircraft. Most estimates put the number of aircraft at somewhere between 4000 and 12,000. Some US estimates were as high as 10,000 even in 1939, while the British estimates from that time were between 4000 and 5000 aircraft. It is difficult to compare these estimates with reality, since sometimes it was stated whether these figures referred to first-line strength, and sometimes not. There were also considerable divergences between estimates in time and between different observers, even from observers from the same country.

Since the total SAF strength was nearly 21,000 aircraft on the 22 June 1941, all estimates, even the higher ones, were clear underestimates. On the other hand only 16,502 were serviceable at that date and 13,211 were combat ready.[16] But even the last figure is higher than the highest estimate of the whole 1939–1941 period. It seems that the US estimates, in general, were closer to the truth than the British estimates. Available American estimates of tank strength were very scarce during the period, but the British made some. Even though most estimates were considerably lower (never more than 12,000) the highest one, form June 1941, put total strength at 18,000. It is hard to say how many of these tanks that was immediately battle-ready, but the actual total tank strength in June 1941 was 22,600 (14,200 in the field forces).[17]

The manpower size of the Armed Forces as such was more correctly estimated. In 1939 most observers believed that the Red Army's manpower
strength was somewhere in excess of 1.5 million men, rising to 2, 3 and even 4
million men later on. No estimate was higher than 5 million during this
period. Some US observers believed that 5 million men was the maximum
wartime size of the Red Army. It hard to distinguish between US and British
estimates regarding this matter during the period, and there is no conclusive
evidence that US observers estimated the size of the Red Army to be higher
than the British did, or the other way around. Already by 1 June 1938 the Red
Army numbered a little more than 1.5 million, but it was only slightly larger
on 1 September 1939. In December 1940 it exceeded 4.2 million men and in
June 1941 it was close to 5.4 million men.[18] The Armed Force's total personnel, including the Navy and NKVD troops, numbered 5 million men by
1940.[19] It can possibly be said that the observers underestimated the size of the
armed forces somewhat, at least during the end of the period, since it actually
was larger than the maximum estimated wartime strength even in peacetime.
But in 1939 and early 1940 some overestimated its manpower size somewhat.

Another factor connected with the Red Army's size is the Soviet mobilization
capacity in the event of war. This factor was not touched upon so very often
but the US military attaché mentioned the extensive pre-military and paramilitary training of a large number of citizens. The actual manpower reserve pool
by 1941 amounted to 14 million, probably not including the pre-conscripts.[20]
But since doubts were expressed over the Soviet ability to expand its Armed
Forces for other reasons, it seems that figures like these have little meaning.

Size is one thing but efficiency is another. Many observers made several
assertions about the deplorable state of the Red Army, its poor performance
in the field and its low efficiency in general. But in many respects their assessments were right. Even at the very top of the military command structure, at
the beginning of 1941, there was a state of paralysis due to political interference and frequent changes in command personnel. This situation brought
uncertainty and a lowering of the general quality of strategic leadership, as well
as affecting the ongoing Red Army reform programme. A similar situation
prevailed throughout the whole command structure of the Red Army:
"Operational force command and control organs, prospective wartime *fronts*
and armies, were also insufficiently prepared for war, both in terms of their
organizational structure and in terms of personnel training and readiness."
Other problems, affecting the readiness of the Red Army, were flawed mobilization and operational plans.[21]

The purges were, without doubt, a problem, even though, as already discussed,
they were not as comprehensive as earlier supposed. Glantz states: "Nothing
had a more debilitating effect on the pre-war Red Army than the military
purges that commenced in 1937 and continued unabated through 1941." The
removal of older experienced officers forced the Soviets to fill the ranks with
younger personnel who had less experience. Most of the Red Army officers,
from regimental commanders and up, were removed from their posts as a

result of the purges, even though not all of them were executed.[22] The purges were at their worst in 1937–1938, but continued right up to the start of the Soviet–German war, although on a much more limited scale than before. The purges produced very serious negative effects on the military efficiency of the Red Army, of which the highest Soviet leadership themselves were aware.[23] To counter some of these effects the dual command system with political commissars was abolished in August 1940[24] – a system which some Anglo-American observers considered as hampering the efficiency of the armed forces.

But the purges, it can be argued, also produced a Red Army that was very loyal to Stalin. However, this loyalty had its price since it was based on "abject and paralyzing fear, which stifled any creativity, initiative, or flexibility". The former revolutionary spirit was also affected by the purges. But the Finnish war produced some positive effects, such as an accelerated training programme for its personnel. Glantz describes the Red Army as being partially reformed by June 1941.[25] As we have seen, a few observers noticed improvements after the Finnish war. Since the Red Army had expanded so dramatically from 1939 to 1941 the training of its personnel had suffered, not only as a result of the purges. This situation had very adverse effects on military efficiency.[26]

Several observers stated that the Red Army would do better in defence than in attack. This notion is hard to evaluate since the Red Army was not involved in any large-scale defensive operations in 1939–1940, and the offensive operations of the period was relatively limited in scale. The largest offensive action was without doubt the Finnish war, which relatively speaking was a poor showing; but on the other hand the offensive action against the Japanese in August 1939 was much better. It can be argued that the Anglo-Americans, and even the Soviets themselves at the time, underestimated the Red Army's performance in Finland.[27]

The Soviet soldier was described in many reports as either being uneducated, untrained, tough, fatalistic, fanatical, apathetic or undisciplined. In some reports the morale of the Soviet soldier was described as good and in others as bad. But on the whole Soviet soldiers were considered as inferior to their western counterparts, especially when led by Soviet officers and commissars. According to Reese many of the conscripts in the expanding Red Army of the 1939–1941 period served very reluctantly, suffering from the social chaos of civilian society and under their deficient military leadership. Reese also describes the soldiers as unmotivated and uncooperative, being mostly of peasant origin as well as harbouring hostile feelings towards their leaders and the communist regime.[28] Glantz considers Reese's description of the social nature of the Red Army as the most "convincing assessment yet to be advanced".[29]

So it seems that much of the criticism that many Anglo-American observers expressed concerning the motivation and training of Soviet soldiers was right, although in practice their achievement in the war against the Germans also showed that they could fight. In practice, the Soviet troops fought against the enemy with determination in 1941 and often continued to fight against hopeless odds.[30] Reese argues that although the Red Army largely fought inefficiently in 1941, and therefore was beaten by a more skilled enemy, it nevertheless was effective in the sense that it basically carried out the tasks it had been ordered to do.[31]

It can be said that many observers were right in general concerning Soviet military efficiency, with some notable exceptions. But were they right in their assessments concerning the economy and society in general? We have already seen that the different estimates of industrial production were correct, with only minor deviations. Reese describes the conditions in Soviet civilian society as being "characterized by labor indiscipline, work turnover, and shortages of competent and trained managers".[32] This description seems to correspond pretty well with many reports from 1939 and 1940. Some of the assessments made concerning industry were about stagnating or declining labour productivity, deficient product quality and stagnating or even declining industrial production. Soviet industrial production had increased constantly during the 1930s, something that was noted in some reports, but shortly before the Third Five Year Plan (beginning in 1938) industrial growth stagnated, relatively speaking. The decline in industrial growth during the 1937–1941 period can be attributed to several reasons: over-investment, the rearmament drive and the purges, which deprived industry of many of its key personnel. Of these three the last two were the most important.[33] During the 1930s, labour productivity in industry grew very rapidly and by 1940 it was four times as high as in agriculture.[34] Nevertheless, it seems that labour productivity increase in industry declined during the 1938–1940 period compared with earlier years, and can, on average, almost be seen as stagnating.[35] On the other hand, even though industrial productivity as a whole could by no means measure up to the levels in US industry, "the basic production process of Soviet engineering plants approached American levels of productivity".[36]

The transport sector was possibly considered to be the greatest single problem in the economy, and the observers were at least partly correct. In this context the railways are of importance, since they stood for 85 per cent of all transport in tonne-kilometres during 1940.[37] Railway investments were very limited in 1930s compared with industrial investments, but nevertheless traffic increased, which sometimes caused transport crises.[38] Even though both the capacity and the productivity of the railways increased steadily during the 1930s this was not enough to prevent problems.[39] In 1939 and 1940 insufficient railway capacity had some hampering effects upon the economy. The territorial expansion in 1939–1940 also put additional strain on an already overburdened railway system, since the Baltic and Polish lines generally had a different gauge than the Soviet system. The Finnish war really did create serious problems for the railway system, especially in Moscow and Leningrad. In February 1940 the transport situation impaired factory production in both these cities. After the Finnish war a rapid recovery took place, even though the railways were still afflicted by problems.[40]

Another conception in the minds of many observers was that the economy as a whole was severely strained by a high degree of war preparedness. This was, of course, in some sense true, since the whole of society in many ways had been prepared for war for over a decade. During World War I Imperial Russia was economically backward compared with the other Great Powers of Europe, and this played a very big part in Russia's defeat.[41] In addition, Russia had to import a considerable amount of raw materials and industrial products needed for sustaining a war effort.[42] These (and other) historical lessons, and the Soviet regime's ideological conviction that a war with the capitalist powers was inevitable, shaped the economic build up during the Five Year Plans.[43] The expansion and construction of heavy and capital intensive industry was a priority, along with economic autarky.[44] Defence industry was the single branch that expanded most during this period (1928–1941), and much of civilian industry had been prepared for defence needs in wartime.[45] The Soviet economy was by 1940 "highly militarized by peacetime standards".[46] But the mistake that was made by the observers was that they believed that the economy was already close to breaking point, and that any further efforts to mobilize the economy would fail.

Notes

1 Fedotoff-White (1944), 350.
2 Kahn (1978), 445–61; Jackson (2000), 237, 291; Kahn (2009).
3 Ferris (1995), 137; Jackson (2000), 15; Herndon (1983), 297–319.
4 Neilson (1993), 189.
5 Fedotoff-White (1944), vii.
6 It is interesting to note that Leshuk claims that US assessments became "more rea-listic" during 1939–1940, after the departure of Ambassador Davies and Colonel Faymonville; we should remember that these two at least had a more positive outlook on Soviet strength (although they were not entirely correct) than their successors, all of whom systematically underestimated Soviet economic and military strength in most important respects. Leshuk (2003), 117; Herndon & Baylen (1975).
7 See, for example, the official figures used by Baykov in his *The Development of the Soviet Economic System* (1946) and also later by Nove in his *An Economic History of the USSR* (1992).
8 See, for example, Davies (1998).
9 In some cases the assessments regarding industrial physical output figures have been left out of the text, despite the fact that reports containing such figures have been commented upon. The reason for this is that these figures were just repeti-tions of earlier assessments, and, as noted, not in any major way differing from the official output figures anyway. The figures regarding physcial industrial output can be compared to the following sources in order to ascertain how close to "reality" they were: Harrison (1985), 253; Davies et al (eds.) (1994), 296; and Harrison (1996), 68–69, 195.
10 Nove (1992), 230.
11 Davies et al (eds.) (1994), 298
12 Kennedy (1989), 324, 354; Harrison (2002), Table 4.2.
13 Glantz (1998), 187, 193.
14 Koenig & Scofield (1983), 102. According to Whiting the "overwhelming bulk of the aircraft it [the Soviet Air force] received was obsolescent". Whiting (1978), 66.
15 Mayer (ed.) (1977), 166–167, 174; Whiting (1978), 65–66. Marshal Zhukov stated in his memoirs that between January 1939 and June 22 1941 the Red Army

received 17,745 combat planes, of which 3719 were of the latest types. Whiting (1978), 66.
16 Only 7133 Red Army aircraft were stationed in the Western military districts on 22 June 1941, excluding any aircraft from the long-range bomber force, the Navy or training aircraft. Glantz (1998), 21.
17 Glantz & House (2000), 306.
18 Glantz (1998), 107.
19 Harrison (1996), 270.
20 Glantz (1998), 107.
21 Ibid, 25–26.
22 For example, the purges affected all military district commanders, most army commanders, 80 per cent of all corps and division commanders, most brigade commanders and 91 per cent of all regimental commanders. The NKVD troops were also heavily hit by the purges. Ibid, 26–31.
23 Ibid, 26–31.
24 Ibid, 32.
25 Ibid, 31–33, 40, 55.
26 In the words of Glantz, referring to the military situation in the spring of 1941: "commanders were unfamiliar with their forces and modern and tactical techniques, staffs were understrength and unaccustomed to performing as teams, units and formations had not been welded together into coherent combat forces, and service arms were not able to function together. Combat and combat support personnel had not mastered the new equipment coming into the inventory." Ibid, 40.
27 Reese (2008); Kahn (2012).
28 Reese (1996), 5, 187, 203.
29 Glantz (1998), 77.
30 Johansson (1991), 327.
31 Reese (2011).
32 Reese (1996), 5.
33 Davies (1994), 157.
34 Wheatcroft & Davies (1994), 129–130.
35 Harrison (1985), 7; Davies et al (eds.) (1994), 280, 299–300.
36 Lewis (1994), 196–197.
37 Davies et al (eds.) (1994), 304.
38 Westwood (1994), 158–161.
39 Davies et al (eds.) (1994), 306–308.
40 Westwood (1994), 167–168.
41 Davies (1998), 6–16.
42 Fedotoff-White (1944), 282.
43 Harrison (1985), 46–47; Samuelson (1996), 1.
44 Davies (1994), 137–138.
45 Davies (1998), 44, 59; Davies (1994), 146; Davies et al (eds.) (1994), 299–300; Harrison (1985), 8; Harrison (1998b), 272.
46 Harrison (1998b), 272.

10 The beginning of Soviet–German war
Assessments during Operation Barbarossa

As we have seen the German build-up for the attack on the USSR begun already in 1940 and they attacked in the early hours of 22 June 1941. The German High Command wanted to secure a line deep into Soviet territory, running along the objectives Archangel-Kotlas-Gorky-Volga-Astrakhan in five months.[1] In fact, Hitler and his generals counted on a much quicker defeat of the whole Soviet system, and its ability to produce armed resistance. Woodward states that the Germans believed they could reach Moscow in three weeks and that the whole campaign would be over in two months.[2] Hitler's infamous statement probably summarizes his perceptions regarding the Soviet ability to resist: "We have only to kick in the door and the whole rotten structure will come crashing down." He also compared campaigning in the USSR to child's play in a sandbox.[3]

His overconfidence is perhaps not that strange, considering the easy German victories in the war so far, the Red Army's poor performance in Finland, and his own racist predispositions. But the military force he had assembled for the invasion was also the most powerful the world had ever seen so far. The front stretched all the way from the Baltic Sea in East Prussia down to the coast of the Black Sea. A geographically separate and militarily much smaller front was also soon established along the Finnish–Soviet border, and the border area between German occupied Norway and the USSR. The German striking force was composed of between 3.2 to 3.5 million men (depending on source) divided into 153 divisions (and some smaller independent units). These troops were, among other things, armed with 3330 tanks. The *Luftwaffe* had 3032 operational aircraft at its disposal.[4] In addition to these troops, Germany's Axis allies contributed with 14 Finnish divisions, 13 Romanian divisions (and 8 brigades), 2 Hungarian divisions, 2 Slovakian divisions and eventually an Italian force would join them.[5] Only counting the original invasion force, more than half a million men were from the Axis minor nations.[6] The Axis minor nations also contributed with around 900 aircraft.[7] Other smaller Axis contingents would eventually participate in the war, for example a Spanish division. From 22 June 1941 onwards the major military effort of Germany would be in the East against the Red Army, and the overwhelming majority of her combat troops and replacements would be consumed in that struggle.

The only other country that numerically could match this powerful force at the time was the Soviet Union, who actually had more troops at its disposal than the Axis, even though the Axis had an initial numerical superiority at the borders, since much of the Soviet troops was stationed inland. However, the foremost Axis advantage was not in numbers, but in the professionalism and efficiency of the German Army and the *Luftwaffe*. Germany's troops had gained almost two years of combat experience since 1939 and their military operational art, characterized by the so-called Blitzkrieg concept, was still way ahead of anything that the Soviets or any other nations could accomplish at the time. The British Army had met the German Army in combat on several occasions 1939–1941, and had so far been defeated each and every time.[8] After the war General-Lieutenant Martel, who had combat assignments against the Germans during the war,[9] believed that the German Army that faced the Soviets in June 1941 "probably was the finest military machine that has ever been produced".[10] Smith believes that one of the chief reasons the British were so soon to write off Soviet staying power in the summer of 1941 was the fact that Germany had had such spectacular victories in 1940 and early 1941.[11]

The Axis had another advantage on the 22 June, and it was the fact that they could take the Soviet troops by surprise. The Red Army was not, as it should have been, on high alert. The surprise effect contributed to the Red Army's tactical and operational unpreparedness. The USSR's long-term war preparedness was profound, but it seems that Stalin counted on the war starting at a later date than it did. The Soviets actually had access to excellent intelligence regarding German troop dispositions, and even spies who supplied them with accurate information about when Barbarossa was to begin. Stalin chose to believe that the intelligence available to him was nothing more than false information and deception. The accurate intelligence pointing in the direction of a massive attack in late June was dismissed. This was a great blunder of Stalin, even though it is easy to see why he was deceived. From Stalin's point of view the British had everything to gain by bringing the USSR into the war, thereby increasing Germany's strategic commitments and buying the British precious time. He also regarded much of the intelligence as a deliberate attempt on the side of the British to accomplish this. Furthermore, from the strategic point of view it was of course a great gamble for Germany to attack the USSR, since Germany still was at war with the British Empire. The possibility of war with the United States could also not be excluded in the long run, and Germany would then face an Anglo-American coalition in the West that between them disposed of more than half of the world's industrial output. But unlike Stalin, Hitler was not aware of the Soviet Union's war potential, and as we have seen Hitler counted on defeating the USSR before an American war entry would come into effect. For Hitler the invasion was just a stepping stone that would enable him to withstand and possibly overcome the Anglo-Americans easier in the long run.

Germany had not only easily defeated her adversaries before June 1941, but her war potential had also been augmented considerably with access to the resources of the occupied countries. During World War I, Germany was subjected to sea blockade by the Entente, which made conditions harder and more complicated for her population and war effort. Germany was not then able to exploit the occupied areas of Eastern Europe sufficiently enough to neutralize these problems.[12] In June 1941 conditions were markedly different, since Greater Germany had the resources of continental Europe at her disposal.[13] Most of the countries that Germany occupied from the outbreak of war in 1939 – Poland, Denmark, Norway, Luxembourg, The Netherlands, Belgium, France[14], Yugoslavia and Greece – were regarded as industrialized by the time, and one of them, France, before the war (1938) was the world's fifth largest producer of industrial goods.[15] Apart from the countries occupied by Germany there were many countries that were allied to her – Italy, Slovakia, Hungary, Romania, Bulgaria, and, as a result of the imminent campaign, Finland.[16]

Germany consequently commanded over considerable military and economic resources. According to the British, German strength was even greater than in reality, since they overestimated the German capacity to manufacture munitions. According to the MEW, Germany produced 25 to 125 per cent more munitions than she actually did during the first two years of the war (1939–1940), concerning fighter aircraft, bombers, tanks and artillery. In 1941 the MEW estimated that the output of fighter aircraft, bombers, and artillery was 45 to 50 per cent larger than it actually was; but curiously enough they underestimated tank output by 10 per cent. German oil output was overestimated by 45 per cent. Later in the war (1944) the Planning Division of the US War Production Board overestimated the total German munitions output for the three years of 1939–1941 by 71, 97 and 128 per cent, respectively.[17] Even if Germany's military capabilities and economic resources by June 1941 do not in a strict sense say anything about the Anglo-American estimate of the Soviet war potential, it reveals something about why they were so willing to write off Soviet resistance in the face of the German onslaught.

10.1 The border battles and the summer: German victories and the possibility of a Soviet collapse

When the first German attacks struck the Soviet defences in the early morning of 22 June,[18] almost all Red Army forces was taken by surprise. The border defences were shattered in a matter of hours.[19] The scale and effect of the surprise attack have been compared to a middle-sized nuclear attack.[20] German Air Force Marshal Kesselring referred to the initial air battles as "child murder".[21] Reality at the front was worse than anyone among the leadership in Moscow could imagine. But in a matter of days the enormous proportions of the initial disasters became apparent.[22] Soviet losses in men and material were of course catastrophic; already on the first day 1200 aircraft were destroyed.[23]

The German forces were divided into three army groups – North, Centre and South – with general initial objectives in the direction of Leningrad, Moscow and the Ukraine. During the first days and weeks of the campaign it seemed that these objectives could be reached. The German armoured spearhead, covered by the *Luftwaffe*, cut through the Soviet forces like a hot knife through butter. Huge Red Army forces became encircled in these battles during the summer and Soviet losses could be counted in hundreds of thousands, eventually culminating into several millions before the end of the year. The disastrous losses in manpower were accompanied by huge losses of military hardware.

In the beginning everything went according to plan for Germany and their Allies, but soon things became a little harder. First of all, the expected breakdown of the Soviet system and state apparatus did not take place, despite the large losses in troops and landmass. The collapse could of course happen at a somewhat later date, but already during the summer the Germans could notice that they had underestimated Soviet military strength. General-Colonel Franz Halder's detailed war diary has often been quoted regarding the history of Nazi Germany for this period. He was at the time the German Army's chief of the General Staff, and one of the most important military men in Germany. He stood in close contact with Hitler and resigned from his post in 1942 due to differences in opinion with Hitler. As early as 15 July 1941 he noted: "The Russian troops now as ever is fighting with savage determination and with enormous human sacrifice."[24] It is apparent from his notes that he still underestimated the Red Army's frontline strength and the USSR's mobilization capacity, counted in divisions, but on 11 August he wrote: "The whole situation makes it increasingly plain that we have underestimated the Russian Colossus, who consistently prepared for war with that utterly ruthless determination so characteristic of totalitarian States. This applies to organizational and economic resources, as well as the communications system and, most of all, to the strictly military potential. At the outset of the war we reckoned with about 200 enemy divisions. Now we have already counted 360. These divisions indeed are not armed and equipped according to our standards, and their tactical leadership is often poor. But there they are, and if we smash a dozen of them, the Russians simply put up another dozen. The time factor favors them, as they are near their own resources, while we are moving farther and farther away from ours."[25]

The Anglo-Americans was of course not yet aware of these circumstances in June 1941, and there seems to have been little difference between their and the German perceptions regarding Soviet strength and staying power. Sir Kenneth Strong, a WO intelligence officer who later in the war became the Allied intelligence chief in the CCS, claimed that the officers who had studied the USSR in the WO "were convinced that Russia would offer an easy conquest for the Germans".[26] Some authors claim that the British MI considered it unlikely in June that the Red Army could put up any successful resistance against the German Army. According to one assessment it would only take six to eight weeks for the Germans to defeat the USSR, and according to another assessment it would only take three to six weeks. The highest military leadership generally shared these opinions, as did the FO and the MEW. The

FO discussed various problems that could occur if the USSR entered the war, and worried, among other things, about how a wave of public discontent could be avoided when Soviet resistance broke down.[27] The British Chief of the General Staff (CIGS) General John Dill and the Joint Planners were also among those who saw a quick end to Soviet resistance.[28] Even Stafford Cripps stated in Cabinet on 16 June that it was likely that the USSR could hold out for three to four weeks if the Germans attacked. According to some, Churchill was notable in the British government for his reluctance to totally write off Soviet chances in the event of a German attack.[29] But Churchill's private secretary recorded in his diary for 21 June, the day before the attack, that: "The P.M. [Prime Minister] says a German attack on Russia is certain and Russia will assuredly be defeated."[30]

Almost everyone within the US military establishment believed that Soviet resistance would collapse relatively quickly, and (as we have seen) US military intelligence predicted a rapid German victory.[31] The same general opinion about Soviet chances prevailed among Western diplomats in Moscow.[32] There existed some divergent opinions[33] about the Soviet ability to resist the attack, but in general the picture was very pessimistic. Johansson claims that the US leadership calculated on the possibility of a total German and Japanese domination of Eurasia in a not too distant future.[34] It is uncertain where President Roosevelt stood on this question at the time of the German attack; but later in July, under the influence of his (relatively) pro-Soviet adviser Harry Hopkins and the former Moscow ambassador Davies, he adopted a markedly more positive stance concerning Soviet chances than his diplomatic and military advisors.[35] This may be contrasted with the advice that Henry Stimson, the US secretary of state for war, gave to the president on the authority of the General Staff. Stimson considered that it would take Germany a minimum of one and a maximum of three months to beat the USSR.[36]

Yeaton burned all his files in July in the belief that the Soviets would immediately collapse and the Germans would soon be in Moscow.[37] He regarded the great majority of the population as disillusioned. One of the reasons for him being so sure that the Germans were winning was because he thought that anti-Soviet fifth columns were in full operation in the Baltic States, the Ukraine and in Georgia. The WD was doubtful about this aspect of his reporting, since the British Mission in Washington had heard nothing of this from its people in Moscow.[38] By late July and early August G-2 assessed that the Germans would probably reach the Volga, and a push to the Urals was not excluded.[39]

The initial British predictions showed that they still had to worry about renewed German attacks on British interests. In July some new reports were presented by the JIC.[40] These indicated that the JIC more or less counted on either a complete collapse, or at least a major destabilization of the central government. The JIC tried to guess where the Germans would attack after the Russian campaign, and they were still (as were the COS) worried about an invasion of Britain. The defeat of the USSR was not a foregone conclusion, but her survival was without a doubt questioned; as was her capacity to defend herself against Germany.[41] In fact Victor Cavendish-Bentinck, a FO official and the head of the JIC,[42] and Lord Mountbatten, the head of the Combined Operations, were, in the words of Cradock "one of the very few people in Whitehall [who] believed that Russia would survive" the invasion.[43] But nevertheless, Cavendish-Bentinck wrote on 10 July in a FO report that preparations should be made to destroy the Caucasian oil industry within four week, as a precaution against a German capture.[44] Woodward states that by mid-July the "average" British assessment was that the Germans would have reached the Caucasus around the turn of August–September.[45]

However, it seems that at least British assessments changed significantly later in the summer. In late July both the head of the British 30 Mission in Moscow, Lieutenant-General Sir Noel Mason-MacFarlane, and his principal liaison in Whitehall, the Director of Military Intelligence (DMI), began to change their minds concerning Soviet chances.[46] According to a report that reached Whitehall at the end of July from a Swedish source with contacts in the German OKH, the OKH by then estimated that it would take at least three months to defeat the USSR. By 1 August, a JIC paper was so optimistic concerning the continuation of Soviet resistance that Churchill and the COS decided to step down from the highest state of readiness against a possible German invasion of the British Isles. Furthermore, a week later the JIC was of the opinion that the Germans would not be able to undertake any full-scale operations anywhere outside the Soviet–German front.[47] On 14 August the FO sent a telegram to the Tokyo embassy, in which it was stated that Soviet resistance had upset the German timetable, and that even the Germans were counting on a longer campaign than first expected. A Soviet collapse was not excluded, but even so some sort of anti-German resistance was expected east of the Volga.[48] By late August a widely distributed MI14/MI3 report stated that there was no imminent sign of a Red Army collapse. It was also hinted in the report that the German Army might be immobilized on the Soviet front when winter arrived.[49]

Since the Soviets and the Anglo-Americans now were allies in practice, and in the case of the Soviets and the British even formally so from 12 July 1941, this ought, of course, to have opened up the possibility of establishing a freer flow of information between them. However, the direct flow of intelligence and information from the Soviets to Western Allies was very limited. Both the British and the Americans received direct information from Stalin about the military situation and some economic aspects by the turn of July–August. Stalin informed both Hopkins and the head of the British Military Mission that the Soviets would hold Leningrad, Moscow and Kiev and that he felt that the USSR had adequate capacity for a war of three to four years, provided the Soviets could overcome their serious aluminium shortage. But it is difficult to know in most cases what the Anglo-Americans really thought about Stalin's information.[50] As we already have seen there was a mutual atmosphere of mistrust between the Soviets and the Anglo-Americans, now being allied more or less as a necessity in the face of a common enemy. There were instances where the Soviets apparently gave accurate information to the Western Allies, but even in those instances there was no way of knowing from the Western perspective if this information was true or not. Even if they believed that the Soviets were giving them information with an honest intent, circumstances at this early stage in the war was changing so quickly that such information could soon be outdated anyway. It was, for example, obvious soon after Stalin's assurances that Kiev was falling to the Germans. The Western Allies continued to produce their own assessments, that stood in contrast to the more optimistic predictions delivered by the Soviets.

10.2 The Soviet economy under attack (and Soviet prospects)

From the beginning of the Soviet–German war, assessments became more comprehensive, more elaborate and directly connected to the ongoing war effort. The character of the economically oriented assessments from now on was often connected to the USSR's need for foreign aid, and/or if the existing resources – still under Soviet control – would be sufficient for the continuation of the war effort. The German advance was so swift that a lot of the European part of the USSR, with all its economic assets, increasingly came under German occupation. The economic system was of course also under pressure simply due to the mobilization, the conversion to a war economy and the potential and actual threat that German aerial bombing constituted. The British and the Americans were interested in giving material aid to the USSR, and they eventually did, but if the help was to become effective it was paramount that Soviet resistance lasted, and that the economy was able to absorb the help. Otherwise scarce Anglo-American resources, needed to counter Axis moves in other parts of the globe, would be frittered away to no use.

Already on 30 June 1941 a report entitled *Economic Aid to Russia as a Means to National Defense* had been prepared in haste by the US Army Projects Division and the Army Planning Division, in cooperation with the Office of Administrator of Export Control. According to the report, the general idea was that US national defence would be best served by those actions which would maintain a Soviet government that could resist the Germans, and prevent Germany from the exploitation of conquered peoples and resources. The report was in many ways about Soviet inefficiency, and in that sense it repeated many of the assessments of the economy which were made during the 1939–1941 period.[51]

The Soviets' primary immediate needs were thought to be military supplies (especially aircraft and aircraft parts) and transport equipment.[52] It was regarded as improbable that the USSR could produce more equipment of this kind during the initial phase of the war, unless a more efficient use of productive facilities was introduced, or Anglo-American engineers and technicians could be sent in sufficient numbers to the USSR, and be given broad directive powers over strategic industries. Another need was identified, although having a lower overall priority – namely, consumer goods.[53] US aid was described as a way to overcome the shortage. The supply of strategic consumer goods was expected to maintain the morale of the working and fighting population.[54]

Without specifying a time frame, it was assumed that "the next stage of the war" would involve a major Soviet retreat over the whole front, with the Urals as the most probable area of withdrawal. The war effort could be supported with shipments of supplies into Siberia, and the extreme eastern section of the European USSR. The specific Soviet needs during the initial and later stages of the war were not only seen as confined to the already mentioned goods; but would also include petroleum products (aviation gasoline and fuel oil), machinery (machine tools, oil well-drilling and refining machinery), metals and alloys of many kinds, especially when the Soviets would be confined to the Urals and Siberia.[55]

A review of the general productive capacity and the Soviet political situation was also included. The remarkable expansion of industrial plant since the end of the 1920s was not disputed. However, the figures indicating the marked capacity expansion tended to give a false impression with respect to the actual productive output. Several sectors of the economy were identified as extremely inefficient or operating at extremely low efficiency: refining methods in the petroleum industry, the metallurgical plants, the factories (in general) and the railways. The inefficiency in the last three sectors was explained by a lack of full integration in industrial planning; the defective character of Soviet materials and machinery, mistreatment of industrial equipment; and the high incidence of accidents and breakdowns. The goods actually produced were regarded as deficient in quality. The crucial bottlenecks in industry were identified as the lack of specialized machines, machine tools, freight cars and locomotives. The authors of the report estimated that US technicians would be able to perhaps double the output of many metallurgical plants in a comparatively short time. It does not seem like the authors mistrusted all and every production figure, since many figures – apparently originally derived from official Soviet sources – were commented on in the report without any signs of doubt, despite the fact that these figures portrayed Soviet success in some fields.[56]

All of the problems were due to what the authors of the report viewed as the great fundamental weakness of the Soviet Union – the lack of technical ability, not only in management and planning, but throughout the whole rank and file of skilled labour in factories, railways and mines. The origins of the labour force were in, a general way, described as the root of the problem, since the industrialization process brought large numbers of peasants with little or no education into urban factories: "It is impossible to take [... the peasants] with such a background and give them hasty courses in machine processes, put them in masses into large factories and expect to get efficient results. This lack of technical ability is the greatest economic weakness of Russia at the present time."[57]

The internal political situation was also under review, involving economic aspects. The USSR was extremely unstable politically. Widespread revolts were anticipated in the Ukraine and the Caucasus, if Hitler's forces defeated the Soviet Army. The liquidation of Stalin, Molotov (the Soviet Minister for Foreign Affairs) and the rest of the men around them was expected. A military regime, with a new capital in the Urals, was an alternative. The question of whether or not this new government would continue the war would depend partly on the military situation, but more largely on economic factors. Therefore US aid was very important.[58]

In late July G-2 and the British JIC separately produced two reports which resembled the US Army Projects Division report in certain respects, and they were more or less as gloomy about Soviet future prospects. The G-2 report, signed by Brigadier-General Sherman Miles, the acting assistant chief of staff, G-2, and the chief of Army intelligence, considered the Volga River as a logical line of withdrawal, which in turn would result in the loss of around 70 per cent of the USSR's resources. Despite the logic of the Volga line a retreat to the Urals was not excluded. An almost identical report was distributed by 1 August to the secretary of war, and other prominent members of the military establishment.[59] The British JIC seems to have been of the same opinion, although they specified instead as that around 30 per cent of the industrial capacity would remain if the Soviet regime could establish itself east of the line Archangel-Volga-Caspian Sea. This territory would be able to support itself with food and other supplies, and some 40–50 divisions (not including the Far East Army in these divisions). However, it was certain that several kinds of economic shortages – possibly causing internal stability problems – would appear in the long run, and a lack of skilled workers.[60]

These reports contained no concrete estimates[61] regarding munitions output; but G-2 believed that, despite increased defence output since 1939, the output of heavy armaments was insufficient. In addition, it was stated that industry was disintegrating due to the strain of war and enemy destruction, and a shortage of essential items for further military operations was expected. Despite the alleged weakness of Soviet strength, and without downplaying the military–industrial importance of the industrial centres at Moscow and Leningrad, the country was thought to be able to survive without these centres. Industrial self-sufficiency was stressed, even though several flaws in efficiency throughout industry were pointed out. The output and production of consumer goods was, for example, a weakness of the system, with output completely inadequate for the country's needs. Economic help from the USSR's was regarded as essential in order to uphold effective military operations. As for the immediate pre-war military resources, it was assessed that the Soviets had about 90 per cent of the manpower reserves and supplies ready for 250 infantry divisions.[62]

It does seem like the perceptions of Soviet economic ineptitude and inefficiency persisted during this period, even though it also appears that the Soviets were willing to at least show some of their resources more openly. In early August members of the British Air Mission – a part of the 30 Mission – were allowed to inspect aircraft factory Number One in Moscow. The British also invited

Yeaton and Lieutenant John Alison of the US Air Corps, and the later reported back to the MID in Washington about the inspection. What he called the
British factory expert stated "that the plant was laid out in accordance with
the best American and British principles", and that the plant was adapted for
the use of a "high percentage of unskilled labour". However, no statement
was made as to the overall efficiency of the plant.[63]

As we have seen, the general impression gained from Western, especially
US, engineers stationed in the USSR, was one of inefficiency and factory
personnel unable to handle their equipment and factory management. It
seems that the Anglo-Americans still relied upon information of this kind. In
early September the MID interviewed an US engineer, regarded as reliable
and with "considerable experience in Russia". According to him the Soviets
had great theoretical knowledge but they lacked practical engineering skills.
In order to make US help effective, American engineers had to be on the spot
to install, operate and supervise industrial plants. According to the report his
opinion had "been generally confirmed by similar sources".[64]

10.3 The autumn 1941 situation

Even though the most pessimistic predictions proved to be wrong, the Germans
were still clearly winning and the Red Army was retreating with huge losses.
By the beginning of September the Germans had over-run the Baltic States in the
North, and were in the process of cementing the encirclement of Leningrad.
Army Group Centre had conquered Smolensk and in the South the Germans
and their Allies had taken the Ukraine up to the river Dnepr. During the
third quarter of 1941, in this case including 22–30 June, the Soviets lost over
2.8 million men. Due to the fact that the German had trapped several Soviet
Armies in large pockets, many of these troops had become prisoners, and
therefore the permanent, or irrevocable, losses were over 2.1 million men.[65] By
comparison, German ground force losses in the Barbarossa campaign, from
22 June to 3 October, amounted to less than 565,000 men, of whom considerably more than two-thirds were wounded.[66] Wounded could often eventually return to active duty.

The Soviets were very interested in receiving material aid from the Western
Powers. According to a telegram sent by Stalin to Churchill on 3 September, the
Soviets would be defeated, or so seriously weakened, that they would be unable
to undertake any active operations against Germany if it did not receive material help from Britain, and without the opening of a second front in France or
the Balkans.[67] The next day Ambassador Cripps sent a telegram, distributed
to Churchill, the War Cabinet and the FO. Cripps urged British action in
order to create a diversion from the hard-pressed Soviets, otherwise a collapse
would commence.[68] Three days later he sent another telegram to the FO and
the War Cabinet, describing a meeting with Stalin. On a direct question Stalin
was uncertain as to whether or not the Soviets could hold out until the spring.
But by this Stalin did not mean a separate peace, but outright defeat, even

though he did not see this happening and rather implied prolonged retreat, possibly to the Volga.[69]

As already stated, it is hard to know what the Anglo-Americans really thought about statements from Soviet officials. The Soviets could benefit from portraying their situation and future prospects as worse than they really were, in order to put pressure on the Anglo-Americans to send more aid or even to undertake military action against the Germans in excess of what they were already doing. The Soviet pressured them to open a so-called second front in Europe. On the other hand, it can be argued that it was in the interest of the Soviets not portray their own situation as hopeless. If the situation was hopeless there would be little meaning for the Anglo-Americans to send scarce resources to bolster an already lost cause.

When he spoke to Stalin they also touched upon the loss of economic assets due to the German advance. If he received this information specifically from Stalin or not is unclear, but Cripps nevertheless stated that the loss of (and up to) the Donets Basin, Moscow and Leningrad would mean a loss of two-thirds of the capacity to supply the front.[70] Without these areas the USSR would be forced to abstain from active participation, and withdraw to a defensive position. If the Donets were lost Stalin believed that they would need steel and coal, otherwise the railways would not function. In addition there would be a greatly enhanced need for aircraft and tanks, but most of all for aluminium. Stalin saw no need for food imports during the winter, except for some wheat to the Far East.[71] The need for aluminium was also stressed in Stalin's telegram to Churchill from 3 September.[72] In a despatch from Cripps dated 15 September he stated that he had heard rumours concerning the serious food situation in some outlying districts, due to the worsening of the civilian transport situation as a result of the war.[73] In late October Cripps informed the FO that several sources reported about a "serious food shortage".[74]

In a message dated 17 October, Eden told Cripps that he had spoken with Soviet London Ambassador Ivan Maisky about the progress of the war. Eden guessed that about 40 per cent of the war industry would be left if Leningrad, Moscow, Kharkov and Rostov should fall into German hands, a figure that Maisky confirmed. But he also added that when the industries being relocated from Leningrad and Moscow to the East were back in production, the figure would be higher.[75]

A more encouraging view of the situation was delivered by a Mr. Ingersoll, who was described as Roosevelt's unofficial emissary to the USSR. At the end of September the FO received a telegram – shared with the War Cabinet – from a representative in Cairo, who recited Ingersoll's experiences. He "had long talks with Stalin" and had "carefully studied the Russian situation". Ingersoll concluded that morale was "extremely high", that there were no indications of political instability, and that Stalin was "determined to fall back indefinitely if necessary". He was probably the only observer so far who actually believed that the transportation system was working well. The evacuation of factories and workers to the East was noted, and considered as "orderly". Apart from the British, Ingersoll had only shared his information so far with the US Moscow embassy. The British Cairo representative regarded the information as very "encouraging".[76] Ingersoll's observations can be regarded as an exception on the positive side at the time.

Another relatively positive voice was Mason-MacFarlane, who on the 22nd had informed London that the Soviets "would fight on to the end" and that Leningrad would hold out. The DMI agreed. Lord Beaverbrook, Churchill's friend, a member of the War Cabinet and at the time Minister of Supply, returned from Moscow, after his attempt to arrange for economic assistance (28 September–4 October). According to Smith he and his team considered the overall Soviet military situation as being far from hopeless.[77] However, other sources reveal that at least Beaverbrook himself believed that unless the Soviets received a substantial offer of material aid, they would not stay in the war.[78]

At the beginning of October the Germans launched their great and "final" offensive against Moscow, which soon rendered the Red Army huge losses. The British military attaché in Tokyo reported that the Japanese General Staff considered the Soviet resistance to be a surprise. Nevertheless, Hitler would capture Moscow soon and drive the Red Army towards the Urals.[79] The members of the 30 Mission believed that Moscow would fall. Churchill assessed in late October that there was a 50–50 chance that Moscow would fall before the winter, and the DMI was even more pessimistic.[80] Perhaps the actions of the Soviets themselves contributed to the pessimistic predictions, since they chose to evacuate several important parts of the government to the interior (Kuybyshev) of the USSR, including Moscow's foreign diplomatic representatives. From now on many Western observers reported about the Soviet situation from Kuybushev instead. The evacuation, which also included preparations for the destruction of important economic installations, resulted in a short outburst of disorder and panic in the city. Stalin remained in Moscow, which probably contributed to calming down the situation.[81]

Cripps and the rest of the British embassy, including the 30 Mission, had been ordered to leave for Kuibyshev on 15 October.[82] Ten days later Cripps expressed his deep concern about the situation in the USSR in a telegram to the FO. He stressed the feeling of isolation in the USSR, concerning the inability of the British to give practical help to the Soviets. Cripps also pointed out the food problem, and feared a general decline in morale that would get worse with the onset of winter. The "disappointment" and "disillusionment" and the accompanying decline in morale, feared Cripps, might even lead to the USSR leaving the war. If the British did not intervene more actively in the war with armed force, Cripps predicted a "crack" in morale and a possible collapse. The heads of the 30 Mission agreed with Cripps's opinions.[83]

In the autumn of 1941, according to Smith, all levels of G-2 in Washington were overwhelmed by negative and defeatist notions regarding the USSR.[84] It is easy to see why this was the case, considering some of the circulated memorandums produced and seen by top officials. A very gloomy picture was presented in a 6 October memorandum, signed by Assistant Chief of Staff

Colonel Hayes Kroner, distributed to the secretary of war, the secretary of state, the chief of staff, the COI, and others. According to Lieutenant-Colonel Solberg, who had prepared the memorandum and was described as something of an expert on Russia, even urgently delivered supplies would make it impossible to avert "disaster". He speculated about a Soviet–German separate peace, an option not entirely rejected by G-2 and Kroner. Kroner believed that Solberg's views were worth serious consideration.[85] Solberg argued that if Stalin were forced to sue for peace due to the impossible situation, the population would not revolt against the regime. But if the war continued, famine, pestilence and misery would follow, and the masses would revolt.[86] In an 18 October MID memorandum Miles made what he called a conservative estimate; predicting that in the spring of 1942 the Red Army would at best be disposed generally along the Volga, and at worst along the Urals, with a Soviet pocket of resistance in the Caucausus in either scenario. He regarded Western aid of the utmost importance if the USSR was to have any chance to continue effective fighting.[87]

Yeaton was another representative of this negative view.[88] A widely distributed telegram of his, received by the WD on the 10th, included the statement: "In my view it is possible that the end of Russian resistance is not far away."[89] Hopkins, on the other hand, rejected Yeaton's opinion as being unrealistic, and listened to Colonel Faymonville (Yeaton's predecessor) who believed that the Soviets would hold out.[90] During September and October Yeaton regularly recommended that Washington should not send supplies to the USSR because the Germans would soon overrun the whole country. He was withdrawn to Washington on 21 October and his assistant, Michela, replaced him and was only slightly more optimistic than Yeaton.[91] When Averell Harriman (head of the US mission to the Moscow Conference) visited Moscow in September–October, General Martin F. Scanlon of the Army's Office of the Chief of Air Staff, found it necessary to send Harriman private and confidential reports to indicate that not all US military officials regarded the situation as hopeless as Yeaton and Michela did.[92] When returning from Moscow Harriman was more convinced than ever that the Soviets would withstand the German onslaught. At the end of October he held a radio broadcast and a public speech, in which he told the American public "that the Soviet Union would not collapse". It could of course be argued that he was biased in his opinions, since he stated this as a means to promote the shipment of Lend-Lease supplies to the USSR.[93]

The German eastwards advance became markedly slower in November. At the beginning of the month Cripps reported that according to a member of his staff, who had travelled for nine days from Archangel to Kuibyshev, both civilian and military morale seemed to be high.[94] But according to another report dated just one day later Cripps stated that Mr. Russel had said that the morale in the city of Moscow was not good.[95] Cripps seemed to explain Mr. Russel's statement with reference to the special conditions prevailing in Moscow.[96] Personally, Cripps seemed to believe that Soviet morale was still "fairly good".[97]

In a COI organization memorandum dated 16 November the Soviets were not expected to stop the Germans before they reached the Caucasus.[98]

All of these predictions and assumptions about the Soviet situation were, of course, backed by several assessments regarding the economy and military strength. From the autumn onwards more extensive papers and reports on this subject were being produced. These reports are of great interest since they not only contained views on the Soviet ability to survive, but also presented a more or less complete picture of Soviet war potential. In the middle of September the British JIC and the MEW cooperated in an attempt to study how the German advance was affecting the war potential.[99] The paper was distributed among the members of the COS, and according to the JIC, was to be regarded as an "approximation by broad lines with a considerable margin of error".[100] The report was also distributed to the G-2, first in a summarized form by cable, and then in a complete version at the beginning of October.[101] A similar US report, dated 19 September, was an attempt to coordinate information received from the SD, the WD, the Department of Commerce, and the Foreign Export Administration, and also to utilize the best Soviet sources of a general character. The American memorandum was first presented in a preliminary form to Colonel Donovan, then the COI, one week earlier.[102] Even though the two reports considered almost the same subject, the US memoranda displayed somewhat older figures, and the British report contained more detail.

The JIC paper was based on an attempt to estimate how much of the war potential that would remain along different lines running from North to South. The four lines were called A, B, C and D. The A line was the frontline as it stood on 6 September, and the other lines represented possible frontlines further ahead in time. The D line was as far east as the Ural River. The estimate included many different branches and individual industries, but also an estimate concerning the overall general war potential. The present line (A) would in the short run preserve 95 per cent of the pre-war potential, but only 75 per cent after the passing of three to four months. That would be sufficient for the maintenance of 225 field divisions, in addition to the estimated 40–50 divisions in the Far East. The pre-war potential was sufficient for around 300 divisions. A Japanese attack in the Far East would, of course, put an additional strain on resources and lower the capacity to maintain divisions against the Germans. The other lines, B to D, would only permit that 70, 40 or 35 per cent, respectively, of the war potential could be preserved.[103] Compared to the actual German advance, line B was approximately tantamount to the situation prevailing at the furthest extent of the German advance at the beginning of December. Line C never happened since it would mean an advance all the way up to Volga, and therefore line D was never reached either.

Therefore, around 70 per cent of Soviet war potential would remain in Soviet hands at the end of 1941 according to this assessment, and this would be sufficient for 210 divisions. It is clear that the Soviets in reality could keep more divisions in the field than the one's stipulated by the line B assessment, but on the other it is hard to know what the JIC meant by a division. A Soviet pre-war division was much larger in terms of manpower and equipment strength than the actual fighting units in December. What the JIC considered as the war potential was more or less equal to the Soviet capacity to produce armaments.[104] The situation never got as bad as alternative C and D; but line B can be seen as a rough approximation of the real frontline during the last weeks of 1941, when the German offensive was halted, and also for long periods during 1942 and 1943.[105]

The paper contained more detailed assessments concerning certain branches. Several of these details concerned raw material output, but the actual fighting would of course be done by military units and these could only be built with manpower and military equipment. According to the line B estimate, 62 per cent of the pre-war population would be on Soviet territory, and as for the industries with the direct capacity to produce munitions, the following would be left: aircraft, 83 per cent; tanks, 59 per cent; guns, 92 per cent; small arms, 70 per cent; and shipbuilding, 18 per cent. This means that most of the munitions capacity for ground and air warfare would remain in Soviet hands, but since the paper contained no estimates regarding the absolute output level it is hard to say what that really meant. Even if the potential would remain, we know that most, if not all, observers counted on a decreasing munitions output – regardless of territorial losses – due to the stress that war in itself would bring the USSR. However, the war potential and the number of divisions could be increased, if the USA and Great Britain sent help to the USSR, which would remedy the worst shortages.

The JIC assumed that the population loss would approximately balance the diminishing food output, and consequently the food situation would not be a problem. They were aware that some of the military–industrial capacity could have been moved eastwards since the start of the war. Therefore, it was not excluded that the relatively low figure for remaining war potential east of line D could be higher. It was also feasible that construction in accordance with the Third Five Year Plan (beginning in 1938 and originally planned to end in 1942) could proceed in the eastern parts of the country, possibly shifting the geographical gravity of war potential. But the authors of the paper were not able to measure these possible effects statistically and therefore they felt obliged to ignore them. The paper also pointed out the possibility of flaws in the economic planning, which occur during the sudden shift to a war economy, and which would almost certainly bring problematic bottlenecks.[106]

Later in September (the 18th) the JIC was asked by the COS to comment on Władysław Sikorski's opinion concerning the Soviet situation. Sikorski was the prime minister of the Polish Exile Government in London, and the highest commander of the Polish Armed Forces in exile in the West. He believed that the economy suffered large losses due to the German advance, but he did not regard the situation as acute with respect to food, manpower and oil. As the Germans continued to close the Leningrad ring, and advance towards Moscow and the Donets Basin, an immediate loss of industrial capacity was to be counted on. However, more severe problems could be anticipated in 1942 if the Soviets would lose the Donets Basin and Leningrad, while at the same time the area around Moscow would become "impaired". This is actually what happened in reality, with the exception that Leningrad was not lost but instead cut off from the rest of the country. Sikorski stated that a scenario like this would make it unlikely that the Soviets could re-equip the Red Army during the winter without foreign help.[107] Churchill and the Secretary of State Anthony Eden also noted Sikorski's estimate. He had prepared an estimate of the economic situation dated 17 September for Churchill – most likely the exact same commented on by the JIC.[108] According to the JIC their earlier September paper did not differ much in general from Sikorski's appreciation.[109]

There is reason to believe that the JIC paper from 6 September was handed over to the Americans, at least in a summarized form. The COI organization report *The Economic Effects of the German Advance on Russian War Potential – Summary* has a striking resemblance with JIC's paper. Even though it is shorter, the report contains some interesting information that was not displayed in the (available) JIC version. One assumption in the COI report was that the equipment of Soviet divisions in steel products would be equal to that of British divisions. Even though this was considered an overestimation even in the report, it underscores the difficulty of comparing British estimates of the number of Soviet divisions with reality.[110]

The newly formed agency the Office of the Coordinator of Information, led by the COI (Colonel Donovan), had an important research topic concerning Soviet capabilities. Since the ignorance on this subject was considerable it became a research area of high priority. Donovan recruited one of the few Americans who qualified as an academic expert on the USSR, Columbia University's Geroid T. Robinson, to lead an important study on the current economic situation.[111] Robinson recruited other academic experts, among them the economist and Russian emigrant Simon Kuznets.[112] The COI group relied on incomplete information from the State, Commerce, and War Departments as well as their own research into Soviet sources. Their work resulted in the memorandum "Losses of Russian Industrial Production Resulting from the Eastward Movement of the War Front; General Geographic Distribution of Russian Industry".[113]

Just like earlier assessments, the losses in raw material output, due to the German advance, were noted and described as very serious. The loss in the manufacturing capacity of machinery and metal products up to mid-September was estimated to 25 per cent, and increasing considerably if Eastern Ukraine was lost – which it soon was in reality. The supply situation was extremely critical, although they admitted that the real situation might be different from what they could conclude from these uncertain and somewhat outdated figures. The location of stocks and the eastward movement of machinery and stocks could also alter this perception positively. On the negative side there were bombing, transportation difficulties, and the pre-war interdependence of the economy.

The report also contained some heavy industry output figures which appeared to have originated from official 1938–1940 Soviet sources.[114]

A revised and extended version of the COI report dated 13 October had a few more industries added and some new sources consulted. The effects of a possible German advance up to the Ural region were now taken into consideration. Due to the rapidity of their advance in the Ukraine, the report was outdated in some respects just a few days after its completion. Robinson concluded that the economic losses (in goods and plant) had been enormous and critical. For the very important heavy industries of coal, pig iron, steel and aluminium, the losses, if the Eastern Ukraine fell (which soon was a fact), were estimated to 60, 60, 50 and 60–80 per cent, respectively. Machinery and metal products output losses were estimated to 33 per cent. The losses in these five branches, if the Germans reached the Urals, the Caspian Sea and seized the Trans-Caucasus region, would be 70 per cent for the first three, 65–85 per cent for aluminium and 90 per cent for machinery/metals. Such an advance would also rob the Soviets of an estimated 90 per cent of their crude oil output, among other things. The report also contained a short assessment of the geographical location of armament output.[115] It was estimated that 23 per cent of pre-war tank production, 13 per cent of aircraft production, and 30 per cent of gun production, as well as 20 per cent of naval construction were located in the Ural Region and in Asia.[116]

In a MID memorandum to the Chief of Staff, dated 18 October, the possibility of supplying the USSR was examined. Even though the memorandum was mainly about possible ways to deliver supplies to the USSR, it also contained a section on the military-economic situation. This section was signed by Miles and distributed to many government officials and departments, including the president, the secretary of war and state, the chief of staff, and Colonel Donovan. The review of the losses in industry was more or less the same as in the 13 October COI organization report, although somewhat more effort was spent on considering the effects on agriculture. Millions of heads of livestock were lost. In this report the area to the east of the Volga line was estimated to contain approximately 35 per cent of the June 1941 war potential, and the area to the east of the Urals to contain a maximum of 30 per cent.[117]

According to the report no less than 65 per cent of the aid requested by the Soviets consisted of food and raw materials. The interpretation of this was that the USSR's overall economic potential was seriously impaired. But it was also a sign of Soviet confidence in the ability of the Siberian industry to produce war materials. The Soviets were regarded as selective in their general requests for military equipment, showing more interest in obtaining quantities of relatively few items, such as aircraft, tanks, anti-aircraft and anti-tank weapons. Western material assistance was essential if the USSR was to continue to fight effectively.[118]

On 23 October, Lord Beaverbrook spoke to the House of Lords concerning what he had learned about the Soviet industrial situation during the Moscow Conference. He considered the losses in industry as great, both in coal and heavy industry. Losses in heavy engineering were not quite so severe, but the loss of aluminium production was very serious. But taken as a whole his message was rather that industry would regain lost ground, partly due to its movement to the East. Considering that he spoke to a wider audience than the War Cabinet, it is hard to know whether or not there was an element of keeping British morale high by playing down the problems of an ally.[119]

10.4 Munitions

As we have seen, the Anglo-Americans believed that the German onslaught had robbed the Soviets of much of their capacity to produce munitions, but very few of these estimates included concrete output figures. But there is no doubt some officials in both Washington and London concerned themselves with these problems. In late June Miles regarded aircraft as outdated copies of older foreign models and inferior to German aircraft. He did not believe that Soviet industry would function adequately during war conditions. He predicted the production of aircraft at 240 per month at the time of mobilization, 300 per month 30 days after mobilization, and 350 per month 180 days after mobilization.[120] The latter figure is equal to an annual output of 4200 aircraft.

This estimate was, as we already have seen, far from actual Soviet output. At this point the Soviets were actually revealing the actual aircraft output figures, but it seems like the Anglo-American observers did not trust them. Stalin informed Hopkins at the end of July, when the later was visiting Moscow as Roosevelt's envoy, that the Soviets were producing 1800 aircraft per month and that they expected to reach 2500 (excluding trainers) in January 1942. When the US General Arnold heard of these production figures – he was involved in supplying Lend-Lease to the USSR – he remarked: "I think that we should ask them for help."[121]

They were also observers that had a somewhat more sober perception regarding the quality of Soviet military aircraft, although once again it is hard to know what the Anglo-Americans made of this information. At the end of August Major Bonner F. Fellers, the US military attaché in Cairo, reported to the MID on the observations made in the USSR by former Yugoslav Air Attaché Major Astanoylovitch, considered as reliable by the MID. He was stationed in Moscow until 12 June and stated that one third of Soviet aircraft were modern, but he also considered that even the older types were good.[122]

In late September, at the request of Lord Beaverbrook, the British Parliamentary under-secretary of state for air produced a report on the general Soviet aircraft situation. He concluded that the Soviets could build "first class" aircraft and engines, and that output was relatively high. According to information from Commissar Shakhyrin (see below), aircraft production was as high as 70 aircraft per day (equivalent to 25,550 aircraft per year). Apparently, Stalin had supplied Lord Beaverbrook with the same figure. Shakhyrin had told British Air Vice-Marshal Collier in private that the Soviets seldom supplied figures, but when they did they were true. The under-secretary believed the figures, based on two factory visits and information from other sources. He also thought that these figures conflicted with earlier Air Ministry estimates, but that they had underestimated Soviet resources. Aircraft factory no. 1 was described as very large, with the very latest machine tools and machinery of US, German and Soviet design, producing the MiG-3 fighter, which he considered almost comparable to the Spitfire.[123]

US Army Air Corps Major-General J.E. Chaney visited the same factory in October. He also commented on the general state of aircraft production and concluded that output actually was increasing rather than decreasing, despite the loss of territory.[124] Chaney told Washington that aircraft factory no. 1 was producing ten or more modern aircraft per day. Michela replied to Washington (regarding Chaney's information): "his report astounds me", and hinted that the Soviets might have "hoodwinked" him.[125] Chaney explained the general output increase by the evacuation of plants to the East, which according to him could be back in production after only three or four weeks. He furnished this information in person to Miles and other intelligence personnel on 31 October in Washington. He estimated present daily aircraft output at 70. Furthermore, he estimated monthly tank output to 1400.[126]

It seems highly likely that Chaney had received his information from Shakhyrin, the Soviet Commissar for Aircraft Industries, who, according to another MID report, had been observed by Chaney and Colonel Lyon when they were in Moscow in October. According to Lyon Shakhyrin had stated that the Soviets could produce 70 aircraft a day, or 20,000 aircraft per year based on a six-day week. Lyon, who was writing earlier in October, thought that the information that was published about aircraft performance underrated the actual performance of the aircraft that the Soviets now had in serial production.[127] Lyons repeated this in a report to the chief of the US Army Material Division, also adding that Shakhyrin's claim was not "extravagant", considering the production factors, men, management, machines and materials. His information was based largely on observations in factories no. 1 and 24, which he considered to be more efficient in their production than the aircraft industry, in general. According to what he could observe in these factories combat aircraft were of high quality, but the bottleneck in the aluminium supply had to be overcome, if Shakhyrin's claim were to be realized.[128]

The same month the MID received information from the US military attaché in Australia, who estimated aircraft output at 50 per day (equivalent to an annual production of around 18,250). The MID had no comment on this information and it was not clear from the report whether or not this output referred to the situation in June 1941, or in October.[129] This report can be contrasted with information available to the MID from the French air attaché in Moscow, who in November estimated that monthly output had fallen from 1200 to 1500 aircraft in June to approximately 800 aircraft (tantamount to around 9600, annually).[130]

In the first (available) Anglo-American estimate regarding tank output since 1939, in the form of a draft report prepared for the WO from late July, the absolute minimum annual output was estimated at 2640, but they also considered that output could be double that figure.[131] Lord Beaverbrook and Harriman received some information about tank capacity from Stalin when they met him at the end of September.[132] This meeting was held within the framework of the Moscow Conference, a three-power meeting with the purpose of discussing the need for material help to the USSR.[133] Stalin was asking for very large amounts of armaments and other war material, especially tanks and aircraft, but also revealed that the Soviets were producing 1400 tanks per month. It is hard to know if Beaverbrook and Harriman believed in Stalin's figure, especially since he gave them a lot of other information related to military matters that was of doubtful value considering its reliability. Stalin grossly overestimated the number of German forces operating in the USSR while he at the same time underestimated the qualitative value of some of these troops.[134] Under the general direction of Beaverbrook, Major-General H.S. Ismay, one of Churchill's closest military aides,[135] repeated Stalin's figure in a paper printed for the War Cabinet concerning the Moscow Conference. According to the paper Stalin also stated that monthly tank output was 2000 units before the invasion. Ismay concluded that the Soviets only asked for the military equipment they really needed, since they were not interested in British offers of modern field artillery and machine guns. Instead, they stressed the need for the "new" arms of this war, like tanks, anti-tank guns and anti-aircraft artillery.[136]

It seems like Stalin's information at least made some impression upon the British. According to another report originating from the WO files, dated October 1941, probably addressed to Mr. Postan at the MEW, the Soviets had told the British that they were currently producing 1,400 tanks a month, but as many as 2000 tanks a month before the German invasion. According to the author of this report these figures were to be taken seriously. One can assume that these figures emanated from Beaverbrook's encounter with Stalin in September.[137]

Regardless of what the Western observers believed about the Soviet output figures for the moment they also noted that the Soviets had weapons that they themselves did not have. In August some members of the 30 Mission could observe how the Soviets used their "rocket bomb", fired from an aircraft. Mason-MacFarlane was impressed and the British had no equivalent to this weapon at the time.[138]

In a late October telegram from Cripps to the MEW, also seen by the FO and the War Cabinet, it was stated that the Soviet authorities had told Mason-MacFarlane that all tank, aircraft and artillery factories had been "successfully" transferred to the East from the territory now being occupied. The armoured-plate rolling mills at Mariupol had been transferred three months before. Cavendish-Bentinck was not entirely convinced of this, but he did at least believe that "a remarkable number" of large industrial enterprises, machines, and personnel had been successfully evacuated. He also noted that this was the first German antagonist that had seriously attempted such an enterprise, and that the Soviets also had carried out a great deal of demolition. Several other FO officials commented on the telegram and they seemed a little doubtful as to whether or not it was true.[139]

Based on information from the SAF Liaison Officer Colonel Beliaev, the chief of the British Air Staff was informed in September that the Soviet "air supply [...] position [... was] fairly good".[140] In a telegram from Cairo to the FO, dated 29 September, it was revealed that Mr. Ingersoll believed that the USSR was "relatively weak in tanks and air but all right in artillery".[141]

10.5 The size of the Armed Forces and their efficiency

Despite the magnitude of the Soviet–German was relatively little was reported regarding the Red Army's size and efficiency during this specific period. Perhaps the Anglo-Americans felt content for the time being with the pre-Barbarossa assessments. In his June memorandum to the Chiefs of Staff, Miles described the SAF as suffering from poor organization, training, equipment and morale.[142] Fellers's August report to the MID contained Astanoylovitch's estimate regarding the size of the SAF: 15,000 aircraft; 10,000 bombers and 5000 fighters. Since Astanoylovitch was stationed in Moscow until 12 June, one can assume that these figures referred to the pre-Barbarossa situation.[143] As apparent, his figures were higher than the figures in the Anglo-American pre-Barbarossa estimates.

In the message to the British chief of air staff from the beginning of September, based on information from Colonel Beliaev, Soviet air training was described as "fairly good".[144] Lyon added in his October report to the chief of the US Army Material Division that US officers in Archangel held the abilities of Soviet pilots in high regard, based on observations during September.[145]

From Solberg's October memorandum to the chief of staff it is apparent that he held the Soviet soldier in high regard, but thought very little of his military leaders: "The Red soldier is an excellent fighting machine and perfect cannon fodder. He fights under orders without soul or nerve but with a will to victory. He is inured to the fatalistic hard conditions of life, without a trace of the softening influence of western civilization, but by the same token he has no spiritual reserve or initiative to fall back upon when the leadership fails him. And the leadership may well fail him for it possesses an extremely nimble, opportunistic mind, completely devoid of honor and integrity of purpose in our sense of the word."[146] In the 18 October MID report Miles believed that the Soviets were suffering from defective command, but German strength and combat ability was the main reason for the Soviet defeat in the field.[147]

The Anglo-Americans made estimates and received information regarding Red Army losses, but the intelligence flow seemed to be sporadic, although confirming that Soviet losses were huge. According to a September report signed by the FBI Director E.J. Hoover, also addressed to the assistant secretary of state and the assistant chief of staff (G-2), aircraft losses only during the first six days of war were over 4100.[148] In early October the MID estimated total Soviet losses up to date at between 2.25 and 2.5 million in dead, wounded and missing. Losses of aircraft and tanks were estimated at 7000 and 12,500, respectively. The total manpower available to the USSR was estimated at 13 million, of which 6.5 million were trained or partly trained first-line reserves, and the remainder to be untrained reserves.[149] It is hard to know if the figure of 13 million included the personnel already at the front, or if it only referred to available manpower in excess of the frontline strength. It seems, however, that this estimate at least stands partly in contrast to a statement made by Churchill on 9 September in the House of Commons: "A considerable part of the munitions industry and iron and steel production of Russia has [... been lost]. On the other hand; the [... Soviets have ...] anything from 10 million to 15 million soldiers, for nearly all of whom they have equipment and arms".[150] There is no explicitly British assessment available regarding the size of the Soviet Armed Forces at the time to compare with, but it is not impossible that his statement was little more than morale boosting propaganda, since the estimated (or the real) actual fighting strength never was as high as 10–15 million men. The peak strength of all Armed Forces personnel was in this interval later in the war, but this also included administrative and supply personnel.

On 18 October G-2 estimated overall losses to date at 2.5 to 2.7 million men dead, missing (prisoners) and wounded. This was compared to an unofficial British estimate, dated September 19, which stated that the losses amounted to approximately 3 million men up to that date. The British estimate was considered by the G-2 to be a "definitive overstatement". The total material losses, according to the G-2, were 7000 aircraft and 12,500 tanks.[151] The military-economic potential was estimated with reference to the number of troops, and productive capacity. The strength of the army facing the Germans was thought to be about 3.15 million men. In the interior military districts, and in the Far East, it was estimated that there were more than 750,000 troops (including the equivalent of seven to eight armoured divisions). In addition to approximately 4 million men under arms, the available military manpower was estimated as in the early October MID report.[152]

An MID memorandum from 21 November estimated losses up to date at 3.3 million men, losses in tanks at 12,500, in aircraft at 8400, and in guns to 8400.[153] Military events at the front were continually updated and commented on in "Current revision of the U.S.S.R. combat estimate", an internal G-2 paper.[154] On 6 December, an update was made in the light of events between 22 November and 5 December. The fact that the German offensive broke down during that period was explained as being due to lack of German coordination, and growing Soviet strength. Total Soviet losses up to date were estimated at 3.44 million men, 12,900 tanks, 8600 aircrafts, and 14,400 guns.[155]

Actually the G-2 underestimated total manpower losses, since they were nearly 2.82 million during the third quarter (including 22–30 June) of 1941 and nearly 1.66 million in the fourth quarter. The material losses was also probably underestimated, since actual guns losses from 22 June until 31 December were

40,600, and tank and aircraft losses during the same period were 20,500 and 21,200, respectively.[156]

Notes

1 Willmott (1992), 134.
2 Even the German generals who regarded the Eastern campaign as a mistake believed in victory before the end of 1941. Woodward (1971), 2.
3 Van Evera (2001), 21.
4 Bellamy (2007), 169, 172.
5 Glantz (2010a), 20; Salmaggi & Pallavisini (1997), 140.
6 Kershaw (2000), 24; Smith (1996), 29.
7 Bellamy (2007), 172.
8 Keegan (ed.) (1989), 40, 42–46, 54.
9 Martel was also the head of the British Military Mission to the USSR for some time during the war.
10 Martel (1949), 218; Smith (1996), 144.
11 Smith (1992), 53.
12 Taylor (ed.) (1974), 92.
13 Greater Germany comprised Austria and large parts (*Sudetenland*) of what today is the Czech Republic, which in turn included a great part of contemporary Czechoslovakia's heavy and other industrial resources. Before the war in 1939 Germany also subdued the rest of Czechoslovakia, transforming the Czech part (Bohemia-Moravia) into a protectorate, and the Slovak part into a puppet state. That Germany could gain control of the Czech munitions industry was without doubt very important. For example, in 1941 about one fourth of all German tanks were of Czech manufacture. Keegan (ed.) (1989), 37; Klein (1959), 257; Shirer (1984), part II, 170–171, 188–207; Milward (1965), 26–27; White (1979), 108; Ránki (1993), 316.
14 The remaining part of France (Vichy France) became an ally of Germany.
15 Kennedy (1989), 330. See Pollard (1992), 314 for a description of which countries could be regarded as industrialized shortly after World War II.
16 Keegan (ed.) (1989), 38–45, 54–57, 130.
17 Klein (1959), 101–102.
18 On the same day the American press reported on Soviet strength. Many newspaper clippings were collected by G-2 with telling headlines: "Soviet Russia's Military Power Estimated: Reds May Have Largest Army in World – 5,000,000 or More; Air force A Secret; Industry and Transport Are Question Marks", or "Greatest Army or Hoax?: Russia's Fighting Strength Is Military Mystery". 22–6-1941, "Soviet [...]", Communiques, Box-3160, Entry-77, RG165; 22-6-1941, "Greatest [...]", Communiques, Box-3160, Entry-77, RG165.
19 Glantz (2001), 35.
20 Erickson (1984), 376.
21 Johansson (1991), 325.
22 Glantz & House (2000), 51.
23 Johansson (1991), 325.
24 Halder, Volume VI.
25 Halder, Volume VII.
26 Strong also thought that "the general opinion in Britain and the United States at the time was that if Russia lasted three months against the Germans she would have done well." Strong (1968), 73.
27 Smith (1996), 12–14; Woodward (1970), 615.

28 The Parliamentary Under Secretary for War Edward Grigg claimed that 80 per cent of the WO considered that Soviet resistance would last for ten days. Beaumont (1980), 26.
29 Clarke (2002), 220–222.
30 Carlton (2000), 84.
31 Herndon & Baylen (1975), 500. According to Joseph Persico the US secretary of war, Henry Stimson, believed that the USSR would surrender even before being attacked. Persico (2001), 100; Harriman & Abel (1975), 14.
32 Herndon & Baylen (1975), 500.
33 One example is Roosevelt's personal representative in Moscow, Harry Hopkins, and the US Colonel Philip Faymonville, the former US Moscow military attaché. Salisbury (1980), 33; Herndon & Baylen (1975), 500.
34 Johansson (1991), 330.
35 Gaddis (1972), 4–5; Carlton (2000), 106; Divine (1969), 80.
36 Beaumont (1980), 26–27.
37 When Harry Hopkins went to Moscow in late July to negotiate with the Soviets about US help, he was very careful to keep both the military and civilian dignitaries in the US embassy at arm's length, due to their anti-Soviet attitude. Smith (1996), 33.
38 Smith (1996), 33–34.
39 30-7-1941, "Subject: [...]", Box-3108, Entry-77, RG165; 1-8-1941, "Subject: [...]", Box-3108, Entry-77, RG165.
40 Hinsley (1981), 67–68.
41 17-7-1941, JIC(41)287, CAB81/103; 18-7-1941, JIC(41)289, CAB81/103; 22-7-1941, JIC(41)295, CAB81/103; 23-7-1941, JIC(41)294(0), CAB81/103; 26-7-1941, COS(41)460, CAB80/29; 28-7-1941, JIC(41)288(Final), CAB81/103; 28-7-1941, JIC(41)296(Final), CAB81/103; 31-7-1941, JIC(41)290(Final), CAB81/103. By August officials at MI3 were concerned about British press reporting, since they thought that the rosy picture it painted of the Soviet–German war might fool the public into thinking that the Soviets might soon defeat the Germans. If the Soviets should collapse this might dampen British morale and make the public think that the British government had let the Russians down. 12-8-1941, "D.D.M.I. (I.). thro' M.I.3. Colonel", WO208/1776.
42 Cavendish-Bentinck was head of the JIC almost during the whole war (7–12–1939 to 14–8–1945). JICMtg1–14(7-9-1939–7-12–1939), CAB81/87; 14–8–1945, JIC(45)55Mtg, CAB81/93.
43 Cradock (2002), 19; Dear & Foot (eds.) (1995), 763. Strong claimed that Lord Mountbatten believed that "the pattern of 1812 would be repeated and the Russians would hold out for one or two years at least." Strong (1968), 73; Hymoff (1972), 169.
44 8–7-1941, N3519/3014/38, FO371/29561.
45 British military experts suggested that the British should offer to assist in the destruction of the Caucasian oil fields. Woodward (1971), 2.
46 Smith (1992), 51–53; Butler (1972), 133. The CIGS Lieutenant-General Sir John Dill told Mason-MacFarlane, shortly before the latter departed for Moscow in late June as the head of the 30 Mission, "that he did not think his mission would last very long". Six months later Mason-MacFarlane stated in an *Isvestia* article that he became convinced of a failure for the German *Blitzkreig* even during the first week of his stay in Moscow. Butler (1972), 133–134; Smith (1996), 26.
47 Hinsley (1981), 67–68, 70.
48 14–8-1941, N4685/78/38, FO371/29489.
49 27–8-1941, "Review [...]", WO208/1778.
50 Hinsley (1981), 71.

51 The slackening of the increase in industrial output since 1937 had several reasons behind it according to the report. The purges and the dismissal of foreign experts were two causes. The report referred to earlier information indicating a decline in labour discipline during the last three years, which according to them perhaps depended on the dismissal of foreign experts. A third reason was emphasized, namely the reorganization of the administrative planning units within the government, involving the decentralization of the large commissariats. Yet another reason was that industrial equipment of all kinds had been very badly mistreated, so that cumulative replacement needs on a large scale had begun to overtake some of the largest plants, and consequent breakdowns had occurred. 30–6-1941, Report 1732, Reel-6, M1499, Entry-16, RG226.

52 The need was especially for freight cars, locomotives, rails and motor trucks. It was estimated in the report that Soviet rail transport was used to handling 90 per cent of all distribution inland; waterways the other 10 per cent. Highway transport was regarded as practically negligible. 30–6-1941, Report 1732, Reel-6, M1499, Entry-16, RG226.

53 The required goods were especially foodstuffs, textiles, leather, and possibly clothing and shoes. The report's authors argued that because the Five Year Plans had focused on heavy industry, at the expense of consumer goods, and the war preparations since 1937 had infringed on the standard of living, there were serious shortages of manufactured consumer goods. 30–6-1941, Report 1732, Reel-6, M1499, Entry-16, RG226.

54 Ibid.

55 The view taken by the authors of the report regarding Soviet needs is not surprising, in view of their belief that the Germans would be capable of occupying practically the whole of the European USSR, including the oil producing regions of the Caucasus. The picture was not all black, since they also reasoned around a long-term plan to help to the USSR, a plan that included an expectation of Soviet resistance for more than 18 months. 30–6-1941, Report 1732, Reel-6, M1499, Entry-16, RG226.

56 30–6-1941, Report 1732, Reel-6, M1499, Entry-16, RG226.

57 The best-trained personnel were to be found in the army, according to the report; but even there, there was a serious shortage of technical ability. Ibid.

58 Ibid.

59 30–7-1941, "Subject: [...]", Box-3108, Entry-77, RG165; 1–8-1941, "Subject: [...]", Box-3108, Entry-77, RG165; Herndon & Baylen (1975), 501.

60 If the Japanese should succeed in blocking the import of supplies from the Far Eastern ports the situation would almost certainly result in the regime's downfall and chaos. 31–7-1941, JIC(41)290(Final), CAB81/103.

61 Apart from some scattered figures concerning the capacity of some factories in Siberia. 30–7-1941, "Subject: [...]", Box-3108, Entry-77, RG165; 1–8-1941, "Subject: [...]", Box-3108, Entry-77, RG165.

62 The first version of the memorandum contained a passage that was excluded in the 1 August version: "Unless the fall of the Stalin regime hastens the disintegration of the armed forces, the Soviet field forces will probably hold out for six months. Prior to that time material aid will be required to strengthen the Soviet Armed Forces to a point where they can effectively conduct military operations and contain the major portion of Germany's army". It is impossible to know why this passage was omitted in the later version, but the point basically seems to be that the Soviet Armed Forces probably had no chance to check the Germans even if material help should arrive within six months, and no chance at all unless help did arrive within that specific time frame. Ibid.

63 5–8-1941, "Inspection [...]", Box-3155, Entry-77, RG165. According to another report the MID in Washington had also received a cable from the SD that stated

that Yeaton "was much impressed by the size and capacity of the installation".
7-8-1941, "Aircraft [...]", Box-3155, Entry-77, RG165.
64   4-9-1941, "Current [...]", "Comments [...]", Box-3172, Entry-77, RG165.
65   Krivosheev (1997), 94.
66   Halder, Volume VII, 8–10–1941.
67   24 November, 3 September, "Telegrams [...]", CAB120/678.
68   4-9-1941, No. 1090, AIR8/565.
69   7-9-1941, No. 1107, AIR8/565.
70   7-9-1941, No. 1107, AIR8/565.
71   Ibid.
72   24 November, 3 September, "Telegrams [...]", CAB120/678.
73   15–9-1941, No. 52, FO418/87.
74   25-10-1941, N6169/78/38, FO371/29492.
75   17-10-1941, N6040/78/38, FO418/87.
76   29-9-1941, No. 3045, AIR8/565.
77   Smith (1996), 69, 86.
78   "Subject: [...]", CAB121/461.
79   10-10-1941, "Subject: [...]", WO208/1789.
80   Smith (1996), 75, 84.
81   Glantz & House (2000), Chapter 6.
82   Clarke (2002), 232–233.
83   25-10-1941, N6169/78/38, FO371/29492.
84   Smith (1996), 34, 73.
85   6–10–1941, "Subject: [...]", Box-3126, Entry-77, RG165.
86   6–10–1941, I.B.136, 387USSR, Box-1047, Entry-47, RG319.
87   18-10-1941, "Future [...]", Box-3178, Entry-77, RG165; 18-10-1941, I.B.142, 400.3295USSR thru 12–31–42, Box-1048, Entry-47, RG319.
88   Smith (1996), 34, 73.
89   10-10-1941, "Paraphrase [...]", Box-3157, Entry-77, RG165.
90   Hopkins had sent Faymonville back to Moscow as a representative in the Lend-Lease negotiations. Herndon & Baylen (1975), 500; Vagts (1967), 85.
91   Smith (1996), 34, 73.
92   Smith (1996), 34, 73; 6–11–1941, "Soviet [...]", Box-3100, Entry-77, RG165.
93   Harriman & Abel (1976), 108.
94   3–11–1941, N6356/78/38, FO371/29493; 3–11–1941, No. 6, FO181/963/7.
95   4–11–1941, N6375/78/38, FO371/29493.
96   Cripps described Moscow as a beleaguered city, with a population critical of the government due to its transfer to Kuibyshev, exposed to German propaganda distributed by aircraft and agents. 3–11–1941, No. 6, FO181/963/7.
97   3–11–1941, No. 6, FO181/963/7.
98   16-11-1941, R&A#68, M1221, RG59.
99   Hinsley (1981), 68.
100 It was named "The effect of Russian war potential of successive withdrawals". 13–9-1941, JIC(41)357(Final), CAB81/104 and 121/464.
101 2–10–1941, No. 44731, 320.2USSR, Box-1040, Entry-47, RG319.
102 Pressure of time did not permit the utilization of data scattered in Soviet periodicals and newspapers. According to the East European Section, statistics published by the Soviet Government were to be regarded with some caution. Furthermore, since some vital economic statistical data was not published by the Soviet Government during 1939–1940, they had to rely upon estimates made by the US Moscow Consulate, on the basis of incomplete information. 19–9-1941, R&A#66, Report 2, Reel-1, UPA1977.
103 The calculations were made with consideration to the loss in population, normal peace time industrial production, the production of munitions before the war, the

supply of raw materials, and the wartime production potential, which was seen as a correlation between the resources in raw materials, manpower, and total industrial production. 13–9-1941, JIC(41)357(Final), CAB81/104 and 121/464.
104 Ibid.
105 13–9-1941, JIC(41)357(Final), CAB81/104 and 121/464, in comparison with Glantz & House (2000), 84, 109, 118, 161.
106 Ibid. The report showed that even a German advance to line C would not seriously threaten the Soviet oil position. But the British were still worried about the possibility of the Germans capturing them. The idea of destroying the Soviet oilfields in the Caucasus was on the COS and the Joint Planning Staff agenda again in the fall of 1941. CAB121/463. According to a paper produced by Lord Hankey's Committee on preventing oil from reaching enemy powers, dated 2 August, Stalin was determined that the Caucasian oil fields should be destroyed rather than fall into German hands. 2–8-1941, POG(41)11, CAB104/259. In August 1941, the current annual oil output was estimated at 30 million tonnes by the British Committee for the coordination of Allied supplies. 7–8-1941, CAS (41)190, CAB104/259; 13–9-1941, JIC(41)357(Final), CAB81/104 and 121/464.
107 19–9-1941, JIC(41)373, CAB81/104.
108 17–9-1941, N5445/78/38, FO371/29490.
109 23–9-1941, JIC(41)376(Final), CAB81/104.
110 "The [...]", Report 940, Reel-3, M-1499, Entry-16, RG226.
111 Kestner (1999), 19–21.
112 Kuznets's works during the 1930s served as a basis for national income accounting, an essential foundation for post-war Keynesian economics. Kestner (1999), 22.
113 19–9-1941, R&A#66, Reel-1, UPA1977; Kestner (1999), 23–24.
114 19–9-1941, R&A#66, Report 2, Reel-1, UPA1977.
115 13-10-1941, "Lines [...]", Report 2, Reel-1, UPA1977.
116 Ibid.
117 18-10-1941, "Future [...]", Box-3178, Entry-77, RG165.
118 Ibid.
119 23-10-1941, N6156/3084/38, FO418/87.
120 28-6-1941, "G-2/2090–259", Box-3152, Entry-77, RG165.
121 Lukas (1970), 32, 96.
122 27-8-1941, Report No. 1978, 580Russia, Box-1052, Entry-47, RG319.
123 30-9-1941, "Note [...]", AIR20/2386.
124 Smith (1996), 73, 86; 31-10-1941, "Memorandum [...]", Box-3155, Entry-77, RG165.
125 Smith (1996), 34, 73; 6–11–1941, "Soviet [...]", Box-3100, Entry-77, RG165; 17–1-1942, "Michela, [...]", Box-1, MECF1941–42, RG84.
126 31-10-1941, "Memorandum [...]", Box-3155, Entry-77, RG165.
127 8–10–1941, "Notes [...]", Box-3155, Entry-77, RG165.
128 17-10-1941, File No. 400-A, Box-949, Entry-300, RG18.
129 22-10-1941, "Soviet-German [...]", "Estimate, [...]", Box-3175, Entry-77, RG165.
130 18-11-1941, "Production-General.", Box-3155, Entry-77, RG165.
131 26-7-1941, "This [...]", WO208/5173.
132 Harriman & Abel (1976), 86–87; Dear & Foot (eds.) (1995), 117.
133 Keegan (ed.) (1989), 86.
134 Harriman & Abel (1976), 87–88 compared to Dear & Foot (eds.) (1995), 109–113.
135 Colville (1981), 161.
136 8–10–1941, 6–10–1941, WP(41)238, CAB121/459.
137 17-10-1941, "Russian [...]", WO208/5171.
138 Smith (1996), 67.

139   Cavendish-Bentinck also believed that the Soviet evacuation and scorched earth policy was one of several disappointments which Hitler and his generals experienced in the ongoing Russian campaign. 28-10-1941, N6244/78/38, FO371/29493.
140   3–9-1941, "ACASI/359/41", AIR8/564.
141   29–9-1941, No. 3045, AIR8/565.
142   28–6-1941, "G-2/2090–259", Box-3152, Entry-77, RG165.
143   27-8-1941, Report No. 1978, 580Russia, Box-1052, Entry-47, RG319.
144   3–9-1941, "ACASI/359/41.", AIR8/564.
145   17-10-1941, File No. 400-A, Box-949, Entry-300, RG18.
146   6–10–1941, I.B.136, 387USSR, Box-1047, Entry-47, RG319.
147   18-10-1941, "Future […]", Box-3178, Entry-77, RG165.
148   9–9-1941, "John […]", Box-3158, Entry-77, RG165.
149   3–10–1941, "Subject: […]", Box-3127, Entry-77, RG165.
150   No. 49, FO418/87.
151   18-10-1941, I.B.142, 400.3295USSR thru 12–31–42, Box-1048, Entry-47, RG319.
152   18-10-1941, "Future […]", Box-3178, Entry-77, RG165.
153   21-11-1941, "Russian […]", Box-3147, Entry-77, RG165.
154   Even though "Combat estimate" primarily was about military matters, it also contained some information about political and economic events. 6–12–1941, "Current […]", Box-3159, Entry-77, RG165.
155   6–12–1941, "Current […]", Box-3159, Entry-77, RG165.
156   Krivosheev (1997), 94, 248–254.

11 The first turning point of the war
The Soviet winter offensive

In the history of World War II it is often popular to talk about different turning points, and many events can qualify for the title. The end of Barbarossa campaign and the beginning of the Soviet winter offensive in early December 1941 is definitively one of these. The German Army and Air Force committed the lion share of its total strength and failed in its task. The USSR was the first country invaded by the German Army that avoided ultimate defeat, and, moreover, while at the same time inflicting palpable losses on the Germans. The German losses in the East, from 22 June 1941 to the beginning of December, far exceeded the total combined losses of all previous campaigns. Of course, Red Army losses were several times that number, but from the German point of view the losses suffered so far was largely unexpected. In addition, a large part of the losses had struck the combat infantry units, which depleted the offensive capacity of the Army. This fact would have serious repercussions for the resumption of offensive operations in 1942. Hitler and his top officials had counted on a quick victory against the sub-human Soviets, but was now instead engaged in the largest land war so far in human history. The German offensive had not only reached its offensive limit in the USSR, facing their first winter in Russia, but was now also forced to defend against a Soviet offensive that begun just a few days into December.

The war entry of the United States a few days later actually provided a short term relief for the Germans considering the global situation. Due to the fast and victorious onslaught of the Japanese in the Pacific region, some Anglo-American resources had to be diverted there, in order to stem the tide. However, since the German military engagement with the British was relatively minor and the engagement with the Americans virtually non-existent at the time, the relief only had a very limited military value. But in the medium term perspective, and especially in the long run, the entry of the US was very serious for Nazi Germany. The US was the world's largest industrial nation which now could begin to mobilize for war. The material support to her Allies could be stepped up, and the creation of an Army and Air Force for future offensive operations against the Axis could begin. All of this made it all they more important for Germany to quickly subdue the USSR, but first the winter had to be endured.

The Soviet winter offensive 1941/1942 was the first successful large-scale offensive against the German Army in World War II. Despite the fact that Soviet military losses amounted to nearly 4.5 million men (as much as 70 per cent being irrecoverable)[1] from 22 June to 31 December, a figure almost as large as the total size of the Soviet Armed Forces before Barbarossa, the Red Army could launch an offensive over large parts of the front from early December. The offensive would press the Germans hard, especially along the central parts of the front near Moscow where the Soviet effort had its main focus, but would of course also exact a heavy toll on the already battered Red Army.

The Soviet winter offensive begun 5 December but it took a few days before the change, from a German to a Soviet initiative, was noted by the Anglo-Americans. According to Harriman there was still a question of whether or not the Red Army would hold out at the time of the Japanese attack on Pearl Harbor (7 December).[2] But already on 10 December 1941 Churchill told the War Cabinet that the Germans had suffered a serious defeat. In December, according to Hinsley, Churchill and the COS "no longer doubted that Russia had demonstrated her capacity to avoid defeat". On the 23rd Churchill considered it as almost miraculous that the Soviet offensive continued at a steady pace in the centre, and that the attacks were being extended to the northern and southern parts of the front.[3] In late December Cripps stated in his diary, in sharp contrast to his earlier views from June, that he had never thought that the Germans would defeat the Soviets. Instead he now thought that the Soviets would "wear down the Germans".[4] The optimism was apparently not shared by General Alan Brook, the CIGS, since he in January 1943 stated that he a year before [i.e. January 1942] had felt that Russia could never hold."[5] At the beginning of February Sir Orme Sargent, deputy under-secretary of state in the FO, wrote a minute on the possible development of the war, speculating about its long term implications. Present Soviet strength prompted him to speculate about a possible Soviet victory in 1942 and the inability of the Anglo-Americans to counter a Soviet march into Germany at the moment, even though such events were unlikely.[6] Nevertheless, the British should foster good relations with the Soviets – with this "unlikely" possibility in mind – and work for the establishment of a treaty regarding an alliance. This would, in turn, mean concessions from the British, for example regarding the Baltic question.[7]

Later in February Eden presented a memorandum to the War Cabinet, which was a copy of a letter he had written to Lord Halifax, now British ambassador in Washington but still in practice a member of the War Cabinet. Eden believed it possible that the Soviets could defeat Germany more or less on their own before the Western Allies had time to develop their own military potential to the full. Apart from the prestige that such an achievement would bring the Soviets, it would also allow them to divert resources from German industry and use them to rebuild Soviet industry. This would make the Soviets more independent of US and British aid, and less likely to comply with their policies. Therefore he argued that the British should establish close cooperation with the Soviets as soon as possible, while the outcome of things was uncertain, which would also mean concessions from the British. He argued in practice that the British should recognize Soviet demands regarding the Baltic States, since Stalin might anyway "have asked for much more".[8] The FO wrote to the MEW on 6 March in asking them to investigate to what extent the USSR would need Anglo-American help after the war.[9]

In February Cripps stated his opinion to the British press concerning his opinions on the Soviet war effort. The Red Army would defeat Hitler, but only if the USSR received maximum British and US support in the form of material help. Cripps was quoted in several British newspapers, which in turn were noted by the US embassy in London. The London embassy forwarded the information to the US embassy at Kuibyshev. Cripps had now recently resigned as ambassador to the USSR, and was appointed a member of the War Cabinet on 20 February and leader of the House of Commons. Cripps stated his opinions to the press before assuming his new responsibilities, but after leaving his post as ambassador. According to the *Manchester Guardian* he was very disappointed with the British war effort, in comparison with the Soviet effort.[10]

Two reports from the British embassy from February and March, reflecting the views of the embassy official Lacy Baggally[11] and the British oil expert E. A. Berthoud,[12] assessed the military situation as rather bright, and counted on the Soviets holding in 1942, even if faced with considerable territorial losses.[13] Baggally believed (in a widely distributed dispatch) that the situation as a whole was such that both the Soviet regime and the Soviet people could face a renewed German offensive during the spring with "reasonable confidence". Provided the government could solve the food and transport problem, Baggally saw no reason why the Soviets could not continue their fight even if much of European Russia was lost to them. He was still not convinced though, that the Soviet organizational effort was optimal. If he only considered the "evidence" – recent Soviet military successes, the effort to supply and equip the armed forces, the evacuation of industry to the East, and the preservation of 70 per cent of its industrial production – the Soviet leadership were masters of organization. Yet, based on his personal experience, he had a hard time to believe that this was really the case. He concluded that even though the men at the top of the administration were able men, the whole system was suffering from "excessive centralization". If the men at the top were interested in a specific matter, or their immediate subordinates had a clear mandate, things worked well; otherwise "endless" and "unnecessary" delays would result.[14]

E. A. Berthoud, who was reporting around two weeks later, had a slightly more pessimistic view on Soviet prospects than Baggally. He had travelled to the USSR three times since the start of the Soviet–German war. According his observations most competent military observers in Moscow at the end of February believed in a 50 per cent chance of a Soviet decisive defeat of the

Germans before the end of the winter. Berthoud was writing on 9 March, and he then considered that things had gone wrong with the Soviet winter offensive, and therefore a German spring offensive could be expected. Such an offensive might result in the fall of Leningrad and Moscow. But whether or not the German offensive was successful the Soviets would be fighting at the end of the year. Just the fact that the Soviets still was standing, and that the Red Army had been able to launch an winter offensive, apparently prompted him to use the phrase "Russian successes", which he explained in the following way: "The main reason is probably that the Russians have had for 20 years many of the advantages enjoyed by Germany only since 1933, namely an economy planned on a totalitarian basis for maximum industrial output and efficiency, and latterly for a maximum war potential." He also considered that many of the recently built factories were constructed for evacuation.[15]

The British paid much attention to the intelligence provided by Colonel Pika, the head of the Czechoslovak Military Mission to the USSR. He was sent to Moscow in April 1941 by Edvard Beneš, the exile President of Czechoslovakia in the UK.[16] Many of Pika's reports had ended up in Whitehall even before Barbarossa. In August Mason-MacFarlane stated that the Czech and Polish military representatives in Moscow had better access to both official and unofficial sources than he had.[17] Many of Pika's reports were seen and sometimes commented on by FO officials and the MI, and they were even noted by the Secretary of State for Foreign Affairs and by the Prime Minister.[18] In a November War Cabinet memorandum he was described by Eden as a person who "knows Russia intimately and is regarded as one of the soundest observers of present-day Russia".[19] A 21 February Pika report was noted by the FO's R. H. Bruce Lockhart (soon also the director-general of the propaganda organization Political Warfare Executive[20]) and sent to Sargent.[21] Bruce Lockhart was regarded as a USSR specialist in the FO Northern Department.[22] Pika believed that the Red Army was in a much better state than the previous year, and he even harboured hopes of some kind of spring offensive. As for the expected German spring offensive; if sufficient help from the Western Allies arrived – in tanks and aircraft – it would be contained after some initial German successes. He was impressed by the evacuation of industries and he also stated that the basic industries in the Urals and Siberia had been expanded.[23]

A month earlier Pika stated that transport was the weakest link in the war organization, due to poor organization and slowness, in addition to a lack of organs of control and trained personnel. The effects of this were reflected in problems with the transportation of troops and supplies, evacuation difficulties and the "total inability to keep any timetable".[24] He also expressed these opinions in a report dated two days earlier, and added that things were "not nearly so bad as I expected them to be".[25] In the 21 February report he described transport as a problem within the context of the general economic system, due to deficient organization, the frosty winter weather, and a lack of coal supplies.[26]

In another report, seen by the MI and dated 22 February, he considered that a quick success of a German spring offensive could produce a breakthrough but not the destruction of the Red Army. It was however evident that he at least considered it possible that the Red Army might be forced to retreat to the Volga in the spring.[27]

In a "USSR Combat estimate" dated 10 January 1942 G-2 summarized the Red Army's offensive operations from 27 November until the report date. Soviet operations were characterized as a strategic success in several respects, with economic and military-political implications for the future conflict. G-2 estimated that an industrial recovery of 80 per cent, as compared to the June 1941 level, was an absolute maximum. But at that time industrial recovery was far from 80 per cent.[28] Some of the American observers had a more depressing outlook despite the current Soviet success. A 23 December COI organization memorandum, signed by Robinson, evaluated the Soviet–German position with respect to current military and possible political developments during the spring. From a purely military perspective the prediction was that the advantage of winter might last for the Soviets during the spring thaw. However, it was judged that the productive advantage still was with the Germans, as it had been from the beginning. Because of this it was probable that Germany would have a significant advantage in tanks, planes and other military equipment during the spring. The possibility of a mutual beneficial Soviet–German separate peace was not excluded.[29] According to Pogue, the intelligence advisers of the US Chief of Staff George C. Marshall doubted by the beginning of 1942 if the Soviets "could last through the rest of the winter".[30]

Notes

1 Krivosheev (1997), 96–97.
2 Harriman & Abel (1976), 112.
3 Hinsley (1981), 85–86.
4 Clarke (2002), 227.
5 Alanbrooke (2001), 355.
6 He considered that some interest should be taken in the possibility of a total Soviet victory over Germany, even in 1942. This would mean, Sargent argued, that the Red Army marched into Germany, settling its own "uncontrolled" peace in opposition to British political interests. Since he did not consider that Anglo-American troops could intervene in Europe in time to stop this – in the unlikely event of a total German collapse – the British, and the Americans, would have to rely on the goodwill of the Soviets and their supposed need to restore its economy with US and British economic aid. 5-2-1942, N885/30/38, FO371/32905.
7 Ibid.
8 Eden also considered that it would be wise to keep on good terms with the Soviets due to the need of keeping Germany contained after the war. 24-2-1942, WP(42) 96, CAB66/22; Cantwell (1993), 4.
9 5-2-1942, N885/30/38, FO371/32905.
10 February 1942, "Great Britain", Box-5, MECF1941–42, RG84.
11 Merritt Miner (2014), 354.
12 FRUS (1961), Document 356.

13 25–2-1942, N1585/30/38, FO371/32906; 30–3-1942, N1911/80/38, FO371/32921.
14 25–2-1942, N1585/30/38, FO371/32906.
15 30–3-1942, N1911/80/38, FO371/32921.
16 MacDonald (1998), 78.
17 Smith (1996), 32–33.
18 26–4-1942, N2214/30, FO371/32907.
19 4–11–1941, WP(41)256, CAB66/19.
20 Cantwell (1993), 133.
21 25–2-1942, N1129/30/38, FO371/32906.
22 Folly (2000), 5. Bruce Lockhart had been a diplomat in Russia already during World War I. In 1918 he was accused by the Bolsheviks for trying to assassinate Lenin. His dramatic experiences were described in his 1934 memoirs (which also became a movie). Bruce Lockhart, 2011[1934].
23 25–2-1942, N1129/30/38, FO371/32906.
24 23–1-1942, N514/30/38, FO371/32905.
25 23–1-1942, "Sir [...]", FO800/874.
26 25–2-1942, N1129/30/38, FO371/32906.
27 1–3-1942, "Sir [...]", WO208/1794.
28 10–1-1942, "Combat estimate", Box-3159, Entry-77, RG165.
29 Several ways of Western Allied military intervention were suggested by the COI organization to ensure that the USSR remained in the war against Germany. 23-12-1941, R&A#810, Reel-1, UPA1977.
30 Pogue (1966), 240; 10–1-1942, "Combat [...]", Box-3159, Entry-77, RG165.

12 The spring, the coming of summer and continued worries

The Soviets did last through the winter but by the end of it their offensive power petered out. A repetition of Napoleon's catastrophic retreat in 1812, which apparently haunted Hitler's mind, had been avoided.[1] Fighting still commenced into the spring but the real danger to the German Army had been averted by then. Some of the sections below (despite the chapter-title) include Anglo-American assessments that was made during the winter months.

12.1 Soviet prospects and economic resilience

During the spring some British reports became more pessimistic again. On 5 March, Cavendish-Bentinck commented on a report by Air Vice-Marshall Collier, who in turn had received information from the Soviet General Beliaev. Collier argued that the Russians could not handle a long war and Cavendish-Bentinck agreed. He feared that unless some apparent success in the war came, the Soviets would "crack up", regardless of the strong morale. Cavendish-Bentinck used historical examples; the Crimean war, the Russo-Japanese war, and World War I to support his arguments. Another FO official was not sure that this scenario was valid, since the prediction was based on pre-revolutionary conditions.[2]

According to Hinsley, when German resistance was stiffening again, the British Joint Planners informed the COS, in view of the military situation, that the USSR was in need of urgent help.[3] In March the US military planners stated that Soviet strength had been underestimated by military authorities in the past, but that the "true test of Russia's capacity to resist the enemy will come this summer". Brigadier-General Eisenhower, then assistant chief of staff at the War Plans Division, believed by the end of February that "Russia's problem is to sustain herself during the coming summer".[4]

Bruce Lockhart wrote on 25 March that the war was now approaching a decisive stage. Everything was possible, both a successful Soviet defence against a German spring offensive, and a Soviet collapse. He wondered how the Western Allies could possibly win the war if the latter alternative should happen. Therefore he recommended that the Soviets should be encouraged in every way, including some kind of satisfaction for political demands.[5]

After the end of the winter campaign the COI organization summarized both the Soviet and the German military and economic situation. Basic industry losses were estimated to 40–50 per cent as a result of the German occupation of Soviet territory; but the loss of munitions output was thought to be lower. Even though Soviet operations during the winter were not regarded as overly successful, the intensity of Soviet opposition to the German offensive in 1941 was regarded as the major factor in limiting the extent of the German advance. German supply problems were played down, and their permanent losses (dead, missing and permanently disabled) from the start of *Barbarossa* were estimated at 1.3 million men.[6] This was a hefty overestimation of German irrecoverable losses.[7]

The COI concluded the report by citing the former Harvard economist Edward S. Mason.[8] He assessed that the British clearly had a more positive outlook on Soviet prospects, and that he at least regarded the situation as more serious, even though there apparently existed US views that saw the Soviets as already crushed. According to him there were three very general views of the present situation in the Soviet-German war:

1   Because German losses had been less serious than Soviet losses, Germany remained the stronger and had a reasonable prospect of success in a new offensive.
2   Soviet strength had been completely crushed and the Germans had already won the war. All the Germans had to do was hold the Eastern Front with containment forces and strike elsewhere with major force.
3   The British view stated that the balance of strength between Germany and USSR was relatively more favourable to the Soviets than in June 1941.

The chances of German victory, according to the third view, were therefore not good. Mason regarded the methodology of the British sources as sound, but most Americans regarded British estimates as affected by wishful thinking. Mason himself was inclined to the first of the three views. Some individuals cited in the report suggested that morale as a factor might have altered to the advantage of the Soviets.[9] But as we have seen from British opinions cited above (and below), at least some British observers believed that the Soviets faced a much more serious situation, than the one called the "British view" by Mason.

In March Michela (from 15 December 1941 the new military attaché)[10] believed that the Red Army could in some way make a stand during the summer, and that by the end of 1942 both combatants would face each other in a weakened condition.[11] This was quite a change in attitude, after his and Yeaton's prophecies during the autumn. He also estimated that the USSR had lost 30 per cent of its industry so far.[12] Three days later he estimated the population loss as of 12 March 1942 to 33 per cent, that the industrial output fall was 35 per cent, and that the USSR had lost 18 per cent of its farmland.[13] Other intelligence reports available to the G-2 by this time suggested that the Soviets would not be defeated, but that the Germans might well reach the

Urals by the summer.[14] During a conversation with Harriman in April, concerning the merits of a possible Western Allied landing in France by 1942, US Army Chief of Staff Marshall expressed concerns over whether or not the Soviets would stand up to the expected German summer offensive.[15]

In a 20 March report the US Kuibyshev embassy could not guess whether or not the coming German offensive would succeed. Even if the Soviets would be able to withstand it, they would do this with the narrowest of margins.[16] However, according to the report the economic system, seen as largely directed towards war, had stood up to the test of war. The total loss of industrial assets was estimated to 40 per cent since 22 June. By taking account of the eastward transfer of industry, it was estimated that about two-thirds of industrial capacity was still in operation. The conversion to war production was described as successful. Some of the industries unaffected by the invasion were had fulfilled or even exceeded their production plans. But it was doubted that the Soviets, with their present industrial capacity, would be able to maintain their effort once again in the summer of 1942, if subjected to the same German offensive as in 1941. Therefore US and British material aid might have a decisive importance. According to the report the railways had done their job well, considerably better than expected. But the war in itself was seen as exerting a great strain on transport, and the railways were still described as a weak link in this system.[17]

Two British reports from about the same time also shone some light on the perceived transport situation. From secret contacts close to someone in German headquarters, British MI laid their hands on a German estimate of the situation on and behind the Soviet front as of 1 Mars. In a report dated 25 Mars the German view was presented regarding transport and other matters. The railways were working normally, since, during the 1941 retreat, the Soviets evacuated around 80 per cent of the rolling stock and locomotives from the lost territories.[18] In a telegram from Sir Archibald Clark-Kerr – the new British ambassador to the USSR until 1946 – dated 26 March, the transport situation was still problematic. Road and railway mileage was "notoriously low" in relation to the vast spaces of the USSR. About 40 per cent of the existing lorries were out of action, and due to the shortage of skilled workers prospects regarding this matter were bleak.[19] In a FO summary of three Pika reports from April, transport was claimed to have "failed badly" during the winter. The transport situation would improve with the spring opening of the waterways, but was anyway "the weak spot". Cavendish-Bentinck considered Pika's views as "objective, and probably correct". The Foreign Secretary and the Prime Minister regarded the information as "most interesting".[20]

Another March US embassy report, also noted by the British FO in April, gave a contradictory picture of the military prospects. Opinions ranged between no German offensive at all and the Germans being able to deliver crippling blows to the Soviets.[21]

In was stated in the extensive G-2 report "Russian Combat Estimate",[22] from 1 April, that the Germans would force the Soviets to yield considerable territory during the summer and the autumn. It was not certain that Soviet resistance would be able to protect her remaining vital centres during the coming campaign. Fears of a Japanese intervention (against the Soviet Far East) were expressed, and the sudden neutralization or collapse of the USSR under the full simultaneous impact of Germany and Japan was not a remote possibility. A resumption of a major German offensive was expected within the next 90 days.[23]

Despite the present danger to survival, the USSR was described as potentially the strongest military power by March 1942 (although this was not clearly stated, it can be assumed that this opinion referred to a comparison with Germany), but with serious problems to realize this potential for practical purposes. The whole USSR was portrayed as one great defence organization. The entire economy was tuned to defence, which according to the G-2 it had been for several years. The government had, of course, an obvious role in this, working in close cooperation with the military leadership to provide for the defence of the country. Military plans were not just considered as part of the general foreign policy pursued, but also as inseparable from the industrial basis on which they depended for fulfilment. Procurements for military purposes were not perceived as major problems, since the G-2 considered that, in a dictatorship, all activities are command functions rather than coordination functions. The high degree of centralization was instead something that facilitated the transition to a war economy. There was little criticism of communism in itself, with respect to the organization of the economic system, since it was appropriate to the stage of cultural and industrial development in the USSR. Problems were identified, such as labour skills and productivity incentives, but the G-2 stated: "it is probably the most effective regime which the Russian people could have at this stage of their history".[24]

However, this did not make the current military-economic problems disappear. It was estimated that the war potential was two-thirds of pre-war capabilities, due to loss of territory, bombing and serious logistical failures. The transport sector was the weakest link in the defence chain, and not sufficient for the needs of the economy. Transportation of vital supplies and raw materials was barely able to keep up with peacetime needs. The war caused further disruption, which was thought to be slowing down production. The industrial evacuation during 1941 was another factor causing problems for transportation, especially as G-2 thought that there were no factories ready to receive the machinery, which in turn resulted in machinery being left in the open, exposed to the harsh conditions of the winter 1941/1942. G-2 thought that the disruption of transport was recognized by the Soviet general staff, which was supposed to have made an attempt to build up adequate stocks of munitions in all sectors that would become vital for defence during the initial stage of the war. The deficiencies in transport were perceived mainly as a question of railways, and its main problem described as a lack of skilled workers. The G-2 reasoned that the combination of bad highways, inefficient railways, the slow antiquated horse transport, and the lack of road discipline, would most likely cause a breakdown in the Red Army supply system. Since industry was not able to update its machinery, obsolescent and even obsolete types of war matériel and equipment transportation were still in production. Due to losses in territory, factories and population it was doubtful whether the economy could maintain 200 or more divisions in the field for over six months.[25]

According to a 17 April G-2 memorandum, signed by Lieutenant-Colonel Arthur L. Richmond, overall Soviet military capabilities seemed so weak that Germany might be able to launch an all-out air offensive against Britain while the bulk of German ground forces were able to maintain "a reasonable status quo" on the Soviet–German front. As for the Soviet winter offensive the German defence was achieved with German forces reduced both in quality and in quantity, and that the failure of the German offensive in December 1941 was as much a question of weather and bad timing as any evidence of Soviet strength.[26]

G-2 reported on the opinions of Michela on 23 April: "Believe summer will find Soviets still in war even if Japs and German attack and all the more so if a second front develops. Soviets prepared to fall back to Urals and Volga river resisting all the way. Loss of Moscow will not be so disastrous as last December."[27]

On 20 April a MI3(c) report mentioned nothing about large inevitable Soviet territorial losses, and the Red Army would be able to hold a continuous front, "provided that no major disaster occur." But the Soviets would not at first be able to prevent a major German breakthrough in the South, and the Germans would probably reach and capture Stalingrad.[28] Even though he feared German military might, the British Chief of the Imperial General Staff (CIGS) General Alan Brooke wrote to his colleague General Archibald Wavell on 5 May that he did not believe that the Germans could muster enough troops to "finish of Russia and penetrate to the Caucasus".[29]

In May Fellers sent a report to the MID which quoted information from the former Yugoslav military attaché in the USSR, Colonel Jarko Popovich, who now served with the British. Popovich was considered reliable by the MID, even though the information he actually supplied was in contrast to the beliefs of most US observers by the time. There was no sound basis for the conclusion that the Germans could win a victory against the Red Army in 1942, and the Soviets were becoming relatively stronger. There were no concrete comments regarding the content of Fellers's report.[30]

Another observer of Slavic origin was Pika, who in May did not especially fear a Japanese attack in the Far East, neither for the reason of it being probable, or with respect to the Soviet capability to withstand it. He also argued that even if the Japanese should attack and succeed in occupying Eastern Siberia this would not seriously influence the European situation. The position would become serious only after the Japanese reached the Novosibirsk area. He stated that the Soviets were fortifying parts of Siberia to counter even this far-fetched possibility.[31] On 7 June he predicted that the Soviets would withstand the coming German summer offensive. The Soviets would be ready for the winter, even though they still were in great need of help from the West.[32]

By 20 May the Joint US Strategic Committee, a working subcommittee to the Joint Planning Staff (JPS), received the task of writing a memorandum on the strategic policy of the United Nations and the United States on the collapse of the USSR. One of the guiding assumptions was that by the summer the USSR would be so impotent, or so weakened, that her military forces could be contained by approximately half of the German forces, an assumption that was noted by the Joint Psychological Warfare Committee on 1 June.[33] In May the British JIC presented two hypotheses regarding the Soviet situation in 1942: "that the Russia had been defeated by October 1942 … or that Russia was still in the war in 1943 'but had suffered heavily in manpower and materiel'".[34]

By this time the Soviet winter offensive was long over even though heavy fighting still was taking place along the long front. Basically though, the Red Army had more or less gone over to the defensive in April, but in May the Soviets tried to launch a local spring offensive near Kharkov, which after some initial success proved to be a costly failure. Around the same time he Germans laid siege to the fortress of Sevastopol, which was taken after heavy fighting at the beginning of July. But the most important event was the beginning of the German summer offensive, which eventually would lead up to the battle of Stalingrad. This offensive was launched at the end of June, and only directly affected around one third of the common Soviet–German frontline. The Anglo-Americans were aware of the German build-up for the offensive and more extensive JIC reports on the subject were made in June.

Judging by a British JIC assessment from 1 June, which received much praise from Churchill, the British seemed to regard Soviet strength as greater than comparable American estimates during the spring of 1942. From the economic point of view, the Soviets could withdraw several hundred miles if necessary. They estimated that even the loss of Leningrad, the Moscow industrial area, and the Caucasian oil fields would allow the Soviets to maintain substantial air and land forces in the field for a considerable time.[35] The report had been approved by the COS, with the comment that it "may be slightly over-optimistic from the Soviet point of view". The US JIC received a note on Soviet capabilities from the Secretary of the British JIC in Washington, which summarized the British report. The note was transformed into a report, dated 13 June, and then submitted to the CCS. The US JIC was at variance with several views in the British report.[36] But the general conclusions in the report were accepted and the US JIC was in "broad agreement".[37] A 30 Mission report from 20 June stated that a loss of territory such as that described by the JIC above would not be the cause of any optimism, with regard to the Soviet ability to maintain troops in the field.[38]

Some representatives of the British military establishment still had their concerns about the Soviet ability to survive. In a meeting with representatives from the COS on 13 June, Mason-MacFarlane reported on his views.[39] He believed that "there was now a distinct possibility that the Russians would avoid being knocked out this summer". Mason-MacFarlane considered the next six weeks as a critical period, especially the next two to three weeks.[40]

A report on Soviet capabilities was approved at the 18th meeting of the US JIC, on 18 June. It was seen and commented on both by the JCS and the British JIC during the summer.[41] The general conclusion of the report, concerning the Soviet ability to defend itself against a coming German onslaught, was relatively bright (in comparison to earlier assessments). The Soviets would be capable of engaging "the entire available striking force of the German Army and Air Force", which was thought to consist of 180–200 divisions and 2500–3500 first-line aircraft. The Red Army was expected to delay and cause heavy loss to the attacker, but in the end be forced to give ground. It was stated that the USSR would be able to continue to wage war after the offensive, but "on a greatly reduced scale". The forces in the Far East were estimated to be capable of defending themselves, without additional resources from the Western USSR, for a maximum of six month against 25–35 Japanese divisions. In general, it was regarded as probable that the Red Army could be able to keep up a defence even after the end of the 1942 campaign.[42] The British JIC was of the opinion (11 July) that Soviet Far East strength was underestimated, on account of the numerical superiority of their Air Force, and their "formidable submarine force".[43]

The tremendous losses in Soviet industry were highlighted by the US JIC, although it was admitted that the calculations were based on outdated figures. The loss of production regarding agricultural and transport equipment was 69 per cent and 35 per cent, respectively, 21 per cent concerning automobiles and tractors, and 21 per cent regarding all other machine-building equipment. Despite the heavy loss of industrial production, it was argued that the fall in the production of finished military materials was not as great.[44] The British JIC had another somewhat lower estimate of industrial losses.[45] The difference between US and British assessments regarding raw material output was in some cases very significant, as was the estimated output loss due to the war. The greatest difference concerned steel and aluminium, which of course were two of the most important inputs in munitions production: steel for everything and aluminium especially for aircraft. While the British assessed annual output to 16 million tonnes for steel and 120,000 tonnes for aluminium, the Americans estimated output to 9.8 million tonnes and 30,000–50,000 tonnes, respectively. The Americans estimates were also lower in general for most (if not all) other raw materials that were of importance for heavy industry and munitions production.[46]

The US JIC regarded transport as a problem, both in connection with other sectors of the economy, and in itself. Its inadequacies – both rail and road – were a factor hampering both industrial production and military operations. The increase in military traffic since the start of the war was in itself described as a factor curtailing economic activities. The locomotives and railway cars that had been evacuated to the Soviet controlled areas would contribute to the railway capacity.[47] When the British JIC commented on the report on 11 July they were not as worried about the railway situation, and it was suggested that the US estimate was too pessimistic and that the railway capacity was underestimated.[48] In their 1 June report the British JIC described the transport sector as weak, even weaker than before the war, but it was impossible to estimate statistically the adequacy of transport facilities. The report contained a sentence stating that the motor transport situation probably was very strained. When Churchill commented on the report he agreed.[49]

During this period several reports from many Anglo-American institutions pointed to the lack of raw materials. It seems that the only exception to this was the aforementioned "Russian Combat Estimate", which concluded that the supply of natural resources was fairly sufficient for the war economy. The COI organization (in January and May) and the MEW (in May) was worried about a possible deficit of rubber needed for the economy and industrial production. The second COI report emphasized the large output increase of the synthetic rubber industry, and the world-leading experience of the USSR in this field. The problem was that the invasion had created an almost certain shortage of rubber, which on the other hand was alleviated to some extent by rationalization and economizing.[50] The MEW feared that not even the addition of rubber from stocks, reclaimed rubber, home production of natural rubber, and Lend-Lease deliveries would be sufficient to fulfill the needs for the second half of 1942.[51]

In May the COI made another in-depth analysis with reference to the raw material situation, investigating the effects of territorial losses on the petroleum position. Even though the general opinion seemed to be that the petroleum situation was fairly under control, further large losses of territory would produce a very serious situation.[52]

The British JIC, in its report from 1 June, made some comments on oil and the economic situation. Even though it was estimated that the loss of all the Caucasian oil fields would deprive the Soviets of 75 per cent of their oil production; accumulated stocks were thought to be considerable. If civilian consumption were curtailed and military consumption reduced by 25 per cent below its present level, the JIC expected that the Soviet capacity to carry on the war would probably not be limited by lack of oil for about a year after the loss of the Caucasus.[53]

Later in the month (7 June) Pika estimated that the raw material situation was not good. He also believed that most of the industry evacuated from the Ukraine, from the Donets Basin, and the Moscow area was now operating at 68 per cent of its capacity further to the East. To replace the industries which had been destroyed new ones were being built, and old ones were being extended. The transport system had improved much for the better. In spite of this, it was not used to its full capacity.[54] Additional analyses of the industrial situation were made during the summer by some institutions. The MEW had prepared a report on the output of the machine tool industry in June, which the G-2 managed to come across. The enemy advance, evacuation and the conversion of production to the manufacturing of war materials had damaged pre-war production. The MEW stated, regarding the present output: "An estimate of the present-day output of machine tools in USSR would, therefore, be an output at the rate of 70,000 units less 19,400, i.e. 50,600 units per annum or about 72 % of what was originally planned for this year."[55]

On 1 July, while the German summer offensive in the South gained momentum, the WD issued a report prepared by G-2's Eastern European Section, concerning Soviet military capabilities: "Determination of fighting strength, USSR". This report was very elaborate and had a somewhat more positive tone regarding the situation than G-2's earlier "Russian Combat Estimate". The total loss of productive capacity was estimated at a maximum of 35 per cent. The term "productive capacity" referred to the loss of industrial production, rather than total national income. Some vital industries were, of course, harder hit than others. No specific production figures were given for machine tools, but the present output was reduced below the 1938 figure of 53,900 units.[56]

Soviet self-sufficiency in raw materials, food and industrial goods was not considered to be as great if compared to the opinions expressed in the (1 April) "Russian Combat Estimate". The need for shipments from the Western Allies was stressed. Marked shortages in several materials of strategic value were noted (e.g. many strategic metals, rubber, aviation gasoline, lubricating oil, machine tools, machinery, trucks, tractors, chemicals, medicine and some agricultural goods). An improvement in the production of several strategic metals was unlikely. A shortage of horses for army, agriculture and transport needs was stressed. Shipping capabilities were not regarded as sufficient to cover the needs of shipments from the Western Allies. Nevertheless, the USSR was still largely self-sufficient from an economic standpoint. It was also estimated that within the next six months, moderate increases in the production of some metals and raw materials would occur in steel, copper, lead, zinc, coal, petroleum and aluminium. The same was estimated for some important foodstuffs. The production of several other metals, ferro-alloys (vanadium, tungsten, etc.) and industrial materials was inadequate due to inefficiency, insufficient resources and production. The time element was regarded as the most serious limiting factor in efforts to develop new mineral resources and industrial plant, in combination with labour shortages, and the general inefficiency of industry.[57]

Due to the evacuation of industries, production in the unoccupied regions was estimated to be about 10 per cent higher than before. Soviet claims of increased output during the preceding months were perceived as exaggerations, even though some of the alleged increases were seen as true. Some of the claimed production increases in mines and metallurgical plants during the late spring of 1942 were dismissed as seasonal, since during winter the extreme cold interfered with operations. But the general increase in some branches of industry was regarded as due to pressure exerted on the workers, longer hours, and perhaps improved organization leading to greater efficiency.[58]

Some advantages were identified by the G-2 regarding transportation in "Determination of fighting strength, USSR" – for instance, a large overall railroad carrying capacity, and some relatively good railroads and supporting roads at a regional level (e.g., around Moscow).[59] Partly in contrast to the "Russian Combat Estimate", Soviet resistance was regarded as adequate to protect her vital centres, even in the advent of a Japanese attack. On the other hand, if the Soviets were to have any chance of expelling the Germans from their territory, and effectively open up a Pacific theatre, large quantities of material and considerable numbers of first-rate troops from the United States and Great Britain were necessary.[60]

12.2 The Soviet population and the war effort

Largely in contrast to many pre-Barbarossa assessments, we can see that the tone of the reporting regarding the population had changed considerably. It seems implicitly that most observers now believed that the population stood behind the regime, at least concerning the war effort. The possible collapse of the regime and the state apparatus, which was as it seems not yet entirely excluded by the some observers, was closely connected to morale of civilian population and the internal stability. A few days after the beginning of the Soviet winter offensive Mason-MacFarlane reported to the DMI (through the WO) that the morale in Moscow appeared to be neither good nor bad, but instead that the mood was one of fatalism, with a "certain amount" of apathy.[61] In late January Michela reported: "With one exception there have been no known instances of a break in civil morale. This exception took place in Moscow the day after foreign diplomats were evacuated." The ability of the government to control the population was good: "So long as there is a Stalin – or his successor – and so long as there is the communist party organization and the N.K.V.D. troops are maintained, the morale of the people of the U.S.S.R. will never be seriously considered by the heads of the government. Decrees will be issued and enforced without regard to effect on the population. Civil morale [...] is not an important factor in the present war – what is more important is a keen knowledge of the national psychology and national capacity to withstand oppression. The present leaders [...] have this knowledge and also know how to use it."[62]

Pika's report from 21 January stated that at present morale was "very high". He argued that except for a very small part of the population everyone was united in its effort to "intensify" the war.[63] The day after he concluded that in spite of the great hardships of the population "the internal situation remains firm", and their great sufferings were such as no other "European could endure". The population was partly driven by hatred of the enemy, and the motto "everything for the front", but also by the watchful eye of the NKVD. When the MI3(c) summarized his report on the 25th they argued, partly in contrast to his opinions, that the population's "dissatisfaction with the existing regime" was on the increase. However, they also concluded that the population, with due consideration to the food shortage and the possibility of further reverses, would stand another winter.[64]

In February Baggally stated in February that the morale of the population was high.[65] The same impression was given by the Berthoud report.[66] The newly appointed War Cabinet member Cripps was quoted in a "Daily Mail" article from March, where his belief that Stalin's position had been greatly strengthened, since the beginning of the Soviet-German war, was expressed.[67] Privately Cripps had expressed as early as in December 1940 that the "half-Asiatic propensity of the Russians [made them] ... admire a strong and cruel ruling hand".[68]

On the American side G-2 considered civilian morale as high in a few editions of combat estimate during the winter months, but in the 1 April issue the increasing food shortage was thought be lowering it. This problem, in combination with increasing outbreaks of disease on the Volga and in Turkmenistan, made G-2 consider that the problems on the home front had assumed dangerous proportions.[69] In the 1 April "Russian Combat Estimate" the war morale of the civilian population was considered high, despite terrible and increasing hardships on the home front. The Russian mentality of obedience, nationalism, hatred for the Germans, a hard and ruthless regime, and the ordinary man's hope for a better tomorrow were factors that held)morale together.[70]

According to an April ONI report the US Assistant Naval Attaché Lieutenant Roullard stated that: "In spite of food shortage, poor distribution, and civilian inefficiency Soviet morale still remains unshaken. Invariably complaints are loudly aired in Soviet home circles about the high prices, poor quality, and other domestic grievances which is [*sic*] only a natural condition, but the people are none the less, fully behind the Red Army and 100% behind the present government."[71] At the beginning of May the US military attaché in Finland, (now) Colonel Huthsteiner, reported on the situation in the besieged city of Leningrad, based on information provided to him by the Finnish General Staff. Civilian morale in the city was very bad, as well as the general living conditions of the population.[72] That the population of Leningrad might had worse morale – in reality – than the rest of the population is not that strange, in view of the situation for the besieged city.

In May James O. Boswell, the US Assistant Military Attaché to the USSR, forwarded the opinion to the MID that "The people live badly but the morale is generally excellent."[73] According to a MI3(c) report forwarded to the FO in May, concerning the views of a Captain Boseley, a former member of the 30 Mission, the regime had a very tight control. This "purely autocratic" rule had its effects both on private life and on the war effort; an effort "second to none in the world". The authorities could maintain control and push the population to hard work by dictatorial methods, but the "main bulk of the population" had faith in communism. The NKVD was an important element in this control.[74]

The British JIC, in their 1 June report, expressed that the Stalin regime would be strong enough to withstand major reverses. The government was regarded as probably being stronger than ever, supported by a vigorous nationalism. But a collapse was not ruled out (neither was a German one in the long run), before the onset of winter.[75] Pika reported in his 7 June report on the high morale of the population in the face of great sufferings.[76] When

Warner of the FO commented on the stability of the regime in June he summarized the views of the whole FO Northern Department. The NKVD
troops were crucial for the survival of the regime. If these troops were intact,
and not used up in battle, they thought that the regime would survive even in
the face of major defeats.[77] According to a FO minute from the beginning of
July morale was declining somewhat, and the authorities were taking steps to
counteract the situation.[78]

By 18 June the US JIC considered civilian morale to be high, influenced by
the defensive struggle, propaganda, self-interest and the secret police.[79] In the
1 July "Determination of fighting strength, USSR", special emphasis was laid
upon the strength and stability of the Soviet leadership, the government and
the forcefulness of Stalin. He was seen as the latest in a long historical line –
represented by figures such as Ivan the Terrible, Peter the Great and Catherine
the Great – of strong, and even ruthless, leaders. With them, according to G-2,
Russia had been victorious; without them, Russia had crumbled. G-2 saw
several advantages in the rule of Stalin, concerning Soviet fighting strength.
The country had been unified, all dissident elements were eliminated, and all
efforts had been directed towards maximum national strength. This effort was
perceived as manifested through the Five Year Plans, with their maximum
backing for military effort, defence related propaganda and successful military
conscription.[80] The G-2 also identified some problems in the Soviet style of
government. The regime was strong, but power without responsibility was a
major problem. The regime had earlier made many costly and terrible mistakes,
and promoted incompetent people, such as the two Marshals Voroshilov and
Budenny,[81] whose blunders in the war before their removal nearly caused a
Soviet collapse.[82]

The population in itself, and its relationship to the economy was also analysed
by the Anglo-Americans. The actual German advance into Soviet territory
had reached a line that threatened its most vital (remaining) centres. Before
the German summer offensive in 1942 this line approximately stretched from
(omitting the limited areas occupied in the far north) Leningrad to (somewhat
west of) Moscow, and from there down to the Sea of Azov somewhat west of
the Rostov-on-Don. Geographically, the area lying to the West of this line
contained around half the European USSR (counting from the 21 June 1941
borders). Worse still, from the Soviet perspective, this area was relatively
densely populated; especially the Ukraine.

In mid-January 1942, the US embassy estimated the population of the
unoccupied territories to be at least 130 million, including 20 million refugees.[83]
On 10 March Michela reported to the MID that the USSR had lost 33 per cent
of its population due to the war so far.[84] The embassy believed in their report
that the agricultural sector was suffering from a lack of skilled personnel.[85] In
March the embassy stated that 8 million men had been withdrawn from
industry and agriculture due to military mobilization, which had resulted in a
serious shortage of labour. According to the report the authorities had met this
problem with an extensive labour mobilization, including the increased use of

women and children, as well as by a considerable tightening of labour discipline. Up to 60–75 per cent of the labour force used in industry was female according to one source, and an even higher percentage was thought to be female in agriculture. A lengthening of the working week was one measure taken by the authorities. The working week in some factories could be as long as 66 hours.[86]

In G-2's "Russian Combat Estimate", labour and its relation to production were regarded as the weakest link in the economic chain. The very large yearly turnover of factory workers was no longer a problem, since the introduction of drastic and severe labour laws in 1940. Most of the difficulties in production were not arising from organization, but from disaffection due to political interference, low living standards, lack of training, and irregularities in deliveries of basic necessities. However, factory managers were regarded as fairly successful in their management of large enterprises.[87]

In March the MEW estimated the 1942 workforce engaged in large-scale industry, handicrafts, construction, transport and communications at an average of 22 million.[88] The MI3(c) report about Boseley's views revealed that he assessed that the majority of the population actually believed in communism. But he also thought that the draconic measures taken by the authorities and the NKVD helped to keep the workers in their place. Failures, laziness and even being late for work were severely punished.[89]

The British JIC stated in June that the total population was 130–140 million in the unoccupied parts of the USSR, with an "industrial" manpower of 65–70 million.[90] Pika reported on 7 June that the Soviets suffered from a shortage of skilled labour.[91]

In the July "Determination of fighting strength, USSR", the G-2 almost praised the centralized organization of the economy. The difficulties were thought instead to be of a different kind: technological, due to inadequately trained personnel; low standard of labour productivity; and political attempts to keep "labour's enthusiasm for a socialist economy at fever heat." We have seen that G-2 estimated that some of the increase in industrial output was due to the better utilization of labour resources. Reports indicated that personnel in some of the more important factories were receiving better food, which was one of the reasons for increased production in those facilities. The mobilization of human resources was at an absolute maximum. The available labour force was estimated to about 28.3 million, excluding the Armed Forces. Of these, 11.6 million were occupied in industry, and 17.6 million in agriculture, in addition to about 10 million auxiliary workers. The education and training level of the population was regarded as low, but with some military value. Soviet technological advancements were praised for a few military inventions, but not for having any general reach. Invention was seen as hampered due to lack of experimental methods and a real machine-tool industry, and by political interference.[92]

An adequate food supply was an important prerequisite for an effective labour force. As we have seen, the pre-war assessments were not particularly bright regarding the food situation, even under peacetime conditions. Not surprisingly, the food situation was seen as very serious by many observers during this period of the war, at least later in the spring. Even though there were several unofficial warnings to the contrary from Soviet officials, the chargé d'affaires of the US embassy, Walter Thurston, reported to Washington in January 1942 that he personally believed that the food situation was not yet so serious that it would lead to hunger. The worries of Soviet officials were discounted as a means to receive more supplies. Thurston argued that the population's ability to withstand hunger might permit even more greatly reduced rations, that there probably existed large grain reserves, and that it was possible to expand production in the territory still under Soviet control. But he admitted that there was a shortage of food, augmented by the large number of refugees and the many men under arms who had to live on the diminished farm lands now left in the hands of the Soviet regime.[93]

In Pika's 22 February report the situation for agriculture was seen as very difficult, with shortages of mechanics and mechanized equipment for the spring sowing. Nothing was mentioned about any acute food shortages. When the MI3(c) commented on Pika's report they stated the Soviet system of collective agriculture was "now proving a disadvantage".[94]

Michela reported to the MID in February that the Soviet authorities admitted for the first time that the food situation was becoming serious.[95] On 10 March he reported that the Soviets had lost 18 per cent of their agricultural land.[96] In the COI organization report from the end of the winter it was regarded as easier to estimate the Soviet food potential, and Robinson felt that the food difficulties had been considerably exaggerated, at least in relation to the industrial problem. He cited the evidence of Lend-Lease Administration officials that, when the Soviets had to choose between war materials and food for transport, they invariably chose the shipment of war materials except in the case of trucks.[97]

The seriousness of the food situation was a subject in many reports from the US Moscow embassy during the spring. Many of these referred to the situation in Moscow and others were about the starvation in the besieged Leningrad.[98] In a despatch from March it was estimated that 44 per cent of the cultivated area of the country had been lost. The remainder of Soviet territory would not be able to produce enough food for the population. Soviet requests for food from the Western Allies were now an indication of the seriousness of the situation.[99] According to a US embassy official reporting in April, the "best foreign observer in Russia" considered that the situation was so serious that famine already existed in many parts of the USSR. His opinion was that the situation would become "catastrophic" shortly, possibly in two to three months.[100]

The food situation was analysed in several reports produced and commented on by the FO. Clark-Kerr wrote at the end of March that even if food were sufficient, distribution would cause problems.[101] The next day he repeated his worries in another telegram to the FO, fearing that many people might die of starvation before the harvest of the year reached the population. However, as he saw it, this would not be a problem for the war effort in general, since the starvation would affect the part of the population that was the least important in relation to it. He also stated that the population was "accustomed to periodic famines", and therefore they would not expect everyone to be fed during times of war.[102]

The FO noted an April MEW report, which in turn was a comment on some of the information sent from the Kuibyshev embassy. The MEW believed the situation being less serious than Clark-Kerr assumed. There was a relative shortage of meat and sugar, but there was a sufficient supply of bread so far.[103] In May Cavendish-Bentinck criticized the opinions of the Polish General Anders. When interviewed by the British, Anders was pessimistic concerning the food situation, and considered it very serious. The Soviet authorities did not possess the necessary organizational ability to solve the situation. Even though Anders's opinions did not differ to any great extent from those presented by other analysts the FO often referred to, Cavendish-Bentinck argued that the Poles had been badly treated by the Soviets, that they disliked and feared them, and therefore their opinions about the USSR would be coloured.[104] MI3(c)'s May report concerning Boseley's views described the food situation as the greatest of all the Soviet Union's present problems – a great danger. But according to him these problems did not affect the Armed Forces.[105]

On 1 April the G-2 considered the food situation to be a critical problem from an economic perspective, with only Lend-Lease shipments to relieve the situation until the summer harvest.[106] In the "Russian Combat Estimate" the essentials of living were considered as very difficult to obtain for the average person, and the food available barely averted starvation. Losses in agricultural land, and usable agricultural machinery resulting from the demands placed on industry due to the needs of war, were perceived as lowering the food supply to a dangerous level.[107] In his May report to the MID Boswell stated: "The food situation is generally bad, due in no small measure to poor distribution."[108]

Pika's 26 May report described the food situation as serious, and one which was the object of great efforts to come to terms with.[109] Although food rations had been reduced since the summer of 1941, the British JIC still (1 June) considered the USSR to have just about enough food. The main difficulty was distribution, and it was probable that the Army, industrial workers and school children were fed adequately, but that other town dwellers were short of food to a greater or less extent.[110] In its 18 June report the US JIC described the food situation as troublesome, especially if the harvest should turn out badly. Harvest surpluses from 1939–1940 were regarded as negated by the now relatively larger population (due to the refugee situation) in the unoccupied areas. Shortages of equipment, material, animals and manpower (due to the war) in agriculture, in combination with inadequate transport, were pointed out as the main problems.[111] The British JIC was not quite as worried as the Americans when they commented on the report on 11 July, since the rationing system would ensure that those consumers who were more important for the war effort would be the last to suffer. They also thought that the number of refugees was closer to 10 than 20 million people, which was the US estimate. They stated, however, that there might be acute local food problems.[112]

In the 1 July "Determination of fighting strength, USSR" three principal factors were identified as seriously limiting the Soviet capacity to increase food production, and for supplying its deficit areas. The first was "technical" factors, including frequent breakdowns and stoppages of tractors and combines, shortage of spare parts, and waste of fuel, which were in evidence already during peace time. Furthermore, wartime conditions added to these defects a shortage of labour, horses, seed, tractors and fuel. Recent reports indicated that many tractors had not been repaired as a result of a shortage of mechanics and a lack of spare parts. Another factor was the transport problem, since grain production was not evenly distributed over the country. The third factor was the harsh climate of the eastern parts of the USSR. The potential grain production, not counting increased plantings, was estimated to be between 60–70 per cent of normal. The food situation as a whole was critical, and even with maximum expansion of grain acreage and favourable weather, a grain shortage of 2 million tonnes was probable. G-2 feared that if drought occurred in some of the principal agricultural regions, then famine would result.[113]

G-2 related the renewal of production within industry to the food supply. The heavy workers received about 50 per cent more food than non-manual workers, and dependents and children somewhat less. The Army, NKVD and Communist party members were regarded as better fed than the average citizen. But since the Russians was accustomed to deprivation, the food shortage was not perceived as being as serious as in more well off countries, even if it was thought that the lowering of dietary standards would result in weakening resistance and disease. Health conditions were incredibly bad, and it was assumed that the civilian deaths in the war equalled the number lost in action. Apart from the food problem, a severe housing shortage was thought responsible for this.[114]

12.3 The Red Army and its munitions

As seen above this period was one of partial reassessments, even though much uncertainty still persisted regarding the ability of the USSR to survive the war. At the heart of this ability were, of course, the Soviet Armed Forces and the supplies the war economy could furnish them. The Soviet capacity to mobilize and supply troops in the field had been seriously underestimated so far by the Anglo-Americans, and some of the reports discussed in another context above indicate that this might still be the case. On the other hand, they knew by now that the Soviets at least had withstood nearly all the Germans could throw at them, and still be able to hold on to their capitol and even launch a winter offensive. It is important to remember that the Anglo-Americans knew that the lion share of the German Army – the best army in the world at the time – and most of the *Luftwaffe* were committed against the Soviets.

The changing fortunes of the war were accompanied by a change in assessments regarding the size and the military efficiency of the Soviet Armed Forces. It is hard to know if the change was inspired by the different frontline situation, or by a more thorough analysis of Soviet capabilities; or both in combination. The most positive observer was Pika, which perhaps was not that surprising considering his earlier relatively more optimistic stance regarding the Soviet situation. His 21 January report had an addendum in the FO version, which stated that the Soviets had "100 reserve divisions in training".[115] In his two February reports (noted by the FO), Pika considered the supply of manpower as good, with many soldiers still being of a satisfactory military age. Many new divisions were being formed to replace the ones destroyed earlier. In this respect his estimate was very high, since he mentioned something in the order of 250–260 infantry and 20–30 cavalry divisions. The MI3(c) considered these figures too high. Pika also reported that motorized and/or mechanized divisions were being created, and tank brigades.[116]

According to the secret German report (dated in March) obtained by the British MI, the Soviets were estimated to have, by 1 May, between 3500 and 4000 aircraft in the first line, and at least 4000 tanks, predicted to increase in numbers. The number of divisions was 290. The Soviets did not suffer from a manpower shortage, and would have 6 million men in military training, in addition to 10 million men of military age not yet conscripted.[117] But by 20 April the MI3(c) considered that the Red Army would be somewhat at a numerical disadvantage contra the Germans regarding army equipment. The Soviets had not better than numerical parity regarding tanks and even fewer aircraft. Unit by unit the Germans were better equipped. However, the Red Army would have at least as many troops in the field as the Axis, and be able to maintain that size for at least several months.[118] When Cavendish-Bentinck commented on a report from the 30 Mission in March he believed that the Soviets had "inexhaustible resources of manpower". Furthermore, "the extent to which they had been able to arm this manpower has up to date proved one of the few pleasant surprises of this war".[119]

The ability to arm manpower was, of course, dependent upon pre-war stocks, domestic war output and the possibility to import munitions. The by far most important of these three for the USSR during the war was domestic output during the war. As we have seen, munitions output was partly reassessed during the autumn, but it is difficult to know what the Anglo-Americans really believed about the figures given to them by Soviet officials. When Eden was visiting Moscow in December he received some information regarding aircraft output from Stalin. Eden made a summary of a conversation with Stalin on 18 December 1941, and sent it to the COS. Eden stated that Stalin had admitted an output slump of military equipment for a period, but that phase was now over. Output of aircraft had fallen to a low point of 30 per day (tantamount to 10,950 annually) but was now increasing. Earlier output (before the slump) was stated to have been about 70–80 per day. Tank output was larger than pre-war, and the artillery position was described as "very good". An earlier fall in rifle output had been remedied. Eden stated: "In general the equipment situation does not cause any anxiety." However, he regarded it as necessary for the Soviets to receive tanks at that moment.[120]

The 19 January Pika report stated that some of the evacuated war material factories already had begun producing again. Despite some wastage in the factory transfer process, the army would have enough war materials in the spring, with the possible exception of tanks.[121] Two days later he gave the impression that the Soviets had managed to reconstruct the armament industry transferred to the East, but that a crisis still existed in tank and aircraft production due to the transfer. The capacity in this respect had not caught up with German output.[122] When Cavendish-Bentinck commented on Air-Vice Marshall Collier's report regarding the Soviet military position (based on information from General Beliaev) in March, he argued that the SAF was receiving more and more aircraft. Even though the waste of planes was considerable, present output was larger than wastage. But he also considered that this condition (output larger than wastage) would not be maintained once the Germans had launched their spring offensive.[123]

According to the British March report containing secret information from German headquarters, the Soviets were able to produce equipment between 1 March and 1 May for approximately 30 rifle/cavalry divisions and 20 tank brigades. Since the Germans believed that a Soviet tank brigade consisted of 96 tanks (and 15 armoured cars) of various weights, they must have considered the monthly tank production to be approximately 960 vehicles (mostly light ones), although the report stated that the Germans had no available figures for output. The monthly output of aircraft by 1 March was estimated at 1150, including 200 training planes. No British comment was added to these figures.[124]

Information available to the FO and the British Moscow military attaché in May indicated that the Soviets had a relatively high munitions output (compared to estimates from before the Soviet–German war). By the middle of May the military attaché had spoken to a SAF general about Soviet production of war material. The general spoke in confidence about the rising and "staggering" production of war material. Both the evacuation of factories eastward and the conversion of factories to war production were described as a successful and speedy process. According to one FO official, this information was "very satisfactory", if not merely propaganda. Either way, the Soviets were making use of the aircraft and tanks given to them by the Western Allies.[125] A late May FO report described the experiences of a Mr. Potts of the British National Union of Railwaymen, who had visited the tank factory at Chelyabinsk, where he studied the production of tanks. He stated that the potential capacity of the plant was 100 tanks per day, when not interrupted by lack of armour, guns or mountings. No comment in the FO minute to this telegram, originating from the military attaché in Moscow, was made as to the production figure, but Mr. Potts was considered to be a man with "technical qualifications".[126]

According to a June FO report, the president of the USSR, Mikhail Kalinin,[127] had stated in an article that the whole war industry had been evacuated to safety in the East. Furthermore, almost all of it was already in operation and its production was increasing every month; in addition, overall production was higher in June than in June 1941. Kalinin had also repeated the last item of information to Baggally in person. Furthermore, Kalinin told Baggally that the production of arms had to become much higher before the Armed Forces would have all they needed. In a telegram to the FO (also forwarded to the MEW) from Clark-Kerr, Kalinin's statements were considered to be somewhat exaggerated, but nevertheless correct in the sense that Clark-Kerr believed that the war industry had made an almost complete recovery, in contrast to industry as a whole.[128] The AI3(a) commented on Kalinin's information a few days later and dismissed statements about increasing monthly industrial production, and a war material production higher than a year ago, as exaggerations.[129]

Pika's 26 May report stated that the building of munitions production capacity was proceeding rapidly, and that by the autumn of 1942 the war industry would produce more munitions than at the beginning of the war. The supply of arms to the troops was now guaranteed, but he also recognized that this effort was achieved at a very heavy price to the civilian population, since all agricultural and civil production had been curtailed.[130] In early June he stated that the Soviet authorities had made "superhuman efforts to organize the production of war materials and have achieved remarkable results." He no longer saw any crisis in this sphere of the war effort, and the Soviets had enough equipment to "withstand" the Germans, although he did not believe that the Red Army would gain any material superiority over the Germans in 1942.[131]

British assessments regarding the size of armed forces were scarce during the spring until the 1 June British JIC report; in which the estimate of the number of troops was as of 15 May. It was stated that the Red Army had superiority over the Germans, counting divisions and aircraft (4000–4500 against 3500), but an approximate equality in tanks. However, the numerical superiority of the Soviets was not seen as overwhelming, with consideration to all the opposing forces. The total number of men of military age was estimated to be about 17 million. Since no figure was given for the number of tanks, or the strength of infantry and cavalry divisions, it is hard to know how many troops the JIC really imagined that the Soviets had. It seems that they really thought that the Soviets had more men than the Germans but it is also probable that they underestimated the number of Soviet divisions.[132] When Churchill commented on the report, based on his secret conversation with Molotov (see below), he considered the estimated German strength as being underrated and the Soviet number of divisions as somewhat overstated. But the Soviets had considerable reserves in training.[133]

The report also contained an estimate of tank and aircraft output: more than 2000 tanks per month, with a growing proportion of heavy and medium tanks. Aircraft output was estimated to be some 2000 operational types per month, even though the JIC did not believe that the Soviets had large stored reserves. For guns, small arms and their supplemental ammunition, the estimate was that the production was at least higher than in June 1941. The production of mortars was considerably higher than in June 1941, and increasing.[134] As we have seen, the COS considered that the JIC report showed a picture of Soviet prospects that was somewhat too favourable. This was particularly true with reference to aircraft production.[135] According to the War Cabinet Deputy Secretary, Major-General Ismay, Churchill had received information from Molotov in "a very secret and personal conversation" (probably when Molotov was visiting London in May), on which Churchill based his comments on the JIC report.[136] Churchill wrote that the Soviets produced about 600 to 700 aircraft per month during the winter, but that the production in April was 1500 "combat" aircraft. In addition, this figure would rise eventually as more "factories [were] now completed".[137]

Mason-MacFarlane, reporting to the COS on 13 June, stated that there was "no shortage" of small arms and guns in the Red Army, although he identified a shortage of anti-tank guns.[138]

The British did not present any estimates for the total size of the armed forces during this period, but according to a MI3c report from October (1942), their "speculative" estimate in July (1942) was that there were some 9–10 million men in all the armed services.[139] On the other hand, estimates regarding the total size of the Armed Forces often say little about the actual size of the field force. The reason for this is that the total size includes all personnel enlisted, regardless of their actual contribution to the military power projected against the enemy. One good example of this phenomenon is total German Armed Forces strength, which often was far in excess of the number of combat troops.

During the winter several British observers seemed to have obtained a more positive outlook on the efficiency and morale of Red Army troops, at least in comparison to earlier assessments. According to Lieutenant-General A. Nye, a member of Eden's entourage to Moscow in December 1941, Soviet Army morale was high, in the conduct of its present offensive. But the Soviets overestimated their military efficiency vis-à-vis the Germans, and that the only way they would achieve any "striking successes" was if the German morale "cracked".[140] From 26 to 28 January 1942 Mason-McFarlane visited the front. His impression was that the Soviets were not as bad as first supposed. He praised both officers, commissars and soldiers, and believed that they knew what they were doing. He had nothing critical to say about the Soviet effort, except that staff work and administration was less efficient at higher levels.[141]

In two February reports from Pika the morale and training of the troops was seen as very good. The experience of men and officers was described as greatly enhanced since the previous year. But there were still problems, such as faulty command and the negative influence of political commissars on the command situation. Nevertheless, the commissars could have some positive effects on the morale of the troops and hinder sabotage. MI3(c) added in a comment that the "Centralization [of the highest] command in Moscow has led to rigidity."[142] Baggally revealed in his despatch from late February that he was more or less of the same opinion as Mason McFarlane regarding the efficiency of the Soviet military administration. The administration of the lower levels in the field was relatively efficient, but at the higher level there existed delays, lack of organization and coordination.[143]

According to the British MI report compiled from secret German information, the Red Army was suffering from the inability of higher-ranking officers (from colonel and up) to handle large numbers of troops in an effective way, or to conduct combined arms operations efficiently. Although all officers were brave, only junior officers (major and down) were seen as good. The whole army suffered from a general shortage of senior officers. The same source also thought that the discipline of the Red Army was good, without even a slight sign of "deterioration".[144]

A MI3 report from 11 April referred to the "over-centralization" of the military as a "curse". On the other hand, the report also referred to Mason-MacFarlane, who had a positive impression of the senior officers he had met at the front, and the "staunchness" of the soldiers.[145] In a report dated 20 April, MI3(c), the Red Army was considered to be inferior to the German Army with regard to higher command, staff work, organization, training of soldiers and mobility. But Red Army morale was high.[146] In the summary of the three Pika reports from April, forwarded by the FO to the secretary of state and the prime minister, the "spirit and morale" of the reserve troops were considered to be high. They were also considered as being well trained by experienced officers.[147] He stated in his 26 May report that the training of military reserves was suffering due to the lack of real weapons during training sessions, since all real equipment went to the front units, and the reserves were using wooden dummies instead.[148]

In the 1 June report the British JIC considered the efficiency of the German Army to be greater than that of the Red Army, due to the relative Soviet inferiority in training, mobility and high command leadership. But the balance was not weighted against the Soviets to the same extent as in 1941. Soviet experience had gained somewhat on the Germans, and the relative difference in morale had diminished.[149] Morale in the Air Force was described as very high, and likely to survive even heavy reverses. But pilot training was summarized as the "survival of the fittest", even though results were better than might be expected in view of the shortage of experienced crews.[150]

In an April report to the air assistant chief of staff (intelligence, A.I.1), a British Air Force officer gave his description of Soviet pilots. He had nothing to complain about regarding their courage or morale, but they were not very good pilots. According to British standards their training was "absurdly inadequate", with too little training time. A Soviet officer had informed him that many Soviet pilots were practically illiterate.[151]

On 13 June, Mason-MacFarlane informed the COS that Soviet staff work had gained in experience. It was good at divisional level and down, but less successful at levels above that, at least when it came to supply and transportation. On air activities, Mason-MacFarlane thought that the Air Force had a lower strategic mobility than the German *Luftwaffe*, and that maintenance was wasteful by British standards. He also commented on the activities of the partisans, which he described as being under the control of the Soviet division on their particular sector of the front. His view was that the partisans contributed to stretching German resources.[152]

On 10 January 1942 G-2 estimated the mobilization capacity as being at an (average) steady rate of 15 divisions per month. The strength of a division was estimated at 17,200 men in general, with about 25 per cent at reduced strength (10,000 men).[153] According to the British Air Ministry's Weekly Intelligence Summary as of 1 January, also noted by G-2 later in January, aircraft strength on all fronts was 5670 operational aircraft (3410 on the Soviet–German front).[154] In a US embassy despatch from the same month it was stated that the USSR had 12.5 million men under arms.[155] In March the embassy estimated the size of the Armed Forces to about 10 million men.[156]

Although seen as uncertain, the COI organization believed by the end of the Soviet winter campaign that the number of divisions was between 320 and 325. It was clear to the COI that these divisions were much more lightly equipped than they were in 1941.[157] The estimate in the 1 April version of the "USSR Combat Estimate" was 325 divisions, with 6750 aircraft, 7250 tanks and 26,500 guns. The number of divisions had increased by 50 since the 10 January version. The report did not state whether the number of aircraft was first line, or total available numbers, or if it included military non-combat aircraft. This estimate was revised in April and May, but no major changes occurred.[158]

The assessments in the "Russian Combat Estimate" were as of June 1941, with corrections up to March 1942 wherever possible. One of the most interesting features of the Armed Forces analysis concerned manpower reserves; based upon demographic figures for the whole population. The total population as of June 1941 was estimated at 193 million. According to both British and US estimates, the USSR had lost some 61 million (30 per cent) of the total population during the first six months of war. To G-2 the importance of calculating population changes was related to evaluating the number of military personnel. The size of the Armed Forces was estimated to almost 10.2 million men as of January, of which nearly 1.5 million had been in the Armed Forces in June 1941. The number of available pre-conscripts (16- to 17-year-olds) was estimated at about 2.15 million, and available men without military training between the ages of 18 and 50 were estimated at nearly 13 million.[159]

In June the Red Army's size was estimated to between 4 and 5 million men by the US JIC, excluding several million men in what they called "immobile home guard units". They stated that the limiting factors on the size of the armed forces were logistical considerations and lack of equipment. The tank strength assigned to combat units, including 1400 tanks in the Far East, was 7400. The estimated number of aircraft in combat units was 6100, including 1100 in the Far East. The total number of available tanks, operational aircraft and guns (larger than 37 mm in calibre) was estimated to at least 11,000, 5800–12,500 and slightly more than 25,000, respectively. In general, the position with respect to munitions was good, but meagre in comparison to the June 1941 situation.[160]

The JIC argued that there were no problems with manpower, since they estimated that the Armed Forces could be nearly twice as large as they actually were (given the necessary equipment and logistical conditions), even though some of the manpower was only partially trained. A pool of 20 million fit men of various ages was still available for military service.[161] The British JIC (11 July) agreed in general with this estimate, since they considered the pool of men to be 19–20 million, even though the estimated practical reserves only was about 4 million. The British highlighted the connection between industrial and military manpower, and stated that the manpower requirements of the army would always have priority, although equipment would be the ultimate limiting factor. It was pointed out that further mobilization of manpower, in the long run, could reduce the economic potential.[162]

The British also believed that the US JIC estimate for the first line strength of the Red Army was too low. The accurate strength was at least 6 million men, and stated at the same time that the Soviets themselves had estimated that they had 8 to 9 million men under arms in January, possibly including the navy and the NKVD. But the British figures were not adjusted for the losses sustained by the Red Army from May onwards. The British estimated the total aircraft strength on all fronts to 6720–7220, and the number of tanks to be 14,000. The British and the US estimate of the size of the navy was divergent in some respects, although neither of them considered the Soviet Navy as a major threat to the Axis, except that the British believed that the Far East submarine force could be a more serious threat to the Japanese than the Americans did.[163]

In the "Determination of Fighting Strength, USSR" (1 July), the total number of men at the front was estimated at 4.15 million, including the troops in the Far East, with another 6 million men organized in various supply, Home Guard and other second-line units. The total number of men in action or in training was thought to be about 12 million. A total of approximately 5000 aircraft and 6000 tanks were thought to be in action at the front.[164]

It clear that US assessments concerning munitions output changed considerably during this period. In late February Michela reported to the MID about a lecture given by a supposedly high-ranking member of the Soviet communist party. The lecturer stated, among other things, that the production of aircraft was 2500 per month. Michela commented on this information: "No observer here believes that [...] production can be in excess of 2,000 planes per month and that the true figure is probably in the neighbourhood of 1500 planes monthly."[165] Considering his assessments in 1940, this was a huge change.

We have seen that by the end of the Soviet winter offensive, the COI organization estimated that the decrease in munitions output was smaller than the loss in overall economic capacity. Nevertheless, the level of munitions output was below the pre-war level. According to Robinson, munitions was the chief bottleneck to the Soviets, in contrast to Germany, whose chief bottleneck was described as manpower. No estimates of Soviet war matériel production were presented, since this was not regarded as measurable due to lack of statistics.[166]

According to the 2 March "USSR Combat Estimate", US Lend-Lease deliveries were still accelerating, but the British contribution was regarded as a major factor in the Soviet supply situation, and was thought to be affecting Soviet war potential very markedly. Total British shipments up to 31 January were estimated at 800 to 1000 tanks, and 900 to 1000 aircraft.[167] This assessment was, of course, an indication pointing to that G-2 still believed in a relatively modest Soviet munitions output. In the 1 April "Russian Combat Estimate", G-2 stated that the USSR would be practically dependent on the Western Allies for the maintenance of her armies in the field with reserves of equipment – apart from artillery and small arms ammunition – and supplies in general. This condition would last for a long time, should another German offensive be launched in the near future. Heavy military matériel was qualitatively deficient, because of the alleged fact that the economy was not able to keep up with the rapid changes in modern matériel.[168]

In the (1 April) "USSR Combat Estimate" the major limitation on the growth of ground and air forces was considered to be supply, since manpower was assumed to exist for 500 divisions. The Soviet productive capacity was very large, and G-2 estimated that the annual average output of combat aircraft, tanks and guns during 1939–1941 was 5000, 6000 and 9000 units, respectively.[169] This implies that monthly output by the spring of 1942 was considered lower. It is apparent that the G-2 considered the 1939–1941 productive capacity as something more or less constant, which was not augmented by the outbreak of war. Instead the total supply of heavy war material available arising from Soviet production during nine months of war (22 June 1941 to 30 March 1942) was estimated at 6000 guns, 4500 tanks and 3750 aircraft. The loss of production capacity since June 1941 was 35 per cent. These losses were offset by complete industrial and labour mobilization, and by considerable quantities of Lend-Lease supplies.[170]

G-2 estimated that the Soviets had produced equipment for 60 divisions since the beginning of the war, including the guns and tanks mentioned above. They assumed that the reduced regular divisions had been restored essentially to normal strength (17,200 men), while those wiped out had been replaced by 10,000 men reserve divisions, and about 43 per cent of all divisions were reserve divisions. Just assuming that the equipment for the 60 new divisions was meant to be for the regular ones (17,200 men[171]), and recalculating these to reserve strength meant that they were equivalent to about 103 10,000 men divisions.[172]

The aircraft factories was described as modern in relation to equipment, and modelled after foreign factories.[173] However, aircraft production was suffering from numerous and serious handicaps. Some of the most serious shortcomings were described: lack of trained and competent personnel in all branches of the industry; shortage of well-equipped laboratories engaged in necessary research; failure to create standardization of machinery (e.g., mass production machinery was adopted from US models while laboratory machinery and apparatus was adopted from the Germans); and failure to bring in foreign specialists due to distrust and suspicion. Generally the aircraft industry was ridden with excessive centralization and characterized by mediocrity. Excessive political interference (e.g. the purges, paucity of engineering skill, low productivity of labour, and inefficiency in planning) were the perceived reasons behind the mediocre status of the industry. These perceptions were, of course, in line with what pre-war observers had identified as the problems of Soviet industry. The estimated monthly output of military aircraft appeared to have reached an all-time high during the first six months of 1941, when the seven factories producing the bulk of production had manufactured 372 aircraft per month.[174]

One aspect of Soviet mobilization revealed in the report, with implications for G-2's view on the whole war economy, was the notion that the USSR was pursuing a policy of building up munitions stocks rather than depending upon increase in plant capacity when an emergency arose. The high military preparedness of the economy was stressed, and even in peacetime it was something of a war economy. The assessment was that, if physically possible, the requirements of the munitions industry should be met, no matter what happened to other branches of industry.[175] According to an April report from Fellers to the G-2, relying on "reliable" Yugoslav military sources, the Soviets produced 1000 planes per month (800 military aircraft) during 1940. The Yugoslavs considered that the aircraft industry lacked qualified workers, which in turn gave an incentive for the use of the most modern and automatic machinery; introduced already by the first Five Year Plan. However, due to the lack of trained personnel it was not possible to utilize factory capacity to the full extent. Yeaton did not put much credence in the picture the Yugoslavs painted.[176]

According the US JIC (18 June), the production of aircraft, tanks and guns (larger than 37 mm in calibre) for the period of 22 June 1941 to 1 May had been 5800–8000, 6000–10,000 and 9000, respectively. The British JIC believed in July that the US estimate was too low. The British on their part concluded not surprisingly that aircraft output had been 12,000, tank output 10,000–12,000, and that the estimate for guns was too low in general. The supply of small arms, light artillery, and ammunition was regarded as comparatively abundant.[177] On 1 July, in the "Determination" report, the G-2 estimated that the current annual output of aircraft, tanks and guns was 2100, 3900 and 5850 units, respectively. The aircraft industry was estimated to have lost at least 40 per cent of its productive capacity since the war started, due to the capture or destruction of factories. The G-2 did not consider that there was enough matériel to go around for the Armed Forces. They did not believe that there was enough military equipment available to permit any major offensive operations, or even to replace heavy losses.[178]

The difference between US and British assessments during this period was definitely significant even a year after the beginning of the Soviet–German war. Considering the great importance of munitions for the war potential of a nation during World War II, the difference was of no small importance. Even British observers were still not convinced by this time that the Soviets actually could stand up to the test of war in the long run. In 1917 Russia pulled out of the war after considerably smaller losses in manpower, territory and economic potential, despite the fact that she was facing a relatively smaller share of German military power than in 1942. The dire situation could of course be mitigated if the Red Army's fighting skills and efficiency had improved a lot since earlier in 1941.

Michela's report to the MID in March left not much hope in this respect, since he estimated the relative combat efficiency between Soviet and German troops as two to five, in Germany's favour. The offensive power of the Red Army was not held in high regard, and much of the credit for stopping the Germans in 1941 was credited to partisans, the immense defensive networks created by the civil population and the poor weather.[179] He made some additional comments on Red Army efficiency a few days later (noted in a G-2 report): "Above the division, leadership is weak, mobility is absent due to bulkiness, great use is made of horse-drawn transport; tank units and air force are of the best, but shortage of tanks necessitates organization of independent tank brigades; in winter maintenance work is quite effective, but in general it is of a low order; and tactical operations are slow but tactical principles well applied."[180]

In the "Russian Combat Estimate" (1 April) the Red Army's combat efficiency was regarded as relatively low, compared to the world's others armies, not least due to a supposed poor military leadership in the higher ranks. G-2 concluded that the bulk of the Red Army's rank and file was recruited from primarily backward agricultural and illiterate people, and the leadership was composed of practical but uneducated and even ignorant men. The purges were one reason for this, but G-2 thought that there was more hope for the younger and more educated generation of officers.[181]

However, the efficiency of the Armed Forces was not in all ways seen as substandard. The great masses of troops were regarded as effective in defence, despite being depicted as poorly equipped, supplied and led. The efficiency of the tank forces and the artillery was regarded as higher than other arms. The problems of the Air Force were not perceived to be merely about obsolete aircraft, since G-2 was of the opinion that the experience and training of the other leading world powers had gone beyond the scope of Soviet training. Nevertheless, they regarded Soviet fighter aviation as effective when equipped with modern planes. Bomber aviation, on the other hand, was described as ineffective even with modern aircraft. No decisive remarks were made about the efficiency of the navy. The general state of morale in the Red Army was rated as fair to good, after the successes of winter warfare.[182]

The morale of the Armed Forces, or more specifically its morale organization, was the subject of special attention from the COI organization in April. The ability of the Armed Forces to maintain morale and discipline among their personnel was good. Attention to the men in the services, severe discipline, indoctrination, traditional Russian patriotism and Russian stamina were some of the most important reasons for this state of affairs according to the COI organization.[183] After a front visit in May Michela's opinion of the Red Army and its morale was changed for the better. According to a G-2 report: "Soviet troops confident, excellent morale", and "[Michela's] general impression favourable and opinion of Red Army raised."[184]

According to the 18 June US JIC report, the Red Army was to a great degree a "reserve" army, since the regular army had been largely annihilated by now. However, despite this it was recognized that the troops had some combat experience, especially at small unit level. The training and leadership of low-level units was regarded as good (especially in defensive and guerrilla tactics), in contrast to larger units, whose staff work, coordination and communications were weak. The ponderous handling of large units put them at a disadvantage when "coping with German strategy and major tactics". The general lack of transport facilities was regarded as a factor enhancing the inadequate manoeuvrability. The morale of the army were "exceptionally high", characterized by an "intense spirit of resistance" and a "determination [...] to fight". There was good reason to assume that the trend of high morale would continue.[185] The British JIC regarded the US picture as too gloomy with regard to the transport situation near the front.[186]

In "Determination of Fighting Strength, USSR", the defensive capabilities of the army and the air force were stressed, as well as the tenacious and extensive support the armed forces received from the population.[187] On the other hand, Red Army operations, staff work, liaison and communications were poor. It seems as if the Red Army was chiefly regarded as efficient at a tactical level, even though some top commanders were praised for their ability. In general, a ratio of 2:5 in relation to German efficiency seemed justified. This ratio was also what Michela suggested in March. The navy was praised for some minor operations, even though its general efficiency was rated as fair. Soviet intelligence and counter-intelligence were regarded as outstanding, but the conclusions the Soviets drew from the intelligence information had been erroneous.[188]

No information is available from the spring regarding British notions on Red Army efficiency and military morale, but in June a few observers made a few comments. Cavendish-Bentinck argued in a FO minute from June that the Soviet High Command had improved since June 1941.[189] After a front visit Colonel K. G. Exham of the 30 Mission reported back to London on a rather positive note regarding the Red Army, its morale and capabilities. Michela visited the same part of the front at approximately the same time. He reported that he had gained a somewhat better impression of the Red Army after this visit. Even though he did not believe that the morale of the Red Army was particularly good he regarded the discipline as "superb".[190]

On 20 June the 30 Mission reported to the WO that it was probable that the disparity between Soviet and German troop efficiency had been reduced a great deal since 1941, especially concerning Soviet defensive skills. German commanders were still seen as superior at the level above divisions. Red Army morale was described as "very high", and the troops were not considered to have any of the "inferiority complex" vis-à-vis the Germans that they showed during 1941. The "traditional national hate" of Germans was also an important factor affecting military morale. The ability to take very heavy losses in the field was another aspect of military capabilities, and the Soviets was exploiting what the 30 Mission called "unlimited manpower" in an attempt to wear down the Germans. This was in line with the "ruthless outlook" of the regime and its leadership. Even if the Red Army were defeated in the field, the regime would still be in power (in the absence of decisive military defeat it must be assumed that the authors meant), and partisan warfare was considered to be large scale in any case. Partisan warfare in conjunction with the vast area of the country would force the Germans to keep large occupation forces in the East according to the report.[191]

These assessments reveal that there had been improvements in military efficiency and morale since 1941, but that the Germans still essentially had the upper hand on the battlefield. The estimates regarding relative losses made during the same period basically confirms that picture.

In March the assistant military attaché in Kuibyshev, Captain Robert E. McCabe, stated that the total (killed, captured, missing and wounded) military losses of men up to 28 February probably were 3.5 million men.[192] A few days later Michela stated that the losses as of 12 March amounted to 3.5 million and 12,000 aircraft and 15,000 tanks.[193] The manpower losses were confirmed in a US embassy report a week later.[194] According to the "Russian Combat Estimate" (1 April) Red Army losses (killed, wounded and captured) during the first six months of the war was well over 5 million.[195] In June, Yeaton, now lieutenant-colonel and the chief of MID's Eastern Section of the European Branch, referred to one of Michelas's earlier reports and added (apparently from Michela's own figures) that cannon losses had been 20,000 (of all kinds) up to 28 February.[196] The June US JIC report estimated losses in heavy munitions since 22 June 1941 to be 15,000–22,000 aircraft, 6000–10,000 tanks, and 20,000 guns (larger than 37 mm in calibre). Permanent military manpower losses were considered to be approximately 5 million.[197] In "Determination of Fighting Strength, USSR", the extent of the losses were regarded as a weakness, despite the fact that the losses quoted in the report (allegedly) were founded on official Soviet sources. Up to 23 June the total number of losses admitted by the Soviets was 4.5 million men, even though it was not stated if this referred to permanent or total losses. If the figure really was based on official Soviet sources it probably referred to total losses. Admitted material losses were 22,000 guns, 15,000 tanks, and 9000 planes (a figure considered as too low by the G-2).[198]

As usual, Pika had an interpretation of the situation that was more positive to the Soviets than other observers. It was stated in the summary of the three Pika reports from April that German losses only in killed from 1 December to 31 March were half a million men, in addition to 250,000 soldiers who had frozen to death. Even though he considered Soviet losses as being heavy, they were smaller than German losses. Based on WO figures, the British JIC head Cavendish-Bentinck commented that he believed Pika's estimate of German losses as somewhat exaggerated, but he did not comment on Pika's estimate regarding Soviet losses.[199] On 20 April the MI3(c) stated that Soviet losses of men and matériel had "been immeasurably greater than those of the Germans".[200]

Notes

1   Jones (2010), "Preface".
2   5–3-1942, N1333/30/38, FO371/32906.
3   Hinsley (1981), 90.
4   Harrison (1951), 11.
5   25–3-1942, "Sir [...]", FO800/877.
6   R&A no. 535, M1221, RG59.
7   According to German High Command statistics from 16 March, German causalities (including wounded) in the Soviet–German war were somewhat over 1 million men. General Halder stated on 1 March that total causalities instead were 1.5 million. However, permanent losses were the lesser part of total causalities, and therefore the COI organization's claim was an overestimation. Salmaggi & Pallavisini (1997), 173, 223.
8   R&A no. 535, M1221, RG59; Katz (1989), 5.
9   R&A no. 535, M1221, RG59.
10 17–1-1942, "Michela, [...]", Box-1, MECF1941–42, RG84.
11 10–3-1942, "Military [...]", Box-3142, Entry-77, RG165.
12 10–3-1942, 370.2USSR thru 6–30–43, Box-1045, Entry-47, RG319.
13 13–3-1942. "M/A [...]", Box-3146, Entry-77, RG165.
14 19–3-1942, "Current [...]", Box-3142, Entry-77, RG165.
15 Harriman & Abel (1976), 133; Keegan (ed.) (1989), 214.
16 20–3-1942, 2–6-1942, Despatch No. 1491, Roll-22, T1250, RG59.
17 20–3-1942, 2–6-1942, Despatch No. 1491, Roll-22, T1250, RG59.
18 25–3-1942, "U.S.S.R. [...]", WO208/4563.
19 26–3-1942, N1658/1375/38, FO371/32988.
20 26–4-1942, N2214/30, FO371/32907.
21 10–4-1942, N1877/30/38, FO371/32907.
22 This was not to be confused with the ordinary "USSR Combat estimate". The "Russian Combat Estimate" was submitted to the CCS, and dated 1 April 1942. This extensive and comprehensive report analysed practically the whole of the USSR from the perspective of national defence and war potential. 1–4-1942, "Russian [...]", CCS350.05USSR, Box-212, RG218.
23 1–4-1942, "Russian [...]", CCS350.05USSR, Box-212 (211), RG218.
24 1–4-1942, "Russian [...]", CCS350.05USSR, Box-212, RG218.
25 Ibid.
26 17–4-1942, "Subject: [...]", 384Russia, Box-1047, Entry-47, RG319.
27 23–4-1942, "From: [...]", Box-3172, Entry-77, RG165.
28 20–4-1942, "Soviet [...]", WO208/1804.
29 Dunn (1980), 12.
30 13–5-1942, Report No. 2437, 381USSR, Box-1046, Entry-47, RG319.
31 1–6-1942, "Sir [...]", FO800/874.
32 22–6-1942, N3416/30/38, FO371/32909.

33 7–8-1942, "Strategic [...]", ABC384USSR(6–1-42), Box-472, Entry-421, RG165; 1–6-1942, JPWC17, ABC384USSR(6–1-42), Box-472, Entry-421, RG165; Cline (1951), 146.
34 Harrison (1951), 25.
35 1–6-1942, JIC(42)200(Final), CAB121/464; Smith (1996), 93.
36 13–6-1942, JIC25, CCS381USSR, Box-214, RG218.
37 Hinsley (1981), 98.
38 13–6-1942, N3429/30/38, FO371/32909.
39 2–8-1942, "War [...]", CAB121/464; Smith (1996), 22.
40 15–6-1942, N3098/30/38, FO371/32908.
41 18–6-1942, JIC18thMtg., JIC25/1, Box-214, RG218, NACPW in comparison with 24-12-1942, JIC45th Meeting, JIC25/5, Box-214, RG218; 19–6-1942, "Memorandum [...]", Box-214, RG218; 8–8-1942, JIC25thMtg., JIC25/2, Box-214, RG218.
42 18–6-1942, JIC18thMtg, JIC25/1, Box-214, RG218.
43 6–8-1942, JIC25thMtg, JIC25/2, Box-214, RG218.
44 18–6-1942, JIC18thMtg, JIC25/1, Box-214, RG218.
45 6–8-1942, JIC25thMtg, JIC25/2, Box-214, RG218.
46 18–6-1942, JIC18thMtg, JIC25/1, Box-214, RG218; 6–8-1942, JIC25thMtg, JIC25/2, Box-214, RG218.
47 18–6-1942, JIC18thMtg, JIC25/1, Box-214, RG218.
48 6–8-1942, JIC25thMtg, JIC25/2, Box-214, RG218.
49 1–6-1942, JIC(42)200(Final), CAB121/464; 1–6-1942, JIC(42)200(Final), CAB120/681.
50 6–1-1942, R&A#74, M1221, RG59; 11–5-1942, R&A#631, M1221, RG59. Mason transmitted the May report to the SD. 15–5-1942, 861.654/12, Roll-27, T1250, RG59.
51 14–4-1942, No. 1843, Roll-26, T1250, RG59.
52 20–5-1942, R&A#646, Reel-1, UPA1977.
53 1–6-1942, JIC(42)200(Final), CAB121/464.
54 22–6-1942, N3416/30/38, FO371/32909.
55 16–6-1942, "Present [...]", Box-3109, Entry-77, RG165.
56 1–7-1942, "Determination [...]", Volume I, Box-1602, Entry-47, RG319.
57 Ibid.
58 Ibid.
59 1–7-1942, "Determination [...]", Volume I, Box-1602, Entry-47, RG319.
60 1–7-1942, "Determination [...]", Volume I, Box-1602, Entry-47, RG319; Glantz & House (2000), 117–119.
61 7–12–1941, "8 A", WO106/5729.
62 25–1-1942, "War [...]", Box-3118, Entry-77, RG165.
63 23–1-1942, N514/30/38, FO371/32905.
64 1–3-1942, "Sir [...]", WO208/1794.
65 25–2-1942, N1585/30/38, FO371/32906.
66 30–3-1942, N1911/80/38, FO371/32921.
67 7–3-1942, N1291/30/38, FO371/32906.
68 Clarke (2002), 209.
69 1–4-1942, "USSR [...]", Box-3159, Entry-77, RG165.
70 1–4-1942, "Russian [...]", CCS350.05USSR, Box-212, RG218.
71 15–4-1942, "USSR [...]", Box-3084, Entry-77, RG165.
72 4–5-1942, Report No. 520, 319.1 Situation, Leningrad, USSR, Box-1053, Entry-47, RG319.
73 16–5-1942, "Comment [...]", Box-3172, Entry-77, RG165.
74 11–5-1942, N2547/80/38, FO371/32921.
75 1–6-1942, JIC(42)200(Final), CAB121/464.

76 22-6-1942, N3416/30/38, FO371/32909.
77 13–6-1942, N3429/30/38, FO371/32909.
78 30-6-1942, N3499/30/38, FO371/32909.
79 18–6-1942, JIC18thMtg, JIC25/1, Box-214, RG218.
80 The Five Year Plans were not considered to be completely successful, since they failed to achieve all they promised and had cost enormously in lives and effort; but G-2 was of the opinion that the plans had succeeded in raising the country's war potential to a significant extent. 1–7-1942, "Determination [...]", Volume I, Box-1602, RG319.
81 These two men were Stalin's old-time cronies and they did not perform well in the new military environment created by the German *Blitzkrieg*.
82 1–7-1942, "Determination [...]", Volume I, Box-1602, RG319; Glantz & House (2000), 391, 413.
83 15-1-1942, Despatch No. 1468, 861, Box-9, MECF1941–42, RG84.
84 10-3-1942, 370.2USSR thru 6–30-43, Box-1045, Entry-47, RG319.
85 15-1-1942, Despatch No. 1468, 861, Box-9, MECF1941–42, RG84.
86 20-3-1942, 2–6-1942, Despatch No. 1491, Roll-22, T1250, RG59.
87 1–4-1942, "Russian [...]", CCS350.05USSR, Box-212, RG218.
88 6–3-1942, "7A, [...]", WO208/1784.
89 11–5-1942, N2547/80/38, FO371/32921.
90 The JIC used the word industrial, but they must have meant total workforce considering its size. 1–6-1942, JIC(42)200(Final), CAB121/464.
91 22-6-1942, N3416/30/38, FO371/32909.
92 1–7-1942, "Determination [...]", Volume I, Box-1602, Entry-47, RG319.
93 15-1-1942, Despatch No. 1468, 861, Box-9, MECF1941–42, RG84.
94 1–3-1942, "Sir [...]", WO208/1794.
95 28–2-1942, 467839, Box-1856, Entry-141A, RG169.
96 10-3-1942, 370.2USSR thru 6–30-43, Box-1045, Entry-47, RG319.
97 R&A no. 535, M1221, RG59.
98 Roll-23, T1250, RG59.
99 20–3-1942, 2–6-1942, Despatch No. 1491, Roll-22, T1250, RG59.
100 10-4-1942, N1877/30/38, FO371/32907.
101 26-3-1942, N1658/1375/38, FO371/32988.
102 30-5-1942, N2849/1375/38, FO371/32988.
103 11-4-1942, N1901/1375/38, FO371/32988.
104 7–5-1942, N2488/80/38, FO371/32921.
105 11–5-1942, N2547/80/38, FO371/32921.
106 1–4-1942, "USSR [...]", Box-3159, Entry-77, RG165.
107 1–4-1942, "Russian [...]", CCS350.05USSR, Box-212, RG218.
108 16–5-1942, "Comment [...]", Box-3172, Entry-77, RG165.
109 1–6-1942, "Sir [...]", FO800/874.
110 1–6-1942, JIC(42)200(Final), CAB121/464.
111 18–6-1942, JIC18thMtg, JIC25/1, Box-214, RG218.
112 6–8-1942, JIC25thMtg, JIC25/2, Box-214, RG218.
113 1–7-1942, "Determination [...]", Volume I, Box-1602, Entry-47, RG319.
114 Ibid.
115 23-1-1942, N514/30/38, FO371/32905.
116 18-2-1942, "Sir [...]", WO208/1794; 25-2-1942, N1129/30/38, FO371/32906.
117 25-3-1942, "U.S.S.R. [...]", WO208/4563.
118 20-4-1942, "Soviet [...]", WO208/1804.
119 19-3-1942, N1480/30/38, FO371/32906.
120 18-12-1941, No. 25, AIR19/293; December 1941, "Report [...]", CAB121/459. Stalin's comments to Eden were also noted by G-2 in January 1942. 9–1-1942, No. 46167/MMT, 350.09 Intelligence*Russia, Box-1045, Entry-47, RG319.

174 The spring, the coming of summer and continued worries

121 23–1-1942, "Sir [...]", FO800/874.
122 25–2-1942, N1129/30/38, FO371/32906.
123 4–3-1942, N1333/30/38, FO371/32906.
124 25–3-1942, "U.S.S.R. [...]", WO208/4563.
125 15–5-1942, N2597/30/38, FO371/32908.
126 26–5-1942, N2968/80/38, FO371/32921.
127 Kalinin was a Soviet career politician who had been the president since the USSR's inception. Despite his title, and although he was a full member of the Politbureau since 1926, his actual influence over Soviet politics was very modest.
128 23–6-1942, N3295/30/38, FO371/32909.
129 26–6-1942, "No. 135/ [...]", AIR40/2344.
130 1–6-1942, "Sir [...]", FO800/874.
131 22–6-1942, N3416/30/38, FO371/32909.
132 1–6-1942, JIC(42)200(Final), CAB121/464.
133 1–6-1942, JIC(42)200(Final), CAB120/681.
134 1–6-1942, JIC(42)200(Final), CAB121/464.
135 6–6-1942, WP(42)246, CAB120/681.
136 13 June and 16–6-1942, "Prime Minister" and "C.I.G.S.", CAB120/681; Cantwell (1993), 5.
137 13 June and 16–6-1942, "Prime Minister" and "C.I.G.S.", CAB120/681.
138 2–8-1942, "War Cabinet, [...]", CAB121/464.
139 10-10-1942, "The [...]", WO208/1805.
140 December 1941, "Report [...]", CAB121/459.
141 "Summary of telegram received from General Mason McFarlane regarding his recent visit to the Russo-German front 26–28 January, 1942.", WO208/1755.
142 18–2-1942, "Sir [...]", WO208/1794; 25–2-1942, N1129/30/38, FO371/32906.
143 25–2-1942, N1585/30/38, FO371/32906.
144 25–3-1942, "U.S.S.R. [...]", WO208/4563.
145 11–4-1942, "MI3/C/DDMI/I/9/42", WO208/1798.
146 20–4-1942, "Soviet [...]", WO208/1804.
147 26–4-1942, N2214/30, FO371/32907.
148 1–6-1942, "Sir [...]", FO800/874.
149 If the Germans would use poison gas during their summer offensive, the Soviets were thought to be at an initial disadvantage, since the JIC had evidence indicating that the Soviets were not fully equipped for chemical warfare. 1–6-1942, JIC(42)200(Final), CAB121/464.
150 Ibid.
151 10–4-1942, "Report [...]", AIR46/21.
152 2–8-1941, "War Cabinet, [...]", CAB121/464.
153 10–1-1942, "Combat [...]", Box-3159, Entry-77, RG165.
154 19–1-1942, "Soviet [...]", Box-3154, Entry-77, RG165.
155 15–1-1942, Despatch No. 1468, 861, Box-9, MECF1941–42, RG84.
156 20–3-1942, 2–6-1942, Despatch No. 1491, Roll-22, T1250, RG59.
157 R&A no. 535, M1221, RG59.
158 1–4-1942, "USSR [...]", Box-3159, Entry-77, RG165; 24–4-1942, "Revised [...]", Box-3159, Entry-77, RG165; 12–5-1942, "Revised [...]", Box-3159, Entry-77, RG165.
159 The Armed Force's (including the NKVD) total manpower strength on 1 June 1941 was estimated to 4.97 million men. 1–4-1942, "Russian [...]", CCS350.05USSR, Box-212, RG218.
160 18–6-1942, JIC18thMtg, JIC25/1, Box-214, RG218.
161 Ibid.
162 6–8-1942, JIC25thMtg, JIC25/2, Box-214, RG218.
163 The Americans estimated that the navy had more submarines but fever battle-ships. The estimate for cruisers and destroyers was approximately the same. 18–6-

1942, JIC18thMtg, JIC25/1, Box-214, RG218; 6–8-1942, JIC25thMtg, JIC25/2, Box-214, RG218.
164 1–7-1942, "Determination […]", Volume I, Box-1602, Entry-47, RG319.
165 25–2-1942, "Comments […]", Box-3127, Entry-77, RG165.
166 R&A no. 535, M1221, RG59.
167 2–3-1942, "USSR […]", Box-3159, Entry-77, RG165.
168 1–4-1942, "Russian […]", CCS350.05USSR, Box-212, RG218.
169 It seems that guns with a calibre in excess of 152 mm were not included in the estimate. 1–4-1942, "USSR […]", Box-3159, Entry-77, RG165.
170 Ibid.
171 In another 1 April G-2 report the estimated June 1941 infantry division size was 17,750 men, the 1939 size was 17,200, and the February 1942 size was any number from 10,000 to 18,000 men, probably averaging 12,000 to 15,000 men. 1–4-1942, "Russian […]", CCS350.05USSR, Box-212, RG218.
172 From another 1 April report it can be assumed that the G-2 knew that newly created Soviet divisions did not have the same allotment of equipment as a June 1941 divisions. They even suspected that some newly recruited divisions during the winter of 1941–1942 had little more than rifles and small arms. Ibid.
173 G-2 estimated that at the time of the German invasion the number of factories making aircraft in the Soviet Union was 32. By October 1941, at least 7 of these were thought to have been in the hands of the Germans, and 19 of the remaining factories were considered as being within a 300-mile radius of the German front line. Ibid.
174 Ibid.
175 Ibid.
176 4–4-1942, "Estimate, […]", Box-3175, Entry-77, RG165.
177 18–6-1942, JIC18thMtg, JIC25/1, Box-214, RG218; 6–8-1942, JIC25thMtg, JIC25/2, Box-214, RG218.
178 1–7-1942, "Determination […]", Volume I, Box-1602, Entry-47, RG319.
179 10–3-1942, 370.2USSR thru 6–30–43, Box-1045, Entry-47, RG319.
180 13–3-1942, "General […]", Box-3142, Entry-77, RG165.
181 1–4-1942, "Russian […]", CCS350.05USSR, Box-212, RG218.
182 Ibid.
183 3–4-1942, R&A#620, Reel-1, UPA1977; 3–4-1942, Report No. 32, 353.8 Morale-Russia, Box-1045, Entry-47, RG319.
184 25–6-1942, "Michela's […]", Box-3126, Entry-77, RG165.
185 18–6-1942, JIC18thMtg, JIC25/1, Box-214, RG218.
186 6–8-1942, JIC25thMtg, JIC25/2, Box-214, RG218.
187 The Soviets were considered to be masters of fortifications. 1–7-1942, "Determination […]", Volume I, Box-1602, RG319.
188 Ibid.
189 19–6-1942, N3218/30/38, FO371/32909.
190 Smith (1996), 97–98, 117.
191 13–6-1942, N3429/30/38, FO371/32909.
192 10–3-1942: From M.A. Kuibyshew, Box-3146, Entry-77, RG165.
193 13–3-1942: "M/A […]", Box-3146, Entry-77, RG165.
194 20–3-1942, 2–6-1942, Despatch No. 1491, Roll-22, T1250, RG59.
195 1–4-1942, "Russian […]", CCS350.05USSR, Box-212, RG218.
196 15–6-1942, "Current […]", Box-3159, Entry-77, RG165.
197 18–6-1942, JIC18thMtg, JIC25/1, Box-214, RG218.
198 1–7-1942, "Determination […]", Volume I, Box-1602, RG319.
199 26–4-1942, N2214/30, FO371/32907.
200 20–4-1942, "Soviet […]", WO208/1804.

13 The first year of the Soviet–German war

How realistic were the assessments?

Obviously, assessments were more realistic in the sense that a Soviet defeat was no longer more or less assured, but instead a possibility. The defeat seemed more probable to the Americans than the British and therefore the British by now had acquired a more realistic perception of Soviet war potential. An analysis on a more detailed level seems to confirm this conclusion. Most of the assessments still support the notion that the Anglo-Americans underestimated the Soviets, even though the estimated Red Army losses are an exception in this respect. Actual Soviet losses were higher than the estimates, and the notion that German losses were higher than Soviet losses during the winter period was incorrect. Total Soviet losses from 22 June 1941 to 31 March 1942 were nearly 6.33 million men, of which more than 3.81 million were irrecoverable (permanent). Losses during the winter campaign, defined as taking place from 5 December until 30 April, were over 2.85 million, of which nearly 1.25 million were irrecoverable.[1] By comparison, German losses (excluding medical causalities) from 22 June until 31 March had been almost 1.11 million men, of which nearly 285,000 were counted as killed or missing.[2] On to this came the losses of Germany's Axis allies in the East, but their total combined losses were a fraction of German losses during the same period.

It is, of course, not that surprising that the Anglo-Americans underestimated Soviet losses (and thereby actually indirectly overestimated military efficiency) since they had little reliable information to base their estimates on, and also had uncertain information regarding the size of the Armed Forces and the capacity of the mobilization system. There were relatively few estimates produced regarding the size of the Armed Forces during the summer and autumn of 1941. There were some estimates concerning the number of divisions, but since it was not stated how large these were it is difficult to draw any precise conclusion. In addition, nothing was stated about various support troops at corps, army and front level. The G-2 estimated in October that the Soviet Army had 3.15 million men on the Soviet–German front, and an additional 750,000 men in the Far East. The Army's actual personnel strength at the time was likely considerably higher.[3] When Churchill told the House of Commons in September that the Soviets had 10 to 15 million men, of which nearly all were armed, it is hard to believe that he actually meant combat or front strength (or that it was anything other than morale-boosting propaganda). The MID stated in October that available manpower was 13 million, of which half had some kind of military training. By the end of June, 5.3 million reservists (including the pre-war mobilization) had already been called to active duty. More than 10 million men were mobilized during the first eight months of the war, and total wartime mobilization amounted to more than 29.5 million.[4] Since it is hard to know what the G-2 meant by "available" manpower, a comparison is impossible to make. G-2 estimates of manpower losses in October and November were somewhat understated, since these were actually over 2.7 million men during the third quarter of 1941.[5] Material losses during the same period were underestimated.[6]

When the Anglo-Americans tried to assess the size of the Armed Forces and mobilization capacity from the start of the Soviet winter offensive up to the German summer offensive, they (or at least the Americans) clearly seemed to underestimate the number of military aircraft available to the Red Army. Even by 1 January 1942 the total number of combat aircraft used by field forces numbered 5400, and the total available numbers amounted to 12,000, not counting military non-combat aircraft. Since actual Soviet output increased during this period (see above), it seems fair to assume that the first line strength would have increased during this period. The first shock of German airpower had already been absorbed during 1941, and poor weather during the winter hampered air operations.[7] On the other hand, the estimates of Soviet tank strength seem not to have been too low, possibly the other way around, since by 1 January the tank strength was 2200 in the field force and a 7700 total.[8] Information from another source indicates that the tank strength rose during the winter and spring of 1942.[9] It is very difficult to judge from the available information if the US estimate of gun strength was too high or low. However, according to Glantz & House (2000), gun and mortar strength as of 1 January was 48,600 and 30,000 in the field forces.[10] Since the output of guns really stepped up during the spring of 1942 it is likely that the US figure (26,500 guns, from 1 April 1942) was an underestimate.

It was not believed that there was any shortage of military manpower, but apart from Pika's optimistic assessments it seems that the military mobilization capacity was underestimated. The mobilization system raised 194 new divisions, and 84 separate brigades (with a theoretical strength of 4400 men each) up to 1 December 1941. After that date the Soviets formed an additional 86 rifle brigades up to early 1942. During the first eight months of the war more than 10 million men were mobilized.[11] By 31 December 1941, the mobilization had created the equivalent of "285 rifle divisions, 12 re-formed tank divisions, 88 cavalry divisions, 174 rifle brigades and 93 tank brigades". However, the figures in the last sentence also included 97 divisions transferred from the Eastern part of the country, and 25 relatively inferior "People's Militia" divisions.[12] Since the frontline strength of the Red Army increased from nearly 4.2 million men on 1 December to more than 5.6 million men on 5 July 1942,[13] despite the heavy losses in May and June, it seems fair to conclude that the

Soviets were able to mobilize more troops than most observers believed even in 1942. On the other hand, it also seems that these figures correspond rather well with estimates of active frontline strength during the period.

To compare the assessments regarding military efficiency (apart from caus-alities) with reality is in many ways complicated, since this covers many levels, from the highest command down to the single soldier in the field. Not much was reported on military efficiency during the very first months of the war, but the little there was did not present a very positive picture. It is hardly necessary to point out that Red Army's military efficiency was very inferior compared to the capabilities of the German *Wehrmacht* during this period of the war. This inferiority was of course also a reality for the other armed forces that faced the Germans at the beginning of the war in Europe and North Africa. For the Soviets this problem was of a persisting nature. Roger Resse states: "Poor training from the beginning – even before the German invasion – resulted in heavy casualties which necessitated quick reinforcement by large numbers of personnel and thus resulted in abbreviated training, thereby creating a per-manent cycle of poor training and high casualties, and excessive loss of mate-riel." The training of the higher military leadership also left much to ask for, and the problem of the poor training-high casualty cycle also applied to the officer corps. The training and education of officers and even generals during the war was not up to the standard it should have been.[14]

The tactical performance of the Red Army front-line troops was on a low level and the lack of training was one of the factors that accounted for this situation. The poor performance of the Armoured Forces during the beginning of the war could be attributed to the low level of tactical proficiency and training among officers, which in turn resulted in problems of control, command and inter-arms coordination. The lack of experience in armoured warfare, especially compared to Germany's *Panzer* troops, was also a contributing factor. Similar problems were affecting all other arms of the Red Army. During the summer of 1941 examples from actual combat demonstrated that the military units involved suffered from: "poor combat training [...] poor cooperation [...] low discipline", poor top-level administration, "insufficient training of comman-ders and staff", and "poor reconnaissance and intelligence gathering".[15] The Anglo-American assessments changed somewhat from the winter offensive onwards, even though they still correctly recognized that the Red Army stood at a disadvantage regarding military efficiency against the Germans even in 1942. However, it seems fair to say that the changing assessments also reflec-ted a real change in the combat capabilities of the Red Army, which improved over 1941 in 1942.

In 1942 almost every report on the subject noted the high morale of the Armed Forces. This certainly seems true. Those soldiers who had not been convinced opponents of the Germans and fascism at the start of the war had changed their minds in 1942, in the light of the brutal and criminal behaviour displayed by the German occupation forces. The political administration of the Red Army made sure that these facts became known to all Soviet soldiers, in case that they had not already experienced it first-hand.[16] It is probably also true that the very fact that the Soviets had manged to survive the German onslaught in 1941, and launch an offensive of their own, had contributed to strengthening the morale.

During the autumn of 1941 many commentators questioned Soviet military prospects and the very existence of the regime, but despite this, civilian morale was considered as being high by most observers. Even though some people in the USSR in reality, mainly in the western – newly annexed – parts of the country, welcomed the German invader temporarily or at least refused to fight for Stalin's regime, most people in the country, in the words of Reese: "remained loyal and supported the [Soviet] regime against the invaders".[17] This need not have to translate into high morale during every stage of the war, since even a low civilian morale does not necessary mean a lack of support for the regime. But it nevertheless indicates that the fundamental basis for high morale was there, and that the population in general supported the war effort. The short October unrest in Moscow, connected to the German offensive against the city, was only of a temporary nature and was not really a revolt towards the regime as such. In 1942 reporting on civilian morale and internal stability became more distinct, and as we have seen, the internal stability of the country and the regime was not questioned in general, even though there were some deviant opinions on this subject. And, as we have seen, the identification of a high civilian morale did not exclude continued worries for a faltering or even a collapse of the Soviet war effort.

Civilian morale was indirectly connected to the food situation. Even though there were some references to a food crisis during the fall of 1941, the scarcity of food was not seen as a major problem by most observers until the spring. Then many – especially American – observers predicted a very serious food situation that could lead to starvation and famine. Food was without doubt a scarce resource in the USSR even as early as the spring of 1942, but apart from the deaths caused by starvation in the besieged city of Leningrad, the situation could be described as serious but not critical. No large-scale outbreaks of starvation occurred – outside Leningrad – and the people of the most importance for the war effort had their food supply secured. This was also noted by some observers during the spring of 1942. On the other hand the food rations for the larger part of the population was meagre, and the overall health situation was affected to a certain extent by the scarcity of food already in 1942. Apart from the Leningraders, it was probably the inmates of the Gulag system who suffered the worst by the deteriorating food situation.

It is therefore hard to say that the Anglo-American observers were wrong, in general, concerning the seriousness of the food situation and the way in which the Soviet authorities managed the situation, although they were wrong in those cases (for obvious reasons) when they thought that it might lead to a collapse of the war effort. Therefore, it may be concluded that at least a few US observers during this period somewhat overestimated the difficulties caused by the food shortage. It is also worth noting that many Anglo-American observers, before Barbarossa, described the food situation as already being very strained.

The actual overall food situation was connected to the contraction of the economy, and especially the decreasing agricultural output caused by the turmoil of invasion and war. Many observers still noted the problems of the economy after the German attack, even though the focus shifted to the loss of economic resources due to the loss of territory. The notion of a declining national income was not mentioned by any observers; attention was instead on industrial production, agriculture and transport. Total actual industrial output (as well as national income) plummeted during the first six months of the war. According to Harrison the 1941 level of industrial output was as high as 98 per cent of the 1940 level, and the 1942 level was 86 per cent.[18] These figures indicate that all observers during the period overestimated the fall in industrial output, some of them to a considerable extent. On the other hand, there were very large declines in the output of certain industrial materials and in some specific branches, especially and specifically regarding civilian industry, which also was noted by the observers. Up to November 1941 the USSR lost between half and three-quarters of its production capacity in coke, iron ore, pig iron, coal, aluminium, crude steel and rolled steel. The loss in electricity output and railway lines was over 40 per cent.[19] Therefore, it is fair to say that the estimated temporary loss in output was correct in many ways, but that the total negative effects of the losses were clear overestimates. The figures for these branches in physical units show that the fall in actual output persisted during 1942. The first half of 1942 was the low point of heavy industrial output. This trend applies to all branches of industry except defence products.

Some of the estimates made during the spring and early summer of 1942 indicated that the British overestimated the economic capacity in certain respects. When the MEW (indirectly) estimated annual machine tool output at 49,000 units they definitively overestimated output, just as the JIC over-estimated the labour force when they estimated it to 65–70 million people. Actual Soviet machine tool output and labour force figures amounted to less than 23,000 and 55 million, respectively, in 1942. The true figure for labour also included the 11.3 million soldiers in the Armed Forces.[20] These figures may be compared with G-2's estimates, which estimated the workforce at 39 million and the machine tool output at 5500 units. The different estimates concerning basic industry output were more in line with reality than the figures quoted above, even though they at times revealed some overestimates. When the US and the British JIC assessed raw material and heavy industry output in June/July the Americans were closer to the truth, while the British overestimated output to a greater extent.[21] So while the output of some branches was overestimated, total industrial output was underestimated. This is, of course, not surprising when considering the importance of defence industry production during the war, and the fact that the output of this sector was underestimated. While basic industry, the consumer industry and engineering industry experienced falling output from 1941 to 1942, the defence industry increased its output from 148 per cent of the 1940 level in 1941 to 307 per cent in 1942.[22] The measurement here is economic value at constant prices, and does not fairly reflect the output increase in units since units prices decreased when output increased.

These figures included naval equipment and a more detailed overview of the weapon systems that was produced only for the Red Army reveals an even more impressive increase. Unit output of military aircraft, tanks, guns and mortars during the second quarter of 1941 (basically a peacetime quarter) stood at 2979, 1366, 6600 and 5100; increasing to 6600, 1981, 13,815 and 21,150 during the third quarter (which was completely dominated by war). Output of artillery shells increased from 15.8 to 29.7 million tonnes. There was a slump in output during the fourth quarter associated with the eastward evacuation of factories and the loss of territory/resources, but output soon picked up again during the first quarter 1942, and continued to do so during the rest of the year. Using the second quarter of 1941 as a benchmark reveals that munitions output (in units) increased by the following percentages to the last quarter of 1942: military aircraft, 179 (even more only counting combat aircraft); tanks, 383; guns, 496; and mortars, 865. The expansion of artillery shell output was more modest, only increasing by 179 per cent (measured in tonnes).[23] Even though these figures capture the combat value of the manufactured units better than using the economic values, it still does not tell the whole story. The tanks and aircraft (and to some extent the guns) produced in late 1942 were generally heavier (especially regarding tanks), and of a higher quality (in terms of performance) than the munitions produced in the second quarter of 1941. This clearly indicates that the various estimates of the output of war materials were a gross underestimate.

As we have seen, the assessments regarding munitions output had gone through revaluations during this period. During the summer and autumn of 1941, both US and British estimates put output at a few thousand tanks and aircraft per year, even in wartime. These assessments and perceptions, were changed radically during the Moscow Conference in October 1941, most probably as a result of information given to the Western representatives from Soviet officials. But these perceptions apparently made no lasting impression on the intelligence community in Washington and London, since later assessments – at least American – from 1942 once again put output at a much lower level than reality.

Judging by the low estimates concerning munitions output it is obvious that the Anglo-Americans underestimated Soviet industrial contingency capacity, and the ability of the Soviets to raise defence industry productivity. According to Harrison, while the productivity of the civilian industry fell during 1941– 1942 (98 per cent of 1940 productivity during 1941 and 82 per cent during 1942), the labour productivity of the defence industry increased to 149 per cent of the 1940 level in 1941 and to 234 per cent in 1942.[24] It is also hard to believe that the Anglo-Americans really knew the full extent of the military build-up during the 1930s. We have already seen that the Anglo-American estimates before the start of the Soviet–German war underestimated the actual peacetime munitions output. We also know that the actual military-industrial build-up during the Five Year Plans (1928–1941) before the war was massive.

There were also specific defence industry targets, established for the contingency of war. According to Samuelson there is indication that a central concern of the Soviet authorities during the early and mid-1930s was the enhancing of this capacity and guaranteeing a sustainable production of munitions during war. Soviet defence planning had two aspects: one plan for the actual production of armaments during peacetime, and one for war. Wartime contingency plans, of course, called for a much higher production of munitions than during peacetime. The capacity of the civilian industry to produce war material was one decisive aspect of the contingency capacity. The general economic development was therefore in many ways determined by the military dimension.[25] It is even fair to say that industry was built up with regard to its wartime capacity. Soviet contingency planning also tried to ensure the safety of industry from potential enemy invasion and bombing by the establishment of industrial evacuation plans. Many industrial enterprises close to the 1938 border were to be moved to their "shadow doublets" (companies that would be able to manufacture the same equipment as their mother companies during wartime) further to the East in the event of war.[26] It is obvious that many observers knew that Soviet industry had been transferred to the East during the war,[27] but it also seems that none realized the full extent of Soviet contingency capacity.

During the spring of 1942, US as well as British observers believed that Germany was producing more munitions than the Soviet Union. This was a gross relative underestimate of Soviet capacity in this respect, since in 1942 the comparable real value of German munitions output (including naval munitions) was about half that of the USSR.[28] If only munitions most important for ground warfare are compared, the Soviet advantage was much higher. But this mistake on the side of Anglo-American observers can probably also be attributed to their belief that the Germans had produced more munitions than they actually did.

The quality of Soviet armaments was also revalued to some extent during the first years of the war. Since they mostly underestimated the quality of Soviet munitions before the war this was of course a step in the right direction. The Soviets had also started to produce more modern aircraft by now, since the manufacture of many modern planes just had begun shortly before the war. When the full military-industrial mobilization ensued these production lines stepped up output, and the older models were phased out. This was also true to some extent regarding other weapon systems.

Munitions production, and the whole war effort for that matter, was dependent on a functioning transport (and especially railway) system. The transport situation was regarded as a major problem for the economy and a coming war effort during the whole period before 22 June 1941. Despite the forecasts from before the war (and in some cases at the beginning), the railways did not collapse due to the strain of war. In reality, the railway and transport sector in general was hit very hard by the war and the invasion. During the second half of 1941 transported railway freight was only about two-thirds (in tonnes/kilometre) of the traffic during the first six months of the year, and in 1942 it was only about half of what it had been in 1940. The productivity of the transport and communications sector (per worker) fell by about 14 per cent from 1941 to 1942.[29] After 22 June the transport sector was not only burdened by massive troop transports, enemy capture of transport resources and bombing, but also by the large-scale eastward transfer of industrial enterprises. That the USSR was able to maintain its war effort on an increasing scale, despite this situation, implies that the Anglo-Americans underestimated the capacity of the transport sector. On the other hand, some improvements were noted over time, and the very fact that transport did not "collapse" – in the sense that the war effort grinded to a halt – was, of course, evident to all observers.

Notes

1 Krivosheev (1997), 96–97, 104.
2 Halder, Volume VII, 293.
3 Glantz (2001), 68.
4 Glantz & House (2000), 292.
5 Ibid, 68, 298.
6 This conclusion can be drawn by studying pp. 293–294 and 306 in Glantz & House, (2000).
7 Glantz & House (2000), 87, 306.
8 Ibid, 306.
9 Ellis (1993), 230.
10 Glantz & House (2000), 306.
11 Ibid, 61, 63, 68.
12 Glantz (2001), 68.
13 Glantz & House (2000), 301–302.
14 Reese (2000), 123–126.
15 Ibid, 130–133.
16 Reese (2000), 113–114.
17 Ibid, 112–113.
18 Harrison (1996), 59, 93.
19 Harrison (1985), 64.
20 Harrison (1996), 272; Harrison (1985), 253.
21 See the indicated reports above compared to Harrison (1985), 253.
22 Harrison (1996), 68–69, 71; Harrison (1985), 254.
23 Harrison (1985), 251; Harrison (1996), 180; Samuelson (1999), 258.
24 Harrison (1996), 88.
25 Samuelson (1996), 243–250.
26 Samuelson (1999), 254, 263.
27 This fact stands in sharp contrast to Leshuk's statement that: "Major movements of people and equipment which would affect Soviet wartime military-industrial capabilities were missed by Western analysts." Leshuk (2003), 249.

28 In 1942 the Soviet Union produced munitions worth about 11 billion US dollars in 1945 prices, while Germany at the same time produced munitions to a value of 5.5 billion dollars. These figures can be derived by comparing Harrison (1994), 242 with Harrison (1990), 587.
29 Davies, Harrison & Wheatcroft (eds.) (1994), 305, 323.

14 The German summer offensive and Soviet prospects

For Hitler and the *Wehrmacht* the only way of winning the war in 1942 was to decisively defeat the USSR. Even though the German war effort against the Western Allies so far had been very limited their potential military strength was enormous. Germany would surely lose the war if she was forced to have the lion share her armed forces tied up fighting the Red Army, while at the same time being forced to fight the United States and the British Empire. Fortunately for Hitler and his followers, the United States was still only at the beginning of her mobilization process. After the losses suffered by the Germans so far, and the Soviets' tenacious defence and troop mobilization, the German Army only had the strength to attack concentrated on the southern third of the Soviet-German front (stretching from Leningrad to Rostov) this summer. The objective of the offensive was primarily to strike into the Caucasus region, where the major part of all Soviet oil output took place, and eventually also to reach the Volga and cut of the freight traffic on the major river. The mid-sized industrial city of Stalingrad, bearing the name of the supreme Soviet leader, was situated on the Volga's western bank. The Germans amassed large Armour and Air Forces for the offensive, which began in late June.

For the Soviets and the Red Army the winter offensive had been a strategic, albeit costly, success that pushed the Germans back from the Moscow. However, renewed setbacks had occurred during the spring and early summer in the Kharkov region and in Crimea and at Sevastopol. The Red Army suffered heavy losses in these operations. Even though the Soviet Armed Forces was a better fighting machine than in June 1941, it still had a long way to go in order to catch up with the skill and experience of the *Wehrmacht*. The German offensive quickly gained momentum and by the end of the summer the Germans was swarming over the North Caucasus region in the south-east and had reached Volga to the north-east of that region.

Even though the situation now was regarded as considerably brighter than a year ago, as we have seen, not even the British JIC – which by June was one of the most optimistic observers regarding Soviet strength and future prospects – did completely exclude a Soviet collapse before the winter of 1942/1943. The resumption of the German offensive prompted further concerns among some observers. The possible collapse of the USSR was especially a concern for the Americans. The JCS, the Joint Psychological Warfare Committee, the JPS and other institutions highlighted the subject from June to September.[1] In the latter half of July the tone was somewhat less optimistic regarding Soviet prospects among US military observers than it had been earlier in the month. On behalf of the Operations Division of the US General Staff, Assistant Chief of Staff Brigadier-General T. T. Handy requested an evaluation of the "Russian situation" on 8 July from Assistant Chief of Staff, G-2, Major-General G.V. Strong. Handy stated in his request that he wanted an evaluation relating to the situation as of 20 July, since a decision on "emergency operations in the European Theater in 1942 must be arrived at no later than August 1".[2] Strong replied in a memorandum dated 20 July, first describing the force and rapid progress of the German offensive in the South. No large-scale Soviet counter-offensive was foreseen and the German capture of Leningrad and Murmansk was anticipated, as was a German advance to the Volga between Saratov and Stalingrad. A German advance into the Caucasus was not credible in the near future; but on the other hand Strong did believe that the Germans would inflict a "crippling blow" on the group of armies around Moscow. As a result the Red Army would be forced to withdraw to the Volga. His report stated that by the beginning of the winter the USSR would have only around 50 to 60 per cent of its present "fighting power". Therefore he considered that the German could remove between 30 to 40 per cent of their ground forces and half their air forces from the USSR, and use them in other theatres.[3]

The tone also changed among the British. By mid-July, just as the German offensive had gained momentum, recent developments were commented on by the MI3(c). The Soviet Kharkov counter offensive (in May, see above) was described as a "fairly disastrous battle for the Red Army", even though the Sevastopol battle, relatively speaking, was (again) considered to have proven the Red Army's defensive ability. However, the easy German breakthrough in the South prompted the MI3(c) to revise its earlier estimates of the Soviet power of resistance. The Germans had been underestimated and the Soviets overestimated. How far the Germans would advance was an open question.[4] In a review written by Churchill, dated 21 July, possibly presented to the War Cabinet, the Germans were described as being militarily very powerful. This situation would continue into 1943–1944, and the Germans could always put up a "holding front" in the East, and bring back at least 50 to 60 divisions to the West.[5]

On 17 July the British Joint Planners still contemplated the possibility of a Soviet defeat and its implications for Allied strategy. But at the same time the JIC was convinced that the USSR would not collapse, even though they admitted on 30 July that it was possible that "light" German troops could reach Iran by November. On 2 August, and again on 19 August, the JIC took the view that not even the loss of Stalingrad and the North Caucasus would cause a Soviet military collapse before the winter.[6] By the end of July the British Air Ministry doubted that the Red Army could hold Stalingrad and

North Caucasus, but they saw no immediate reason to conclude that the Soviet army would be destroyed before winter.[7] The FO received reports from the Czechoslovak Minister to the Soviet Union by the beginning of August, which stated that the Soviet regime would not collapse even in the event of the German offensive being very successful.[8]

At the beginning of July Clark-Kerr reported to the FO that the position of Stalin's regime was firm. The risk of military defeats, even the loss of Moscow and Leningrad, would not alter that situation in his opinion, even if the regime were to be seriously shaken. The food situation was considered to be a more serious threat than military defeats, and Clark-Kerr did not believe that there was any alternative to the present regime or another kind of political alternative that the population could gather around. Apart from the food situation he also argued that if the NKVD and the militia should lose much of its power, the regime would in turn lose much of its grip over the population.[9]

When Cavendish-Bentinck minuted on Clark-Kerr's telegram a few days later he was more pessimistic about the regime's ability to survive in the face of military defeat. He referred to the Tsarist regime during World War I, and commented that "Russia had never been good stayers in long wars." He even went so far as to count the Soviets out of the war after February 1943, if they did not receive "tangible – apart from supplies – encouragement". If the Soviets did not defeat the Germans during 1942, or if the Western Allies did not open a second front, Stalin's position would be "shaken". But at the same time he argued that if a second front was launched, and it resulted in a military defeat of the invasion force, the situation would be even worse with respect to the stability of the regime. Clark-Kerr argued broadly along the same lines, when he stated that the Anglo-Soviet treaty (established in May) would not be enough to strengthen Soviet morale, unless backed up by a second front.[10]

As the beginning of August the MID made an estimate concerning Soviet war potential after Germany had conquered the Moscow Area, Southern USSR to the Volga and the Caucasus. Nothing was stated about the probability of this happening; but just the fact that such an evaluation was undertaken indicates that at least some in the MID considered it possible.[11] Harriman believed at the end of August (when attending a Lend-Lease Administration meeting) that there would be a Russian front in 1943, but that it was doubtful how effective it would be. He saw it as "fantastic" that the military in the United States and Great Britain did not recognize that the whole course of the war depended on the Soviet–German front.[12]

Notes

1 1-6-1942, JPWC17, ABC384USSR(6–1-42), Box-472, Entry-421, RG165; 8 August, JPS43, ABC384USSR(6–1-42), Box-472, Entry-421, RG165; 8–9-1942, "Notes [...]", ABC384USSR(6–1-42), Box-472, Entry-421, RG165.

2 8–7-1942, OPD381Russia(7–8-42), 319.1 Situation USSR, Box-1040, Entry-47, RG319.
3 20–7-1942, MID904(7–20–42), 319.1 Situation USSR, Box-1040, Entry-47, RG319.
4 15–7-1942, "M.I.3 Colonel.", WO208/1777.
5 21–7-1942, WP(42)311, CAB66/26.
6 Hinsley (1981), 101–102.
7 2–8-1941, "War Cabinet, [...]", CAB121/464.
8 8–8-1942, N4170/30/38, FO371/36911.
9 3–7-1942, N3485/80/38, FO371/32921.
10 Ibid.
11 4–8-1942, MID904(8/4/42), 091.3USSR, Box-1038, Entry-47, RG319.
12 Harriman & Abel (1976), 168–169.

15 The Anglo-American assessments in the context of the possibility to establish a Second Front in 1942

Even though the war in Europe was not of such immediate importance to the Americans as to the British, President Roosevelt laid great emphasis on the Soviet war effort. In November 1941 he declared that the survival of the USSR was vital to the defence of the United States, and ordered the inclusion of the Soviet Union in the Lend-Lease programme. On more than one occasion in 1942 he praised the great importance of the Soviet military effort against Germany. In May he wrote to General Douglas MacArthur, the commander-in-chief of the US forces in the South-West Pacific: "the Russian armies are killing more Axis personnel and destroying more Axis material than all other twenty-five United Nations put together". Three months before, sitting at his headquarters besieged by the Japanese on Corregidor in the Philippines, MacArthur cabled that "the hopes of civilization rest on the worthy banners of the courageous Red Army."[1] But according to A. Harrison (1951) and Matloff & Snell (1953), in anticipation of the German summer offensive on the Soviet-German front 1942, there were still serious doubts among US military authorities (including the JPS) as to the ability of the USSR to withstand the coming German onslaught (i.e. their summer offensive). The US planners believed that the outcome of this coming engagement "was the key to the European and possibly to the world situation". In June the general opinion of most British and US high-ranking military officials was that "they would be lucky if Russia managed to stay in the war through 1942".[2] As we have seen earlier, this was not quite true, at least and especially concerning British perceptions, even though a Soviet collapse was not completely excluded even by the British JIC in June. Of all observes, with the exception of Colonel Pika – who was not British and seen as overoptimistic by some British observers – the JIC was the most positive regarding Soviet future prospects. However, the essence of the last quote, attributed to most US and British high ranking officials, seem to be an exaggeration. They all feared that the USSR could be knocked out of the war, but the situation was perceived a markedly different than in the summer of 1941.

If one considers some of the reports from the early summer of 1942, it cannot be said that the British or the Americans believed that they "could be lucky" if the USSR stayed in the war during 1942. They reveal an attitude that actually counted on the USSR still putting up a front against the German Army at the end of 1942, although possibly far to the east of Moscow (of course this implies a much weakened USSR). It is therefore possible to conclude that at least most US observers believed very strongly in a Soviet collapse by the winter and spring of 1942, but that they changed their assessments during the early summer if one considers the 18 June US JIC report and the 1 July WD report prepared by the G-2. But later in July, when the German summer offensive was well under way, US assessments changed again. In the 20 July G-2 report it was anticipated that the Red Army would be forced to the Volga and that Soviet "fighting power" would be reduced almost by half. Since nothing was stated about a corresponding loss of German strength (it was believed instead that the Germans could transfer large amounts of troops to the West) this must have been a very depressing insight indeed. Furthermore, this report was prepared at the highest G-2 level with the specific assumption that it should form part of the basis for a decision on "emergency operations" in Europe. Even at the beginning of August it seems that the MID calculated on the USSR losing Moscow in addition to large areas of territory in the South and the Caucasus. If one considers the report from the Joint US Strategic Committee and other US institutions it seems clear that they too were very pessimistic concerning Soviet military strength during the summer of 1942. As we shall see below these pessimistic perception was seemingly also harboured by Roosevelt.

The question of an Anglo-American invasion of Western Europe, in order to alleviate German pressure on the USSR, was an important consideration for the Western Allies – of course, closely connected to the perceptions of Soviet strength and future prospects. In the summer of 1942 the reality was that Red Army and the Soviet front was holding, and by doing so they tied up the greater part of German military power. By comparison, while the British had a hard time fighting the around 50,000 German and 40,000 Italian troops in North Africa (the only place outside the USSR where the Allies actually fought German ground forces at the time), the Soviets faced nearly 3 million Germans and in addition also several hundred thousand other Axis troops. The home front of the United States, and for the most part that of the British Empire, was untouched by the war, while half of the European part of the USSR had fallen under German occupation. As already mentioned, the Anglo-American block controlled considerably more than half of the world's manufacturing output. The German U-boat menace was of course a very serious threat in the Atlantic, which had to be neutralized, but on the other hand the US and the British Navies were the strongest in the world. The Japanese military offensive since December had scored impressive victories in the Far East and the Pacific, but Japan was, despite her vast territorial holdings on the Asian continent, not a first-class industrial power. She was an industrial dwarf compared to the United States, and her troops stood a long way from the homelands of the Anglo-American powers (with the exception of Australia). Therefore it is not surprising that the Soviets pressed for the opening of a so called Second Front in Western Europe, since the facts of the Western Power's potential strength was not unknown to the Soviets.

It can also be argued that it was in the self-interest of the British and the Americans to invade Hitler's Europe as quickly as possible. Delaying would make it possible for the Germans to fortify and strengthen their positions in Western Europe (militarily as well as economically), and there was, of course, also the danger of a Soviet collapse, or at least a Soviet–German separate peace. With the Red Army out of the war most German troops in the East could be transferred to the West, and probably make it more or less impossible for the Western Allies to invade German-occupied Europe successfully anytime soon. It must also be remembered that due to the attrition and the heavy fighting in the Soviet–German war, not only the Red Army, but also the Germans, was losing a substantial amount of men and munitions on a daily basis.

The very idea of an invasion was not new in 1942, after all; since June 1941, the major part of German military strength was committed in the East. There were even individual G-2 officers already in August 1941 who urged for the creation of a Second Front, as soon as practically possible, in order to divert German forces from the Soviet Union.[3] Roosevelt repeated several times from December 1941 onwards that he wanted US troops in action on the European continent during 1942. In April 1942 the Americans suggested that an immediate build-up of strength should commence in England, in order to enable the Western Allies to launch an invasion in the spring of 1943 (Operation *Roundup*).[4] The option of a 1942 cross-Channel attack – Operation *Sledge-hammer* – was just a contingency plan, or as Averall Harriman put it in his memoirs: "a sacrifice for the common good", in the event of an imminent Soviet collapse.[5] The hope was that such an invasion might keep the Soviets from surrendering, if on the verge of collapse. *Sledgehammer* was an American attachment to *Roundup*, and would be undertaken (if launched) in September, involving a relatively small military force.[6] But Roosevelt's "openly declared position" was that US forces should take offensive action in Europe during 1942, and that this should "take precedence" over the preparations for a 1943 offensive if these two goals "were found to be inconsistent".[7]

Roosevelt's views on this subject were reflected in US military planning. In February 1942 the US War Plans Division wanted large US and British forces to engage an increasing number of German air and ground forces in north-western Europe by the summer of 1942 at the latest. According to Cline, Army Planner Colonel Hardy typified the War Plans Division when he declared: "Germany would completely defeat Russia in 1942 unless we move all possible forces to the United Kingdom for an offensive this year."[8] General Eisenhower concluded in early 1942: "We would be guilty of one of the grossest military blunders of all history, if Germany should be permitted to eliminate an Allied [Soviet] army of 8,000,000 men."[9] By the end of May, Roosevelt considered the situation on the Soviet–German front as "dangerous". By the middle of July Roosevelt still calculated on a Soviet collapse.[10] As early as 9 March Roosevelt "urged the British to consider the second front". On the same date the highest

British military leadership objected to a major landing on the grounds that too little was known of German strength on the continent and that it would be a gamble to use scarce British resources in such an undertaking. As late as 2 July the British had not convinced the Americans about the presumed folly of launching a cross-Channel attack, despite the fact that Churchill had gone to Washington in June to oppose Operation *Sledgehammer*. As late as 12 July, Churchill tried to convince Roosevelt to abandon that operation in favour of a North African attack.[11]

In May, the president made it very clear to his principal military advisers that he expected the creation of a Second Front in Europe during 1942 in order to help the Soviets, and not just a contingency plan.[12] But according to information – intercepted by German military intelligence in late May – that the head of the Coordinator of Information (COI) organization, Colonel William J. Donovan, was providing to foreign diplomats, the Western Allies would not launch a Second Front in 1942.[13] Regardless of Donovan's views actually being shared by the president in May, Roosevelt nevertheless went against his own military advisers in July, abandoning *Sledgehammer* in favour of the British alternative to invade North Africa later that year.[14]

Regardless of how sincere the Americans were in their intention to help the Soviet Union militarily, the Americans suspected the British of being less than sincere in their intentions. In early 1942 there was a widespread suspicion among US military officials that the British were more motivated by political than strategic interests concerning the defeat of Germany. The Americans favoured a direct approach, which included an early invasion of the European continent, and were less interested in the option of an Anglo-American invasion of North Africa (Operation *Torch*, launched in November 1942).[15] Campbell commented on the notion of a British political agenda in the following manner: "The [US] threat to take their resources away to the Pacific, in a word, was used by the Americans as a weapon in a debate about different ways of defeating Germany, in which the Americans early committed themselves to a cross-Channel assault as soon as possible, while they suspected the British, rightly, of backing away from that in favour of Mediterranean operations for which military arguments concealed political purposes."[16] The British and the Americans also had traditionally different military strategies: "The US tradition of military strategy advocated that battle should be joined as soon as possible at the point where the war would be decided, even though this might mean attacking where enemy forces were strongest. This derived from a confidence in the quality and strength of American forces, abundant resources, technological superiority and a preference for the direct approach. British military tradition, especially for a war on the continent of Europe, was quite different. Britain had always favoured indirect methods, stretching the enemy's resources by naval blockade and by involving the enemy in conflicts around its peripheries."[17]

According to Gaddis: "One of the main reasons why American strategists wanted an early invasion of Europe was their desire to help Russia."

Roosevelt was as concerned as his military advisers about the Red Army's capacity to withstand another German summer offensive. In May 1942 the Soviet Foreign Minister Molotov warned Roosevelt that the Germans could defeat the Red Army, unless an Anglo-American invasion could draw off 40 German divisions from the Soviet–German front. Roosevelt promised Molotov that there would be an Anglo-American invasion of Europe before the end of 1942, and WD strategists began planning an invasion of the French coast in the autumn of 1942. Roosevelt even put pressure on Churchill, demanding that he should assist in an invasion of France in August 1942. Churchill and the British COS vetoed this operation in July 1942, which made American military planners react violently.[18] According to archival evidence it can be argued that the British had already decided not to intervene on the Continent by the first half of June.[19] Roosevelt, who placed Anglo-American unity above any other consideration, accepted Churchill's plan for a North African invasion.[20] The British argued that *Sledgehammer* was too much of a risk, and besides, the US Joint Chiefs had to conclude that their position was weak since the British would have had to provide most of the troops for the invasion.[21] According to Gaddis the primary British reason for rejecting a cross-channel attack in 1942 was that they would have to provide the majority of the troops engaged, and that they dreaded the losses that such an operation would entail.[22]

There was probably, as some Americans suspected, politically oriented motives behind the reluctance of the British to invade in 1942. However, there may also be another dimension to this problem – namely, that the British were not as afraid of a Soviet collapse as the Americans were. As already shown there was a clear difference between US and British assessments regarding Soviet strength. The British considered Soviet military strength to be much greater than the Americans did during this period, in almost every respect. Maybe the most striking example of this was the difference in the assessments of Soviet munitions production. This difference alone was also probably the most important, since if the Soviets really did produce so few munitions as the Americans thought they did, it is not surprising that they saw the Soviet war effort as lacking in staying power. If British assessments were closer to the truth, the risk of a Soviet collapse was considerably smaller. A more risk-averse observer (than the British JIC) could of course object that the very absence of a second front in itself was a gamble, since it was possible that the Soviets could be forced out of the war in 1942 (which even the British JIC considered to be a, although remote, possibility). Even if the Germans were unable to completely crush the Red Army the strain of the war on the USSR could have resulted in a separate peace.

However, with hindsight it seems fair to say that the British and Churchill were right in their views regarding this matter. When Churchill and Harriman met Stalin in Moscow in the middle of August, 1942, the prime minister's main purpose in his visit was to tell Stalin face to face that there would be no cross-Channel attack that year. Churchill informed Stalin that the Western Allies could only put ashore six divisions (due to a lack of landing craft) in

September, and that the number of US troops and landing crafts would have multiplied by 1943. There were other arguments but this fact alone must be considered as very convincing.[23] It is easy to agree with FitzGibbon concerning this question: "At a better-informed level the Russians, like the British and American leaders and commanders, knew that a 1942 D-day could only have been a disaster for the forces involved."[24] In June 1942 the Germans had 27 combat divisions in the occupied West (excluding those in Denmark and Norway).[25] According to another source the Germans had 33 divisions in the West by August, but none of them were of the first line. At the Stalin-Churchill meeting the latter had deliberately distorted the facts and told Stalin that the Germans had 25 divisions in France, of which nine were first line.[26] But even so, if the Western Allies had invaded in September, it seems likely that the Germans could have reinforced these troops by transferring at least a few divisions to the West from the 171 German divisions on the Soviet–German front, or the nine divisions stationed in the occupied Balkans.[27] The Germans were not on the defensive in the East by this time, and it can be assumed that a Western Allied landing in Western Europe would have been given the highest military priority by Hitler and the OKW.

To Churchill the situation must have seemed to be even more serious at the time, since he personally believed in July that the Germans could transfer at least 50 divisions from the Soviet–German front, while at the same time containing the Red Army with a holding front (see above). With this perspective in mind, an Anglo-American cross-channel invasion with only six divisions must have been considered to be a very risky affair, to say the least. It must also be borne in mind that at this time the Western Allies had not yet achieved total air superiority over the Continent, in the way they did later in the war.[28] The Western Allies also fought the war in a different political context than Germany and the USSR. Since they were parliamentary democracies they could not fight the war in the same manner as the totalitarian states. Large military losses, especially coupled with defeat, would be received by a much more critical response by the home opinion than in a dictatorship.

Assuming that the British really had a political agenda, we can also be safe in assuming that they hardly wanted the Germans to knock the USSR out of the war. That would have meant that Germany could have exploited the natural resources in the East to a much larger extent than they really did during the war, and that they could have transferred most of the forces fighting on the Soviet–German front to the West and the Mediterranean instead. Furthermore, all the continuous and heavy losses in manpower, ground equipment and aircraft that were expended on the Eastern front every day – the brunt of German military losses during World War II – could have been used or converted to other military resources in a war against the Western Allies instead. In such a scenario, purely due to geographical proximity and overseas dependence, Great Britain would have been a more vulnerable target than the United States.

Therefore, it seems likely that at least a part of the explanation to the question of why the Americans were more eager than the British to invade the continent in 1942 can be found in the difference between these two nations' assessments of Soviet war potential. This can also to some extent explain why the US military were suspicious regarding the sincerity of the British intentions. We have also seen that Roosevelt was very sympathetic towards the Russians and the Soviet war effort, just because they were carrying a heavy burden in the war. According to Persico "Roosevelt was highly sensitive to the fact that the Red Army was losing eight Ivans for every Allied soldier killed in battle."[29] Roosevelt's feelings concerning this situation must have spurred his ambitions to some extent regarding his desire to launch a cross-Channel attack in 1942. Implicitly this also means that Roosevelt considered the Soviet military contribution to be very important (and why should he not, considering its magnitude). When he spoke to Henry Morgenthau (the secretary of the US Treasury) on 16 June, he stated: "the whole question of whether we win or lose the war depends upon the Russians".[30] It seems likely that most British observers also recognized the magnitude and paramount military importance of the struggle on the Soviet–German front, but that they were less worried about a negative outcome (i.e. a major Soviet defeat or a total Soviet collapse), since by the summer of 1942 they estimated Soviet military-economic strength as much greater than the Americans did.

There is no doubt that the Soviets put considerable pressure on the Western Allies during this period. Ambassador Standley sent information back to Washington about the grave political consequences for Allied unity if a large-scale Second Front did not materialize quickly. Furthermore, Roosevelt seemed to have really believed that "the Russians' assertions that their ability to stay in the war depended on relief from the pressure on their front". Standley reinforced him in his beliefs regarding this matter.[31] And, once again, there was plenty of US intelligence indicating that the Soviets really needed relief. Another factor probably exerting some pressure on the US decision-makers was the domestic press which was impatient and critical of US passivity.[32]

But the difference between US and British intelligence assessments regarding Soviet strength during this period add another dimension to the Anglo-American dilemma concerning a 1942 cross-Channel attack. It does not explain why the invasion did not take place, but it does to some extent explain why the Americans were eager to invade while the British strongly objected to the idea.

The discussion above also sheds some light on the former views concerning Anglo-American assessments of Soviet military prospects during 1942 (i.e. probable breakdown and disaster, mainly but not only displayed in the works of G. A. Harrison and Matloff & Snell in the first half of the 1950s). This picture is to a large extent still valid when consideration is taken of the somewhat larger array of sources used in this study. This question becomes even more interesting since Smith (1983) seems to suggest that the JCS (by referring to one JCS report from 20 June 1942) more or less counted on the USSR to stand up to the "full force of the German Army and the Luftwaffe" in 1942, even though she would not be unshaken. This would in turn (according to Smith) give the United States the time needed to attain full mobilization and develop her armed forces. Smith furthermore argues that the JCS strategy of avoiding a direct ground confrontation with Germany in 1942 depended "for effect on a cold calculation that" the Soviets could withstand German military pressure.[33] The report Smith refers to is without doubt the 18 June report cited in Chapter 12. Even though this report must be considered as bearing considerable weight, since the US JIC issued it, it was not the only report on the subject at the time. Furthermore, it must be regarded as something of an exception since it was the only US report from the period that actually predicted that the Red Army would be able to bear the German onslaught without any serious consequences, if the statement that the USSR would be able to continue to wage war after the offensive, but "on a greatly reduced scale", is not counted.

It was also stated in the report that the Soviet Union would be able to continue to wage war after the German offensive, but "on a greatly reduced scale". The fact that the Soviets could be able to hold a front would not mean that they would be able to damage the invader in a serious and aggressive manner, as they actually did in the Stalingrad offensive in November. If the Soviets should be very hard pressed, the Germans might get an opportunity to transfer large number of troops to the West, which was feared in other US reports from the period and by Churchill. At any rate, Roosevelt and the Americans continued to press for a Second Front well into July.

Notes

1 Gaddis (1972), 5, 37; Keegan (ed.) (1989), 72–73, 214.
2 Harrison (1951), 11, 25; Matloff & Snell (1953), 180–181, 221–222.
3 Matloff & Snell (1953), 177.
4 Greenfield (1963), 12–13, 58.
5 Harriman & Abel (1976), 132; Greenfield (1963), 13.
6 Even if it were considered an unlikely event at the time, *Sledgehammer* would also be launched if the Germans should crumble, in order to finish them off. Greenfield (1963), 28.
7 Greenfield (1963), 59.
8 Cline (1951), 149–150.
9 Gaddis (1972), 67.
10 Bennett (1990), 56, 59.
11 Dunn (1980), 192–193.
12 Harrison (1951), 11, 25; Matloff & Snell (1953), 180–181, 221–222.
13 Persico (2001), 185.
14 Greenfield (1963), 13.
15 Gaddis (1972), 66–67; Keegan (ed.) (1989), 116–117.
16 Campbell (1985), 222.
17 Folly (2002), 44.
18 Gaddis (1972), 67–70; Dunn (1980), 13.
19 In fact, already by 8 June, at a COS meeting attended by the prime minister, it was stated: "It should be made clear that a 'SLEDGEHAMMER' could only be undertaken this year as a contribution to the speedy downfall of the Germans, after the Russians had succeeded in undermining their resistance." 8-6-1942, COS (42)51stMtg.(0), CAB121/459. A document dated 26 June originating from the Air Ministry, addressed to many of the highest ranking British military officials and

the minister of defence, stated: "As you will be aware it has been found necessary to abandon the idea of substantial land operations on the Continent this year." 26–6-1942, "Webber W.681", CAB121/459.

20 General Eisenhower, who later led the North African invasion, was bitter over the cancellation of the European invasion. Gaddis (1972), 67–70.
21 Greenfield (1963), 57–58.
22 Gaddis (1972), 69–70.
23 Harriman & Abel (1976), 152.
24 FitzGibbon (1976), 273.
25 Ellis (1990), Table 35 (Statistical Appendix).
26 Dunn (1980), 190–191.
27 Ellis (1990), Table 35 (Statistical Appendix).
28 Dear & Foot (eds.) (1995), 20, 22.
29 Persico (2001), 299. The final ratio of Soviet contra Anglo-American soldiers killed was much higher. It was more than double the ratio that Roosevelt referred to. Dear & Foot (eds.) (1995), 290.
30 Bennett (1990), 57; Dear & Foot (eds.) (1995), 758.
31 Bennett (1990), 58–59.
32 Poulsen (1982), 235.
33 Smith (1983), 142–143.

16 The autumn assessments and the battle of Stalingrad

Even though the German offensive appeared menacing during the summer, it soon bogged down during the autumn. In the Caucasus, which at the beginning had been the prime target for the offensive, the oil wells in Maikop and Grozny fell into German hands. But the real prize in terms of oil output, the Baku wells, could not be reached by the *Wehrmacht*. The German troops established contact with the Volga further to the North but they had still not taken the whole city of Stalingrad. Street fighting with heavy losses on both sides commenced during the autumn. Hitler continued to underestimate the Red Army and the USSR, and the Germans were basically unaware of the Soviet offensive preparations. They prepared two great offensives, Operation Mars and Uranus. The first was directed towards Army Group Centre, but ended up in a costly failure, apart of course from the fact that it drew German reinforcements and attention during a critical time period.

The second offensive would become much more famous since it successfully encircled the Germans and other Axis forces around Stalingrad, ultimately sealing their fate. Even though the fighting in Stalingrad was connected to the offensive on a strategic level, it were largely separated operationally, since the objective of the forces participating in Uranus was to punch a hole in the Axis front, north and south of Stalingrad, and not to participate in the city fighting. The operation also opened up a wide whole in the German front, through which the Red Army could advance relatively quickly. The offensive brought the frontline back into Eastern Ukraine, before stabilizing, forcing the German troops in the Caucasus to evacuate the region. A German attack in order to relief the encircled Stalingrad troops failed, and at the beginning of February the still surviving troops in the pocket surrendered. For the Red Army this was a victory of the first magnitude, which also proved that the Soviets successfully could stage an offensive involving fast mobile mechanized troop.

16.1 Prospects and civilian morale

The Anglo-Americans continued to observe the internal situation and Soviet prospects during the fall. Four US reports from August to November – from the Joint US Strategic Committee[1], the US Consular-General at Vladivostok[2] and the OSS[3] – did not reveal much new information in principle about the internal situation, but rather confirmed that it was stable and that the population was behind the war effort. Reports from Pika and British MI in October gave the impression that the Soviet internal situation was satisfactory. Pika believed in his 7 October report that despite the hardships suffered by the population, the situation as a whole would proceed "satisfactorily" since he considered that there were "no limits to the toughness of the Soviet population".[4] Through a most secret official Hungarian source – the Hungarians were waging war alongside the Germans against the Soviets – British MI learned in October that the Hungarians considered that the Soviet internal situation was not yet critical, despite difficult economic conditions. It appears that MI3c agreed with the Hungarian point of view.[5]

At the 161st British Joint Planners meeting, held on 1 October, Admiral Miles, who had followed Mason-MacFarlane to the USSR in 1941 as the head of the Naval Section of the 30 Mission, expressed his worries about a possible breakdown in civilian morale during the winter, due to the shortage of fuel and food.[6]

In a report to the War Cabinet dated 2 December, also seen by the US JIC, the British JIC took the position that although the population was experiencing hardship and privation, civilian morale was good. In any case, possible problems with civilian morale were not likely to spill over to the military or the essential industrial workers.[7] The US JIC, which commented on the British report in January 1943, was in general agreement with the British regarding civilian morale.[8]

Other reports from the US embassy,[9] from British intelligence[10] and the FO[11] – in December and January 1943 – all indicated that the morale of the civilian population in the USSR was high. In a late January 1943 report prepared by the G-2 (signed by Lieutenant-Colonel W. S. Culbertson), the possibility of a Soviet–German separate peace was examined. The general trend of their findings seemed to be that the possibility of a separate peace was slim. Several factors were analysed in the report. Civilian morale was considered high and there was no danger of a Soviet collapse.[12]

At first the Anglo-Americans did not expect a Soviet winter offensive, not even the usually optimistic Pika, although he changed his mind later on. He stated in a late September report that it was improbable that the Soviets could stage a major offensive due to a shortage of tanks and aircraft.[13] According to another Pika report, originally from 3 October, commented on by MI3(c) and MI14 later in October to form an abridged version, the Soviet ability to continue the fight against the Germans was not in jeopardy, despite the earlier German breakthrough and the critical situation.[14] In yet another report from Pika, dated 19 November – the very same day the Soviets started their (Stalingrad) winter offensive – but commented on somewhat later by the FO, he expressed the belief that there would be some sort of major Soviet offensive during the winter.[15]

Through the official Hungarian source, British MI had received a summary of the political and military situation in the USSR as of 1 September. In late

October the MI3(c) commented on and agreed with several points the source made. Even though the Red Army could not be completely defeated in 1942, it was seen as probable that it could be so weakened that it could not offer any threat to the Axis forces during 1943.[16]

Apparently the British JIC did not entirely exclude the possibility of some kind of Soviet defeat as late as 18 September, and once again in October.[17] But on 2 October they argued that the Germans would not be able to make any more progress in the Caucasus before the spring. No major threat to Persia and Iraq was foreseen before the spring of 1943.[18] The COS accepted the JIC's assessment, but not until the beginning of November did they conclude that any further German advance was unlikely.[19] Nevertheless, in November the JIC showed continued concern for the Red Army's ability to defend the South of Caucasus (the Germans were occupying the Northern parts). The Soviets were considered able to defend the Southern parts of Caucasus at least until April 1943.[20] This assessment implies that they counted on that the Germans could hold on their positions in the Caucasus until the spring.

The British JIC paper on this matter was noted at the US JIC's 45th meeting on 24 December.[21] In a report issued 13 January 1943, discussed at the 48th meeting, the US JIC concurred with the British view of the Soviet ability to defend South Caucasus. And they pointed out that there were current indications that the Soviets might not have to worry about this problem within the contemplated period.[22] By the time the report was issued the German Sixth Army was already surrounded in the Stalingrad area, and the Red Army was shattering the larger part of the German Southern Front, and chasing the Germans out of the Caucasus.[23] At the 58th meeting of the British JIC, held on 1 December, Clark-Kerr attended and answered the question of a possible Soviet–German separate peace during 1943. He believed that it was not possible on the condition that the United States and Great Britain continued their offensive against Germany. Morale in the USSR was good, but if no second front materialized during 1943 the situation could change for the worse.[24]

When the last German troops surrendered in Stalingrad on 2 February 1943, the German Army had suffered a very heavy defeat over the whole southern wing of the Soviet–German front.[25] On the very same day the OSS director Donovan wrote a letter to Brigadier-General John R. Deane, attached to the JCS. The letter not only highlighted Donovan's views concerning Soviet future prospects, but also considered some important differences regarding this subject between the British MEW and the OSS. The OSS had a group in Great Britain that was working with the MEW on Soviet capabilities. Evans, Morgan, Robinson and Morse of the OSS were involved in the discussion, and according to them all the OSS R & A personnel, who had been working with the British, had experienced what Donovan referred to as "British over-optimism". According to the very preliminary conclusion of Robinson, "the resources behind the Russian front are diminishing and the effort being made by the Russians at the front cannot be continued for long at the present scale". According to Morse's very tentative conclusion it was not possible for the Soviets to "win a decisive general victory over the Germans", if the British and the US effort continued to be limited.[26]

According to the OSS there were three probable explanations for the current heavy Soviet effort: "A. Prior to an enforced reduction of Russian effort, the Russians are counting on early development of heavy Anglo-American operations. B. The Russians are counting on a possible situation to be produced by their present heavy expenditure in which the Germans will not attempt a large-scale offensive against them in 1943, and as a result a relapse into defensive warfare of low military expenditure by both powers on the Russian front. C. Russians are counting on this heavy expenditure to produce a separate Russian compromise and a trading position with the Axis." There were fears of a separate peace, and large sacrifices were expected from the British and the Americans to keep the USSR in the war in order to prevent even greater Anglo-American sacrifices in the future.[27] At about the same time Roosevelt was also among those who feared a separate peace.[28]

16.2 The economic situation

US assessments regarding the economic performance of the economy continued to be rather depressing during the late summer and autumn. In a special study dated 1 August 1942, G-2 analysed the machine tool position. In the war industries of the time machine tools were the instruments used to manufacture most of the parts that went into munitions. The total 1941 output was estimated at 26,700 units, in addition to an import of about 2500. Depending upon which figure you believe in the report, the total number of machine tools at hand in 1941 was either 339,316 (as of 1 December) or 411,314. The quality and complexity of the machines was not up to US standard. G-2 stated that the USSR "did not have an adequate machine tool base for a prolonged war" when the Germans invaded, and the prospects for building up a machine tool industry during wartime were not considered bright. They estimated that 78 per cent of total production capacity was lost as a result of enemy occupation, or in the eastward evacuation process. Therefore the annual production capacity left was only 5500 units.[29] Furthermore, the losses and change inflicted on the industry had reduced its productivity. It was stated: "The drop in production has been so great that the industry today provides virtually no base whatsoever for adequately supplying the munitions industries, etc. with new machines to carry on the war."[30] The estimated annual output was much below the actual level (22,935 lathes and 2210 presses);[31] it was also far below the level estimated by the MEW earlier in the year.

Around the same time (the beginning of August) the MID estimated that if the Soviets were forced to withdraw to a position where only the Urals and Siberia would be left to them, they would not have the strength to launch any sustained offensives. This area of the USSR was estimated to have between 40 and 50 per cent of the economic war potential of the whole country at the beginning of hostilities in 1941. Judging by the concluding remarks in the memorandum, these percentages probably referred to the armaments and munitions production capacity of the area. But several serious weaknesses were identified in the economic branches supporting this potential effort, mainly in transport, food, clothing and consumer goods.[32] Even though it is hard to exactly establish how large the munitions capacity of the Ural-Siberia was in June 1941, it seems that the MID figure was too high, since the transfer of war important industries to the east had not taken place yet at that time. However, the actual capacity of the region in the late summer of 1942 probably was higher than 40–50 per cent.

In their August report the Joint US Strategic Committee analysed the whole Soviet economy. The economy was still suffering from the same problems now, as at the beginning of the war, regarding the handling and production of industrial goods and raw materials. But it was also recognized that the economy "stood up under attack very much better than was feared". The total loss of production capacity was estimated to be at least 35 per cent. That the Soviets were still resisting was seen as an indication of "a hidden plus-factor in the resources of Urals-Siberia". The Committee argued in the following manner: despite the fact that the invasion had robbed the USSR of vital resources, and reduced her economic war potential, she could still maintain her troops on a broad front due to the unexpected and increased productive resources of the Urals, the Caucasus and other areas. The loss of the Ukraine was seen as a major setback to the economy, which would have serious consequences in the long run. In the short run, however, the loss could be compensated by large stockpiles. The estimated overall loss of raw material production capacity was extra severe with respect to aluminium (60–80 per cent), and coal, iron ore and pig iron (60 per cent in all cases), but somewhat less concerning steel (50 per cent). The capacity loss regarding electric power, manganese ore and nickel was 35, 30 and 30 per cent, respectively, while the output loss in petroleum and copper was estimated as only "negligible". The USSR almost entirely lacked tungsten, molybdenum, cobalt, vanadium, tin, antimony and magnesium. The output capacity of the machinery and metal goods sector had fallen by 40 per cent.[33]

If true, the last figure especially would have been very serious, since output in this sector during wartime more or less was tantamount to munitions output; but as we already have seen the fall in total industrial output in 1942, compared to 1941, was much more modest, and munitions output (if counted as a separate sector) had, of course, increased drastically.

According to another estimate the same month, made by an "ordinarily reliable source", submitted to Assistant Secretary of State Adolf A. Berle and US military intelligence by FBI Director Hoover, the Soviets had lost the following within the designated production areas: steel, 60 per cent; iron ore, 65 per cent; coal, 50 per cent; aluminium, 80 per cent; cereal grains, 30 per cent; and sugar beets, 90 per cent.[34]

Despite the fact that the loss of raw materials and natural resources was stressed in several reports during 1941–1942, some observers pointed out that the Soviets had rather large reserves of raw materials at hand. In a report from early September, discussed during the US JIC's 29th meeting, the loss of the oil and manganese resources in the Caucasus region was not considered to have serious implications in the short run. The stockpiles of oil and manganese were sufficient to mitigate the effects of the eventual Caucasian raw material losses on military strength for a year.[35] A similar opinion was expressed at the 161st meeting of the British Joint Planners, when on 1 October, Admiral Miles – who had followed Mason-MacFarlane to the USSR in 1941 as the head of the Naval Section of the 30 Mission – stated that even if Stalingrad fell, the oil position would not be affected for a "considerable" time.[36] Reports produced as a result of correspondence between the FO and the Ministry of Fuel and Power during the first half of August also confirmed that the Soviets could manage for a long time, at least 12 months, despite the possible cutting of the major part of the Caucasus supplies. This was mainly seen as possible due to production from other oil wells and due to stocks.[37]

Otherwise British reporting on the economy during the late summer and autumn was relatively scarce. When Churchill visited the USSR in August he and Stalin discussed some aspects of the Soviet need for war resources. Stalin stated that the Soviets were very short of aluminium for the remainder of 1942. Their discussion was later produced as a part of a War Cabinet paper.[38] In early August Clark Kerr submitted a memorandum from Kuibyshev, written by the embassy's First Secretary Lambert. His impression was that the economy was wasteful and that too little attention was paid to maintenance. Even though the USSR was seen as an improvement over Imperial Russia, he connected the general inefficiency of the county with "Slav mentality". In the long run he saw potential for improvement. One specific Russian problem was that the abundance of resources made the economy, organization and the full exploitation of resources lax. One FO official commented that Lambert's report (in general) was superficial, since he had been there for such a short time (four months) and only socialized with diplomats and journalists.[39]

As usual, information from Czech origin painted a brighter picture of the situation than most Anglo-American assessments. Reporting from the Czech minister to the USSR, noted by the FO in August, indicated a growing war industry in the Urals and the Kuzbaz areas, and that the country was self-supporting in raw materials.[40] In a Pika report from 7 October, also later signed by Bruce-Lockhart, the economic situation in the face of winter was partly seen as worse than last year. The additional losses of agricultural land and some industries this year were considered as something that would be "severely felt". But he also identified some positive aspects in the overall economic situation, as he considered that transport had improved and that the experiences from the last winter could be used this time. He estimated that industrial production for civilian needs was about 40 per cent of the original plan, a condition that would mean much suffering for the population. It was noted that considerable restrictions had been introduced for the first time in the use of oil, fuel and petrol.[41]

In November the MEW also noted the problematic raw material situation, or more specifically the shortage of coal, in a report that also was sent to various US agencies the following month. The perceived shortage had a negative impact on the war potential, which was caused not only by the fall in output but also by the alleged fact that the distribution of the coal to the production centres was disturbed by transport problems.[42]

In late 1942 the OSS, successor to the COI organization and the CIA's forerunner, produced what by all accounts was their first comprehensive report on Soviet war potential, in a series called "Military Potential of the Soviet Union". The third part, from late November, was about basic industry capabilities. Like other observers this autumn, they also wrote about coal shortages (estimated annual output 80–100 million tonnes), mainly due to transport problems, that affected steel output negatively. A steel shortage was therefore in effect. The annual steel output of 10 million tonnes was considered enough to match the current quantity of steel the Axis powers were committing to the Soviet front, in the form of armaments and ammunition, but not sufficient for non-military needs. The minimum annual requirement of steel was estimated to 12 million tonnes. But it was impossible to estimate whether or not there was sufficient plant capacity in the machinery and metal-working industries in the Soviet-controlled area to convert the 10 million tonnes of steel into munitions to the full amount. Therefore it was seen as uncertain if the Soviets could actually match the Axis expenditure on arms and ammunition on the Soviet–German front.[43]

The output of non-ferrous metals was estimated as being below the actual requirements with regard to aluminium (60,000–75,000 tonnes and 132,000–171,000 tonnes required), copper (160,000–200,000 tonnes of black copper and 203,000–243,000 tonnes required), lead (maximum of 90,000 tonnes and 135,000–174,000 tonnes required), zinc (56,000–58,000 tonnes and 98,000–100,000 tonnes required), nickel, and tin (2000 tonnes and 20,000 tonnes required). Most of the requirements, except in aluminium and nickel, were considered as being satisfied by Lend-Lease or other imports. The current requirements of oil could not be estimated, but the greatest problem in this respect was not considered to be either the output (29.6 million metric tonnes of oil and gas on an annual basis) or the refining capacity (a minimum of 24.4 million tonnes), but transportation problems. The Soviets had around 400,000 machine tools, with enough existing plant facilities for the fulfilment of the most current replacement needs for machines. The Soviet request for more machine tools via Lend-Lease was seen as an indication of a need for certain machines in excess of domestic output.[44]

In an early December British JIC report on Soviet strength during the winter of 1942–1943, shared with the Americans[45], it was estimated that the "industrial potential" was 60–70 per cent of the pre-war level. The non-military output was considered as reduced to a minimum, since the main industrial effort was spent on munitions. The JIC identified some deficiencies in certain commodities, primarily aluminium, tin, nickel, copper, special steels and rubber. Even though no shortage of oil was foreseen, it was predicted that a shortage of certain oil derivatives, such as some forms of aviation sprit, could occur. Allied shipments were considered to have alleviated at least some of these commodity shortages.[46] In mid-January 1943 the US JIC commented on the British paper in a report, examined during their 48th meeting. The overall losses of industrial potential were estimated instead to be close to 50 per cent. But the Americans considered that it was better to estimate losses within certain branches, and to take account of their specific importance for the war economy. The shortages in some strategic commodities were not quite covered by western aid. Aluminium and nickel were two of these, since the Soviet aluminium requirements were estimated at 132,000–171,000 tonnes per annum, and the total available supply was estimated at 108,000–123,000 tonnes, and the annual nickel deficit was estimated at about 10,000 tonnes, which was not entirely made up by the Allied deliveries of 7200 tonnes.[47]

The US military attaché in Turkey, Colonel C. C. Jadwin, reported to the MID in January that the Turkish ambassador to the USSR (rated as fairly reliable by the MID) believed that it did not appear as if the Soviet Armed Forces was suffering from any imminent shortages of petrol or oils.[48] According to a MI3(c) report from January on the observations of a US military visiting the Don front in early December, the industrial output of the USSR was overstrained, and was expected to continue to be so in a war of attrition.[49]

As evident from the above the transport sector was regarded as insufficient in the sense that it hampered the operations of other branches. A few reports also touched more specifically on the transport problem. The (August) Joint US Strategic Committee report described the transport system as one of the greatest problems of the war effort, and the poor state of rail and road transport was a "serious limitation", both to military operations and to industrial production.[50] British MI reported in September on the problematic labour and organizational conditions that affected the efficiency of the railways.[51] Pika was less gloomy when he in his 7 October report described improvements in the organization of transport and in distribution, and argued that railway transport had undergone a considerable improvement.[52] The same month the British MI received information from a military source stating the rail transport had "been steadily improving".[53] However, in December the British JIC came to the conclusion that transport was the most important limiting factor on the war effort, both with regard to industrial output, distribution of food, and the mobility of armies. But the main transport branch, the railways, was – although operating under considerable strain – regarded as in a good enough state to operate sufficiently.[54] In a January 1943 report, examined at their 48th meeting, the US JIC stated that they were in general agreement with the British regarding transport, with some minor exceptions.[55] The JIC assessments can to a certain extent be seen as a turning point in Anglo-American perceptions regarding the railways and the transport sector. The earlier fear that this sector would bring about a collapse of the war effort seems to have disappeared, even though the transport sector's limited capacity still was regarded as a factor that hampered the war effort in general.

A 10 December telegram from Brigadier-General Patrick Jay Hurley to President Roosevelt described a visit undertaken by a delegation of US officers to the Stalingrad front. Hurley had been the secretary of war (1929–1933) in Hoover's administration, and was now travelling around the world as Roozevelt's representative. Even though he saw improvements in the military efficiency of the Red Army, its transport and supply problems would become more and more difficult. His inevitable conclusion was therefore that the defeat of the Axis in the USSR must "depend more and more on supply assistance from the United States".[56] Many British institutions, including the FO and Lord Halifax, also noted Hurley's report in December.[57] Hurley's aide at the front visit, the assistant US military attaché Lieutenant-Colonel Richard Park, Jr., reported in January 1943 to the Joint Strategic Committee on the rudimentary conditions of supply transport to troops at the front. Park later reported that supply communications were not good, and that the main rail line lacked necessary facilities. The supplies were brought by train to the railhead and then dumped, and then the troops had to collect them. This was done in an *ad hoc* manner with help from the local peasants: "Anybody with a one horse cart, or horse, or a wheelbarrow, are put in the communication line." Park saw this as a key to what he regarded as Soviet success in supplying the troops. Nevertheless, the US Mission saw many trucks being used on their visit in the area.[58]

16.3 Food supply

Anglo-Americans expressed concern for the food situation during the earlier part of the year. This concern was not surprising, considering that the Germans had occupied the Ukraine and other agriculturally important areas of the USSR. It must be remembered that a problematic food situation played a part in the downfall of the war efforts of Imperial Russia and of Germany in World War I, something that most observers of the Soviet situation probably were well aware of. In the summer of 1942, even more fertile agricultural lands were taken away from the Soviets as the German troops advanced in the North Causcasus region.

The German advance in the South prompted further concerns among the British about the food supply in several reports. This can in some respects be seen as a shift away from the more optimistic British assessments, which were made during the spring and early summer. In a late July report from the Air Ministry this was described as the potentially most dangerous situation, even though the word starvation was avoided in most reports.[59] The critical food situation was confirmed by several FO reports during July, August and September.[60] In a report from the CIGS to the DMI it was considered that the food situation might curtail the Soviet will to resist in the autumn. The 1 July grain area under Soviet control was estimated at 75 per cent of the pre-war area.[61]

The MEW produced a report on the food situation in relation to the war potential, dated and presented to the War Cabinet 21 July, which pictured a very serious situation, but no starvation except in Leningrad. Further German occupation of grain land could be handled. The system of differential rations for different groups of workers was giving assurance for the war effort. It was stated that the Soviets controlled 75 per cent of the pre-war grain producing area, with 75 per cent of the original population. According to a FO minute on the report, the productivity of the unoccupied areas had been reduced by 30–40 per cent in comparison to the pre-war situation, due to a shortage of draught power, skilled workers and agricultural machinery.[62] This report was probably sent to the MID in Washington by the US assistant military attaché in London.[63]

Other information received by the FO from the Czech minister to the USSR in August confirmed the picture that there was no acute food crisis despite the further loss of territory. The reason forwarded to support this conclusion was that the harvest everywhere had been good.[64] In mid-August Clark-Kerr seemed to have backed from his earlier pessimistic outlook expressed during the spring. Famine had not been reported anywhere according to him and the favourable weather had made almost all Soviet areas self-supporting this year. He stated in his telegram to the MEW (commented on by the FO): "The importance of the food situation as a possibly critical factor in determining how long Russia can hold out has thus greatly diminished."[65]

According to a FO report from mid-September the Norwegian ambassador in the USSR had spoken to Molotov, who informed him that the situation was better than previously expected, due to an excellent harvest and effective methods of collection. The report was distributed to the MEW.[66] In September the US assistant naval attaché in Vladivostok stated in a report to the ONI that the food situation in the city was "critical at the present".[67]

In October Clark-Kerr and the MEW expressed somewhat different views on the food situation. Clark-Kerr still feared a crack in resistance more as an effect of the food situation rather than any military setbacks.[68] Even though the report concluded that food shortages would persist, and that they might even become acute in certain areas due to transport problems, the MEW did not believe that the situation would be so serious that it would impair the war effort during the harvest year 1942/43. One FO official commented that he felt the conclusions of the MEW report to be "sound" in general.[69]

Later, in early December, the British JIC commented on the food situation in a similar fashion, and concluded that even now, after the losses during the summer, there was enough food to prevent dangerous shortages. But local food trouble was expected in certain areas during the winter, due to transport difficulties. Nevertheless, the food system with its differential rationing was expected to assure that no one directly involved in the war effort would go without food.[70] On the 58th meeting of the JIC on 1 December, Clark-Kerr stated that the food situation was "satisfactory", even though there would be shortages during the spring, which however could be controlled.[71] In a late

November report originating from the British Ministry of Food, noted by the MEW and the FO, it was stated that industrial efficiency could be maintained as high as possible due to the careful rationing of food to individual needs.[72]

The food situation was discussed during at least three US JIC meetings in the autumn and winter of 1942. In October it seems that the JIC believed that the armed forces and the important war workers could be fed adequately, but that much of the civilian population would have to suffer shortages. However, the general food situation was regarded as "a somewhat unfavorable factor in Russian military capabilities".[73] In the second version of the report, dated 11 November, this sentence was altered and a subordinate clause was added, with the sense that the food situation would not affect military capabilities in such a way as to be decisive for the war effort.[74]

In the OSS series "Military potential of the Soviet Union", two separate but consecutive reports were issued in November and December about what they labelled "The food problem". The conclusion of the first report was that the unoccupied territories of the USSR were not self-sufficient in food before the war, apart from bread grains, wheat, rye and the catch of fish. Even though it was calculated that there was a substantial deficit of many foodstuffs (e.g. the grain total, potatoes and animal fats), it was also assumed that there was an accumulated surplus of bread grain in the unoccupied areas possibly amounting to 15–20 million tonnes at the time of the German attack.[75] The second part quoted the US embassy and the US Supply Mission in the USSR, in their belief that there would be no starvation before the next harvest, if the United States successfully completed the food deliveries of the Lend-Lease program, the Soviets did not increase food rations and the food was distributed in a carefully planned way.[76] In the quoted embassy telegram original, from November, it was also stated that the urban population was "suffering from undernourishment to such an extent that its normal capacity for work is being hampered". Many people would die of undernourishment before the end of spring.[77] The OSS believed that the USSR had a deficit of bread-grain amounting to 4.5 million tonnes.[78]

The US embassy in Kuibyshev reported in December that there had been a "marked improvement" in the food situation in Moscow during the last weeks.[79] On 12 January 1943 the US London embassy sent a telegram to the SD, containing information on the food situation from the MEW.[80] Molotov had told a "reliable informant" (according to the MEW) that the food position during the winter of 1942/1943 would "be satisfactory due to a good 1942 harvest". But it would be necessary to draw on the reserves, and a bad 1943 harvest could be more serious, due to the fact that these reserves would then be smaller.[81]

It was apparent that the Anglo-Americans believed that the food situation was very problematic and that it was lowering the war potential to some extent. They correctly assumed that the personnel most important for the war effort also received the most beneficial rations of food. At the end of the period it seems that they did not any longer fear, at least in the short term, a breakdown in the war effort due to the precarious food situation. In reality the food situation without doubt was a very palpable and serious problem for the Soviet home front.

Even though the situation was considered better by the end of 1942 it was still believed that the food situation affected the economic efficiency of the country. The German invasion had very grave consequences for Soviet agriculture. The value of total agricultural production in 1941 was only about 63 per cent of the 1940 level, and only 39 per cent in 1942.[82] Compared to 1940, Soviet citizens received about two-fifths less food in 1942. Judging by the following (post-war research based) quote: "Hunger, cold, malnutrition and disease were almost as great threats to the survival of the USSR as German military power", it can safely be said that the food situation, and the poor general living conditions, were a real threat to the war effort. Much of the population was living on "a level barely above subsistence". In addition, the 1940 living standards were still below the 1928 level.[83]

During the spring and summer of 1942 the FO and the G-2 observed that differential rationing was a feature of the Soviet war effort. This observation was repeated during the autumn, and the British especially seemed to consider this as a factor of importance. Since priority was given to defeating the invaders, the personnel of the armed forces and war industry workers were considered to be the most important groups of the population to supply with food. Several other groups of the population had to suffer, relatively speaking, to ensure the living standards of the first two groups. This was accomplished by a rationing system, just as in other countries during World War II. But according to Barber and Harrison, the rations did not guarantee survival since the regime, due to a shortage of food, could not "feed adequately even the minority of the population entitled to rations". Furthermore, it was just "combat soldiers and manual workers in the most difficult and hazardous occupations [that] received sufficient rations to maintain health". More than half the population was not entitled to rations, and had to get by using local and unofficial resources, such as the "produce from side-line farms belonging to factories and institutions, from the allotments of urban residents, and from the collective farmers' private plots". These resources were indeed crucial for the survival of a large part of the population during the war.[84] It is a fact that undernourishment was a negative factor affecting industrial output during 1942.[85]

16.4 The manpower situation

During the autumn, the Anglo-Americans for the first time during the war noted a manpower shortage. In October the British MI recorded the opinion of a Lieutenant-Colonel Bartnowski. He said that in (Soviet) Turkestan some of the crops could not be harvested owing to lack of workers, and that if the armed forces wanted more recruits it had to enlist personnel at the expense of industry or agriculture, or draw upon "not entirely reliable elements".[86]

The OSS reports about the military potential (see above) were the most extensive studies so far regarding the manpower situation.[87] The parts about manpower were from the beginning of November. The shortage of labour, already a problem before the war, was seen as a major weakness and a serious handicap on the economic life of the country. The decline was not just quantitative, but also a qualitative problem affecting industry, since the loss and mobilization of so many people had to be remedied by longer hours of work, stricter labour discipline, more intensive work, and the increased employment of peasants, young people, and old men and women. Within the agricultural sector it was considered that the problem was being remedied in much the same way by employing more women, and by the conscription of children and townspeople for seasonal farm work. The civilian workforce was estimated at nearly 57 million, and considered as adequate to maintain production at a moderate level, if efficiently directed.[88]

Yeaton reported in November to Colonel D. C. McDonald of the Board of Economic Warfare (BEW) that there were 5 million evacuees in the unoccupied areas, originating from the area under German control. He also stated that the number of civilian casualties in the Soviet Union was estimated at half a million, based on figures from the larger cities and populated areas.[89]

In early December the British JIC estimated that the USSR by then had mobilized all the manpower she could, without damaging the economic effort. A further call up to the armed forces, over and above the regular annual intake, was expected to cause some reduction in either industrial or agricultural output.[90]

16.5 Munitions

In their August report the Joint US Strategic Committee described the Red Army's munitions as modern. However, they regarded the supply of heavy armaments as inadequate, in contrast to the output of small arms, light artillery and ammunition, which by contrast was seen as "abundant". They doubted that the economy alone could maintain 200 or more divisions in the field for more than six months, and that this was not primarily due to losses in manpower and population, but largely due to the inability to produce (especially heavy) armaments in adequate numbers. According to a map attached to the report, the output of aircraft was less than one sixth of the German output. But they did not believe that the general fall in production capacity – at least 35 per cent – could be translated into a corresponding fall in the output of military items. Besides aircraft, no figures were presented for the output of heavy armaments; but the following statement reveals that they regarded the situation as bad: "Outside of artillery and small arms ammunition, the ... [Soviets] is practically dependent on England and the United States to maintain her armies in the field for any length of time."[91] The Committee was, of course, severely underestimating munitions output. Actual Soviet output of munition was higher than Germany's, even regarding aircraft.

In a US intelligence memorandum from mid-August the great importance of Lend-Lease for Soviet air strength, and consequently for the supply of aircraft to the front, was evaluated. The following conclusions, among others, were reached: "On any basis of comparisons of strength, Russia's imports have made it possible to maintain at least numerical equality with Germany, if not numerical superiority." Furthermore, "Without imports, Russia's total air strength would have been so diminished as to suggest the following prob-abilities: (1) her ability to effectively resist German air power would have reached almost the vanishing point, with the result of either immobilizing her air strength, or suffering rapid destruction of her remaining aircraft through abnormally high losses."[92] Needless to say this was also an underestimation, and by implication also an overestimation of the importance of Lend-Lease, which in mid-1942 still was rather modest.

According to a report signed by the MIS, Colonel T. E. Roderick, in August, addressed to the US Chief of Ordnance in Washington, the T-34 tank was considered by several sources to be the "best tank on any battlefield". Roderick believed that it was an opinion that "may very well be well foun-ded".[93] This was quite correct in 1942 since the Germans, or any other power, did not have anything that could match the T-34 (or the KV-1). This would later change since the Germans in late 1942 began to produce the so called Tiger (PzKw VI) tank, and in 1943 the Panther (PzKw V), but these models were only manufactured in relatively limited numbers.

At the August Stalin–Churchill meeting in Moscow, Stalin said that tank production was satisfactory, but the need for trucks was much greater. He wanted 20,000 to 25,000 trucks per month from the Western Allies and no more tanks, in addition to the 3000 trucks the Soviets produced themselves.[94] The information Stalin gave Churchill at this time was quite accurate, but there is no way of knowing if the British really believed it.

In September the US London embassy forwarded a summary of a report from the MEW regarding aircraft production to the SD. The report stated that the July aircraft output had been at a rate of 1500–2000 operational aircraft.[95] The same month a report from some US Air Force officers (members of the US Bradley Mission[96] to the USSR) to the commanding general of the Army Air Force at the WD revealed a rather high regard for Soviet aircraft. The Pe-2 medium bomber was regarded as a "very good" plane and aircraft armament in general was considered good. They even went so far as to state that "plane for plane the Soviets seems superior to the Germans in the air, but are hampered by a lack of airplanes".[97]

In early October, US air intelligence sources repeated notions about the monthly output of 372 aircraft in seven factories that accounted for the bulk of the production.[98] This piece of information was quoted by the G-2 in the spring of 1942, and confirms well with information that Yeaton sent home to Washington in 1941. However, in a 23 November report, noted by the G-2, the Blockade and Supply Branch of the BEW evaluated the aircraft industry with special emphasis on production. The total output of all military types on an annual basis was estimated at 16,000 to 19,000 aircraft and 32,000 to 39,000 aircraft engines.[99] These figures correspond to a monthly output of between 1333 and 1583 planes.

At the 1 October meeting of the British Joint Planners, Admiral Miles stated that even though there was no information about what was happening east of the Urals, it was likely that the Soviets had built a large war industry in the "Magneto Gorsk [Magnitogorsk] area". The production of tanks was "very large".[100] During the second half of 1942, British MI continued to evaluate the tank situation. Information from the press and foreign intelligence agencies was used, among them the OSS.[101]

In the OSS reports about the military potential, the fourth part was on the munitions situation. The report, dated 11 November, was an attempt to analyse production, imports, losses and current strength with regard to planes, tanks and artillery. The report drew on a wide variety of sources.[102] The production figures stated in the report were higher than in any earlier US report. The monthly output figures for combat aircraft were estimated at approximately 2000, and the figures for tanks and artillery pieces were 2000 and 750, respectively.[103] Apart from their reservation concerning tanks (see below), the Americans, through the OSS report, managed to estimate the approximate figures for aircraft and tanks correctly. The figure for artillery, though, was still an underestimation (see below).

In addition to combat aircraft, the Soviets had stated that they produced about 100 DC-3 type transporters every month. Based on interviews with British and US officials, the general impression of the OSS was that Soviet plant efficiency was good. The machinery was very modern, the workers were very skilled and experienced, and the factories were large and well organized. Even though women and boys were used as workers, experienced mechanics and operators held the key positions. But the efficiency of the aircraft industry was considered as somewhat hampered by the relative lack of aluminium. Instead, the OSS identified a considerable use of other materials in aircraft, such as steel, wood, plywood or fabric. But they saw it as questionable whether output could be increased before the Soviets had obtained more aluminium.[104] In general, the OSS regarded Soviet aircraft in series production as being of high quality. The attack aircraft *Sturmovik* (Il-2) received some praise for its ability in combat.[105]

Tank output was estimated at about 1400 tanks per month, and total output from 22 June 1941 to 31 August 1942 was estimated at around 20,000. The only reason that present output, as of November, was considered to be lower, was that the Stalingrad complex was out of production. On the other hand, the OSS considered that the margin of error for the 1400 figure was several hundred vehicles a month up or down. An increase was anticipated, since the important tank factory evacuated from Stalingrad would be back in production. Output was expected to rise again at the beginning of 1943. Although it was not possible for the OSS to break down output by type, they assessed that the proportion of heavy and medium tanks in production had grown substantially since June 1941. In sharp contrast to G-2 estimates from the spring of 1942, the OSS believed that output during the late spring and summer had approached the June 1941 figure, which in turn was estimated to have been 2000 a month. The OSS must have considered the potential for tank production as substantial. According to a quoted British observer, somehow connected with the MEW, the tank factory at Chelyabinsk alone had a "labour force of 50,000 people and machine-tool equipment capable of producing 3,000 tanks a month".[106]

The OSS had a much harder time to estimate artillery output, defined as guns and howitzers of 37 mm in calibre or larger. Minimum monthly output was estimated to 750 pieces, but probably considerably higher. Output was in any case considered to be substantially higher than in June 1941, due to the relatively safe location of the artillery industry, plant conversion, and the development of new plants. The fact that the Soviets had never asked for Western Allied deliveries of artillery, except regarding anti-tank guns and anti-aircraft guns, was an indication to the OSS that the Red Army's supply of artillery was adequate.[107] Actual output was far in excess of the OSS estimates. Output of field artillery pieces of the calibre 76 mm and upwards was around 30,100 in 1942, which translates into more than 2500 units per months. Since output increased during 1942 it is likely that the November figure was substantially higher than 2500. In addition to the field artillery pieces, 1942 output of rocket artillery comprised 3300 units, anti-tank artillery 20,500 pieces and the output of anti-aircraft guns 6800 pieces. These figures do not even include the output of anti-aircraft guns below 37 mm in calibre, or guns of any calibre produced for naval units or aircraft.[108] All of this implies, considering the great importance that artillery had for firepower, that the OSS seriously underestimated the combat strength of the Red Army.

We have seen that the British JIC estimated monthly tank output at about 2000 units by early June.[109] This figure was confirmed in December, and the JIC stressed that a larger quantity of heavy and medium tanks was produced than in 1941. Generally the Red Army had enough equipment (of all kinds) for the most important sectors of the front, even though it was not enough to go around for all requirements. Artillery output was greater than the pre-war level, and the increase in mortar output was seen as substantial. They stated that both the production and distribution of ammunition probably was satisfactory. The monthly output of operational aircraft was estimated at 1500 to 2000. The general production level of munitions was not believed to be higher than 100–110 per cent of the pre-war rate. But the output of certain weapons was believed to be both quantitatively and qualitatively higher.[110] In January 1943 the US JIC commented on the British estimate with scepticism, since they considered that there was no information available regarding the June 1941 munition output level. They believed instead that the British overestimated munitions output.[111] Actually both were wrong since the output level by November 1942 was far above the June 1941 level.

The British JIC commented on the evacuation of aircraft factories, which they described as a well-planned and rather successful operation. New plants were also believed to be in operation. They considered that great improvements in technique and organizations had been achieved with regard to the production of aircraft. The efficiency of production was believed to have improved, and the aircraft produced were "superior in workmanship" to those manufactured during earlier years. According to the JIC, modern Soviet aircraft were comparable to their counterparts in other air forces of "first class powers", although some older types were still in use in the Air Force. The capacity to build larger naval vessels was considered as "practically non-existent".[112]

According to the January 1943 report from the US military attaché in Turkey, concerning the opinions of the Turkish ambassador to the USSR, Soviet military equipment was of "excellent quality" and "still sufficient".[113]

As late as December 1942 the British JIC believed (as we have seen) that the production of war materials was at a maximum of 110 per cent of the pre-war level. But on the other hand, it seems that the production of heavy munitions was not underestimated by as much at that time. It is difficult to know to what extent the 110 per cent-level was an assessment made in the light of a British revaluation of the June 1941 production level. Several estimates made by both the British and the Americans during the war suggest that such revaluations (of earlier estimates) took place more than once.

These production figures reveal that all estimates for all categories of munitions from the start of the war up to the end of 1942 were underestimates. The different figures quoted as a result of the Moscow Conference are, of course, an exception to this rule. At the end of 1942 the British JIC and the OSS approached this reality when estimating the size of aircraft and tank production, although they were still on the low side. In general, and considering the period as a whole, the British were closer to the truth than the Americans.

The quality of aircraft was revalued somewhat by many observers, and during the autumn of 1942 a report considered the T-34 as probably being the best tank in the world. Some reports even stated that Soviet aircraft were almost as good as German aircraft. As we already have seen earlier, the Soviets had begun producing more modern aircraft by the time of the invasion. The production and technical upgrading of these models continued during the war, and in a technical sense many of these models were not inferior to German designs.[114] The KV heavy tank and the T-34 were much better than anything the Germans could field in 1941–1942. During 1942, the T-34 design stood for more than half of all the Soviet tanks produced.[115] On the whole it seems fair to say that most Anglo-American observers correctly assessed the qualitative improvement of tanks and aircraft, even though the report on the T-34 hardly represented a general point of view.

16.6 The size of the armed forces and military losses

During the late summer, autumn and winter of 1942–1943, the estimate of the armed force's size varied greatly between different observers. It is difficult to assess some of the estimates since it is not always obvious whether or not they referred to front strength or total strength. In two estimates from late July and early August, G-2 believed the total number of troops in all formations (including the Far East but excluding Central Asia) to be between 4 and 5 million, in addition to 300,000 men in training and a few cavalry divisions in Asia. Taking into account earlier assessments and the numbers given, G-2 probably referred to the personnel of combat formations, and not all personnel officially enlisted in the armed forces. The total number of tanks was estimated at 6900 and the number of aircraft at 6000. But these figures were revised downwards by the middle of August when the total strength of all formations was estimated at between 4 and 4.5 million, with 5880 tanks and 5780 aircraft, in addition to the reserve and cavalry divisions already mentioned.[116] The British Air Ministry estimated the number of aircraft (report date 31 July) to about 4000.[117] The Joint US Strategic Committee estimated it to 6000 in early August, of which 5000 were engaged in the European theatre.[118]

G-2 estimates from September and November were even lower: 4 million men, 5100 tanks and 5500 aircraft, with 200,000 men in reserve and 12 other varied formations (mostly divisions) in Asia. In two order of battle estimates from 8 and 28 January 1943, the number of troops was fixed at 4.5 million, with 8700 tanks and 5700 aircraft. The reserve forces were believed to be 10–15 divisions (the strength of a division was estimated at 10,000–18,000 men) in training plus 12 formations mentioned in the 8 January estimate, and 25–30 divisions in the 28 January battle order.[119] The ONI issued their own reports based on MIS sources, displaying exactly the same figures for the armed forces strength as the G-2 in two reports of their own from August and September.[120] The same situation applied also to the G-2 report from 8 January 1943.[121]

In the OSS military potential series (from November) the estimated size of the armed forces was about 12 million men, including reserves in training.[122] The lack of reliable information was stressed, but the first line aircraft strength on the Soviet–German front was between 2000 and 4000 planes. A "substantial number of planes" were stationed in the Far East. There were no guesses with regard to the reserves of aircraft, even though it seems that the OSS regarded it as doubtful if there were any large reserves at all. The OSS counted on the fact that the Soviets would add to their strength during the winter of 1942/1943, since they reckoned that replacements would exceed losses.[123] The tank strength was estimated to circa 16,000, but only 9000 were actually considered to be ready for action by 1 September, since 3000 were believed to be used in training or in the Far East, and about 4000 were considered to be in repair. No estimate was made for artillery pieces (defined as guns or howitzers of 37 mm calibre or larger), even though it was believed that the Red Army had a relatively better supply of guns than of aircraft and tanks.[124]

OSS estimated total military casualties (including wounded), from 22 June 1941 up to 1 September 1942, to 5.7 million men.[125] They also tried to estimate munition losses. In doing this they evaluated official German and Soviet communiqués. The span concerning combat losses in aircraft was from 11,000 planes – the Soviet claim – to 30,000 planes – the German claim, since

22 June 1941. The OSS was more inclined to believe Soviet communiqués, and therefore leaned more towards the lower figure. However, there was much reserve even about this figure, since it was believed that the Soviets did not reveal the full extent of their casualties. Furthermore, this was only combat losses, and it was stated that there was considerable aircraft losses due to other operational causes and training accidents. The method for calculating tank and artillery (guns of 37 mm in calibre and larger) losses was pretty much the same as in the case of aircraft: German (higher) and Soviet (lower) statements compared, with a bias towards the Soviet figure. The span in the case of tanks was from 17,500 to 32,500, and in the case of artillery from 25,000 to 50,000.[126]

A G-2 report from 5 December, signed by Lieutenant Colonel Henry I. Szymanski, a US Army liaison officer to the Polish Army, quoted both Czech, Polish and British sources when claiming that military losses up to 1 November were about 7 million. Of the 7 million, 3 million were reported to be dead or so badly wounded they were unfit for service. The other 4 million had been taken as prisoners, and most of these (around 2.6 million) were thought to be dead by this time. According to the report the WO was in agreement with these figures.[127]

In the December British JIC report, shared with the Americans, the manpower of the armed forces, including the navy, air force, and NKVD troops, was estimated at some 9 to 10 million (with 8 to 9 million men in the army alone). The JIC believed this to be the peak strength of the armed forces. After this point in time heavy losses could not be made good without transferring workers from industry and agriculture, which in turn would curtail production. The operational strength of the air force (army and navy) was estimated at between 5220 and 5720, including the Far East.[128] In a January 1943 report the US JIC commented upon these figures, and believed instead that the right number was 7500 aircraft. But otherwise the US JIC agreed in general with the British estimate concerning the number of troops.[129]

Later in the autumn most Anglo-American observers hardly changed their assessment regarding the size of the armed forces, as compared to the spring. Apart from the estimates referring to the total size of the armed forces (12 million, OSS in November), it seems that the front strength of the Red Army was underestimated. The actual size of the armed forces was between 10 and 12 million men during 1942.[130] The front-line strength of the Red Army increased somewhat during the autumn and was 6.1 million men on 2 February 1943. By 1 January 1943 the number of combat aircraft in the field forces was 12,300 and the total strength was 21,900. As for tanks and self-propelled (armored vehicles) guns the corresponding figures were 8100 and 20,600, respectively.[131] Therefore it seems that at least aircraft strength was underestimated by most observes, and probably to some extent tank and front-line strength also.

Total military losses up to and including the third quarter of 1942 were almost 10 million men, of which more than 5.5 million were permanent casualties.[132] This implies that the OSS underestimated Soviet losses in their November assessment, while G-2 and the WO overestimated the losses in December. As for assessments regarding equipment losses, only the OSS made any during this period, and their assessments were clearly an underestimate. Total Soviet losses of tanks and other heavy armoured vehicles with a gun main armament was 35,600 from 22 June 1941 until the last day of 1942. In addition to this 12,000 armoured cars, tractors and other armoured vehicles was lost. Aircraft losses during the same period was 35,900, even though far from all aircraft destroyed was due to combat losses.[133]

16.7 Military efficiency and morale

Even though the events of the winter 1941/1942 had changed Anglo-American perceptions to a certain extent, some older notions were still reflected in the assessments. In August the Joint US Strategic Committee regarded the morale of the Red Army as "a very moot questions". According to the report, many observers still believed that both the morale and the efficiency of the army were still affected by the 1937–1938 purges. Other observers believed that the purges had had little effect. But in contrast to the situation in June, the present morale was not considered as good. The report also commented on the stamina of the Soviet forces: "The Russian soldiers are physically hardy and accustomed to privation and the idea of sacrificing individual liberty and life for the good of the state."[134] Otherwise most British and US reports from this period gave the impression that the morale of the armed forces was high. The critique of military efficiency was – as earlier during 1942 – mainly a question of poor leadership and organizational capacity in the higher military strata. The efficiency of the troops at lower levels was not considered as such a big problem.[135]

The Axis advance during the summer offensive prompted a near panic among the Red Army units in the south, and *Stavka*, the Soviet High Command, issued (on 28 July) their infamous order No. 227, which stipulated an absolute end to retreats. The order included severe disciplinary measures for refusal to obey it.[136] Interrogation of Soviet prisoners of war during the end of July had revealed a low Red Army morale to the Hungarians, who participated in the German offensive. Information about these interrogations reached the British. The British did not agree entirely with the Hungarian information, since they considered that the lowering of morale was only local. The MI3(c) report was from late October, and it stated that discipline had "been tightened up very sharply – not without shootings". The role of nationalism and propaganda was also stressed by the British.[137]

In early September Clark-Kerr sent a telegram to the FO, intended for War Cabinet distribution, which commented on the faltering of morale on the Southern part of the front during the early stages of the German offensive. The fact that Rostov and Novocherkassk fell so easily was blamed on the morale situation.[138] Another Clark-Kerr telegram, sent on 16 September and quoting information from the 30 Mission, argued that there were no notable signs of a weakening military morale in general.[139] When the British Joint Planners considered the USSR at their 1 October meeting, Admiral Miles believed Red Army morale to be high.[140]

It is apparent that the MI3(c) had reassessed their opinion of military effi-
ciency in some ways since the earlier days of the Soviet–German campaign.
According to one MI3(c) official the fighting value of the Red Army in
October was of a "high standard which the recent fighting proves to exist".[141]
In another report the MI3(c) commented upon the improvements in the use
of armoured formations, away from the previous infantry support role. The
training of troops was considered to have improved.[142] Exham of the 30
Mission commented on the abolition of the commissar system in October as
an improvement. In a telegram to the DMI he described it as a way to
strengthen the officer corps and an improvement of the distribution of
resources.[143] The same month, in two separate British (MI) and US reports, it
was seen as improbability that the Red Army would be able to launch a
major offensive in the near future. The incompetence of the leadership was
among the many factors referred to. The US assistant military attaché Park
reported to the MID regarding the low efficiency of high ranking Soviet
military commanders: "This incompetency is typical of the governing bodies
of a great many of the governmental agencies of the present regime, and for
this reason it is doubtful that the army developed by the present regime will
ever, or can ever put on a sustained offensive until it has an overwhelming
superiority in all departments." Park even concluded that Stalin considered
that the lack of Soviet victories was due to the incompetence of the Soviet
commanders.[144]

On 24 October the MI3(c) and the MI14 made a joint comment on a Pika
report from the 3rd. The reasons for the recent German successes were
attributed to their superior organization, staff work and the experience of
senior commanders. They also enjoyed a "complete technical superiority".
The Red Army, on the other hand, was suffering from the "clumsiness" of its
higher command, "weak technical equipment", "lack of technical training",
"poor transport and organization of supplies", and a "lack of properly
trained" non-commissioned officers. However, they did believe that the Red
Army had improved somewhat in defensive warfare since 1941. Morale was
not believed to be broken, since it was stated that the Soviets were awaiting
the summer campaign of 1943 with "considerable self confidence".[145] The
Pika report from 7 October predated this critique of the Red Army, but added
that there were efforts at improvement going on in the areas of front supply
and the training of non-commissioned officers. Younger and more competent
officers had also to some extent replaced older and less able commanders.[146]

In the OSS military potential series Red Army morale was described as
high. This was not just a notion that originated from observers friendly to the
OSS, but also from German sources. Several reasons for the high Red Army
morale were enumerated: the close relationship between the Red Army and
the civilian population; the brutality of the Axis; the political education of
Soviet troops; the fact that the Red Army had the highest priority regarding
resources of any organization in Soviet society, which the soldiers knew; the
inculcation of a tradition of military honour and glory in the Red Army;

"and, for those who required it there [was] ruthless discipline".[147] In the OSS November report on munitions some remarks were made about the relative efficiency of the Air Force. It was assumed that the *Luftwaffe* had a greater strength than its Soviet counterpart, despite a slight inferiority in planes at the front, since it had higher operational efficiency, greater mobility and better equipment. Nevertheless, according to American and British eyewitnesses referred to in the report, Air Force personnel were both skilled, efficient and with a high morale. The pilots were regarded as able and brave.[148]

In the December British JIC report the description of the efficiency of the Red Army was pretty much the same as in earlier estimates – good defensive capabilities at lower levels but poor leadership. At this time (in reality) the Red Army had punched a large hole in the Axis front and surrounded the Germans at Stalingrad, but it was not yet, according to the JIC, able to "maintain the momentum of a large-scale offensive operation." This was not just blamed on the low ability of staff officers, but also on poor signal communications and a lack of mobility. But the JIC expected improvements in the capabilities of staff officers in the future since the Soviets had improved training.[149] The training of personnel within the SAF was not considered to be any better. They assumed that the training of pilots allowed for no more than 30 hours flying time in some cases, compared to the 170–200 hours of training that RAF pilots received before joining operations. The training of bomber pilots was believed to be somewhat better. The efficiency of the navy was described in almost the same way as that of the Red Army – poor higher command but better efficiency at ship level. The navy's support to the army along the Black Sea coast and in the defence of Leningrad was considered valuable. Soviet naval gunnery, in general, received praise, as did the submarine fleet.[150] The JIC described the activities of partisans as something in large part directed by the Red Army. The partisans were recognized as a force hampering the Germans. The morale of the armed forces, including the navy, was considered to be high.[151]

Hurley's December telegram to Roosevelt was also about the Red Army's efficiency. He was impressed by what he saw regarding "the esprit, the morale and the physical strength of the troops in combat", of one division at the front. Hurley observed some improvements since the beginning of the Soviet–German war. The Red Army was considered to be better led and a much better "fighting force" in general. Roosevelt replied to Hurley in a personal telegram the following day, where he expressed his delight with his report and "the magnificent operations and fine morale of the Russian Armies."[152]

According to a MI3(c) report on the views of a US military observer, who visited the Don front in early December – probably a member of Hurley's party – the Soviet soldiers were "brave, able fighters with superb morale". But the powers of the Red Army as a whole were considered as being neutralized by the Germans, and the retreat of the Germans was seen more as an attempt to gain better defensive positions. The USSR was considered to have "enough manpower to defeat Germany but lacks weapons, transportation coordination or the staff competent to conduct a sustained offensive."[153]

When Major Speaks, Jr., of the MIS, interviewed General Bradley in December, Bradley was of the opinion that the SAF was a highly efficient organization – both with regard to it as an operational Air Force and with respect to the morale of the personnel. Bradley also had some criticism, since he stated "that Soviet pilots, due to lack of experience, are not particularly good at night or instrument flying".[154]

In a 31 January 1943 report, the JCS was informed about the remarks the former assistant military attaché, Park, made to the Joint Strategic Committee on 26 January about his experiences in the USSR. The Soviets were considered to be well equipped, very tough, well fed, with high morale and under excellent leadership. Park regarded the pilots as among the best in the world.[155]

We have seen that Anglo-American assessments of Soviet military efficiency changed somewhat during 1942, but it was not until the end of 1942 that a real change took place, although in a rather limited manner. According to Glantz and House, this was also the time when the Red Army began to "blossom into a force that not only could halt the fabled Blitzkrieg offensive but could also conduct its own offensives in all types of weather and terrain". The SAF was suffering from the same problems as the ground forces when the war began – lack of training and "severe deficiencies in leadership at all levels".[156]

As observed by some Anglo-American commentators during the German summer offensive in 1942, Red Army morale faltered in the southern part of the front, which led to draconic measures from the Soviet leadership in order to uphold discipline. But this situation was of a temporary nature. There were, for example, many cases of desertion, many draft evaders and many cases of self-mutilation among the existing and potential Soviet soldiers, but this does not seem to have been a problem that affected the "motivation of the Red Army as a whole to defeat Germany and its allies".[157] It seems fair to say that most Anglo-American observers during this period had a pretty accurate picture of Soviet military efficiency and military morale.

Notes

1   In their August report the committee regarded the Soviet dictatorial form of government as an advantage for the war effort. The Soviet control of their population was showing no sign of breaking. The people were united in their effort to survive, and the "defense spirit will not admit capitulation even if retreat to the Urals occurs." 7–8-1942, "Strategic [...]", ABC384USSR(6–1-42), Box-472, Entry-421, RG165.
2   Smith (1996), 116–117; 18–9-1942, "O.S.S. [...]", WO208/1755.
3   6–10–1942, R&A#673, Report #12, Reel-1, UPA1977; 18-11-1942, R&A#584, Part VI, Report #18, Reel-1, UPA1977; Katz (1989), 141, 150. The morale of the Soviet civilian population was described as high in the report, spurred by the hatred of the brutal Axis invaders and the damage they were inflicting upon their land. Government propaganda was considered effective, as were the efforts of the secret police to counter negative influences. 18-11-1942, R&A#584, Part VI,

Report #18, Reel-1, UPA1977. When the Lieutenant-Colonel Park returned to the US from service in the Soviet Union he reported in January 1943 to the Joint Strategic Committee, among other things, on the Soviet propaganda machine. He described the propaganda system as "great", and thought that the outside world knew nothing about what was happening inside the USSR, while the Soviets knew everything about what was going on outside of the Soviet Union. 31–1-1943, Joint Chiefs of Staff, Memorandum for information No. 45, Box-212, RG218. Most citizens of the USSR were not believed likely to gain anything by a German victory, but instead lose heavily. According to the OSS most national minorities, except in rare cases, had proved their loyalty to the Soviet regime. It was stated in the report that there were signs of weakened morale during the German summer offensive, but that by November 1942 the high Soviet morale had returned. 18-11-1942, R&A#584, Part VI, Report #18, Reel-1, UPA1977.

4   17-10-1942, "Sir [...]", FO800/874.
5   30-10-1942, "M.I.3 [...]", WO208/1805.
6   1–10–1942, JP(42)161, CAB119/38.
7   Conditions were considered to be worse in Central Asia, but, with help from the NKVD, the government's control over the country was regarded as firm. 2–12–1942,   JIC(42)459(Final),   CAB81/111;   24-12-1942,   JIC45thmtg./JIC25/4, 381USSR, Box-214, RG218.
8   14–1-1943, JIC48thMtg, JIC25/6(13–1-1943), Box-214, RG218.
9   The US embassy at Kuybushiev notified Washington in December that morale among the population in Moscow was now higher as a result of the recent military victories. 22-12-1942, "American [...]", Box-3084, Entry-77, RG165.
10 In an unsigned British intelligence report from a visitor (probably a British officer) to the Caucasus, dated 4 January 1943, Russian morale in general was described as good. The morale of ethnical Caucasians was considered to be lower. 4–1-1943, "Soviet [...]", WO208/1750.
11 A FO report from January 1943 confirmed the total dedication and high morale of the population in their effort to win the war. The information originated from a Russian ship crewman. 16–1-1943, N447/52/38, FO371/36944.
12 26–1-1943, "Tendencies [...]", Box-3178, Entry-77, RG165.
13 10-10-1942, "Sir [...]", FO800/874.
14 24-10-1942, N5532/30/38, FO371/32915.
15 28-11-1942, N6194/30/38, FO371/32916; Keegan (ed.) (1989), 104.
16 Since the Hungarian army was fighting against the Soviets at the time, the Hungarians in some respects had better access to the Soviet reality than the British. 30-10-1942, "M.I.3 [...]", WO208/1805.
17 Hinsley (1981), 111–112.
18 2–10–1942, JIC(42)383(Final), CAB81/110.
19 Hinsley (1981), 106–107.
20 14-11-1942, JIC(42)443(Final), CAB81/111; Dear & Foot (eds.) (1995), 198–199. Even though the JIC identified some anti-Soviet subversive activity among some of the Caucasian nationalities, it was believed that the Soviet authorities had the situation under control. 14-11-1942, JIC(42)443(Final), CAB81/111.
21 24-12-1942, JIC45thMtg, JIC25/5, Box-214, RG218.
22 14–1-1943, JIC48thMtg, JIC25/7(13–1-1943), Box-214, RG218.
23 Keegan (ed.) (1989), 106–107.
24 1–12–1942, N6195/1375/38, FO371/32990.
25 Willmott (1992), 252–253.
26 2–2-1943, "Brigadier [...]", Box-212, RG218.
27 Ibid.
28 Persico (2001), 235–236.

29   There were other figures in the report, which more or less speculated that the production could be 7500 units instead, or as low as 500 units during 1942. 1–8-1942, "Special [...]", Box-3109, Entry-77, RG165.
30   Ibid.
31   Harrison (2002), table 4–2.
32   4–8-1942, MID904(8/4/42), 091.3USSR, Box-1038, Entry-47, RG319.
33   7–8-1942, "Strategic [...]", ABC384USSR(6–1-42), Box-472, Entry-421, RG165.
34   12–8-1942, 861.50/960, Roll-22, T1250, RG59.
35   3–9-1942, JIC29thMtg, JIC25/3, Box-214, RG218.
36   1–10–1942, JP(42)161, CAB119/38.
37   6–8-1942, N4055/11/38, FO371/32893.
38   15–8-1942, "Record [...]", CAB121/460.
39   Lambert was the first secretary of the embassy. 5–8-1942, N4516/80/38, FO371/32922.
40   8–8-1942, N4170/30/38, FO371/36911.
41   17-10-1942, "Sir [...]", FO800/874.
42   11-12-1942, No. 6662, Roll-27, T1250, RG59; 22-12-1942, Report No. 52542, 463.1Russia, Box-1050, Entry-47, RG319.
43   25-11-1942, R&A#584, Part III, M1221, RG59; 25-11-1942, R&A#584, Part III, Reel-1, Report #16, UPA1977.
44   Ibid.
45   The JIC report was commented on by the US Naval Attaché in London, who considered the report reliable, although he did not give it the highest rating of reliability, A-1, but instead A-2. 8–12–1942, F-6-e, 23025, Box-723, Entry-98A, RG38.
46   2–12–1942, JIC(42)459(Final), CAB81/111.
47   14-1-1943, JIC48thMtg, JIC25/6(13–1-1943), Box-214, RG218.
48   13-1-1943, Report No. 7576, 350.05 Union of Socialist Soviet Republics, Box-1043, Entry-47, RG319.
49   25-1-1943, "Summary [...]", MI3(c), WO208/1755.
50   7–8-1942, "Strategic [...]", ABC384USSR(6–1-42), Box-472, Entry-421, RG165.
51   At the beginning of September, MI3(c) and MI10(c) cooperated concerning a report on Soviet railway transport. Their information originated from interviews with travellers from the Soviet Union. In the report several reasons were given for the deficient functioning of Soviet railways. The disparity between planning and execution of railway traffic, bad planning, incorrect information, lack of order and discipline, lack of training on the part of railway workers, their hard living conditions, chaotic initial war conditions and "general bad conditions" were regarded as the principal explanatory factors. It was believed that the conditions within railway transport would deteriorate further, due to lack of railway equipment, a shortage of skilled workers, and the general food shortage, which would force workers to search for food instead of work. 3–9-1942, "U.S.S.R. [...]", WO208/1818.
52   17-10-1942, "Sir [...]", FO800/874.
53   21-10-1942, "Notes [...]", WO208/1755.
54   If the military used more transport resources, the JIC believed that the production of armaments would suffer. There was no information concerning any serious failure, and the operations of the railways were thought to be better than during the latter half of 1941. The JIC stated that there was no shortage of locomotives or wagons. The motor industry was, according to the JIC, never strong enough to meet all requirements, and war conditions had aggravated the shortage of lorries. The demand for motor transport could therefore not be met for either economic or military needs. 2–12–1942, JIC(42)459 (Final), CAB81/111.
55   14–1-1943, JIC48thMtg, JIC25/6(13–1-1943), Box-214, RG218.

56 Roosevelt replied to Hurley the next day through a personal telegram. 10-12-1942, No. 411, 820-Secret, Box-48, MECF1944, RG84; 11-12-1942, Roll-6, T1250, RG59.

57 11-12-1942, N6322/30/38, FO371/32916; 14-12-1942, N6335/30/38, FO371/32916.

58 31–1-1943, Joint Chiefs of Staff, Memorandum of information no. 45, Box-212, RG218; 10-12-1942, No. 411, 820-Secret, Box-48, MECF1944, RG84.

59 2–8-1941, "War Cabinet, [...]", CAB121/464. The Air ministry report on the situation in the USSR was also highlighted by the JIC in August. 1–8-1942, JIC (42)297(0), CAB81/109; 2–8-1942, JIC(42)298(0)(Final), CAB81/109.

60 Some examples are the reports from 13–8-1942, N4449/80/38, FO371/32922; 12–9-1942 (stamped and handwritten), N4671/80/38, FO371/32922; and 30–9-1942, N5000/80/38, FO371/32922. One report from July, covering an interview with General Borouta, the former second in command to the Polish General Anders, was very depressing and pictured a situation where starvation would be a fact during the coming winter. Borouta pointed out the Soviet loss of land and the withdrawal of about 300,000 tractors from agriculture to the Armed Forces. He expected that the coming harvest would be only about one fifth of the normal, but that it would be enough to feed the 10 million members of the Armed Forces. A great part of the population would face famine and starvation during winter, and this situation – not the military development – was the reason that the Soviet government was urging for a second front. From the minutes on this report it is hard to say if this really was the opinion of the FO, but nothing was stated in direct contradiction to Borouta's views. 9–7-1942, N3610/1375/38, FO371/32989.

61 (17?)-7–1942, "Food [...]", WO208/1800.

62 A German occupation of more surplus grain land in the South (Azov–Black Sea area and North Caucasus) would reduce these figures to 60 per cent and 65–70 per cent, respectively, according to the estimate. Of course, the MEW saw additional problems with the loss of agricultural land due to the ongoing German offensive, but this would not worsen the situation by much, except perhaps at a local level. Privation would chiefly affect those not directly engaged in the war effort. 21–7-1942, WP(42)309, CAB66/26; 28–7-1942, N4140/1375/38, FO371/32989. The MEW produced similar reports at the beginning of July, which were available to the US embassy in August. 18–8-1942, No. 5087, Roll-23, T1250, RG59.

63 The MEW report was prepared at the beginning of July, and had the purpose of evaluating the food situation in relation to the war potential. The MEW saw no acute danger in the food situation at the time, at least not for the next nine months. Especially since the MEW emphasized that the Soviets were differentiating the food supply to their citizens, depending upon what importance they had to the war effort. Owing to the system of collective farms and the degree of state control in agriculture, it was not believed that there was any risk of hoarding. The 1942 harvest was estimated to be between 60 and 70 per cent of the normal amount. 26–8-1942, "USSR [...]", Box-3107, Entry-77, RG165.

64 8–8-1942, N4170/30/38, FO371/36911.

65 18–8-1942, N4255/1375/38, FO371/32989.

66 14–9-1942, N4746/30/38, FO371/32913.

67 18–9-1942, "U.S.S.R. [...]", Box-3107, Entry-77, RG165.

68 Clark-Kerr transmitted a telegram on 1 October to the FO which showed a somewhat different perspective than the rather optimistic one he had expressed in August. According to several sources, there were once again concerns about famine during the winter. Molotov's private secretary had stated that the Red Army would be fed without problems, but the population in general would "go

extremely short". Clark-Kerr recommended that additional shipments of wheat be sent to the USSR to counter the difficult food situation. 1–10–1942, N5066/1375/38, FO371/32990.

69   The MEW report was from 19 October and analysed the Soviet food situation relative to the war potential of the USSR. The MEW apparently took the possibility of imports into the equation, since it concluded that global food supplies seemed adequate. The Soviet system of differential rationing was also considered as a factor – i.e., more food to the Armed Forces and the industrial workers. Other factors were that the Russians had been "conditioned from time to time" during the last decade to severe food shortages, and that the Allied shipments of "concentrated foodstuffs" could bring some help. 22-10-1942, N5461/1375/38, FO371/32990.

70   2–12–1942, JIC(42)459(Final), CAB81/111. Of course, the horrible conditions in Leningrad were not unknown to the British. According to a telegram from the MEW (to Washington), dated 13 November 1942, the official Soviet estimate of the deaths caused by hunger and exposure during the winter of 1941–1942 in the "Leningrad area" was over 1.75 million. The MEW drew the conclusion that these figures must also include deaths caused by bombing and shelling. 13-11-1942, N5940/1375/38, FO371/32990.

71   1–10–1942, N6195/1375/38, FO371/32990.

72   12-12-1942, N6410/1375/38, FO371/32990.

73   The first report on the subject – compiled after a directive at JIC's 35th meeting on 8 October – dated 21 October, came to the conclusion that it was likely that the USSR would be able to maintain an adequate food level for the army during the crop year of 1942–1943. It was further assumed that adequate bread supplies could be given to the most important war workers, but other foodstuffs would at best be only tolerable. Very limited food conditions were expected for the rest of the urban population, and much of the rural population. The nutrition level of the army and the most important war workers was expected to be sufficient for them, in the sense that these groups would be able to maintain their efforts. 8, 23 October, and 12-11-1942, JIC35th, 37th, and 40thMtg, Box-217, RG218; 21-10-1942, JIC58, Box-217, RG218. The Soviet food situation was also delegated to the CIC, and was subsequently discussed on the 19th meeting of the Combined Intelligence Sub-Committee. 9–10–1942, CISC19thMtg, Box-217, RG218. The OSS made a similar estimate in October, which they handed over to the Enemy Branch of the Board of Economic Warfare (BEW). The OSS believed that the food situation was adequate for the Army and the most essential war workers, but less satisfactory for other categories of Soviet society. The rural population and other categories of urban inhabitants would "face severe food conditions". Even if it was estimated that the food supplied to the army and the essential war workers would enable them to continue their efforts, the Soviet food situation in general was seen as a "somewhat unfavorable factor" in Soviet military capabilities. 20-10-1942, 402033, Box-1619, Entry-141A, RG169.

74   Furthermore, it was added that the army, the important war-industry workers, and the peasants in the food surplus-producing regions, would experience a fairly stable food position during the crop year of 1942–1943. For the rest of the population it was believed that the situation would probably be worse, until next year's harvest. 11-11-1942, JIC58(2d Draft), Box-217, RG218. The second version was read and amended at the US JIC's 40th meeting, resulting in the third draft, which in turn was considered by the JPS. The general drift of the third draft was the same as in the second draft. 12-11-1942, JIC40thMtg, Box-217, RG218; 13-11-1942, JIC58(3d Draft), Box-217, RG218; 14-11-1942, JPS "Memorandum [...]", Box-217, RG218.

75   The first of these reports was called "The Food Problem under Peacetime Conditions", dated 12 December 1942, and analysed the Soviet food situation on the

eve of the German invasion in the parts of the country still held by the Soviets at the time of the report date. Agricultural statistics from earlier years, as far back as the middle of 1930s, were used for this purpose. 12-12-1942, [R&A#584], Part IIa, Reel-1, Report #14, UPA1977.

76 The second but separate part of the report, "The Food Problem under War Conditions", was dated (30 November) before the first part in its preliminary draft form. 30-11-1942, R&A#584, Part IIb, Reel-1, Report #14, UPA1977.

77 17-11-1942, 413902, Box-1675, Entry-141A, RG169.

78 30-11-1942, R&A#584, Part IIb, Reel-1, Report #14, UPA1977. In another OSS memorandum from December, prepared by the R & A branch's East European Section in London and forwarded by the US London embassy to the SD, the Soviet food situation was described as serious. The need for sugar and fats were considered acute. The OSS pointed to the circumstance that the consuming population of the unoccupied area of the USSR had increased, while the production of food had diminished. December 1942, "Subject: [...]", Roll-23, T1250, RG59. This notion was more or less substantiated by another December despatch from the US London embassy to the SD and the Economic Intelligence Division of the BEW, containing information from the MEW about the Soviet livestock position. 18-12-1942, No. 6783, Roll-26, T1250, RG59. The MEW livestock memorandum was forwarded to the US Kuibyshev embassy by the SD in January 1943. 16-1-1943, No. 107, 862.2, Box-26, MECF1943, RG84.

79 22-12-1942, "American [...]", Box-3118, Entry-77, RG165.

80 The telegram was intended for further distribution to the BEW and the Department of Agriculture. 12-1-1943, Number: 309, Roll-23, T1250, RG59.

81 12-1-1943, Number: 309, Roll-23, T1250, RG59; Gaddis 1972, 16. The BEW doubted the reliability of the informant. 11-2-1943, 861.5018/70, Roll-23, T1250, RG59.

82 Harrison (1996), 92.

83 Barber & Harrison (1991), 77–78.

84 Ibid, 79–83.

85 Harrison (1994), 260–261.

86 21-10-1942, "Notes [...]", WO208/1755.

87 In early November 1942 the first report in a series of six about the military potential of the Soviet Union was published by the OSS East European section. The report was divided into two parts. 3–11–1942, R&A#584(Ia), Reel-1 (13), UPA1977.

88 Ibid.

89 4–11–1942, "Subject: [...]", 350.05 Union of Socialist Soviet Republics 5-1-42 thru 8–31–43, Box-1043, Entry-47, RG319.

90 2–12–1942, JIC(42)459(Final), CAB81/111.

91 7-8-1942, "Strategic [...]", ABC384USSR(6-1-42), Box-472, Entry-421, RG165.

92 14-8-1942, "Lend [...]", Box-3155, Entry-77, RG165.

93 18-8-1942, MID470.8U.S.S.R.8-4-42, 470.8USSR, Box-1051, Entry-47, RG319.

94 15-8-1942, "Record [...]", CAB121/460; Harriman & Abel (1976), 163.

95 12-9-1942, 5122, Roll-16, T1250, RG59.

96 The mission, headed by Major General Follett Bradley, was tasked by Roosevelt to coordinate defence preparations with the Soviets in anticipation of a possible Japanese attack on the USSR. Matloff (2003), 100.

97 17–9–1942, "Subject: [...]", File No. 000.800-Misc., Box-949, Entry-300, RG18.

98 This was according to a memorandum dated 1–10–1942, signed by the assistant chief of intelligence for air, Colonel Ralph Stearly, meant for the BEW. 1–10–1942, Box-3155, "Subject: [...]", Entry-77, RG165.

99 23-11-1942, "Russian [...]", Entry-77, Box-3175, RG165.

100 1–10–1942, JP(42)161, CAB119/38; "Assistance to Russia", CAB121/459.

101 "12/zf/1, Holdings + wastage, Holdings", WO208/5171.
102 The sources included official Soviet sources, statements from Soviet officials, American and British intelligence reports, Polish intelligence reports, newspapers, independent authors, British and American officials, and even secret sources. 11-11-1942, R&A#584 (Part IV), Reel-1, Report #17, UPA1977.
103 Ibid.
104 The OSS also pointed out that the practice of using substitute materials in aircraft was used by the British to some extent. The total monthly supply of aluminium was estimated to be about 9000 tonnes, of which about 4000 tonnes were supplied from the US and the UK. The monthly Soviet production was estimated to be about 4000 tonnes, and the amount of aluminium received from scrap was estimated at 1000 tonnes. Judging by the consumption in the US aircraft industry the Soviets would require about 13,000 tonnes of aluminium in their aircraft industry alone, a deficit the OSS reckoned that the Soviets had made good by economizing on the use of aluminium both inside and outside the aircraft industry. The OSS believed it possible that, with consideration to all possible economies, the Soviets had a sufficient supply of aluminium for their aircraft production at the time. Ibid.
105 Ibid.
106 Ibid.
107 Their view in this respect was further strengthened by accounts of the fighting on the Soviet–German front, from both Soviet and foreign observers. Ibid.
108 Krivosheev (1997), 244–250.
109 Apparently the British went to great lengths to investigate the exact location and capacity of the Soviet tank industry and individual factories. Many sheets of information were compiled on this subject left in the WO files. See for example WO208/5173 and WO208/5174.
110 2–12–1942, JIC(42)459(Final), CAB81/111.
111 They did not present an estimate of their own, but thought that the Soviets had enough steel to produce almost three times the volume of armaments produced in 1938. But they were not sure if there were adequate facilities to turn around 10 million tonnes of steel into munitions. Even though they did not present an overall production level regarding munitions, the US JIC had some views on the concrete production figures for planes and tanks. The British estimate of a monthly production rate of 1500–2000 aircraft was not regarded as impossible, but unlikely. The British production figure for Soviet tanks, 2000 a month, was not at all regarded as reliable. For one thing, it appeared to the Americans that the British had not accounted for the evacuation or destruction of the Stalingrad plant. 14–1–1943, JIC48thMtg, JIC25/6(13–1-1943), Box-214, RG218.
112 2–12–1942, JIC(42)459(Final), CAB81/111.
113 13-1-1943, Report No. 7576, 350.05 Union of Socialist Soviet Republics, Box-1043, Entry-47, RG319.
114 Overy (1996), 214, 218–220; Ellis (1993), 285–286, 288, 290, 292; Harrison (1998a), 29.
115 Harrison (1985), 250.
116 23–7-1942, 5–8-1942, 12–8-1942, 19–9-1942, 27-11-1942, 8–1-1943, 28–1-1943, "Battle [...]", Box-3159, Entry-77, RG165.
117 2–8-1941, "War Cabinet, [...]", CAB121/464.
118 7–8-1942, "Strategic [...]", ABC384USSR(6–1-42), Box-472, Entry-421, RG165.
119 23–7-1942, 5–8-1942, 12–8-1942, 19–9-1942, 27-11-1942, 8–1-1943, 28–1-1943, "Battle [...]", Box-3159, Entry-77, RG165.
120 6–8-1942, 14–8-1942, 23025, Box-250, Entry-98, RG38; 22–9-1942, A-6-b, 16382–0, Entry-98, RG38.
121 10–1-1943, F-6-e, 23025, Box-250, Entry-98, RG38.

122 3–11–1942, R&A#584(Ib), Reel-1 (13), UPA1977.

123 11-11-1942, R&A#584 (Part IV), Reel-1, Report #17, UPA1977.

124 The fact that the Soviets had never asked for Western Allied deliveries of artillery, except regarding anti-tank guns and anti-aircraft guns, was an indication to the OSS that the Red Army's supply of artillery was adequate. Their view in this respect was further strengthened by accounts of the fighting on the Soviet–German front, from both Soviet and foreign observers. 11-11-1942, R&A#584 (Part IV), Reel-1, Report #17, UPA1977.

125 3–11–1942, R&A#584(Ib), Reel-1, UPA1977.

126 11-11-1942, R&A#584 (Part IV), Reel-1, Report #17, UPA1977.

127 5–12–1942, "Politico […]", 383.6USSR6–1-43 thru, Box-1047, Entry-47, RG319.

128 The strength of the Soviet Navy was estimated at two battleships, seven cruisers (with fighting value), seven flotilla leaders, 35 modern and old destroyers, 24 escort vessels, 224 submarines of various sizes, and a couple of hundred, mostly smaller, ships with different military purposes. 2–12–1942, JIC(42)459(Final), CAB81/111.

129 The US JIC believed that the number of Soviet submarines in the Far East was 57, instead of 105 as the British JIC had listed. 14–1-1943, JIC48[th]Mtg, JIC25/6 (13–1-1943), Box-214, RG218.

130 Harrison (1996), 270–271.

131 Glantz & House (2000), 306.

132 Ibid, 292.

133 Krivosheev (1997), 252, 254.

134 7–8-1942, "Strategic […]", ABC384USSR(6–1-42), Box-472, Entry-421, RG165.

135 In a US August report from the assistant military attaché in London to Washington, the views of Josef Kalla on the Red Army were expressed. Kalla was the military attaché at the Czechoslovak Legation in London and he expressed a high regard for the stamina and morale of the Soviet soldiers. But he believed that the officers of the higher staffs were suffering from "the national lack of organizing ability". 17–8-1942, "Czech […]", Box-3120, Entry-77, RG165. In an interview at the beginning of September with Commander A. T. Courtney, previously attached to the British Naval Mission in the USSR, MI3(c) learned that Courtney considered Soviet army morale to be very high. 2–9-1942, "Notes […]", WO208/1755; Smith (1996), 110. The US officers of the Bradley Mission (see above) also reported to the WD in September that they considered the maintenance of military aircraft as adequate, although below US standards. Soviet "camouflage discipline" was considered superior. 17–9-1942, "Subject: […]", File No. 000.800-Misc., Box-949, Entry-300, RG18. According to the Hungarian report, which was regarded as fairly reliable by the MI3(c), the Soviet High Command was unable to carry out any large-scale operations. But the resistance capacity of the Red Army was still believed to be considerable, although the "hitting power" of the army was seen as weaker than at the beginning of the Soviet–German war, despite the fact that it now fielded more military formations. But the fighting power, in general, of the troops was regarded as better than at the beginning of the war. According to the Hungarians the principal weakness of the Soviet army was "the higher command, the exhaustion of manpower and the material losses which can only be partly replenished". 30-10-1942, "M.I.3 […]", WO208/1805. Lieutenant-Colonel Bartnowski was of the same opinion regarding the higher Soviet command (the bureaucratic general staff). 21-10-1942, "Notes […]", WO208/1755. On 1 December Clark-Kerr had informed the participants at the 58th meeting of the JIC that he believed the morale of the Red Army to be good, and that he saw the abolition of the commissar system as an improvement in efficiency. 1–12–1942, N6195/1375/38, FO371/32990. The report from the US military attaché in Turkey from January

1943 to the MID, on the views of the Turkish ambassador to the USSR, stated that the morale of the Soviet army was high. 13–1-1943, 350.05 Union of Socialist Soviet Republics, Box-1043, Entry-47, RG319.

136 Glantz & House (2000), 121; Keegan (ed.) (1989), 100.
137 30-10-1942, "M.I.3 [...]", WO208/1805.
138 4-9-1942, N4566/30/38, FO371/32913.
139 1–10–1942, 16–9-1942, N5066/1375/38, FO371/32990.
140 1–10–1942, JP(42)161, CAB119/38.
141 11-10-1942, "M.I.3.(c).", WO208/1805.
142 24-10-1942, "M.I.3/6998", WO208/1805.
143 14-10-1942, MIL7266, FO181/964/4; Smith (1996), 129.
144 21-10-1942, "Notes [...]", WO208/1755; 30-10-1942, "Comments [...]", Box-3172, Entry-77, RG165.
145 24-10-1942, N5532/30/38, FO371/32915; 3–10–1942, "Report [...]", WO208/1794.
146 17-10-1942, "Sir [...]", FO800/874.
147 18-11-1942, R&A#584, Part VI, Report #18, Reel-1, UPA1977.
148 11-11-1942, R&A#584 (Part IV), Reel-1, Report #17, UPA1977.
149 2–12–1942, JIC(42)459(Final), CAB81/111; Keegan (ed.) (1989), 104–106.
150 2–12–1942, JIC(42)459(Final), CAB81/111.
151 Ibid.
152 10-12-1942, No. 411, 820-Secret, Box-48, MECF1944, RG84; 11-12-1942, Roll-6, T1250, RG59.
153 25-1-1943, "Summary [...]", MI3(c), WO208/1755.
154 16-12-1942, "Efficiency [...]", Box-3157, Entry-77, RG165.
155 31-1-1943, "Joint chiefs of Staff, Memorandum of information no. 45", Box-212, RG218.
156 Glantz & House (2000), 37–38, 288.
157 Ibid, 114–117.

17 From Stalingrad to Kursk

After a period of relative lull, during the spring and early summer of 1943, the military duel between the *Wehrmacht* and the Red Army erupted in the battle of Kursk. Even though the turning points in the East can be seen as the most important in the context of the War, considering the large mass of German and other Axis troops engaged there, the end of 1942 and 1943 did also produce turning points on other theatres of war. The Axis troops in North Africa were forced onto the retreat and eventually surrendered in Tunisia. Shortly after the Western Allies invaded Italy, eventually resulting in the downfall of Mussolini's fascist regime. The battle of the Atlantic continued but by the summer of 1943 the U-boat threat was largely under control. The bombing campaign of Germany gained momentum, even though it still was very limited compared to the 1944 effort. In the Pacific Japan's offensive was thwarted, and the Americans was now on the offensive instead. The increasing US mobilization was slowly but surely beginning to produce results on the combat theatres of the globe.

The Soviets benefited from the gearing up of the US war economy, since this allowed for an increase in Lend-Lease shipments to Americas allies all around the world. But despite the increasing Anglo-American strength most of the German divisions actually fighting the Allies was stationed in the East. The fighting in North Africa and later in Italy only drew a very limited number of German divisions and replacements, and the Allied success in the Mediterranean was at least partly due to the fact that the Red Army tied down the bulk of German strength. For the continuation of the war in 1944, it also very important that the Soviets still did exactly that, otherwise an Anglo-American landing in Western Europe would have been a much riskier – or perhaps even a more or less impossible – task.

In time, political attitudes towards the USSR began to alter in the West and the USSR received recognition for her efforts against Germany. Greater respect was also shown for Stalin and the Soviet system.[1] This period also saw a deepening of the cooperation between the Western Allies and the USSR. Two major Allied conferences were held, one in Moscow and one in Teheran.[2] There were also a few Anglo-American conferences with implications for the war on the Soviet–German front. At Casablanca in January 1943 Roosevelt and Churchill decided on future strategy. The British doubted Allied capacity for a French landing before 1944, and they advocated a Mediterranean strategy, while at the same time claiming that the bombing of Germany was weakening her effort in the East. In May 1943, at the *Trident* conference in Washington, the Anglo-Americans agreed to launch a cross-Channel attack in May 1944.[3]

17.1 Military prospects, internal stability and civilian support for the war effort

At the end of the Soviet winter offensive in the south the Red Army became overextended, which opened the way for a German counteroffensive. The Germans had concentrated forces in reserve, after which they struck the Soviets spearheads and then moved on to Kharkov. The Red Army suffered heavy casualties and the Germans could retake Kharkov. The German operation was over in less than a month and then the frontline stabilised. We have seen that at the time of the German surrender at Stalingrad, OSS representatives still doubted the future Soviet ability to continue the offensive against Germany. By March 1943, when the Germans were counter-attacking at Kharkov, the British JIC concluded: "the prospect of a German defeat of Russia has receded to vanishing point". At the end of April the JIC predicted that the Germans would have to face a third winter in the East, and that she no longer could count on reaching a separate peace with the USSR (even if she conquered new territory later in 1943).[4] In their first report on Soviet capabilities after the German Stalingrad surrender, dated 12 March, the JIC commented on Soviet strength as of 1 March. The report was also distributed as a US JIC report at the beginning of April.[5] Civilian morale was seen as high in the report. The Soviet victories, German atrocities and a relatively mild winter were described as some contributory factors. As long as the military situation did not deteriorate seriously and the NKVD could continue its hold on the country, the Government would not have any problem in keeping civilian morale at a level adequate to sustain production and services behind the front.[6]

In mid-February the US London embassy rated civilian morale as high.[7] A week later the OSS stated that the Soviet people felt that they, together with the Western Allies, were fighting the common fascist enemy. The people were united by their hatred of fascism, by nationalism and by the influence of religion. Western Allied progress in North Africa, in combination with declarations from Allied statesmen, was one factor that had strengthened Soviet morale since the summer of 1942. Therefore, despite the enormous sacrifices, the morale of the Soviet people was now "at a very high level".[8] According to an April US Kuibyshev embassy report, the labour force in general endured their harsh labour conditions due to "a combination of fear, ignorance, acceptance of unavoidable circumstance, war 'esprit', and sense of duty".[9]

In April the OSS analysed the Soviet winter offensive in a report intended for internal distribution. The offensive was "the most substantial victory of the United Nations [the Allies] to date." Total Axis casualties were 1.5 million men. But the USSR was straining its economy in a way that could not possibly continue for long.[10] Later that month a joint Board of Economic Warfare (BEW)-OSS Coordinating Committee issued a memorandum that dealt with the Axis economic situation, distributed to Donovan among others. The section concerned with the Soviet–German front revealed some differences between the US and British outlook on Soviet and German strength. The British believed that Soviet military strength was "markedly superior to [...] German", that Soviet output of aircraft and tanks "greatly exceeds German", that the Soviets had "superior forces" (with reference to numbers in the field) and that the economic potential still had not "passed its peak", while German economic and military potential was declining. US military intelligence believed that Germany could more than replace its losses and launch renewed extensive offensives against the Red Army. The committee believed that the British over-estimated Soviet strength and "somewhat" underestimated German strength, but also believed that US military intelligence "continues seriously to over-estimate German strength". The committee believed instead that Soviet military strength would probably "be at least equal" to Axis strength in the summer of 1943, but that Soviet "economic staying power" was deteriorating much faster than German economic strength. Anglo-American operations in the West during 1943 might have a decisive influence on the course of the Soviet–German war, since the Soviet–German forces were now so closely balanced in strength. On the other hand, it was not discounted that the Germans would cripple Soviet armed strength in 1943 to such an extent that Germany would be able to reduce her military commitments in the East, despite the fact that she had failed to do so in 1941 and 1942.[11]

The committee's conclusions are in line with a difference in British and US assessments, which could be discerned already in the middle of 1942. I return to the realism of these assessments regarding the Soviet economy below, but it was clear that the British underestimated German strength when they concluded that Germany's economic strength already had reached its peak. As a matter of fact, the German war economy, which already at the time was rather heavily mobilized, was gearing up even more. This mobilization rendered results in form of a constantly increasing munitions output, which only reached its peak in the late summer of 1944. By then munitions output was substantially higher than at the beginning of 1943, and also in many cases often consisted of significantly better weapons in terms of performance.

Hitler was not prepared to resign his ambitions in the East just yet, and was therefore planning for another summer offensive. This offensive was more concentrated than before. In 1941 the offensive had involved the whole front from the Baltic to the Black Sea (and Finland); during the summer of 1942 the offensive only stretched over the southern third of the front, and now it was only directed against the so-called Kursk-salient. The salient was situated around the city of Kursk and had been formed as a bulge – around 250 kilometres in width from north to south – pointing into the German frontline. Large German forces were concentrated to the north and south of the bulge in order to cut it off. The idea was to catch large Red Army forces in a pocket, and at the same time open up a hole in the Soviet front. Most of the German elite *panzer* formations had been concentrated to the bulge.

In early May the US JIC tried to assess future developments on the Soviet–German front. No definite conclusion was presented regarding the military situation, but a Soviet attempt to reach a separate peace was unrealistic.[12] About the same time Michela, now brigadier-general, shared his personal observations regarding Soviet (and German) capabilities. The MIS stated that his report was "excellent" and in line with their views. This makes Michela's statement concerning Soviet strength all the more interesting: "All in all the future for the eastern front is not black and the chances of the Soviets holding are slightly in their favour, however, a determined German offensive on the southern part of the central front would be a real threat but any operations of the Allies in the west would decrease the chances of German success in the east in direct proportion. If the Allies invade Europe the Soviets could go on the offensive – but not otherwise."[13] Cavendish-Bentinck was more optimistic on 4 June when he wrote: "even if the Germans do not attack in Russia, they will require the forces that they have there in order to withstand a Russian advance".[14]

That civilian morale still was high was indicated by a FO report also presented to the War Cabinet. At the beginning of June a FO official commented on a report from May, describing a trip made by another FO official to Sverdlovsk and Chelyabinsk in the Urals region. The latter had socialized with some ordinary people there. Most of them had lost relatives in the war and saw the pre-war days as better times. They would endure until Germany's defeat without feeling any "defeatism" or "despair", with "a desperate determination to defeat the Germans quickly".[15]

On 25 June, ten days before the German Kursk offensive, the OSS issued an internal report concerning Soviet military potential.[16] Apparently the OSS still believed that Soviet war potential was declining: "The Soviet Union this summer may be expected to offer resistance at least as strong as that shown in the summer of 1942 – but at the expense of a further decline in manpower, a shortage of industrial materials, and a dangerous decrease in its rapidly vanishing food stocks."[17]

On 5 July the German offensive started against the fortified Soviet armies in the Kursk salient. The attack made some hard-won progress at first, but the Red Army was too well prepared. After the huge armoured clash near Prokhorovka on 12 July, at the southern wing of the bulge, the attack bogged down. On the very same day the Red Army began their strategic offensive in the Orel area, to the North of the Kursk salient.[18] This was actually the first time the Red Army managed to successfully launch at summer offensive. The Kursk battle was the largest armoured battle of the war and it drained precious German reserves. Soviet losses were substantially greater but they could better afford to replace them. The failed German offensive seemingly had an impact on the assessments.

On 13 July the British 30 Military Mission in Moscow concluded with confidence that the German Kursk offensive had failed.[19] Pika believed on 23 July that a major Soviet offensive would start in September. When the WO comment on his assessment 30 July they stated that it was too early to expect a major offensive then, but that one might start before the end of 1943 "if the Allied invasion of Europe has made substantial progress by that date". They also agreed with Pika's belief that the population was suffering hardships, but they saw no danger (nor did Pika) of a crack in the civilian morale in the near future.[20] It was not stated whether the WO referred to the invasion of Sicily which begun on 10 July[21], or another invasion at a later date. Actually both were wrong since the Soviet Orel offensive was already in full swing.

17.2 The economy, manpower, food supply and civilian living conditions

We have seen that the Anglo-American, and especially the US, observers perceived the economic situation as very hard pressed. The war effort was straining Soviet resources and the Germans were economically stronger. That these perceptions persisted is not that strange, or rather quite natural, in the light of the fact that Germany occupied most of continental Western and Central Europe, while at the same time having robbed the USSR of approximately half her European land area. In terms of a simple GDP comparison – although not a method used by the Anglo-Americans at the time regarding the Soviet situation – Germany and her Axis allies commanded an area that was much larger than the Soviets. This would, of course, had mattered a little less if the Western Allies at the same time had tied a large part of German military strength, which at the time was not the case. The greater part of German military power was still committed against the Soviets.

This discrepancy between Soviet and German strength, in purely economic terms, was noted by the US Kuybyshev embassy in February 1943. Even though it was clearly stated that the role of foreign aid was not considered, the author nevertheless wondered "how a country which has suffered from such great losses can continue as a military power, or indeed to remain in the struggle at all." There was no explicit explanation for the reason that the USSR had managed to survive against a "superior" industrial and military power such as Germany. But in the absence of purely economic explanations the "determination" and "even ruthlessness" of the Soviet leadership, which managed the war effort, was mentioned. Regarding the raw material situation, Soviet industry did not produce enough industrial raw materials to provide for the supply of a modern fully equipped army.[22] Worries concerning the raw material situation were also expressed by other US observers. In January Lieutenant-Colonel Park reported on his earlier visit to the Soviet front, with General Hurely, to the British Joint Staff Mission in Washington. The British JIC and the FO noted a minute of this meeting at the beginning of February. Park stated that he doubted whether the Germans would attempt to capture Baku during 1943, since they had already reduced the oil flow from Baku to the interior parts of the USSR by about 80 per cent.[23] It is hard to come by estimates regarding how much the flow of Baku oil was curtailed in reality, but Park's assessments seems to be a clear overestimation of the negative effects.

However, in general it seems that at least the British started to change their assessments of economic capabilities, even though the food situation was still regarded as a substantial problem by some observers. The British MI, and Pika, believed in March that there had been "a great improvement in the railway system". Pika claimed that the civilian population was "suffering acutely" from a shortage of food and other supplies. But there was no shortage of bread in the larger cities, not even in Leningrad.[24]

The same month US military intelligence gave attention to an article written by a British military official in India. One of the main points in the article was that it was Soviet industry, built up through industrialization, which had made resistance to the German invasion possible: "Of course, Britain and America have made an enormous [material] contribution [...] but this cannot detract from the fact that without Soviet industry the Red Army would probably have had to give up the struggle at the end of the three weeks' limit which so many sceptical people gave it."[25]

The economic section of the March British JIC report, shared with the Americans, had a clear resemblance with the JIC report from December 1942. Once again industrial output was estimated at 60–70 per cent of the pre-war level. The transportation system was still a major limiting factor upon economic performance, and several commodities were still in short supply. Just as in December no more military personnel could be mobilized, except for the regular annual intake, without curtailing economic performance. Military transport, even though still generally not capable of handling large troop movements efficiently, was no longer impeding economic transport. The continuation of Allied shipments in 1943 was a guarantee against a reduction in the war effort. The oil and steel situation was now improved. This was explained by improved communications with the Caucasus, and an increased steel production (13 million tonnes a year). The Soviets were economizing on the use of steel and was practising raw-material substitution, and had access to a large pre-war reserve of gun ammunition, which in turn made it unnecessary to increase ammunition production to keep pace with the higher consumption.[26]

The increased population, estimated at 10 per cent (13 million people) due to the re-occupation of the Don and North Caucasian areas during the winter offensive, was not a problem from the perspective of food supply. The minimum requirements of the whole population could now be better met by improved communications, increased Allied food deliveries and captured German stocks. Food was not a critical factor in the war effort until the next harvest, although local food deficiencies were not excluded.[27]

Other British observers conveyed a more depressing picture. In April Clark-Kerr sent a telegram to the FO reporting that "all official observers" in Moscow had seen "signs of acute shortage of food". He had learned from a "reliable sources" that during the past months about 300 workers per month in the Stalin auto works in Moscow had died of hunger due to "albumenless swelling". The factory was one of the "leading industrial establishments" in Moscow. The alleged reason was corrupt catering officials.[28]

The same month the very serious food situation and the hardships for the ordinary population were confirmed in a MI14 report. There might soon be a grave danger of famine. However, the food situation in the army was good. The information originated from a journalist, Paul Holt,[29] who was seen as well informed. The manpower problem was also mentioned and the journalist had seen fighting units composed of personnel varying in age from 17 to 50.[30] The next month Holt was interviewed by the MI3(c) when he stated that the manpower situation was "very tight", and that the Soviets lacked reserves (in general) for any large-scale offensive. His assessment regarding casualties was in line with this notion since casualties in general were "at least three or four times [...] the German.", and permanent losses somewhere between 7.5 and 10 million men.[31]

Holt's assessments were partly contradicted by Paul Winterton,[32] another journalist interviewed by the MI3 in May. Winterton considered the manpower situation as "fairly satisfactory". The soldiers he had seen were "neither to young nor to old".[33] His opinion on the food situation was that: "The useless mouths in Russia were starving." However, there was enough food to go around for the troops and people employed in the war effort.[34] Later, in July, MI3(c) estimated that the Soviets had mobilized 20.5 million men out of a total of 23 million available for mobilization. This was taken as an indication that although the manpower situation was tight, it was not as problematic as earlier thought.[35]

In April the MI3 Colonel F. Thornton sent a letter to his colleague Colonel K. G. Exham of the British 30 Mission. Thornton asked Exham about the food situation, since a telegram from the British ambassador in the USSR had depicted a rather "depressing" picture. Exham painted a somewhat brighter picture of the situation. He wrote that: "the people continue to look reasonably fit". Even though he admitted that the unbalanced diet must have unwanted cumulative effects, the situation was under control. From experiences in the recaptured areas of the Donbass Exham had learnt that "strenuous and successful efforts" had been made to cultivate the area again, but that the main problem was the shortage of tractors.[36]

The British MI received information in June from someone concerning a German military high command (OKW) appreciation of the Soviet situation and German intentions. The source was described as "reliable [...] in the past", and might be the same source used by the MI in 1942. The OKW predicted that the food situation was deteriorating rapidly, and that it would be so acute during the winter of 1943–1944 that the USSR would cease to be a serious adversary. The MI3 and the MI14 commented that the food situation was not deteriorating, although it was very serious. It was too early to contemplate a food crisis for the winter of 1943–1944.[37]

In April the OSS presented a more pessimistic outlook on the economic situation, compared to the British JIC in March. The Stalingrad victory and the ensuing offensive were described as a victory of the first magnitude, but the cost of maintaining the military effort was too great: "the Russians have maintained their military effort only at a terrific cost in civilian living standards and capital equipment maintenance. The Soviet Union is stripping its economy to the danger point, and the length of time this process can continue is strictly limited." This state of affairs was the background to the Soviets' constant insistence on a second front.[38]

The OSS analysed the food situation in May and described "food [as] the weakest element in present Soviet capabilities." The only adequately fed group was the Red Army, whose daily calorie intake was compared to US Army rations. Others had less than the international standard: war workers and manual labourers had 2000 calories daily; white-collar workers had only 1600; and adult dependants were "badly underfed". Children had more adequate rations. But the extent of undernourishment was worse than the actual calorie intake indicated, since the quality of the foodstuff was low and therefore had low protein content. They stated that "the poor diet [had] decreased the man-hour productivity of the average manual worker in war work by at least ten per cent". This was "the direct impact of the food shortage on the war effort". US food shipments were described as very important. During the first three months of 1943, US deliveries constituted 17 per cent of the Red Army's food requirements on a calorie basis. OSS argued that if the same amount of food had been taken from war workers and manual workers, they would have suffered from a 38 per cent deficiency in their food intake. The high calorific value of the US shipments was explained by the fact that they consisted mainly of meats, fats, and sugar.[39]

In June the OSS returned to the food situation. They interpreted the Soviet request for large amounts of additional bread grains and cereals, for the Lend-Lease year June 1943 to June 1944, as an indication that the food situation was still critical. The 1942 harvest was 39.1 million tonnes of grains, which left a net deficit of 10 million tonnes for the crop year 1942–1943. The 1943–1944 deficits were 7.6 million tonnes. The rationing system (adapted to the scarce food supply) was not adequate to provide a decent diet for the population, even though this would not affect the Red Army, most war workers, and the majority of the children. The situation concerning consumer goods was described as critical, since the war had reduced output and the Red Army was taking what was left. But with US aid there was at least enough to go around for the needs of the military.[40]

They argued that there existed a general labour shortage, but it had not affected the production of armaments. The problem was a perceived lack of workers with special skills. Despite the introduction of the 48-hour week before the war, and much overtime, it was not enough to offset the decline in average efficiency due to male workers being replaced by women since the beginning of the war. Furthermore, the recruitment of women, children and aged to the labour force was not expected to continue for very long at the current rate. They also highlighted a perceived strain on the transport system, or more specifically the railways. Several problems were identified in basic industry, most notably regarding the supply of non-ferrous metals. If it not had been for Lend-Lease supplies the non-ferrous metals situation would be critical. The need for imports was also noted concerning rubber, and, to some extent, steel. Coal was identified as another problem area. The petroleum output was regarded as more than adequate, except that they raised some concerns about the Soviet capacity to transport it from the production areas.[41]

The BEW-OSS Coordination Committee memorandum from late April emphasized the long term decline of economic strength, eventually affecting military strength. The high commitment of total resources to the war effort, relative to other countries, seriously affected the civilian economy and eroded the maintenance of industrial and transport equipment. The losses of economic resources due to the war were described as further accelerating the strain and erosion off human and physical assets. No forecast was presented as to when this situation would affect munitions output. Due to "a better maintained economic structure", German economic "staying power" was greater.[42]

In Michela's May report to the MID the railways were described as "still greatly overburdened – but apparently getting by". He considered the recently proclaimed Soviet decree, instigating martial law for railway employees, as an attempt to prevent a further deterioration of efficiency, rather than an effort to raise it. He described the transport system's effect on the Red Army's offensive capabilities: "The supply and transport system of the Red Army comprise the one serious but not critical weakness which has not yet revealed itself because no Soviet offensive involving great distance and rapid movements against determined resistance has taken place." He also commented on the food supply and described it as a serious problem. He saw no immediate problem with manpower, since he predicted that the part played by women in the war effort, would allow the Soviets to continue to fill the ranks of the Red Army for the coming year at least.[43]

The same month the US JIC stated: "Limitations to the effectiveness of Russian Armed Forces lie in organization and transport rather than in insufficient supply of manpower."[44] An April report from the US embassy in Kuibyshev, intended for the War Manpower Commission, stated that the limitation of the working force was more a question of skill and efficiency than numbers. The total burdens on the Soviet workers were far more pressing than on their US counterparts. The USSR used women for heavier labour duties than in the US, and teens (from 14 to 18 years) were employed in war production, a measure not undertaken in the US. Several practical conditions within the framework of the economy were factors that impaired the efficiency of the labour force (i.e. the lack of adequate housing and local transport facilities were such conditions).[45]

According to the British MEW, the reoccupation of Soviet soil by the Red Army was another factor affecting the economy. In a memorandum from

April, noted by the FO in May, the MEW concluded that the territory gained from November to March was both a liability and an asset – the liability being the civilian population of the liberated territories, about 12 million people, in need of food and other supplies. However, the advance was also believed to have alleviated the over-all transport situation, which in turn was something that would improve the economic situation. The distribution of Baku oil and other supplies would be eased by this development, as well as more long-term additions of coal, steel and non-ferrous metals and food (if permanently held) from the Donbas, Kuban, North Caucasus, Kursk and Voronezh areas.[46]

The next month the MEW estimated the total number of men mobilized into the armed forces since June 1941 to 17 million (including the 5 million already called up on 22 June 1941). The problem was not the total number of males drafted to armed forces so far, since the men still available for military draft was "enormous", but rather the fact that these men had been taken from the workforce. Therefore industry and agriculture were experiencing an "extremely tight situation" with reference to available labour. Considering military losses and available recruits the MEW concluded that the present strength of the armed forces was at a maximum. One FO official regarded the MEW's conclusions as very speculative, although "broadly true". He stated that the MEW had not taken account of the "widespread" employment of women in the USSR. Cavendish-Bentinck guessed that the Soviets had a considerable numerical superiority over the Germans on the front, somewhere in the range of one million men.[47]

As always information from inside the Axis camp was also used in order to gain knowledge of the Soviet situation. A telegram from the Japanese foreign minister to the embassy in Berlin, decrypted by the British in May, stated that the Soviet industrial potential (and ability to wage war) was "steadily increasing".[48]

Sometimes the economy was analysed more or less out of the context of the war. The FO Research Department was involved in the production of a USSR handbook and stated in a report: "It may be disputed whether the Soviet system has proved the superiority of State ownership of the means of production and distribution over the capitalistic system of private enterprise. But it is important to bear in mind that Russia and the Russian people cannot be compared with Western European countries, including of course the U.S.A. An economic and political system admirably suitable to Russia might be entirely out of place in our country."[49] An analysis like this is actually quite interesting since it shows that the Soviet economic system was not completely rejected by an initiated Western observer. He was actually contemplating that state ownership of the economy might be better than private ownership, and then of course especially in the Russian case.

Another draft paper (for the USSR handbook) made by the FO's Research Department dated 5 July enumerated several "facts" relating to industrial efficiency and labour. Figures relating to the year 1937 were quoted in an attempt to compare productivity per worker in relation to other countries. They revealed that the amount of coal produced per miner in 1937 was 370 tonnes in the USSR, 435 in Germany and 844 in the United States. The figures in tonnes for pig iron per worker in blast furnaces were 756, 612 (Germany) and 1260, respectively. Other pre-war figures (1940–1941) of industrial output were quoted to stress the fact that the USSR was one of the largest industrial producers in the world. The quality of heavy industry products, and especially engineering manufacturing, although not consumer goods, compared well with the product quality of the capitalist countries. However, even though the quality of manufactured goods was better than during the first Five Year Plan, it was in any case regarded as inferior in comparison with British or US products. The "individual efficiency" of labour and its output per man-hour were behind Western capitalist standards.[50]

Bureaucracy in Soviet enterprises was a greater problem than in Western countries. But the lack of a private profit motive was not a major problem: "[its] absence [...] does not, at least in the U.S.S.R., render the heads of enterprise, engineers and technicians unimaginative, unenterprising and apathetic [...] if the lack of competition does to some extent take the edge off the 'push' and inspiration that sometimes animates private enterprise, it has one important advantage. Any new invention, a labour-saving device or a cheaper process, that may be discovered in one [...] factory is immediately made available to all instead of being [...] a trade secret."[51]

A FO Research Department draft paper on agriculture for the Handbook, dated 10 July, included some praise for agricultural science and new innovations in agricultural practices. But the labour productivity standard of farming was far below the level of British agriculture. Soviet agriculture used three to four times more labour relatively speaking. The explanation for this was that labour was an abundant and expendable resource (just as during the time of serfdom in Tsarist Russia) in relation to land and capital. In addition farm labour was less efficient than in the West. The relative level of mechanization was much lower than in Great Britain.[52]

The Research Department argued in another August draft paper, for the Handbook, that the Soviet worker was more of an economist than his Western counterpart, since he realized that he and his fellows could not consume more than they produced. This realization, of being part of a huge common concern, was forwarded as a reason explaining why he could put up with so much repression. It was also stressed that the Russian could not be compared to a Westerner in general.[53]

The report of the FO official who had visited the Urals region (see above) contained information about industrial expansion in the Urals, including the building of new factories and an expansion of existing ones. He also commented on economic efficiency. Labour mobilization was "far less efficient and complete than is often supposed". Mr. Wilson of the FO Northern Department remarked on the transfer of factories and machinery as not being "anything like complete", and he also saw rusty machinery being transferred. Everything that did not matter for war production, or the expansion of it, was being neglected in his view. The policy of "desperate" urgencies, while other things were totally neglected, was a part of the "chaos and confusion", the price being paid for Soviet "forced industrialization". The only way to improve the situation was to overcome the lack of technical and administrative personnel. Another FO official commented and saw the visitor's statement about industrial efficiency as a reinforcement of his belief that "while you can get things done effectively in Russia by being absolutely ruthless and by putting first things first, that does not mean that things are done efficiently and that there is not colossal wastage in the process." When the official was visiting the "Ural-mashzavod" factory in Sverdlovsk he observed a machine working area. To him it seemed that there was no shortage of raw materials and that the machines were working fast.[54]

At an informal British Joint Planning Staff and JIC meeting in June an engineer earlier involved in the delivery of supplies to the USSR reported on Soviet industrial administration. He considered it to be good, with a careful system of planning. He also seemed to think that Soviet industrial planning was more efficient than British planning.[55]

17.3 Munitions

The reality was that by the beginning of 1943 Soviet munitions output was higher than ever, and still increasing in terms of total output. The increase would continue during the year. Even at the end of 1942, British assessments was to some extent in line with what was actually going on in the Soviet munitions industries. The British March JIC report, later issued as a US JIC report, revealed about the same estimate concerning the level of munitions production as in their December 1942 report – 100 to 110 per cent of the pre-war level while the output of certain weapons was qualitatively and quantitatively very much higher.[56] Since actual munitions output was much higher than 100–100 per cent of the pre-war level this estimate was an underestimation, but despite this the JIC got it right regarding some specific classes of munitions. The output figures for tanks and operational aircraft were the same as earlier, around 2000 units per month. An increasing proportion of these was medium and heavy tanks, and most of the planes in production were stated to be fighter planes and light bombers. It was even suspected that aircraft production might reach 2500 units per month.[57]

The 1 March Pika report, commented on and seen by the MI and the FO, stated that the evacuation and reorganization of the war industry had guaranteed a satisfactory supply of equipment and munitions for the Red Army. Tank production was adequate to replace losses, but not yet to gain superiority. Further shipments from the Western Allies were needed of both tanks and aircraft, even though only a small amount of Western supplies had been used so far with the exception of trucks. The MI3(c) agreed with this but made no comment on his views regarding munitions output.[58]

Lieutenant-General Martel and other 30 Mission officials, after a front visit in May, described Soviet military equipment as not being up to Western standards.[59] Another 30 Mission report from June, signed by Martel, described the quality of air-communications equipment and long-range bombers as inferior compared to British standards.[60]

Captain Jack Duncan, the US naval attaché in the USSR, considered that the level of technological advancement in the Soviet Navy was not worth much praise. When the Soviet Navy asked the US embassy to supply them with some of the latest US naval technology in March Duncan reacted with anger. Although he felt sympathy for the Soviet war effort, it would be meaningless and stupid to hand over such sensitive information to the Soviets. He considered them so technologically backward on the naval side that they could not possibly find any use for the information they were asking for in this war.[61]

Michela wrote the following in his May report to the MID: "We can assume that production of war materials is at present better than [ever]. Sufficient time has elapsed to permit all evacuated factories to get into operation." Tank output was 1000 units per month and aircraft output at more than 1,000 units, or possibly as many as 1600 units, depending on how his report is interpreted. Both aircraft and tank production was higher than present losses.[62]

The OSS R & A branch produced several reports that contained information on munitions production during 1943–1944. In a late February 1943 report Soviet measures on the economizing of the use of copper in ammunition was analysed. The report indicated that the US had something to learn from the Soviets in that particular case.[63]

In an internal report from April they presented no concrete figures, but nevertheless estimated that the output of tanks and aircraft was higher than German output. The Soviet ability to replace losses was "far superior".[64] Another internal report from June estimated monthly output of combat planes to 2000, in addition to 200 imported aircraft. The aircraft industry had been consolidated since the previous year and production increased. It was expected that if the importation of aluminium was kept at an adequate level, output might continue to rise during the summer. The figures for tank output (and foreign imports) were the same as for aircraft. No figures were given for other military matériel, even though the estimated output of artillery and explosives was higher than the year before. The output of ammunition was nevertheless too low, due to the perceived steel shortage. The shortage of trucks was blamed on the conversion of the motor industry to tank production. But because of the "high level of imports from the United States" this problem was somewhat relieved.[65]

The British Kuibyshev embassy and the MEW exchanged telegrams in the spring concerning tank production. In March Baggallay of the embassy informed the MEW, partly based on assumed losses, that output might be as high as 6000 units per month. At the end of March Exham of the 30 Mission considered this figure as "fantastic", when compared to the latest WO estimates of German tank production. It was also hinted that the calculation of losses from British experiences were a bad measure of Soviet conditions. This view was repeated in a FO telegram from April to Kuibyshev, which also stated that the MEW estimated monthly output to 2500 units. A later telegram to Kuibyshev revealed that the WO shared the MEW estimate. Based on inclination or intuition Dew of the FO stated a few days later that tank output was much higher than the figures estimated by the MEW or the WO. The correspondence continued. Baggallay informed the MEW on 19 April that the "Uralmashzavoe [Uralvagonzavod]" tank factory was not using conveyor belts in production. On the 27th he persisted in the claim that the Soviets really were producing 6000 tanks per month, with a "considerable margin of error in either [*sic*] direction". The Kirov plant in "Tankograd" was according to him the only plant "organised on conveyor basis". When the MEW answered him in May, after conferring with the WO, they saw no reason to change the estimate of 2500 tanks per month.[66]

According to Air Ministry intelligence from June 1943 the latest Soviet fighter models had achieved "a good measure of success against the [German] Me 109 F." But the Soviet fighters could not match the later Me 109 G model in all-round performance.[67]

The FO Research Department believed, in a draft paper from July, that the experience of the war had shown that Soviet arms of even the most complex construction were "excellent both in design and general quality". They tried to explain this and the earlier confusion regarding such matters: "[the Soviets] had [...] before the war followed a policy of concentrating the best engineers and workers in armament works and equipping them with the best machinery [...] As no foreign engineers were employed in these factories – [...] the very existence of many of these factories was [...] secret – both the quantity and the quality of [...] weapons and munitions came as a surprise to the rest of the world."[68]

17.4 The size of the armed forces and the military mobilization

Just as during earlier periods it is hard to evaluate the different estimates concerning the size of the armed forces, since it is sometimes difficult to know what the Anglo-Americans really considered to be combat troops or not. The actual frontline strength of the Red Army was about 6.1 million men at the beginning of February 1943. The frontline strength continued to be in excess of 6 million men during 1943, give or take a few hundred thousand men depending on month. In addition to this there were about half a million men in the hospital pool. During 1944 and there were around 6.5 million men in the Red Army's frontline strength.[69] These figures do not comprise all personnel in the armed forces, since many was not part of the combat troops and some served in the navy. The total manpower strength of the armed forces (including the navy and NKVD troops) was 11.9 million in 1943 and 12.2 million in 1944.[70] The munitions position of the Red Army was as follows. On 1 January 1943 it had 21,900 combat aircraft, whereof 12,300 in the field forces and 20,600 tanks (and SP guns), of which 8100 were in the field forces. The position for guns and mortars, above 50 mm in calibre, was 161,600 of which 91,400 were in the field forces. The corresponding figures for 1 January 1944 was 32,500 and 13,400 combat aircraft; 24,400 and 5800 tanks; and 244,400 and 101,400 guns and mortars.[71]

In the British JIC report on Soviet strength (as of 1 March) from 12 March 1943 the JIC presented an estimate of the 1 October 1942 Armed Force's size.[72] It was 10 to 11 million men, with 8 to 9 million in the Army.[73] This was the Red Army's numerical peak strength. Except for a general shortage of motor transport, no shortages of equipment existed, at least at the vital sectors of the front. Aircraft strength was 6830, of which 4500 were stationed on the Soviet–German front, mostly fighters and ground attack aircraft. There was not thought to be any stored reserves.[74] The same month (March) the MI3(c) estimated the first-line tank strength on 1 January 1943 to 6600, not including heavy tanks or tanks sent by the Anglo-Americans, since the latter vehicles for the most part were held in reserve for summer operations.[75] In April the FO apparently believed the same regarding the Anglo-American tanks shipped (around 5,000 up to the end of January) to the USSR, while at the same time estimating total "front" tank strength, including 1000 tanks in the Far East, to 8600.[76] According to a British AI report from early May the Soviets had nearly 5100 aircraft in the Western USSR on 1 April.[77] In June, based on German OKW, Finnish and Swedish sources, the MI3 and the MI14 concluded that for the first time in the war the Soviets had gathered a large strategic reserve. The figures varied from 120 infantry divisions and 40 tank brigades to about 200 infantry divisions and 105 tank brigades.[78] It is not possible to assert how large the reserves was in reality (especially since it also is a question of how to define what is reserves and what is not), but these estimates implies that the observers probably believed that the Red Army was not suffering from any acute shortage of troops.

Available US assessments were more conservative during the spring and early summer. In March G-2 estimated the Red Army's ground strength to be between 5 and 6 million men, with about 3.6 million combat troops. These forces were supported by 9100 tanks and 5700 aircraft. Later in March they estimated total armed forces strength at between 6.5 and 7.5 million. By the end of March another evaluation estimated the number of tanks to between 5500 and 5700, and aircraft strength to between 5200 and 5300. At the end of April total armed forces strength was set to 7.56 million, with 7775 tanks.[79] In June the OSS believed that the armed forces had sustained quite large permanent losses, but the Soviets were not suffering from manpower shortages yet. The number of first-line aircraft was 5100 on 1 March 1943, and increasing, and the current tank strength "on the war front" was 17,000–18,000. Since losses were regarded as lower than output, the guess was that the tank force would increase further. Moreover, the relative proportion of heavy and medium tanks had grown, according to the report.[80] This was a gross overestimation of tank strength, if the words "on the war front" are to be taken literally and being tantamount to tanks in the field forces (see above). On the other hand the OSS clearly underestimated aircraft strength. In July G-2 estimated the Red Army's ground forces to about 6.2 million men, with 9230 tanks, in "the West", and in addition to this about 0.75 million men in Asia and Iran (which at the time was under joint Anglo-Soviet occupation), with 1170 tanks.[81]

The same month the MI3(c) compared US and British estimates on the manpower position. The US estimate was from 15 May and the British from 1 July. The Americans believed that there were only 7.6 million men in the armed forces (including NKVD troops and manpower in training, of which nearly 6.5 million were in the Army), while MI3(c) believed that the correct figure was 11.75 million men (nearly 7.9 million in the Army). The British estimate was more elaborate, and the Americans confessed that their estimate in many ways was guesswork. The British believed that another 2.5 million men could be mobilized. By 8 July the Americans updated their assessment and added half a million men to the Army.[82] This was probably the very same July G-2 estimate mentioned above, which also summed up to approximately seven million men as the total Red Army ground force strength.

17.5 The morale, efficiency and losses of the armed forces

After Stalingrad both the morale and the fighting capabilities of the Red Army were seen in a somewhat different light. Of course, as we have already seen, the impression of the armed forces was improving in some respects even before Stalingrad, but afterwards the tone of the reporting changed in several ways. In February the Red Army was still exploiting their successful winter offensive. In February the US London embassy and the OSS described military morale as high, and a British Director of Naval Intelligence report described the morale among the personnel of the Black Sea Fleet as very high.[83] Some observers seemed to think that the reduced influence of the political commissars in the Red Army had contributed to the military success, even though organizational problems still persisted. Parks's February report to the British Joint Staff Mission in Washington (see above), noted by the British JIC and the FO, revealed that he had met officers who appeared intelligent but lacking in necessary coordination skills. The NKVD personnel and the Political Commissars were now subordinated to the military officers in the units. Despite this partial "dethroning" of the political personnel, their presence worked against military efficiency. He stated that the soldiers were well equipped and in high spirits, and that air force morale was high, but also that the air force was not very well organized. He considered the supply organization as "haphazard", but despite this the troops had received what they needed in the field so far.[84]

At the beginning of March Pika analysed the success of the winter offensive. The abolition of Political Commissars, improved staff work and the removal of older and more military conservative officers had contributed. The MI3(c), which commented the report, agreed. Pika also mentioned what he described as a greater degree of cooperation between the various arms, and an improvement in communications between different military units. The MI3(c) also agreed with this and attributed the improvement to better training. Pika assessed that the forces used in the winter offensive had been well supplied with arms, equipment and clothes. The MI3(c) had information which supported that notion too.[85]

In their March report the British JIC concluded that the: "Fighting spirit is at present high everywhere."[86] Red Army training was praised in a more specific way than earlier; its improvement was explained by its increasing ability to learn from experience. The operations since the summer had proved to the JIC that the Soviets had improved their staff work, intercommunications and supply services, the very factors that had made the Soviets inferior to the Germans so far. Opinions from the December 1942 JIC report were confirmed regarding the fighting value of the air force. The same could be said about the navy, apart from a low regard for its ability to conduct combined operations. The partisans had made a significant contribution, especially during the winter offensive. They also praised Soviet strategy. The winter offensive was regarded as a marked development in that respect. Planning, organization and execution were described as a "remarkable success", and the timing of the successive blows was described as "masterly". In the later offensive stages the Soviets had overstretched themselves, which, in combination with favourable defensive conditions, paved the way for the successful German counter-offensive at Kharkov, which was commencing at the time.[87]

When Paul Holt was interviewed in April and May by the MI14 and the MI3(c), he praised the discipline and morale of the Red Army and its soldiers, and also regarded their equipment as "excellent". He described tank and artillery personnel as well trained, but that the infantry had poor training and was of inferior quality. According to his opinion manpower was used wastefully, and the Soviets considered themselves inferior to the Germans with respect to military technique and organization, although they regarded the Germans as the inferior "fighters".[88] According to MI3 Paul Winterton had about the same view as Holt regarding Soviet morale.[89] The MI3(c) also took an interest in an article by the correspondent Godfrey Blunden. According to Blunden's article, published in May, the Red Army provided its troops with light supplies to make them more mobile in the field. The MI3(c) commented that "little baggage and simple diet" was of importance in making the Red Army relatively mobile.[90]

Several observers commented on the Red Army in May. Michela stated in his report to the MID that the "morale of the people and army is decidedly good". He thought that the successes at Stalingrad, the Allied African campaign and the prospects of a second front had made the future considerably brighter. His report also contained information about plane losses, which were 1,000 per month.[91] In an ONI report, based on official Polish exile sources, which in turn had information from the letters ("Feldpost") of German soldiers, revealed a picture of a Red Army relying on numbers but with little tactical proficiency. Soviet forces were suffering heavy losses against the Germans.

Lack of training and individual initiative were mentioned. Red Army infantry was poorly equipped, and the artillery was the only arm that received some praise. The report was regarded as fairly accurate by an ONI naval attaché.[92] The FO was informed by a source in Spain, that according to the Chief-of-Staff to the Commander of the Spanish forces in the USSR, Soviet artillery was superior to German artillery, and that Soviet infantry were inferior to its German counterpart.[93] Spanish volunteers served on the Soviet–German front in their own so called Blue Division (called the 250 infantry division by the Germans).

Martel and other members of the 30 Mission visited the front in May. In the resulting report he praised the high-level planning and considerable strategic skill shown by the Soviets in recent military campaigns, but still considered the handling of Soviet formations as being crude and without refinement. The Soviets had a "shrewd common sense" and a "considerable ability to improvise". The British had nothing to learn from the Soviets as regarded organization and technique. But the British could learn from the "the real value of rocket artillery" from the Soviets. When Martel recalled this visit in his memoirs he praised the individual fighting qualities and high morale of the Red Army soldiers. But he did not value the quality of Soviet Army technique, their ability to wage mobile warfare in comparison with German and British standards, their training and equipment, even though he considered the Red Army to be superior in winter warfare.[94]

The same month the British AI stated that the Red Army's techniques of war to be much below that of the Germans. The Soviets would, for example, have little chance against the Germans in mobile warfare when both sides had equal strength. But the Soviets were superior in winter warfare and very strong in positional warfare. Furthermore, the forces of the Axis minor nations were no match for the Soviets.[95]

A 30 Mission report from June repeated much of this information, but also added that the Soviets had had successes in the air war, and that they were well equipped for trench warfare.[96] In another 30 Mission report, probably written around the same time, described the Soviet soldier: he had "great fighting qualities"; he was "tough", "capable of withstanding great hardship"; he was "patriotic" (with a traditional hatred of the Germans); he was "docile and willing"; and he was trained and experienced.[97]

In late July the WO agreed with Pika in his claim that the Soviets had been effective in their effort to disrupt the German concentrations before their Kursk offensive, and also added that the partisans had played a considerable role in this. He also believed, with which the WO concurred, that the Red Army personnel possessed a "splendid spirit", was well armed, equipped and nourished, in addition to being full of self-confidence.[98]

Notes

1 Smith (1996), 120.
2 Keegan (ed.) (1989), 134.

3 Ibid.
4 Hinsley (1981), 615.
5 12–3-1943, JIC(43)102(Final), CAB81/114; 2–4-1943, JIC25/8, Box-214, RG218.
6 12–3-1943, JIC(43)102(Final), CAB81/114.
7 The report was based on an interview with the French Captain Mirles, who had spent six months in the USSR. 16–2-1943, "Subject: [...]", Box-3118, Entry-77, RG165.
8 23–2-1943, R&A#523, Report #1, Reel-2, UPA1977.
9 14–4-1943, "American [...]", Box-3085, Entry-77, RG165.
10 14–4-1943, R&A No. 841, Report #3, Reel-2, UPA1977.
11 28–4-1943, "Memorandum [...]", Box-614, Entry-141A, RG169.
12 7–5-1943, 211–3(JIC83/1–2d Draft), ABC384USSR(6–1-42), Box-472, Entry-421, RG165.
13 3–5-1943, "Comments [...]", Box-3172, Entry-77, RG165.
14 4–6-1943, N3416/75/38, PRO371/36959.
15 8–5-1943, N3268/52/38, FO371/43349.
16 25–6-1943, R&A No. 917, Report #5, Reel-2, UPA1977; Glantz & House (2000), 166.
17 25–6-1943, R&A No. 917, Report #5, Reel-2, UPA1977.
18 Glantz & House (2000), 166–167.
19 Hinsley (1981), 627; Glantz & House (2000), 167.
20 The FO also commented on the report in August. 30–7-1943, N4516/75/38, FO371/36959; 10–8-1943, N4893/52/38, FO371/36950.
21 Keegan (ed.) (1989), 130.
22 15–2-1943, "Subject: [...]", Box-3175, Entry-77, RG165.
23 3–2-1943, N718/52/38, FO371/36944.
24 5–3-1943, N1539/75/38, FO371/36958.
25 The report was sent to the chief of the MIS by Major Charles S. Cutting, a US military observer in New Delhi, and outlined the content of an article written by Lieutenant-Colonel G. H. Nash. Nash was attached to the British Secretariat in New Delhi. 8–3-1943, "An Introduction [...]", Box-3126, Entry-77, RG165.
26 12–3-1943, JIC(43)102(Final), CAB81/114. Paul Winterton, who spent 14 months as the *News Chronicle*'s correspondent in the USSR, informed MI3 when interviewed by them in May 1943, that "The Russian communications are in exceedingly poor condition [...]." But it seems that it mainly was the roads that he spoke about. 10–5-1943, MI3, "Notes [...]", WO208/1755.
27 12–3-1943, JIC(43)102(Final), CAB81/114.
28 10–4-1943, N2172/52/38, FO371/36946.
29 He was from the *Daily Express*, had a pass to the Kremlin, and appeared to have access to more information than most correspondents. He had been stationed in the USSR for 14 months.
30 30–4-1943, "Some notes [...]", MI14, WO208/1755.
31 31–5-1943, "MI3c/Col/76/43", MI3(c), WO208/1755.
32 The journalist was Paul Winterton, who had spent 14 months as the *News Chronicle*'s correspondent in the USSR. 10–5-1943, MI3, "Notes [...]", WO208/1755.
33 10–5-1945, "Notes [...]", MI3, WO208/1755.
34 Ibid.
35 31–7-1943, "Comparison [...]", MI3(c), WO208/1834.
36 14–4-1943, "MI3/11/43", WO208/1755; 24–5-1943, "The British [...]", WO208/1755.
37 The report indicated that the Germans were not going on the offensive in the USSR during the summer of 1943. The source stated that the OKW was placing reserves to meet an expected Western Allied invasion of Europe during the summer. The OKW

did not believe that the Soviets could penetrate their *Ostwall*, or even that they wanted to do so. 30–6-1943, "MI3/6895/60", MI3, WO208/4565.

38 14–4-1943, R&A#841, Report #3, Reel-2, UPA1977.
39 21–5-1943, R&A No. 1842, M1221, RG59.
40 25–6-1943, R&A No. 917, Report #5, Reel-2, UPA1977.
41 Ibid.
42 28–4-1943, "Memorandum [...]", Box-614, Entry-141A, RG169.
43 3–5-1943, "Comments [...]", Box-3172, Entry-77, RG165.
44 7–5-1943, 211–3(JIC83/1–2d Draft), ABC384USSR(6–1-42), Box-472, Entry-421, RG165.
45 14–4-1943, "American [...]", Box-3085, Entry-77, RG165.
46 29–4-1943, N2887/52/38, FO371/36948.
47 1–5-1943, N2637/52/38, FO371/36948.
48 Hinsley (1984), 20.
49 14–5-1943, N2981/2979/38, FO371/37017.
50 17–8-1943, N4636/2979/38, FO371/37017.
51 Ibid.
52 10–7-1943, N3984/2979/38, FO371/37017.
53 The Soviet citizen was believed to have more interest and show more pride in big industrial constructions, such as the Stalingrad tractor works or the Moscow–Volga canal, than over more traditional national monuments, like the Kremlin. 31–8-1943, N5034/2979/38, FO371/37017.
54 8–5-1943, N3268/52/38, FO371/43349.
55 16–6-1943, "Some [...]", CAB121/465.
56 12–3-1943, JIC(43)102(Final), CAB81/114; 2–4-1943, JIC25/8, Box-214, RG218.
57 12–3-1943, JIC(43)102(Final), CAB81/114.
58 5–3-1943, N1539/75/38, FO371/36958.
59 15–6-1943, "Precis [...]", WO208/1829.
60 6–7-1943, N3880/163/38, FO371/36969.
61 Smith (1996), 117, 140.
62 3–5-1943, "Comments [...]", Box-3172, Entry-77, RG165.
63 27–2-1943, R&A No. 496, M1221, RG59.
64 14–4-1943, R&A#841, Report #3, Reel-2, UPA1977.
65 25–6-1943, R&A No. 917, Report #5, Reel-2, UPA1977.
66 17–4-1943, N2433/52/38, FO371/36948.
67 19–6-1943, "Air [...]", AIR40/1534.
68 17–8-1943, N4636/2979/38, FO371/37017.
69 Glantz & House (2000), 303–305.
70 Harrison (2002), Chapter 5, Table 5.4.
71 Glantz & House (2000), 306; Zaloga & Ness (2003), Chapter 6.
72 12–3-1943, JIC(43)102(Final), CAB81/114.
73 This report not only ended up with the US JIC, but also with the NID and the MIS. According to the US naval attaché in London, the Soviet figures for armed strength were more accurate than the information that "we have previously had". 22–3-1943, "British Official", Box-3148, Entry-77, RG165.
74 12–3-1943, JIC(43)102(Final), CAB81/114.
75 9–3-1943, "MI3/6895/31.", MI3(c), WO208/5171.
76 17–4-1943, N2433/52/38, FO371/36948.
77 8–5-1943, "Soviet Air Force", AI3(d), WO208/1755.
78 At this time British MI calculated on 9,000 men as being the representative figure for a Soviet division. 30–6-1943, "MI3/6895/60", MI3, WO208/4565.
79 11–3-1943, 25–3-1943, 28–4-1943, "Battle [...]", Box-3159, Entry-77, RG165; 17–3-1943, "Manpower [...]", Box-3159, Entry-77, RG165.

80 The shortage of manpower was more due to a shortage of labour than men of military age. 25–6-1943, R&A No. 917, Report #5, Reel-2, UPA1977.
81 8 July (6 July), "Battle [...]", Box-3159, Entry-77, RG165.
82 31–7-1943, "Comparison [...]", MI3(c), WO208/1834.
83 2–2-1943, N717/52/38, FO371/36944; 16–2-1943, "Subject: [...]", Box-3118, Entry-77, RG165; 23–2-1943, R&A#523, Report #2, Reel-2, UPA1977.
84 3–2-1943, N718/52/38, FO317/36944.
85 5–3-1943, N1539/75/38, FO371/36958.
86 12–3-1943, JIC(43)102(Final), CAB81/114; 2–4-1943, JIC25/8, Box-214, RG218.
87 12–3-1943, JIC(43)102(Final), CAB81/114.
88 30–4-1943, "Some [...]", MI14, WO208/1755; 31–5-1943, MI3c, "MI3c/Col/76/43", WO208/1755.
89 10–5-1945, "Notes [...]", MI3, WO208/1755.
90 29–5-1943, MI3(c), "MI3c/Col/73/43", WO208/1755.
91 3–5-1943, "Comments [...]", Box-3172, Entry-77, RG165.
92 7–5-1943, "Serial: 330–43", Box-3155, Entry-77, RG165.
93 7–5-1943, N2784/75/38, FO371/36959.
94 15–6-1943, "Precis [...]", WO208/1829; Martel (1949), 226–227.
95 (11th to 19th) May 1943, "Reports [...]", AIR46/28; 21–6-1943, AIR46/28.
96 6–7-1943, N3880/163/38, FO371/36969.
97 15–7-1943, "The British [...]", WO208/1829.
98 30–7-1943, N4516/75/38, FO371/36959; 10–8-1943, N4893/52/38, FO371/36950.

18 The 1943 cross-channel attack that never was and the "90-division gamble"

Despite preliminary plans and Soviet demands the Anglo-Americans did not invade Western Europe even in 1943. Instead they concentrated on knocking Italy out of the war. Just as in 1942, the American WD planners suspected Churchill of having political motives when he continued to push for additional Anglo-American commitments in the Mediterranean during the summer and autumn of 1943.[1] In August 1942 Churchill had personally informed Stalin that there would be no Second Front in Europe in 1942. Stalin used this situation to put diplomatic pressure on the Western Allies. The US North African invasion, and the ensuing strategy to invade Sicily in July 1943, in order to knock Italy out of the war, made an Anglo-American landing in France impossible in 1943. The decision to postpone the invasion of France until 1944 was taken in practice already at the Casablanca Conference in January 1943, and it was further confirmed at the May 1943 Trident Conference. Roosevelt still lobbied for a 1943 invasion at Casablanca but in the end Churchill's preference for an invasion of Italy won the day. The absence of an Anglo-American landing strained relations with the USSR.[2]

The decision to postpone the invasion of North-Western Europe was, according to Scott Dunn Jr., more the result of a hidden political agenda than based on purely military reasons. According to his assessments the Western Allies could have invaded North-Western Europe already in 1943, with greater relative force (vis-à-vis the Germans) than during the actual invasion in 1944. He believes that the Western Allies were aware of their opportunity. Dunn argues that the British and the Americans did not want a USSR that was too militarily successful and strong after the war. Furthermore, he believes that a 1943 invasion – when the German Army still was engaged in positions deep into the USSR – would have allowed the Western Allies to occupy a larger part of Europe than they actually did in 1944–1945. Instead, it was the Red Army that came to overrun Central Europe. A quicker end to the war would also have saved many lives and much destruction in Europe.[3] Can the decision not to launch a full-scale Second Front in 1943 be regarded as a "daring decision", in the light of Anglo-American estimates of Soviet strength from the abandonment of Sledgehammer 1942 up to the Casablanca and Trident Conferences in May 1943? Was there any marked difference in British and American estimates which possibly can add another dimension to the different outlooks concerning the opening of a second front, and if so, in what respects?

It is clear that the Americans did not evaluate Soviet strength and military prospects in the same way as the British did. They regarded the Soviets as considerably weaker than the British in several respects, even after Stalingrad. It is also obvious that they were more worried than the British about a Soviet–German separate peace. Dunn argues that by the beginning of 1943 the Soviets looked stronger to the Western Allies than they had done six months before, and that the Western Allies recognized this when they met at Casablanca in January 1943 to discuss the future conduct of the war.[4] It is obvious that the British were more interested in following a Mediterranean strategy than the Americans during the first half of 1943. General Marshall wanted to divert resources from the Mediterranean campaign in order to launch an attack in France during the late summer of 1943.[5] Dunn is of the opinion that for purely military reasons the Western Allies might as well have invaded France in 1943, instead of pursuing their goals in the Mediterranean. He also considers that General Alan Brooke, the British Chief of the Imperial General Staff (CIGS), "consistently and Churchill at times believed that the major effort on land should be left to the Russians."[6]

Dunn is convinced that "Churchill wanted a weakened Russia after the war." The Americans wanted to go for a cross-Channel attack in 1943, partly for the reason that they wanted to control as much as possible of Germany by the end of the war. He also thinks that the Americans, in practice, wanted to prolong the war for political purposes. Roosevelt could have allowed the resources spent in the Pacific to be used in the European war instead. The actual situation was instead that Western Allied troops were put to use in the Mediterranean, and in the Pacific, instead of being used in a more direct attack on Hitler's empire across the British Channel.[7]

The German defeat at Stalingrad has often been referred to in the literature as the turning point of World War II.[8] Some Anglo-American observers recognized that "fact" early. In 1947 Major-General John R. Deane, the head of the US Military Mission in Moscow during the war, published his war memoirs. With hindsight he wrote that the tide on the Soviet–German front "finally turned at Stalingrad, and a Russian offensive started which ended only at Berlin".[9] When Deane's British counterpart during 1943–1944, General-Lieutenant Martel, wrote about the turning point in 1949, he referred instead to the summer of 1943 – the Battle of Kursk and its aftermath.[10] As a matter of fact, judging by the Anglo-American assessments, it might be said that some British observers, at the time, believed that Stalingrad was the turning point. The Americans, on the other hand, did not share that opinion, and seemingly some of them did not even fully believe that Kursk was the final turning point (see Chapter 19).

Since the Americans apparently believed that the Soviets were weaker than the British did in 1943, and some even believed that Soviet offensive power might be spent in 1944 (see also Chapter 19), they must have considered the decision to postpone the cross-Channel attack until 1944 as rather risky. This is especially true since (as pointed out above) Soviet weakness meant German strength, and relative German strength meant more US and British casualties. In addition we know that Roosevelt and the Americans feared a Soviet–German separate peace, which would have been more likely if the Soviets were weak. The US assessment of Soviet strength can be interpreted as that they really saw Soviet weakness as a factor that contributed to their willingness to invade France as early as in 1943 – a willingness that was greater on the American side than among the British decision makers. In April 1943 the OSS argued that the reason for the Soviets urging for a second front was that their long-term economic prospects were weak, and that their war effort would suffer from this.

The question of whether the Americans really were taking a calculated risk, when they not used their resources in a cross-Channel attack before 1944, can also be related to the question of the size of the US Army during the war. This concerns the US decision not to raise a large land army in proportion to its manpower and productive resources. As already stated, the US was by far the largest industrial power in the world, and had a population in excess of 132 million; only slightly less than the USSR population within their territory held in 1942, and considerably more than Germany. By the autumn of 1941, in accordance with the "Victory Program",[11] the WD projected that it would take an army of 213 divisions for a successful conduct of the war against Germany. The prospect of a possible Soviet collapse and the fact that the British and the Americans would have to fight an offensive war against the large German army on their own was the underlying assumption guiding this estimate. Throughout most of 1942 it was still believed in the WD that it would be necessary to raise at least 200 US divisions. But Soviet progress, hopes for a successful air bombardment of Germany and the postponement of the 1943 cross-Channel invasion lessened the need for a large US field army.[12]

At the beginning of 1943 discussions were held within leading US military circles, which proposed a mobilization limit of 100 divisions in 1943, and 120–125 divisions in June 1944. Later in 1943 discussions were still being held over the size of the army. This discussion was influenced both by events on the Soviet–German front and the Anglo-American bomber offensive in Europe. In November the President approved 90 divisions as a necessary "cutting edge" to win the war. Matloff refers to the decision to limit the US Army to just 90 divisions as the "90-Division Gamble". Furthermore, he writes: "Of all the calculated risks taken by General Marshall [the US Army chief of staff] in World War II none was bolder than the decision in midwar to maintain the US Army's ground combat strength at ninety divisions. Students of warfare will long debate whether the decision was as wise as it was courageous, as foresighted as it was successful."[13] This question can without doubt be debated from several different perspectives, but since the Soviet capacity to fight the Germans was one of the most important factors in the debate over the size of the US Army, it is of interest to investigate how much of a "gamble" the 90-Divison decision was from that particular angle. If it were still judged that there was any chance that Soviet opposition to the Germans might cease by the time this decision was taken, then it would indeed have been a gamble of major proportions.

This problem is especially interesting concerning the last period of the war, since during 1942 it was still believed that the army should be around 200 divisions. It was only at the beginning of 1943 that the size was revised downwards drastically. This can, of course, be interpreted as an acceptance of the fact that the Allied position as a whole was improving, and that – regarding the Soviet–German front – the Americans estimated that the Red Army now was so strong that it was not necessary to build up an army of more than about 100 divisions. This would, of course, also mean that the responsibility for the land war would more or less in practice have been passed over to the Soviets. But, to use Matloff's words, was this a wise and foresighted decision? Judging by US intelligence assessments from the winter and spring of 1943 it seems not. The OSS doubted the Soviet ability to continue any offensive action by the time of the German surrender at Stalingrad. In April the OSS and the BEW-OSS Coordinating Committee believed that the USSR was straining its economy in a way that could not possibly continue for long. On the other hand the US JIC believed in May that a Soviet attempt to reach a separate peace with the Germans was not regarded as realistic.

In June the OSS concluded: "The Soviet Union this summer may be expected to offer resistance at least as strong as that shown in the summer of 1942 – but at the expense of a further decline in manpower, a shortage of industrial materials, and a dangerous decrease in its rapidly vanishing food stocks." Earlier, in May, Michela believed that the Soviets could hold out fairly well against a renewed German offensive, but that it was impossible for them to go on the offensive if the Western Allies did not invade Europe. The MIS concurred in this.

In August, after the Soviet success in the Kursk battle, Donovan presented a paper to the US JCS with the message that the Soviets would be able to continue their offensive until the spring thaw in 1944 (see Chapter 19). This was, of course, a considerable change in assessment as compared to earlier, but the report was also about declining Soviet strength in the long run. By the summer of 1944 her resources in food and manpower would be so strained that it would reduce her military capabilities. But it was not considered that the Soviets would enter into a separate peace with Germany, a notion that was repeated in an OSS report from September. In November it was expressed in an OSS report that the Soviets would be able to advance beyond the Riga-Odessa line in five to six months' time. It also seems that the OSS had changed its position to some extent regarding long-term economic prospects in November, since it was predicted in another (major R & A) report that the adverse economic trends would not affect military capabilities for the next 12 months. This would mean that the Soviet economy, although seen as weak in the long run, still could support a war effort on the present scale up to the end of 1944.

Other reports from the autumn, of both US and British origin, described a Soviet industrial economy that was increasing in strength somewhat. Although, as we already have seen, many reports described problems in the Soviet economy no acute crisis was predicted. Judging by US JIC and OSS reports from August and September 1943 it seems that the earlier fear that the Soviets might conclude a separate peace with the Germans had been abandoned. This conviction can possibly explain why the perceived weakness of actual Soviet strength had lost its importance somewhat. Even if the Soviets might not be able to continue their present offensive forever, they were at least on the move and so long as they did not conclude a separate peace with the Germans they would still engage considerable German and other Axis forces.

It is obvious that when Roosevelt finally approved 90 divisions as the limit in November, it was far from clear that the Red Army would be able to achieve such success as it really did in 1944. Even though there were several military factors that affected the conduct of the war as a whole by November – the Battle of the Atlantic, the air war over Germany, the Italian campaign and the war in the Pacific – all of which went the Allies' way, the Western Allies were in the process of building up for the invasion of France in 1944. If the Soviets should be unable to seriously challenge the Germans during the summer of 1944 – as US intelligence indicated before the autumn of 1943 – the task facing the Anglo-American forces would, of course, be much harder. In this respect the decision not to expand the US Army in 1943, and instead limit it to about 100 divisions, can be regarded as a gamble. But there was hardly any evidence of a Soviet collapse at the time, so the decision cannot be regarded as a total hazard. When Roosevelt made the final decision, on the other hand, the intelligence picture was different.

Notes

1 Gaddis (1972), 76.
2 Gaddis (1972), 70–73; Dunn (1980), 38–39. In a draft telegram intended for Stalin from mid-June 1943 Churchill outlined his arguments regarding why it was impossible to launch a cross-Channel attack during 1943. Churchill referred to the recent success of the Western Allies in North Africa, and said that a cross-Channel attack would entail slaughter for British troops. Instead he argued for the impending Italian invasion and the escalating strategic bombing offensive over Germany, and the long-term effects of these two campaigns. The COS instructed the Joint Planning Staff to find arguments that would strengthen the reasoning of the telegram. 15-6-1943, "Brigadier Hollis", CAB 119/38.
3 Dunn (1980), 3–4, 266–274.
4 Dunn (1980), 36; Dear & Foot (eds.) (1995), 1095.
5 Dunn (1980), 38.
6 Dunn (1980), 43; Dear & Foot (eds.) (1995), 167.
7 Dunn (1980), 266–269.
8 Müller & Ueberschär (1997), 126.
9 Deane (1947), 90.
10 Martel (1949), 245–254.

11 The "Victory Program" was designed to enable the United States and the British to crush the Axis even if the USSR were terminated as an active belligerent. Greenfield (1963), 54.
12 Matloff (1960), 365–376.
13 Matloff (1960), 365–376; Dear & Foot (eds.) (1995), 719.

19 The Red Army's first major push to the West

After the successful defence of the Kursk bulge, the Red Army's offensive increased in scope and soon involved the whole southern wing of the front, pushing the Germans back in the Ukraine and Western Russia. Soviet losses was as always heavier than German, but the Germans had reached a point when their replacements was significantly smaller than their losses, and therefore the actual combat manpower strength of the German Army was decreasing in the long run. This meant that the combat force that could meet the Red Army in the field was becoming smaller and smaller as the war progressed.

19.1 Soviet military prospects, civilian morale and internal stability

On 9 August, British Intelligence reported back to Whitehall from Switzerland that "'the highest German authorities' recognized that they had under-estimated Russian strength and feared that they might not be able to prevent a break-through".[1] In mid-August Air Vice-Marshal John Babington, head of the Air Section of the 30 Military Mission, considered that there were "indications" that the Soviets would win the war.[2] At about the same time the MIS reported that "Ivan Pouschine", the US representative of the Tsarist pretender (see above), concluded that the Soviet victories at the Orel-Belgorod front, in the aftermath of the German Kursk offensive, could be regarded as a new phase in the war – "the defeat of the German army".[3]

Later that month the US JIC issued an assessment of the psychological situation, and concluded that although the Soviet people were tired and increasingly hungry, they were also "firmly convinced of their ultimate victory and no reliable evidence is at hand that points to a lowering in morale". The Stalin regime was so stable that it could only be overthrown by an "over-whelming defeat".[4] Two days later Donovan presented a forecast concerning the Soviet-American ability to cooperate to Brigadier-General John R. Deane, then secretary to the CCS.[5] In October Deane became the head of the new US Military Mission in Moscow, invited by the newly appointed US ambassador Averell Harriman.[6] Donovan's forecast (mainly the work of Gerard T. Robinson) was soon presented to the JCS. The USSR was expected to have sufficient strength to continue her present scale of operations until the 1944 spring thaw, or maybe even longer. But by the summer her food and manpower resources would be so strained that her military capabilities would be reduced. Despite this it was not expected that the Soviets would accept a separate peace.[7] In September the OSS assumed that the Soviets would not consider a separate peace as an option, even if a German (post-Hitler) military regime should agree to a withdrawal to the June 1941 border.[8]

In September the FO commented on a Polish (Exile) Ministry of Information report about the Soviet economy. The FO put little credit in the economic estimate, and concluded that the Polish were "taking pleasure in collecting intelligence, whether accurate or inaccurate, which would tend to show that the Soviet Union is on the point of collapse; but the country seems resolved to do nothing of the sort".[9] This report indicates that at least some British observers had begun to put more credit into their own assessments, rather than Polish notions.

In two OSS reports from September and November civilian morale was described as "very high" and "high", respectively. In the first report the food situation was something that might affect morale in the long run.[10] In December they analysed the morale of Soviet workers. The labour force's morale was very high in general. The workers were convinced that they really had a direct part in winning the war, and they had "given lavishly of their skill, energy and health". Due to this there had been little need to impose "the severe penalties provided by the law".[11] Later that month the OSS issued a special study about morale. The popular support for the war and the morale of citizens were regarded as high. Hatred for the Germans, Soviet victories, patriotism and the support of the church, were all crucial factors. The secret police was a force that dealt with "occasional evidences of weak discipline or collaboration with the enemy". It was also probable that western supplies helped morale.[12]

A report about the "the secret of the Soviet people's high morale" was given by a member of the Czechoslovak legation in London to Lieutenant-Colonel J. D. Carlisle of the WO in December. This issue was a part of the Pika report studied by the DMI and a FO official in January 1944. Pika presented several explanations: the very rigorous but successful build-up of a powerful Soviet state, without any help from abroad, was a factor that had "hardened the will and toughness of the country", the "energetic concentration" on achieving victory, the hatred against everything German due to German atrocities, the "good political party organisation", and "a general belief that the war will not last any more".[13]

In January Major-General Deane forwarded a report to the MID concerning a Leningrad visit, undertaken by several high ranking US Army officers that month. One of the officers wrote about the high morale, an "unshakeable" spirit, and "defiant confidence" among the people.[14]

An October British JIC report depicted a continued German retreat due to heavy Soviet pressure, and further Soviet gains on the southern part of the front were expected.[15] L. C. Hollis, a senior assistant secretary in the War Cabinet Office, submitted it to Churchill on 5 October, while at the same time informing him that the COS believed that the report gave a "fair picture" of the situation.[16] Later in October a possible Soviet–German separate peace was apparently contemplated by the British JIC, since a 20 October JIC draft report considered this possibility. But it was supposed that the terms would be dictated mainly by the Soviets. The military situation was perceived as very favourable to the Soviets and an increase in Red Army numerical superiority was anticipated. No definite conclusion was made as to the possibility of a separate peace, but it was probably not considered as likely, since it appears that the draft was not proceeded with and no copies were issued.[17]

On 5 November the OSS Current Intelligence Staff issued a report on what they called the "Russian summer campaign", between 10 August and 15 October. Even though the Soviets had recaptured much of the Ukraine during their offensive, the Germans had been able to withdraw, without losing too many prisoners, and making the Red Army pay heavily for their gains. The Germans made the supply problem worse for the Soviets through their scorched earth policy. But despite this it was unlikely that the Germans could hold a position even as far back and shortened as the Riga–Odessa line for more than five to six months, which would be the time required for the Red Army to repair and organize supply in the devastated areas.[18]

In mid-November 1943, just after the Soviets had recaptured Kiev, the British JIC prepared a report concerning the possible transfer of German divisions from the East.[19] It was not specifically stated in the report, but now the Anglo-Americans had established a frontline in Italy against the Germans. The Western Allies had air superiority over the Italian front, and their fleets had more or less established domination in the Mediterranean Sea, but the Germans could still use the railways and roads on the Italian mainland. At the time the Germans had less than 15 divisions at the Italian front. The report was circulated for information more than a week later within the US JIC. The German failure to stop the Red Army since the battle of Kursk was assessed, despite the fact that new German divisions had reinforced the front. The JIC supposed that the Soviets could continue the offensive during the winter, and that they now had air superiority. The Germans could not spare any divisions in the East, if they wanted to avoid disaster. The spring thaw was the first opportunity the Germans would have in order to rest and resupply their troops.[20]

At the Allied "Big Three" meeting in Teheran in November 1943 Stalin told the Western Allies that the Red Army had a military margin of superiority that would enable it to continue the offensive against the Germans, but that he feared that the Germans could strengthen their defences if the Western Allies were unsuccessful in drawing more German divisions from the Soviet–German front.[21] The Soviet offensive continued into the winter and soon all of the Ukraine was freed from German troops. The Red Army also begun to move in strength on other parts of the front. The German encirclement of Leningrad in the north was finally lifted and the *Wehrmacht* was also pushed back on the central part of the front.

In January 1944 the British JIC commented on Soviet military progress: "The Russians hold the initiative everywhere and have marked superiority on land and in the air." They did not expect that the Germans would be able to stop the advance, and the possible defection of some of Germany's Balkan allies was analysed.[22] Already by February the FO (in a JIC report) predicted that the USSR would emerge from the war in a position of considerable strength, despite her enormous losses in men and material. The Soviet Union would be the strongest land power in the world, and among the three strongest air powers.[23] The memorandum was about the impact of Soviet foreign policy upon British strategic interests. No doubt was expressed concerning the Soviet ability to finally win the war.[24] In the same memorandum the JIC made a forecast concerning the state of Soviet society after the war.[25] The victorious conclusion of the war would bring great prestige and further strength to the regime, and no serious internal problems would face it. The Soviet Union's war record, the achievements of the "planned economy" and "socialism in one country", would "continue to arouse widespread sympathy and admiration abroad in many circles".[26]

At the beginning of March the JIC overestimated future Red Army progress. They believed that the Germans could be driven back to the line River Dniester-Warsaw-Riga already by May/June 1944.[27] In reality, the Soviets did not reach a line that approximated that forecast until August/September.[28] On the other hand, the British believed that the Germans would gamble on holding the front with the forces available to them in that theatre by that date (1 March). In April the JIC had instead to conclude that the Germans had moved 17 to 19 divisions to the East from other theatres.[29] In May they commented on the temporary lull on the Soviet–German front, and concluded it had helped the Axis to stabilize their situation. But they expected that the Soviets would launch a general offensive when the Western Allies began *Overlord*, i.e. the invasion in France.[30] A MI3 report from late March 1944 predicted that the Soviets would stage two major offensives against the Axis during the summer.[31]

The OSS tried to predict, in a report dated 20 March, the relative capabilities of the opposing forces engaged on the Soviet–German front as of 1 May 1944. They believed that the Soviets could launch a "powerful offensive" within the next few months, which would be successful. The Red Army's military superiority in men and material would be several times the German strength.[32] In May the US Secretary of War H. L. Stimson worried that the Red Army would stop their westward advance when they had evicted the Germans from their own soil. The Soviets might be "satisfied" with this result, and it is unclear whether or not he justified his worries by a perceived possible exhaustion of Soviet offensive capabilities.[33] Stimson's worries were of course unfounded, but at least in line with general worries that the OSS had expressed earlier (in 1943) regarding a possible exhaustion of Soviet strength in mid-1944. It seems though that the OSS had changed their opinion by now, and they – correctly – expected renewed Soviet efforts on a large scale during the summer.

The British Moscow embassy did not question the strength of the Soviet communist party and its influence over the Red Army, judging by two reports taken under consideration by the FO in May and June.[34]

A COS paper intended for the War Cabinet, dated 15 June, little more than a week before the Soviet *Bagration* offensive, tried to analyse the long-term effects of Soviet policy on British strategic interests.[35] It was based on earlier Post Hostilities Planning Committee (PHP) papers from May and June, also produced for the War Cabinet, containing much of the same information.[36] The paper was written in cooperation with the FO and was not intended as a basis for any executive action, but rather as military advice from the COS. A picture of a victorious USSR was painted in the report, of a country that would potentially threaten British strategic interests after the war, particularly in the Middle East. It was expected that the Soviet Union might take advantage of "the general weakness of the countries of Europe" after the war, and that Britain would have to cooperate closely with other European states, especially France, in order to counter the Soviet influence.[37] They counted on that the British could deal with a Soviet naval threat with their own air and naval forces. Furthermore, the COS believed that the British Commonwealth should maintain strong and highly efficient military forces in order to secure its "vital interest vis-à-vis Russia". But these perceived problems did not hinder the COS from recommending the upholding of friendly relations with the Soviets in order to avoid friction. They did not believe that the Soviet system was in any danger due to the "success" of Stalin's policies and the Red Army.[38]

19.2 The economy, manpower, food supply and civilian living conditions

In August 1943 the US JIC asserted that the economic potential was very much strained by the war and its effects. Despite this: "The Soviet economic organization has, on the whole, withstood the shock of war and, with help from abroad, has supported successfully a great war effort with no decisive signs of flagging." Even though there was still a critical situation in some sectors of the economy, the present level of "military output" could be sustained at least until the summer of 1944. Despite continuing transport difficulties – affecting the distribution of raw materials and farm products – the overall supply of the armed forces appeared to function satisfactorily. Food supply was perceived as the weakest element in the overall Soviet position. A large part of the population was undernourished, and most workers performing below normal efficiency. Even an average 1943 harvest would not save the situation, and it was regarded as likely that the food situation would be even worse, eventually leading to a nutritional situation in 1944 that would damage military strength and war production. A considerable decline in industrial output was foreseen during the early summer of 1944, possibly due to shortages in manpower or food, transport difficulties and capital deterioration. They had clear evidence of a shortage of industrial manpower. It was also probable that there was a shortage of agricultural manpower. But the JIC could not assess the exact economic effects of this. So far, there were no shortages of military manpower for the purpose of maintaining the armed forces at approximately full strength.[39] The JIC did not state at what level industry was producing at the time, but according to a G-2 report from late September the present output at that time was 60–70 per cent of the pre-war level.[40]

In two OSS reports on Soviet capabilities and prospects, from September and November, the food position was the weakest element. The assessments of the population's nutritional standard and civilian consumption were more or less the same as the views expressed by the OSS in May and June. But the liberation of land in the Ukraine since that time was both an opportunity and a liability. Some cumulative effects of this situation on the war effort were seen as unavoidable in the November report, even though it was stated in the September report that the Red Army would have sufficient supplies at their disposal. In the September report a great deficit in food was expected the more land the Red Army conquered from the Germans. If the pre-1939 borders were regained a total deficit of nearly 11 per cent of the 1943 annual requirement of grain for the USSR was possible. This situation, in combination with transport problems, might, according to the OSS, cause starvation among the urban population. In the November report the possibility of a larger harvest in 1944 was expected, but "only a significant increase in consumption can check the moderate cumulative effects of poor nutrition on war capabilities".[41]

The two reports were extensive OSS R & A material that analysed the whole spectra of war potential. The first, issued 18 September, was apparently prepared in 24 hours for the War Production Board. Both reports foresaw long term economic problems, which would hurt the capability to sustain a war effort with high military wastage at the current level. The September report was slightly more pessimistic since it predicted that the Soviets might already experience problems with the economic support of the war effort by the summer of 1944, while the November report predicted that the adverse economic trends would not affect military capabilities for the next 12 months.[42]

The capacity of basic industry was seen as adequate in the November report, and the output of steel and other war-essential industries was expanding. In both reports the annual output of steel was estimated to about 13 million tonnes. According to the September report the output of non-ferrous metals was expanding, but still being below minimum requirements. The dependence on allied supplies was therefore very important, constituting from 8 to 68 per cent of the non-ferrous metal needs (depending on metal). The situation for rubber (with imports), coal and oil was adequate.[43]

Both reports concluded that the transport system had managed the extraordinary strain of the war, but that a future transport crisis was expected which would affect the whole war effort. In September poor maintenance and extended supply lines was stressed as a latent problem, and it was predicted in both reports that the newly liberated territories would cause further demands on the railways. In November they believed that local transport was suffering as a result of the diversion of horses and trucks to the front. Expected future needs of local transport equipment were a potential cause of a crisis. The transport problem, and general problems in the civilian sector of the economy, was expected to create difficulties for basic industry within one year.[44]

In September the manpower problem were not considered to be available military personnel, but rather a shortage of labour. The need to recruit military personnel was a problem in the sense that it reduced the labour force, which in turn pressed industrial and agricultural output downwards. But munitions production was not suffering from any labour shortage. The notion about military manpower was repeated in November. Instead, heavy military recruitment, in conjunction with inadequate nutrition and a generally reduced standard of living, was responsible for a decline in the efficiency of the labour force.[45]

In December the OSS made an in-depth study of the manpower situation. The conclusions reached were much the same as in November. They also stated that labour productivity had been raised in (the non-Axis controlled area of) the USSR since June 1941, but this was described as a result of the labour force working longer hours. It was not much to gain by increasing working hours further. The employment of the elderly, women and children was also an option already largely exploited. Furthermore, undernourishment was a factor working against the labour force. If the current recruitment of military personnel from the civilian work force were to continue, they foresaw a possible reduction by five per cent in food and other supplies available to the civilian population. However, the output of armaments or critical raw materials would not suffer as a result of the labour shortage, even though some problems were identified due to a lack of skilled labour. The recently liberated areas were more a burden than an asset, since they were unable to support themselves up to the 1944 harvest.[46]

By early October the British JIC had recognized the thorough German destruction in the areas they were retreating from. But they were also surprised over the rapid rehabilitation of these areas. In addition they noted that the Soviet food situation was not as critical as it had appeared to be earlier in 1943.[47] More or less the same picture, regarding the rehabilitation of the liberated areas, was presented in a MEW report the same month. No food shortages were identified in the Kuban, the North Caucasus or the Don regions, some of which were newly liberated. They noted that young people (from 15 years of age) were "widely employed" in the industry being re-established in the liberated areas. People younger than 14 were also being used for clean-up work connected to the railways. The MEW also added that there was a shortage of many consumer goods in the USSR. Clothing and especially boots were in short supply.[48]

However, another October MEW report concluded that the land recovered by the Red Army from July to October was more a liability than an asset for a considerable time to come. They stated that local self-sufficiency could be achieved during the harvest year 1944/1945.[49] They noted in November that the bread ration in Moscow and the surrounding districts had been cut. The

Soviet authorities stated that this was necessary to provide for the liberated areas. The MEW considered this to be a sign of a deteriorating bread position, which according to them had been successfully maintained up to date.[50]

Additional MEW reports from October and November recognized that the output of heavy industry was increasing.[51] In November they estimated that the annual output of coke, pig iron and steel had increased from 8.5, 8 and 12.2 million tonnes in September 1942, to 10, 9.6 and 13.7 million tonnes, respectively, in September 1943.[52] Later that month they acknowledged that many new large industrial enterprises had been launched during the war. The estimated annual aluminium output was 71,000 tonnes.[53] Yet another October MEW report analysed the nickel situation. Nickel output was higher at the present than during 1940: 18,000 tonnes as compared to 8650 tonnes. The annual requirements were 19,000 tonnes, and therefore the nickel situation as a whole was favourable.[54]

Even though the British noted some signs of economic recovery there still arrived reports that stressed the relative inefficiency of economic activities. In October Clark-Kerr sent a memorandum concerning the experiences of two British engineers, who had worked for some time in an explosives factory in the Urals. The words deficient, stiff, uncooperative and sub-optimal can be used to summarize their description of the factory management. A rapid turnover of factory officials was noted, as well as worn out and outdated equipment, in combination with a lack of coordination. They noticed evidence of a labour shortage. Clark-Kerr did not necessarily regard the experiences of the engineers as a typical phenomenon, but nevertheless thought it revealed a "comparative backwardness in relation to British standards of quality, craftsmanship and labour conditions". When an FO official commented on the memorandum in November he was not surprised; there was "colossal wastage and inefficiency" in the USSR. He thought that this condition existed both in times of peace and war, although somewhat altering in form, due to over-bureaucratization, muddle and a fear of taking responsibility.[55]

In a (US or British) report, probably written at the end of 1943, and probably presented to the CIC, improvements were noted in the economic position since mid-year. This was the result of the 1943 victories and foreign support. The country had adjusted itself successfully to the earlier shocks and dislocations imposed by the war. But it was also recognized that there were still major problems: "The entire Russian economy is still under immense strain". Steel, food, transportation, and manpower were identified as the critical factors. Manpower was regarded as fully mobilized, and no labour reserves existed. It was stated "that manpower, rather than equipment, is the primary limiting factor in the maintenance of the Russian war potential". Improvements were noted in the food situation, partly as a result of the liberation of more than half the Ukraine. But even though the food outlook was more promising now it was still regarded as uncertain. The annual steel output (13–16 million tonnes) was sufficient for armaments and military equipment, but not enough for industrial maintenance or new construction. The only thing that mitigated the deterioration of industrial plant, according to the report, was foreign deliveries of equipment. One almost new notion in the report was the statement that the railways had "operated efficiently to date". However, the scarcity of steel was described as a major problem for the maintenance of the railways, and the rehabilitation of railways in the liberated territories.[56]

In November Lieutenant-Colonel Henry I. Szymanki, at the Military Attaché's Office in the US London Embassy, sent a report to Major-General George V. Strong, Assistant Chief of Staff, G-2, called entitled *Soviet Agricultural and Industrial Potentialities*. The report was mainly based on information received from Poles in exile with experience of the USSR. The report was criticized by Lieutenant-Colonel Park, now the chief of the MID's Eastern European Section, as being full of old information already in the hands of most intelligence agencies in Washington and London. The report described the Soviets as being in a strong position, considering their economic and industrial capacity, to support the war effort. Szymanki agreed with this picture and stated: "Russia's potential might is on the increase despite war, devastation, famine, and epidemics."[57]

Towards the end of the war the devastation of Soviet territory was recognized more frequently. In an OSS report from December 1943 the opinions of the Soviet economist Eugene Varga were quoted. Varga was regarded as a spokesman for the Soviet leadership.[58] In a newspaper clipping collected by the FO from the British Newspaper *Evening Standard* he was referred to as the "Russian Keynes" in September.[59] According to Varga the destruction carried out by Hitler's armies in the occupied areas of the USSR was "unprecedented in the history of mankind". Even though the OSS had some doubts as to his figures, concerning the material destruction, it nevertheless seems that the OSS did not object to his message in principle.[60]

In the FO report from February 1944, distributed by the JIC, several aspects of the devastated economy were analysed. The ongoing material destruction was "on a scale unparalleled in history." The loss of millions of lives and the enormous demographic relocation was another major factor. Several aspects were considered: the killing of millions (both soldiers and civilians); the abnormally high civilian mortality and abnormally low birth rate; 15 million eastward evacuees; and the westward deportation by the Germans of about 2 million people and the capture by the same of about 3 million prisoners. The process of rehabilitation in the areas that had been and still were occupied by the Axis was a vast task, which would take at least five years to accomplish. But in about ten years' time the economic resources, manpower and industrial capacity would "be immensely strong and, almost certainly, well organized". However, the reconstruction process was not regarded as a walk in the park. To be able to meet the needs of relief or reconstruction, during the first one or two years after the war, the USSR would have to depend on foreign aid. During the period of reconstruction the USSR would avoid war, and hence therefore be no menace to British strategic interests.[61]

The FO judged that the USSR would have to import both industrial and agricultural products in order to reconstruct and further expand the economy. Even if the Soviets should exploit Germany and other smaller countries close to her after the war, it would not be sufficient to satisfy the needs. The chief source of all these very badly needed supplies must come from the Western Allies, and therefore the United States, and to a lesser extent Britain, would be in a position to influence the USSR considerably. But it seems that the FO regarded this point of view as somewhat theoretical, and in practice laid greater emphasis on the vast internal destruction as an argument for the Soviets keeping the peace.[62]

Later, on 20 March, the British JIC commented on the FO paper. The JIC agreed that the reconstruction of the liberated areas would take at least five years, but they also believed that an expansion of industry had been going on during the war in the unoccupied parts of the USSR. Furthermore, while the liberated areas would be reconstructed, expansion of industry in other areas of the country would continue. The JIC believed that the FO overestimated the need for rehabilitation and that it might lead to an underestimation of the military potential.[63] The COS paper dated 15 June stated that the reconstruction and rehabilitation process would go on for about five year after the end of the war. The USSR faced a shortage of manpower as a result of the "enormous casualties" suffered during the war. Forced labour from Germany and other former enemy nations was a remedy for this problem. The shortage of labour was predicted to last for a few years after the war.[64]

In March the R & A branch analysed and estimated the extent of war damage up to July 1944. The Germans were still holding substantial parts of the Western USSR. By estimating Soviet property value (within the pre-1939 borders) as of June 1941, they concluded that 21.9 per cent of all physical property had been destroyed. The value of the destruction was US$18 billion. If the areas incorporated after 1 September 1939 were included, the value would instead be US$22 billion. The Soviets would demand large reparations from the Axis nations, but they could repair the destruction within the time span of one Five Year Plan. An effort comparable to that projected under the Third Five Year Plan would be more than sufficient.[65] In a May R & A report on the housing situation, they estimated that over half of the urban housing and nearly a fourth of the rural houses in the liberated territories were completely destroyed. In addition, half as much housing again was considered as damaged.[66]

Returning to January 1944, a FO official regarded a Pika report (received from the DMI) as very interesting. The report's content shows that it was written during the fall or early winter of 1943. Pika still considered the transport situation as the Soviet's greatest problem, due to the "enormous spaces" and lack of rolling stock. He also described a situation where ordinary people were lacking ordinary commodities and food. The food shortage was extra marked in the cities. Military personnel were better off. On the other hand Pika was also stating that the USSR had "enough food", and that the Russians were "satisfied with incredibly poor nutrition". The agricultural plots allotted to the people around the towns and the villages during the war, which ordinary people could cultivate for themselves, were considered by Pika to be producing good results in terms of strengthening the food intake. On the whole, the Soviets had extended the arable land of their "ordinary" agriculture in Asia to compensate for the loss of the Ukraine. He thought that the amount of cattle in agriculture was increasing; even though it was going to take time. Despite shortages of workers and machinery an improvement in agricultural conditions was predicted, and a future great agriculture crisis was unlikely. The role played by women was very important. The women had "replaced the men very well", also in more physically demanding jobs.[67]

Major-General Deane's January report, concerning the US Army officer's Leningrad visit, contained some comments (written by one of the officers) on factory production: "though factories are primitively organized and conditions are far below American standards, production does continue satisfactorily". He also stated "Russia has a much, much greater supply output than we think".[68]

In March the MI3(c) sent a memorandum, dated 13 February, to the MEW about a tour made by a British officer, from Moscow to Leningrad, during January-February. The officer also visited some parts of the Leningrad front. According to the report the railways had stood up to the test of war, due to an efficient administration and the "devotion" of the railway workers. The food situation was much improved by Western Allied supplies. He based this observation on what he had seen in Leningrad, but also stated that all Soviet towns received aid. When the MEW replied on 16 March they stated that the memorandum was in accordance with information from other sources.[69]

A MEW memorandum from March, received by the FO in April, compared the food consumption in some European countries. It was more or less argued that workers in the USSR received enough food, but that other categories relying on the working population for their support were suffering from shortages, except children. The official rations for miners and "heavy manual" workers were regarded as approximately comparable to conditions in Germany, and even above conditions in Belgium (which was occupied by Germany). This assessment was approximately the same if adjustments were made for food intake above the official rations, even if the Soviet intake was a little less favourable then. The USSR compared favourably even with Belgium concerning the category labelled "light workers", but less favourably with Germany (1750 calories against 2000/2350 calories). The Soviet disadvantage was really apparent first when comparing "dependants", such as children, the aged and infirm people. Both Germany and Belgium had a considerably higher calorific intake than the USSR concerning these categories. In general the British food situation was much better than the Soviet situation. But there was also room for some redistribution of food within families, which in practice made the situation better for children. It was also argued that regardless of calorific intake "children in the U.S.S.R. are usually reported to appear fit". The situation for the other categories of dependants was much worse.[70]

In March the OSS predicted that the Soviets would be able to successfully mount a powerful offensive not too long after 1 May, which would extend their supply lines. The extension would put additional strain on the locomotive and freight car position, even though this would not affect the efficiency of the Red Army, or seriously reduce Soviet capabilities in the rear.[71] They repeated the claim that the food situation was the "principal factor threatening Russian capabilities", although it was not so grave that it would affect military capabilities in 1944.[72]

The Soviet state budget was analysed both by the MEW and the FO in March. According to the MEW the total expenditure on defence, in this case on the Commissariats of Defence and Navy, was 52.3 per cent of the total defence budget for 1944. This was less than in 1943, in which the expenditure was 59 per cent. In actuality the MEW believed that real defence expenditure was higher, since various defence outlays were hidden under other sections of the budget.[73] During the same month, the Moscow embassy's Clark-Kerr also reported that actual defence expenditure was higher (than shown by the budget).[74]

In April the MEW reported on an increase in heavy industry production during the first quarter of the year. The annual rate of production was 18.7 million tonnes for iron ore, 12.5 million tonnes for coke, 9.3 million tonnes for pig iron, 12.3 million tonnes for steel and 9.5 million tonnes for rolled steel. New plants and a fuller utilization of existing capacity explained the increase.[75]

The US military attaché in Stockholm, Colonel Chas E. Fayens, submitted a report in May to the WD, containing information about a survey of Soviet war potential. The survey originated from a person whose reliability was rated as good. According to the survey raw material supply was assured, and industry was capable of satisfying the Red Army's requirements. The westward shift of the battlefront had increased transportation difficulties, and the labour situation was becoming more and more serious. The latter problem affected agriculture the most. The food situation was serious, but under control, with the help of foreign aid, until the next harvest. A poor harvest in 1944 could change this situation in a drastic way.[76]

In mid-June the OSS R & A branch estimated that the production of steel ingots was equivalent to an annual output of 15.35 million tonnes. The total 1944 output was predicted to be 17 per cent below the 1940 level (which in turn was estimated to 18.4 million tonnes). By 1 January 1945 the output on an annual basis was expected to be 16.8 million tonnes, of which furnaces in the liberated territories would provide 1.7 million tonnes. The importance of steel imports for the total supply of steel was "substantial", amounting to over 10 per cent of domestic output between 1 October 1941 and 31 March 1944. The actual imports analysed were not just raw steel but also imports, e.g. tanks, which had to be made out of steel if manufactured in the USSR.[77]

Many other US reports – by the ONI, BEW, SD and MID – from this period, including the period during the first half of 1943 described in Chapter 17, was about the increasing economic and industrial strength of the USSR (from the earlier low points), even though several problems and shortages still existed. The heavy strain on the civilian economy, relative to other countries in order to sustain the war economy, was emphasized by some observers. The great need for Lend-Lease to the Soviets was also repeated in a few reports. The more recent reports generally painted a brighter picture.[78]

19.3 Munitions: output and quality

In their August report, the US JIC believed that the high level of armament output could only be attained at the cost of a very high concentration of all economic resources on war. Declining armament output was predicted in the early summer of 1944, possibly due to food or manpower shortages, transport difficulties and capital deterioration.[79] This assessment was in line with their general belief in an exhaustion of the war effort from mid-1944 (see above), and they were not alone in this opinion. The assistant US military attaché in Cairo, Lieutenant-Colonel Henry I. Szymanski, drew on several sources (Polish, Czech and English officers) when he reported to the MID in September: "The consensus of opinion [...] is that the [military] output [...] in Russia has reached its peak. Factories can supply the needs of the army, but cannot increase production because of the difficulty of getting help and because of wear and tear on the machinery and equipment. Airplane production [...] has not been affected by the above statement and though it has reached its peak it can replace future losses though they may be big."[80] The same month G-2 estimated monthly tank output to between 1000 and 1500 units, mostly light and medium tanks. Monthly aircraft output was between 1000 and 1200 operational units. The general level of weapons production was 110 per cent of the pre-war level. It was not stated whether or not tanks and operational aircraft were included in this production level.[81] The statement "110 per cent" resembles the British JIC assessment from the beginning of the year, and can only be explained by an underestimation of the present Soviet capacity, or a change regarding the earlier, June 1941, level of output. Whatever the reason actual Soviet output of tanks and aircraft was substantially higher than the G-2 estimate. Babington did not think much of the design and efficiency of Soviet military equipment. He stated anyway, in his August memorandum, that the equipment was practical with "the essentially important quality of simplicity." He meant that the crudeness of the equipment corresponded well to the relatively low mechanical skills of its users. The general state of equipment was inferior to German or British standards.[82]

In the September OSS report (see above) the output of planes, tanks, and guns was adequate "to support military activity of a high intensity". Now the monthly output of combat planes was 2200, in addition to 300 imported. Monthly tank and gun output (37 mm in calibre and larger) comprised 2000 and 6000 units, respectively. Ammunition output during the first six months of 1943 was 50 per cent higher than during the same period in 1942. This was explained by an increase in labour productivity and by an expansion of productive facilities. The output of 2.5-tonne trucks was 4500 units per month, in addition to imports of 8000 per month. But despite imports the total supply of trucks was insufficient to replace losses in the long run. The continual decline of the truck park, which would follow from this situation, was predicted to ultimately have serious effects.[83] In the November report the output level was upgraded once again, to 2250 combat aircraft (almost entirely fighters, "Stormoviks" [Il-2s] and light bombers). But tank output was now only 1300 of mostly medium tanks. Monthly imports were stated to be 500 (aircraft) and 250 (tanks) units, respectively. No estimate for gun output was given, but ammunition output had increased from an equivalent of 2.3 million tonnes of steel during the second half of 1942 to 2.8 million during the first six months of 1943.[84] In October the British JIC concluded that the Soviets produced up to date high quality aircraft.[85] About the same time British AI noted that "Germany was drawing on obsolete and obsolescent aircraft, [while] the Russians were building modern planes".[86]

Sometime during the latter half of 1943 the British decrypted a report from the Japanese Ambassador in Berlin to the Foreign Ministry in Tokyo, concerning an interview with the German Field Marshal Milch held at 17 August 1943. Milch stated in the report that the Soviets produced around 2000 aircraft per month, including non-combat aircraft. Furthermore, he was apparently of the opinion that there had been a "great falling off" in the efficiency of Soviet planes recently.[87] According to Harriman Stalin stated in November, at the Teheran conference, that maximum monthly aircraft production was 3000. This probably referred to total military production, not just combat types.[88] G-2 reported in January 1944 the US ambassador in Moscow, Admiral Standley, estimated monthly aircraft output in August 1943 at "possibly" 2000 planes.[89]

By the beginning of 1944, G-2 revised their figures for aircraft output upwards drastically. In January 1944 G-2 estimated total 1943 aircraft output at between 28,000 and 30,000 units, including 6000 to 8000 non-combat types. Almost all manufactured combat types were medium bombers, attack aircraft ("Stormoviks [Il-2s]") and fighters.[90] An internal G-2 memorandum dated 1 January, written by Major Frederic M. Seeger, the chief of the G-2 Eastern European Section Air Unit, estimated November 1943 output at 1120 tactical combat aircraft produced in the Western USSR. However, this figure was based on extrapolations of a 1942 estimate, and by now the G-2 had identified three new factories, producing more than half the total output, judging by the 1942 estimate. The new estimate – considered conservative – was 2000 per month.[91] Several additional US and British estimates referred to in the memorandum corroborated the new estimate. Later in January a report forwarded by the US military attaché in Turkey, Brigadier-General Richard G. Tindall, also confirmed the estimate. Tindall had learned from his Finnish colleague, probably in turn relying on German sources, that the current monthly output was 2000, or even possibly 2500.[92]

The same month the British 30 Military Mission reported that the Soviet Army was well equipped with essential weapons. But at the same time it was short of transport and special combat vehicles (e.g. scout cars and command vehicles).[93] In February, Wing Commander McDonald, head of the British AI3(d), estimated monthly aircraft output at 1500.[94] In a widely distributed NID report, dated 10 March, the total estimated new construction of Soviet Naval vessels during the war was two destroyers and four submarines.[95]

An in-depth sequel, concerning military supplies, to the November 1943 OSS report on Soviet capabilities and prospects, was issued in January. The output figures in the November report for aircraft and tanks was confirmed, and it was added that the monthly output of artillery pieces (with a calibre of 37 mm and above) was about 2800, mostly anti-tank guns. Perhaps the most revealing information was the assessment that the majority of the guns produced were of a relatively light calibre. The output of pieces with a calibre of 76.2 mm or less was estimated to be in excess of 90 per cent of the total. Monthly mortar (not to be confused with guns/artillery) output was at least 10,000 units. Aircraft and tanks output was also more specified in this report. More than 50 per cent of the aircraft was "Shturmoviks [Il-2s]", and almost 70 per cent of the tank output was described as medium (and of somewhat heavier models than earlier). The quality of the aircraft – in terms of performance – was "probably somewhat inferior" to German models, especially with regard to fighters. The trend noted in the November report concerning a long-term increase in ammunition production was also confirmed. Truck output was 78,000 vehicles from July 1943 to June 1944.[96] Two months later the OSS R & A branch updated their munitions assessment to 2350 aircraft and 1438 tanks, on a monthly average basis, per the future date of 1 May. Added to this output came imports of 500 aircraft and nearly 240 tanks per month. Estimated monthly truck output was 8000, and current (monthly) Lend-Lease imports amounted to 11500. The Soviets would be well supplied with guns and ammunition during 1944.[97]

It seems that very few assessments were made regarding munitions output during the late spring and early summer. In a report dated 6 June the US Joint Intelligence Staff estimated the monthly aircraft output to 2200.[98] In the COS paper dated 15 June the COS made some predictions about the development of Soviet strategic bombers. This forecast was more about the post-war situation. It was feared that the Soviets might develop bombers with a range that could reach Great Britain. Other targets, such as vital Empire communications, were also in jeopardy. The COS therefore suggested that the strength of the British Air Force must be in accord with the development of Soviet air power.[99]

All the assessments during this period were much closer to the truth than during the preceding period, but still in some respect an underestimation. Actual tank and aircraft output during 1943 was increasing and continued to do so during 1944. The assessments support this but were still too low regarding tanks. Actual monthly average tank output in 1943 was slightly in excess of 2000, increasing to more than 2400 in 1944.[100] These figures also includes so called SP guns (i.e. tanks without a traversable turret, which in turn often allowed for a heavier cannon). It is common practice to include SP guns in these figures, and it can be assumed that the assessments above included vehicles like this. The cost of manufacturing a SP gun is in most cases close the cost of a tank, and if SP guns are excluded this would lower the output figures of Germany even more than the figures for the USSR. This means that the OSS still underestimated tank output but that the British, for example the MEW, produced fairly accurate assessments, or even slight overestimations.

Actual average monthly military aircraft output in 1943 and 1944 was more than 2900 and around 3350, respectively, of which nearly 2500 and somewhat less than 2800, respectively, were combat types.[101] This means that all observers still somewhat underestimated aircraft output. As already discussed artillery (and mortars), was the most important weapon system for the armed forces in terms of firepower. This can be exemplified by the fact that artillery (and mortar) fire was the most important factor in terms of manpower losses. Much fewer assessments was made regarding artillery than other weapon system, especially when expressed in concrete output figures. The OSS was an exemption in this respect, but their assessments were clear underestimations. Instead of the estimated 2800 units (of 37 mm or larger pieces), actual average monthly output in 1943 and 1944 was close to 4700 and more than 3200, respectively. Output fell in 1944, but this was associated with the fact that the losses of guns decreased. The total stock of field guns, for example, was substantially higher at the beginning of 1944 than at the beginning of 1943. The notion that at least 90 per cent of these guns were of a calibre of 76.2 mm or less might have been correct for 1943, but not for 1944 (in which case it was and underestimation). The USSR also produced many guns with a calibre lower than 37 mm in calibre, and hence not included in the OSS assessment, but it seems appropriate to include rocket artillery, which had a calibre in excess of 37 mm. Including rocket artillery would increase the monthly average in 1943 and 1944 by around 275 and 217 units, respectively.

The OSS also claimed a monthly mortar output of at least 10,000 units. This is actually the first available estimate (in concrete figures) for mortar output, and was at the time (January 1944) a gross overestimation of actual output. However, mortar output peaked already in 1942 with a monthly average of nearly 19,200 units, decreasing to nearly 5700 in 1943 and only circa 167 units in 1944.[102] The explanation for this is that the near catastrophic losses in 1941 and 1942 made it necessary to produce a large amount of mortars. New divisions were created in 1941–1942 in order to replace the one's lost in 1941, and understrength divisions raised in 1941–1942 had to be fleshed out with more men and equipment. Further output in 1943 and 1944 was more directed towards replacing (the now lower) losses in the already existing organization. Nevertheless, it was an overestimation at the time, but it must also be remembered that the production cost of a mortar was minimal in comparison to artillery. According to one available comparison, in 1942 the cost of 50, 82 and 120 mm mortars was 1600, 3200 and 6000 roubles, respectively, while the cost of a 45 (1937 model anti-tank), a 76.2 and a 152 mm gun was 10,500, 28,000 and 77,000 roubles, respectively. All things considered, it seems therefore that the underestimation of gun (artillery) output was relatively more important.

19.4 The size of the armed forces and the military mobilization

In August the US JIC estimated the size of the armed forces at about 10 million men, and the size of the army to around 6 million men, with 4000 combat planes on the Soviet–German front.[103] The size of the armed forces was confirmed in a G-2 report from September, but just as in July the army had 7 million men. G-2 also identified several rear area troops with duties of an administrative character, referred to as "semi-autonomous militarised service forces". The available manpower outside the armed forces was between 3 and 4 million men. The total number of tanks at the front was 5000, in addition to 1170 tanks in the Eastern parts of the country, and the aircraft strength was the same as in the JIC report.[104]

In their September report the OSS estimated the strength of the armed forces to 11.4 million men (9–10 million in the army and the air force), equipped with 6000 operational aircraft (of which 4000 were serviceable on any given day), 16,000 tanks in Europe (9000 in the frontline), and 60,000 guns and howitzers (of 37 mm in calibre or larger).[105] The corresponding estimate in November was 11.9 million men, 4500–5000 first-line aircraft in the Europe by the end of 1943, and 8300 tanks in the frontline. Tank strength was reduced by 1000 vehicles since July, which was explained by the German bombing of the Gorky tank plant. But the tank position was nevertheless favourable, compared with the October 1942 situation.[106] It seems that the OSS by now at least was approaching reality, even though aircraft and gun strength still clearly was underestimated.

During September and October more assessments was made, regarding the size of the armed forces and their equipment, by a US military attaché, the ONI, the British JIC and G-2.[107] The later organization observed the growth of the SAF in several estimates from May 1943 to June 1944. Aircraft in operational combat squadrons as of 1 May 1943 were set to 5400 on all fronts (but including the Far East, although excluding other non-combat areas). This figure was revised slightly upwards later in the year.[108] In 1944 the figure exceeded 7000 in the spring and then 8000 in the summer.[109] Total aircraft strength (i.e. reserves and other tactical aircraft) was also estimated. Apparently G-2 must have revised their assessments of available aircraft outside operational squadrons in a major way between December 1943 and February 1944, since their total numbers were 4050 as of 1 December 1943, and then 10,400 as of 1 February 1944. According to later estimates the reserves were steadily increasing from February to June 1944, being 13,320 on 1 June.[110] The probable explanation for the drastic upward revision of reserves was given in the internal memorandum from 1 January 1944, written by Major Seeger (see above). Since the memorandum concluded that output was much larger than had been estimated earlier this meant a much larger supply, and the residual numbers were put on the "reserve account", instead of a revision of the operational front strength.[111]

In January the British JIC and the OSS both presented assessments. The JIC estimated Soviet Army strength in the European theatre to between 7 and 8.5 million men (excluding the air force), with ample equipment and supported by about 5000 operational aircraft of "improving quality". Some of these forces were coming from a large reserve previously uncommitted during the summer.[112] The following month the ONI rated the report as A-1 in reliability.[113] The OSS estimated the SAF's strength to between 6300 and 6800 combat aircraft in the first line (including the Far East). The frontline tank strength was 9500 (including the Far East as of 1 July 1943), and the total number of artillery pieces (of at least 37 mm in calibre) as of July 1943 were 48,100. Artillery strength had increased since July. The mortar strength as of July 1943 was 115,000, and the total amount of military trucks on the Soviet–German front as of 1 July was around 350,000.[114]

In March the OSS made another assessments; this time predicting the position as of 1 May 1944. The size of the army would be 9.9 million men, with 6.4 at the front, mostly combat troops, and the Soviets would still have sufficient manpower to replace all losses. The SAF would have 16,500 combat aircraft, but only 6500 in front service, and the rest would be in reserve, at depots, and available for training. The total tank strength would be 17,300, of which 12,700 would be available for front action. The Red Army would have 380,000 trucks. No figures were presented for artillery, or ammunition stocks, other than that it was expected that the Red Army would be well supplied with these items during 1944.[115]

In two other March assessments British AI underestimated the SAF's operational and reserve strength and the NID made a fairly correct assessments of the number of ships in the navy.[116]

In May the US JIC estimated the opposing force on the Soviet–German front in an attempt to assess the implications for Operation *Overlord*, the coming Western Allied invasion of France. The SAF's frontline strength was between 5000 and 6000, almost all of them modern models.[117] This can be compared to a US Joint Intelligence Staff report, estimating on 6 June that the Soviets, on 1 June, had a total (everywhere in the USSR) of 8260 operational tactical aircrafts, and a reserve of 13,320 aircraft.[118] In May the British JIC made exactly the same estimate as their US counterpart regarding the SAF's operational strength (opposing the Germans).[119]

In the mid-May report from the US military attaché in Stockholm to the WD in Washington it was estimated that the Red Army had plenty of reserves for the rest of the 1944 military campaign, and no crisis in reserves was expected until the beginning of 1945.[120] It seems that the British considered the Red Army to be much larger than the Axis forces on the Soviet–German front. In a June DMI paper, addressed to the Vice-Chief of the Imperial General Staff (VCIGS), it was estimated that the Soviets outnumbered the Axis by 2.5 to 1 in men and 3.5 to 1 in tanks.[121]

The figures presented above suggest that most estimates of Soviet Armed Forces equipment strength were approximately correct, with the notable exception of combat aircraft in the field forces and the total number of tanks and aircraft in reserve. The air strength was therefore underestimated to a considerable extent. The first line tank strength was overestimated at times, which implies that military wastage was underestimated, since, as we have seen, output was also underestimated to some extent, at least by the Americans. On the whole, considering the large number of tanks and aircraft the Soviets held in reserve, the size of the armed forces were somewhat underestimated during the period.

19.5 The morale, efficiency and losses of the armed forces

In his August memorandum Babington questioned what he regarded as the common view of the "toughness" of Soviet soldiers. To him there was no indication that they had any "exceptional `guts´ or superior endurance". Since at the same time he believed that they were at a disadvantage vis-à-vis their Western counterparts, in education and intelligence, the human factor could not be used as an explanation for Soviet military success. But he did, nevertheless, have some praise for their "effective" military training. The whole Soviet military machine worked under conditions that would seem "impossible" to a Western observer. This state of affairs was a factor that could facilitate mobility in the field, since there was less need to use scarce specialist resources. It appears that Babington regarded Soviet "simplicity" not merely as an advantage, but as a somewhat necessary condition for military efficiency. However, he regarded the Soviet technique of war as considerably inferior to that of the German Army. As for military losses he stated that conservative, non-Soviet estimates varied from 6 to 8 million men, counting only permanent losses. He saw these estimates largely as guesswork, but that Soviet losses could be counted in millions. According to him, the WO estimated losses to be 7.5 million up to 1 April 1943, of which 5.5 million were assumed to be "permanent".[122]

The same month an MI3(c) report gave a partly contrasting view, regarding the character of the Soviet soldier. Several reasons were given as an explanation of why the he "excels in close combat". Two of the reasons were his "unusual power of endurance" and "indifference to personal danger". Other reasons stated in the report were intensive training, the soldier's confidence in his weapons and favourable organizational and mental conditions.[123]

In August Michela forwarded a report to the MID, in which the material losses for the first two years of the war were estimated to 29,400 tanks, 35,000 guns, 50,000 machine guns, 15,000 mortars, and 100,000 motor vehicles. The figures were tentative, especially concerning tanks, since he assessed real tank losses as higher.[124] Later that month the US JIC described Soviet troops as "hard and well disciplined", with equipment comparable to the Germans. The supply position of the army was satisfactory, but the training, command and staff functions were still regarded as being inferior to German standards.

They had evidence that the qualitative difference between the Soviet and the German air forces was still in existence, but that the difference was at the same time diminishing. This was at least partly explained by increasing Soviet efficiency. The transfer of German air forces to other theatres and a lowering of the quality of Axis pilots on the Soviet–German front were other explanations. The Navy was having poor organization and staff work, but with a high morale and in general effective individual vessels.[125]

In September G-2 estimated total military causalities at somewhere between 8.5 and 9 million men, of which 3 to 3.5 million were killed and 2 million taken prisoners by the Germans. Total tank losses as of 1 September were 44,000. Aircraft and gun losses (probably at the same date as regarding tanks) were 31,500 and 60,000 units, respectively.[126] The same month the OSS estimated permanent losses to nearly six million at the beginning of the summer campaign.[127] In an earlier report from June estimated permanent military losses was between 5.5 and 6 million men.[128] In the September report long-term losses of planes, tanks and guns were not larger than the OSS allowed for a long-term increase in numbers available to the Red Army. But losses of trucks were in excess of replacements.[129]

The notion of a high military morale was repeated by the British JIC and the FO in October. The JIC also added that the efficiency of the SAF was improving, and that the Soviets had air superiority, at least on the southern part of the Soviet–German front.[130] The FO summarized the experiences of the *Daily Express* Moscow reporter Jacobs. During his several visits to the front he had observed that the morale and the spirits of the troops were at a very high level.[131] According to an ONI memorandum from the same month the Red Army had improved since the start of the war. The Soviet high command was being largely successful, due to organizational changes, the removal of inadequate commanders and by the training of the staff along modern lines of war. The 1942–1943 winter campaign was proof that the Red Army had learned both to plan and to execute major offensive operations. The ONI's general impression of the naval forces was that they had a somewhat lower efficiency than the naval forces of the western powers.[132]

In November the OSS issued a report concerning "Soviet guerrilla warfare". The report seemed to consider the partisan movement as strong and very disturbing to the Germans, causing considerable havoc and destruction behind German lines. The partisans were also of great value to the Soviets because of the information they provided. They were also largely regarded as an integral part of the military organization – with substantial support from the local population – since they took their orders from the Soviet High Command.[133] The view regarding the control over the partisans was shared by the MI3(c), which in a July report concluded that the partisans, activities were planned and controlled in a central manner by the Red Army.[134]

This month the OSS also made two assessments regarding losses. In one report the OSS estimated permanent losses at between 5.5 and 7 million. Average monthly losses of aircraft (during the preceding year) and tanks were

1900 and 1500, respectively. Since artillery and mortar strength had increased over the last year, it is also apparent that estimated losses were at least lower than production. The numerical increase of artillery pieces and mortars were, in addition to an increase in ammunition supply, one factor in the growing firepower of Red Army units.[135] In the "Soviet agricultural and industrial potentialities" report total estimated casualties due to all causes were 12.5 million. Although not specifically stated, this figure probably included dead, missing, and permanently disabled, as well as civilian casualties.[136]

In January 1944 the FO and the DMI noted a report (the report was probably somewhat older than January since it referred to conditions in September) in which Pika stated that the German Air Force "to-day is not superior [to the Soviet Air Force] neither with regard to the quality nor to the efficiency of the flying personnel and Soviet command. A comparison tends to favour the Soviets."[137] The same month the British JIC probably had a more realistic assessment of the current situation when they stated that the SAF, plane for plane, was "greatly inferior to the Germans". The JIC did, however, regard the SAF as first-class when it came to improvisation, and being "capable of a rough and steady efficiency". But they praised both the fighting efficiency and high morale of the Red Army, and considered that it was increasing its combat experience steadily. Technical and specialist troops were very good, especially tank and artillery troops. The infantry was the least efficient arm. Staff work was now much improved and the Soviets were masters of improvisation.[138] Earlier in January a 30 Mission report stated that compared with British standards Soviet ground support operations were something of a "'hit and miss' affair".[139]

The OSS reported in January that it was "possible [...] in some cases [that] Russian flying personnel is inadequately trained." The high losses of planes were leading to high losses of pilots, which in turn were leading "to a lower average level of experience and to speed-up training." They also saw it as probable that it was the poor maintenance of aircraft behind the front that was the single most important factor in the large wastage of aircraft. As for figures the OSS repeated its November claim regarding losses of aircraft (including non-operational wastage) and tanks. The average monthly losses of guns (equal to or in excess of 37 mm in calibre) and mortars were around 2100 and 8000 units, respectively. These estimates were extrapolations, partly calculating in possible future losses from July 1943 to June 1944. The losses of trucks were big enough to induce a decline in the truck park over the coming year.[140]

In a telegram from Deane to G-2 in Washington, dated 12 January, a trip made by General Connolly and other military officials to the Kiev front was described. Connolly's party had a positive impression of the Red Army. It had a high morale, was well fed, clothed and armed.[141] In February an officer from the 30 Mission informed the deputy (military) secretary of the War Cabinet, Lieutenant-General Ismay, in a report on the "excellent" morale of the army in Leningrad.[142] The Soviet conduct of operations during the Korsun battle in the Western Ukraine was criticized in March by a member of the 30 Mission. It was not considered that they could achieve large-scale encirclements with their operations.[143] Nevertheless, it was apparent, in the report addressed to the MI3(c), that the Red Army had trapped the Germans in the Korsun operation and that it was on the move and victorious.[144] During this battle, also called battle of the Korsun–Cherkasy Pocket, which was a part of the general Soviet offensive through the Ukraine since Kursk, the Red Army had encircled six German divisions (and smaller support units). Some Germans escaped the encirclement, but in the end the battle proved to be a Soviet victory which inflicted relatively large losses in the Germans.

When the OSS R & A branch compared the relative strength of forces on the Soviet–German front in March (predicting the situation as of 1 May 1944), they did not doubt that the Soviets had a massive numerical superiority in tanks and aircraft. But in practice, they argued, this superiority was somewhat diminished, due to the Soviets being less efficient regarding military tactics and maintenance of material. However, this was not entirely seen as being the case concerning artillery, since the assumed Soviet superiority in this arm was more an effect of different artillery practices than a German shortage of guns. OSS stated that the morale of the armed forces would be high on 1 May, and that it would continue to be so as a result of continued military successes.[145]

In March the NID estimated that while the total losses of the Northern Fleet were relatively modest during the war, the Baltic Fleet's losses were 59 per cent of all destroyers and 46 per cent of all submarines. Corresponding losses for the somewhat smaller Black Sea Fleet were 75 per cent and 36 per cent, respectively.[146]

According to the May report (see above) of the US military attaché in Stockholm, the Red Army's "combat quality" had risen, and several "positive factors" were identified. Combat training, new tactics, and the aggressiveness of the high command were among these factors.[147]

At the beginning of June 1944 the US Joint Intelligence Staff estimated the monthly loss rate for aircraft to be 1500.[148]

Notes

1 Hinsley (1984), 20.
2 Folly (2000), 53; 8–10–1943, "ACASI/250A/43", ADM223/506; 16–6–1943, N3557/163/38, FO371/36969; 8–10–1943, "ACASI/250A/43", ADM223/506; 12–8–1943, "Air Section [...]", ADM223/506.
3 13–8–1943, "Subject: [...]", Box-3172, Entry-77, RG165.
4 20–8–1943, JIC72dMtg, 625–2(JIC129)(1st Revision)(20–8–1943), Box-214, RG218.
5 22–8–1943, "Memorandum [...]", ABC336Russia(22–8–1943)Sec 1-a, Box-250, Entry-421, RG165; Deane (1947), 9; Harriman & Abel (1976), 228–229.
6 Deane (1947), 10–12.
7 22–8–1943, "Memorandum [...]", ABC336Russia(22–8–1943)Sec 1-a, Box-250, Entry-421, RG165.
8 14–9–1943, R&A No. 1193, Report #10, Reel-2, UPA1977.
9 11–9–1943, N5282/2759/38, FO371/37015.

10   18–9-1943, R&A No. 1217, Box-3102, Entry-77, RG165; 8–11–1943, R&A No. 1355, Box-3102, Entry-77, RG165.
11   22-12-1943, R&A No. 1670, Report #18, Reel-2, UPA1977.
12   29-12-1943, R&A No. 1355.2, M1221, RG59.
13   23-12-1943, "69A", WO208/1794; 1–1-1944, N131/42/38, FO371/43310.
14   The officers were attached to the Persian Gulf command and the US Military Mission to the USSR. 13–1-1945, "Subject: [...]", Box-3127, Entry-77, RG165.
15   2–10–1943, JIC(43)409(0), CAB81/117.
16   5–10-1943, "Prime Minister", CAB120/744.
17   20-10-1943, JIC(43)421(0)(Draft), CAB81/118.
18   5–11–1943, R&A No. 1460, Report #16, Reel-2, UPA1977.
19   The original British report was dated 15 November. Keegan (ed.) (1989), 126–127; 25-11-1943, "Memorandum [...]", ABC381Germany(29–1-43)Sec 2-a, Box-342, Entry-421, RG165; 15-11-1943, JIC(43)457(Final), CAB81/118.
20   25-11-1943, "Memorandum [...]", ABC381Germany(29–1-43)Sec 2-a, Box-342, Entry-421, RG165.
21   Deane (1947), 145.
22   20–1-1944, JIC(44)21(Final), CAB81/120.
23   11–2-1944, JIC(44)60(0), CAB81/120.
24   10–2-1944, N1008/183/38, FO371/43335.
25   11–2-1944, JIC(44)60(0), CAB81/120.
26   10–2-1944, N1008/183/38, FO371/43335.
27   13–4-1944, JIC(44)138(0)(Final), CAB81/121.
28   Keegan (ed.) (1989), 148–149.
29   13–4-1944, JIC(44)138(0)(Final), CAB81/121.
30   13–5-1944, JIC(44)198(0)(Final), CAB81/122.
31   25-3-1944, "The Russian [...]", MI3, WO208/1849.
32   The approximate superiority in men, aircraft and tanks was nearly 2–1, 4–1 and 4–1, respectively. 20–3-1944, R&A No. 1977, Report #26, Reel-2, UPA1977.
33   Matloff (1959), 377; Dear & Foot (eds.) (1995), 1066.
34   15–5-1944, N3472/1667/38, FO371/43395; 16–5-1944, N2958/1667/38, FO371/43395.
35   15–6-1944, COS(44)527(0)(PHP), CAB121/064; Keegan (ed.) (1989), 148.
36   1–5-1944, PHP(43)1(0).(Final), CAB81/45; 6–6-1944, PHP(44)13(0)(Final), CAB121/064; 15–6-1944, COS(44)527(0)(PHP), CAB121/064.
37   Such cooperation was seen as necessary anyway "in order to prevent the possibility of a new German aggression".
38   15–6-1944, COS(44)527(0)(PHP), CAB121/064.
39   The US JIC report came in two versions, one on 19 August and one on 20 August. The first version referred to the Soviet situation as of 15 August and the second to the situation on 20 August. The second version was read and amended on the US JIC's 72nd meeting. 19–8-1943, 625–1(JIC129), Box-214, RG218; 20–8-1943, JIC72dMtg, 625–2(JIC129)(1st Revision)(20–8- 1943), Box-214, RG218.
40   29–9-1943, "Memorandum [...]", Box-3159, Entry-77, RG165.
41   18–9-1943, R&A No. 1217, Box-3102, Entry-77, RG165; 8–11–1943, R&A No. 1355, Box-3102, Entry-77, RG165.
42   Ibid.
43   Ibid.
44   Ibid.
45   Ibid.
46   30-12-1943, R&A No. 1355.1, M1221, RG59.
47   2–10–1943, JIC(43)409(0), CAB81/117. When Major-General Deane arrived in Moscow in October 1943, as head of the new American Military Mission, he got the impression that it was only the very young or the very old that were under-nourished. Deane (1947), 5–6; Harriman and Abel (1976), 228.

48 19-10-1943, N6382/52/38, FO371/36951.
49 20-10-1943, N6487/52/38, FO371/36951.
50 "Agenda, Notes of economic intelligence for meeting to be held on Friday, 26th Nov 1943", FO837/26; "Agenda, Notes of economic intelligence for meeting to be held on Friday, 19th Nov 1943", FO837/26.
51 "Notes of economic intelligence for week ending, 29th Oct 1943", FO837/26.
52 "Notes of economic intelligence for week ending, 5th Nov 1943", FO837/26.
53 "Agenda, Notes of economic intelligence for meeting to be held on Friday, 26th Nov 1943", FO837/26.
54 26-10-1943, N6280/2759/38, FO371/37015.
55 6–10–1943, N6724/5806/38, FO371/37057.
56 AA02067, CCS320.2USSR(2–11–43), Box-209, RG218.
57 10-11-1943, "Soviet [...]", Box-3100, Entry-77, RG165.
58 13-12-1943, R&A No. 1570, Report #17, Reel-2, UPA1977.
59 3–9-1943, N5090/75/38, FO371/36960.
60 13-12-1943, R&A No. 1570, Report #17, Reel-2, UPA1977.
61 11–2-1944, JIC(44)60(0), CAB81/120; 10–2-1944, N1008/183/38, FO371/43335.
62 10–2-1944, N1008/183/38, FO371/43335.
63 20–3-1944, JIC(44)105(0)(Final), CAB81/121.
64 15–6-1944, COS(44)527(0)(PHP), CAB121/064.
65 8–3-1944, R&A No. 1899, M1221, RG59.
66 25–5-1944, R&A No. 2094.1, M1221, RG59.
67 1–1-1944, N131/42/38, FO371/43310.
68 13–1-1945, "Subject: [...]", Box-3127, Entry-77, RG165.
69 13–2-1944, "Memorandum [...]", WO208/1844.
70 5–4-1944, N2032/106/38, FO371/43329.
71 The park of locomotives and freight cars was 22,000 and 750,000 units, respectively. 20–3-1944, R&A No. 1977, Report #26, Reel-2, UPA1977.
72 20–3-1944, R&A No. 1977, Report #26, Reel-2, UPA1977.
73 28–3-1944, N1868/42/38, FO371/43314.
74 16–3-1944, N2122/42/38, FO371/43314.
75 "MEW, Notes of economic intelligence for week ending 14th April 1944", FO837/28.
76 15–5-1944, "Subject: [...]", "Estimate [...]", Box-3175, Entry-77, RG165.
77 14–6-1944, R&A No. 2160, M1221, RG59.
78 15–2-1943, No. 251, Roll-22, T1250, RG59; 28–4-1943, 42120, Box-614, Entry-141A, RG169; 1–7-1943, Report No. 9587, 16088-T, Box-591, Entry-98A, RG38; 8–7-1943, Report No. 9658, 350.05USSR, Box-1043, Entry-47, RG319; 1–11–1943, 20785-B, Box-529, Entry-98A, RG38; 5–1-1944, No. 130, 800 – Soviet Union – General, Box-47, MECF1944: 800–811.1, RG84; 25–4-1944, No. 386, 850 – Economic Matters, Box-50, MECF1944: 842–850.4, RG84; 25–4-1944, No. 386, Roll-22, T1250, RG59.
79 20–8-1943, JIC72dMtg, 625–2(JIC129)(1st Revision)(20–8-1943), Box-214, RG218.
80 16–9-1943, "Potential [...]", Box-3122, Entry-77, RG165.
81 29–9-1943, "Memorandum [...]", Box-3159, Entry-77, RG165.
82 8–10–1943, "ACASI/250A/43", ADM223/506; 12–8-1943, "Air Section [...]", ADM223/506.
83 18–9-1943, R&A No. 1217, Box-3102, Entry-77, RG165.
84 2–10–1943, JIC(43)409(0), CAB81/117.
85 Hinsley (1984), 21.
86 8–11–1943, R&A No. 1355, Box-3102, Entry-77, RG165.
87 Hinsley (1984), 547.
88 This particular statement was made in the context of a toast to the president and people of the United States, where Stalin thanked the Americans for Lend-Lease supplies sent to the USSR during the war. Harriman & Abel (1976), 277.

89   1–1-1944, "Subject: [...], Estimate, [...]", Box-3175, Entry-77, RG165.
90   29–1-1944 (Handwritten date), "Production [...]", "Estimate, [...]", Box-3175, Entry-77, RG165.
91   1–1-1944, "Subject: [...], Estimate, [...]", Box-3175, Entry-77, RG165.
92   1–1-1944, "Subject: [...], Estimate, [...]", Box-3175, Entry-77, RG165; 17–1-1944, "Subject: [...]", "Estimate, [...]", Box-3175, Entry-77, RG165.
93   4–1-1944, "Report No. 5 [...]", WO208/1829.
94   16–3-1944, "Soviet [...]", "Estimate, [...]", Box-3175, Entry-77, RG165.
95   10–3-1944, "N.I.D. [...]", CAB120/680.
96   15–1-1944, R&A No. 1355.3, Box-3155, Entry-77, RG165.
97   20–3-1944, R&A No. 1977, Report #26, Reel-2, UPA1977.
98   6–6-1944, JIS54, Part 1: The Soviet Union, Records of the JCS, UPA1981.
99   15–6-1944, COS(44)527(0)(PHP), CAB121/064.
100 Krivosheev (1997), 252–253; Harrison (2002), Appendix B.
101 Ibid.
102 Krivosheev (1997), 251–252.
103 20–8-1943, JIC72dMtg, 625–2(JIC129)(1st Revision)(20–8-1943), Box-214, RG218.
104 29–9-1943, "Memorandum [...]", Box-3159, Entry-77, RG165.
105 18–9-1943, R&A No. 1217, Box-3102, Entry-77, RG165.
106 8–11–1943, R&A No. 1355, Box-3102, Entry-77, RG165.
107 The September Szymanski report to the MID stated that (based on the "most reliable source in England") the Red Army had 13 million men, including a reserve of 3 million men, NKVD troops numbering 300,000, "Workingmen Battalions" of 1 million men, and an air force consisting of 1.5 million men. The ability to mobilize new troops from a single annual class of conscripts was between 600,000 and 800,000 men. 16–9-1943, "Potential [...]", Box-3122, Entry-77, RG165. In October the ONI estimated that the ground forces as of 8 July exceeded 6.2 million men, with 9230 tanks. The size of the air force was stated to be 7200 planes on 1 October. The report was a memorandum for the European team of the Joint Intelligence Staff 19-10-1943, "Memorandum [...]", CCS320.2USSR(2–11–43), Box-209, RG218. According to an October G-2 report the total strength of the army, including troops in training, the NKVD and the SAF, was 9.85 million, of which 7 million were in the Red Army ground forces. 7–10–1943, "U.S.S.R.", Box-3159, Entry-77, RG165. By early October the British JIC estimated that the Soviets had at least 5000 first-line aircraft facing the Germans. 2–10–1943, JIC(43)409(0), CAB81/117.
108 6 May, 1 June (handwritten dates), 1 August, and 1–12–1943, "USSR, [...]", "Estimate, [...]", Box-3175, Entry-77, RG165.
109 1 February and 1–4-1944, "USSR, [...]", "Estimate, [...]", Box-3175, Entry-77, RG165; 1 March, 1 May, and 1–6-1944, "Estimates [...]", "Estimate, [...]", Box-3175, Entry-77, RG165.
110 9 December (handwritten date), 1 February, 1 March, 1 April, 1 May and 1–6-1944, "Estimate [...]", "Estimate, [...]", Box-3175, Entry-77, RG165.
111 1–1-1944, "Subject: [...], Estimate, [...]", Box-3175, Entry-77, RG165.
112 14–1-1944, JIC(44)16(0), CAB81/120; 20–1-1944, JIC(44)21(Final), CAB81/120. According to a mid-January report from the British DMI, distributed to some top officials in the military administration, the Soviet Army (on 11 January) had the equivalent of 524 infantry divisions and 234 tank brigades. 13–1-1944, "4/Inf/ 1881", DMI, WO208/1773.
113 2–2-1944, 23025, Box-250, Entry-98, RG38.
114 15–1-1944, R&A No. 1355.3, Box-3135, Entry-77, RG165.
115 20–3-1944, R&A No. 1977, Report #26, Reel-2, UPA1977.
116 In March, Wing Commander McDonald, head of the AI3D, believed that the SAF's operational strength at the Soviet–German front was at least 5000 by the

end of February, with 4600 reserves, alternatively circa 6000 with 2250 reserves. His estimate was shared with Colonel T. D. Lanphier, head of the G-2 Air Section. Major Seeger's memorandum from 1 January 1944 also came to the attention of Lanphier. The NID report dated 10 March was widely distributed and estimated the present strength of the Soviet Navy to be 2 battleships, 6 cruisers, 33 destroyers and approximately 210 submarines of various sizes, in addition to a large array of smaller vessels. 16-3-1944, "Soviet [...]", "Estimate, [...]", Box-3175, Entry-77, RG165; 1-1-1944, "Subject: [...], Estimate, [...]", Box-3175, Entry-77, RG165; 10-3-1944, "N.I.D. [...]", CAB120/680.

117   25-5-1944, "Memorandum [...]", ABC384USSR(6-1-42), Box-472, Entry-421, RG165.
118   6-6-1944, JIS54, Part 1: The Soviet Union, Records of the JCS, UPA1981.
119   13-5-1944, JIC(44)198(0)(Final), CAB81/122.
120   15-5-1944, "Suspect [...]", "Estimate, [...]", Entry-77, RG165.
121   2-6-1944, "VCIGS", WO208/1849.
122   8-10-1943, "ACASI/250A/43", ADM223/506; 12-8-1943, "Air Section [...]", ADM223/506.
123   21-8-1943, "MI3(c)/c/Min/21/43", MI3(c), WO208/1824.
124   11-8-1943, "Subject: [...]", Box-3147, Entry-77, RG165.
125   20-8-1943, JIC72dMtg, 625-2(JIC129)(1st Revision)(20-8-1943), Box-214, RG218.
126   29-9-1943, "Memorandum [...]", Box-3159, Entry-77, RG165.
127   18-9-1943, R&A No. 1217, Box-3102, Entry-77, RG165.
128   25-6-1943, R&A No. 917, Report #5, Reel-2, UPA1977.
129   18-9-1943, R&A No. 1217, Box-3102, Entry-77, RG165.
130   2-10-1943, JIC(43)409(0), CAB81/117.
131   9-10-1943, N6186/52/38, FO371/36951.
132   19-10-1943, "Memorandum [...]", CCS320.2USSR(2-11-43), Box-209, RG218.
133   5-11-1943, R&A No. 1356, Report #15, Reel-2, UPA1977.
134   15-7-1943, "Russian Partisans", WO208/1836.
135   8-11-1943, R&A No. 1355, Box-3102, Entry-77, RG165.
136   10-11-1943, "Major [...]", Box-3100, Entry-77, RG165.
137   1-1-1944, N131/42/38, FO371/43310.
138   20-1-1944, JIC(44)21(Final), CAB81/120.
139   4-1-1944, "Report [...]", 30 Military Mission, WO208/1829.
140   15-1-1944, R&A No. 1355.3, Box-3155, Entry-77, RG165.
141   The telegram was also later sent to the War Cabinet Offices in London. 19-1-1944, "JSM 1433", AIR20/7951.
142   17-2-1944, "Dear [...]", CAB121/464; Cantwell (1993), 5. In another report, probably about the same visit to Leningrad, the morale of the Red Army on the Leningrad front was excellent. 13-2-1944, "Memorandum [...]", WO208/1842.
143   18-3-1944, "Dear Mathews", MI3(c), WO208/1850.
144   In the Korsun-Shevchenkovski operation the Red Army trapped 73,000 German officers and men during January and February 1944 in a salient west of the River Dnieper. Keegan (ed.) (1989), 146-147; Glantz & House (2000), 186; 18-3-1944, "Dear Mathews", MI3(c), WO208/1850.
145   20-3-1944, R&A No. 1977, Report #26, Reel-2, UPA1977.
146   10-3-1944, "N.I.D. [...]", CAB120/680.
147   15-5-1944, "Subject: [...]", "Estimate [...]", Box-3175, Entry-77, RG165.
148   6-6-1944, JIS54, Part 1: The Soviet Union, Records of the JCS, UPA1981.

20 The final phase of the war

From Operation *Bagration* to the surrender of Germany (and the campaign against Japan)

At the end of the spring of 1944 the Soviets and the Red Army could look back upon long series of victories the last ten months. The Red Army's offensive military operations since the middle of July 1943 had pushed the Germans back all over the long frontline. These operations had been very costly in terms of lives and material losses, but the German Army had been severely mauled in the process and was never able to stabilize the front until the spring thaw, which worsened the logistical conditions for the Red Army as well as for the Germans. The Germans still held on to some important parts of the USSR though. They had been thrown out from most of the Ukraine, but Belorussia and the Baltic States was still in German hands.

The greater part of the German Army was still stationed in the East, even though a build-up in the West had taken place in anticipation of a Western Allied invasion of Western Europe. The Anglo-Americans was making progress in Italy but the Germans could retreat slowly and in relatively good order, only employing a small fraction of their total strength. The terrain and width of Italian peninsula was not suited for quick breakthroughs. On 6 June the invasion of German occupied France became a reality. The Anglo-Americans soon established a bridgehead in Normandy, which allowed for a continued build-up of forces. With this build up and the help of their overwhelming air power the Western Allied forces could soon break out of the Normandy region. Apart from their inferiority in the air, the Germans simply lacked the necessary forces to hold the Anglo-Americans at bay.

The relative lull on the Soviet–German front was deceptive, since the Soviets were building up for the single largest Red Army offensive so far in the war. The Operation was codenamed *Bagration*, and was directed towards the German Army Group Centre. The attack begun on 22 June, exactly three years after the start of Operation *Barbarossa*, and soon the Red Army won a great victory.

20.1 Soviet military prospects and internal stability

In general the intensity of the reporting concerning military prospects and internal stability was relatively low during this period. Possible, and more or less obvious, explanations for this, is that the observers probably did not doubt the Red Army's ability to continue its westward advance, and perhaps their intelligence resources was more preoccupied now with assessing phenomena related to the war in Western Europe, due to the recent Normandy invasion.

At this time the Allied advance was swift in the West and the East. By late summer and early autumn, after the German defeat in France, the mood among high ranking US military officials was very optimistic. They were nurturing hopes of an end to the war in Europe perhaps by November.[1] However, in September the Western Allied advance stalled. Their supply lines had become extended and the Germans were able to raise a large amount of new troops by instigating drastic measures. The Anglo-Americans could liberate most of France during the summer, but the Benelux nations and Germany was still denied them. In the East the Red Army had destroyed Army Group Centre, advanced all the way to Warsaw, while at the same time almost trapping Army Group North in the Baltic States. After a failed attempt to invade Romania during the spring, a renewed Red Army offensive was launched in August which defeated the German troops there. Romania switched sides and the Red Army could continue its march into the Balkans.

The speedy advance through Belorussia and Eastern Poland had also extended the Red Army's supply lines. Further preparations were therefore necessary in order to launch a full scale offensive into Central Poland and East Prussia (which was a part of Germany proper). A lull on the central part of the Soviet–German front was therefore in effect until the winter of 1944/45. In the meantime the remnants of Army Group North were decimated, the advance through the Balkans continued and an offensive was launched against Finland. By October Army Group North was separated from the rest of the German front, and what was left of it took up defensive positions in Latvia (the "Courland Pocket"). Finland had surrendered and switched sides, as did the Bulgarians. The centre of gravity of the Soviet–German was now central Poland, and in November the British JIC believed that at present the Germans had a chance to keep the Red Army at bay, since the front had become shorter and the Soviet supply lines longer. It was not obvious to the JIC that the anticipated large-scale Soviet winter offensive would have decisive results.[2] In December Harriman and Stalin talked about the situation. Allied hopes of ending the war in 1944 had been frustrated. Stalin waited for better weather so that the Soviets could resume the offensive in Poland.[3]

For Hitler and Germany December and January was the time for the last offensive of any significance in the war. In December the *Wehrmacht* attacked the Western Allies, but the offensive soon bogged down after some initial success. In the East the Red Army had pushed into Hungary during the autumn and surrounded Budapest. The Germans attacked in January trying to relieve their besieged troops, but the encirclement held. In mid-January the great Red Army offensive in Poland and against East Prussia begun, and in contrast to the fears of the British JIC it yielded decisive results. According to Harriman, by the time of the Yalta conference at the beginning of February,

Roosevelt had made "bets as to whether the Russians would get to Berlin before the US Army liberated Manila". Stalin replied that the German defence was so stubborn that the Americans would surely capture Manila before the Soviets would enter Berlin.[4]

When spring was approaching Hitler's forces were making their last stand against the Allies.[5] In March Harriman asked Stalin about the forthcoming Soviet advance in the light of an earlier forecast made by Stalin that the Red Army might be bogged down by the end of March, due to early spring floods. However, Stalin was confident that, in spite of strong German resistance, the Red Army would overcome all enemy forces.[6] In April the final Soviet drive towards Berlin begun and the city fell after heavy fighting at the beginning of May. A few days later Germany capitulated.

In a report dated 8 May, the day Germany surrendered to the Western Allies (the official surrender to the Soviets was 9 May), the British JIC tried to estimate Soviet economic and military strength as of 1 July. Judging by the undertone of several paragraphs, and the fact that hostilities were assumed to end about 1 June, the report was not about Soviet capabilities in relation to the German war, or even Japan, but about the Soviet ability to wage war against other great powers, presumably Great Britain and the United States.[7]

Later that month the British Joint Planning Staff issued a report in which war with the USSR was contemplated. The operation, called Unthinkable (supposed to begin on 1 July), was about imposing "the will of the United States and British Empire" on the USSR in order to reach "a square deal for Poland". This plan was seen and commented on by several British top officials during May and June, including Churchill, who seemed to at least have been one of the principal persons responsible for the idea, although he hoped (on 10 June) that it "still [was] a purely hypothetical contingency". When Field Marshal Alan Brooke, and other high-ranking military officials, commented on the plan on 8 June they believed that it was "beyond [Western Allied] power to win a quick but limited success and we should be committed to a protracted war against heavy odds." When Churchill commented on a COS appreciation of the plan on 10 June he wrote that it was free for the Soviets to march to the North Sea and the Atlantic if the Americans withdrew from Europe. The discussion about Unthinkable sparked another report from the Joint Planning Staff, dated 11 July, apparently as an answer to a minute from Churchill. It seems that the planning for Unthinkable led to concerns about the defence of the British Isles. It was, however, concluded that it would take many years of Soviet build up to enable them to invade Britain.[8]

A COS report made by the Post Hostilities Planning Staff, dated 29 June, made some forecasts about Soviet strength in the future and its implications for British policy. The report was primarily about the future and in the 1955–1960 period it was only the Soviet threat that was regarded as realistic.[9] A July report signed by Sargent, called "Stocktaking after VE-day", was about the new political situation in Europe and the World after the German surrender. The USSR was weakened by the war and not in a position to pursue its policy in the face of determined opposition. He did not believe that Stalin wished or could afford another war in Europe.

The demobilization and withdrawal of Soviet troops from Central Europe interested the British. In a late June 1945 report from the WO to the prime minister, signed by the VCIGS, it was stated that the Soviets had told them that they would demobilize 40 per cent of their troops in Europe. In addition the WO believed that the Soviets planned to withdraw large forces from Central Europe to the USSR.[10] The British, as well as the Americans, had always tried to keep track of the number of Soviet troops in the Far East during the war, facing Japan. In late June the British JIC noted the build-up of Soviet strength in the Far East.[11] This build-up was of course only natural in the light of the Soviet commitment to attack the Japanese Empire. This attack, beginning on 8 August, was the last large scale land offensive of World War II, involving nearly 1.6 million Soviet troops; against more than one million men of Japanese (and Japanese allied) troops. The Japanese stood little chance against the more battle hardened and well-armed Red Army; now utilizing the skills they had paid so much blood to learn in the Soviet–German war.

Just as concerning military prospects the intensity in the reporting regarding internal stability and civilian morale was lower than before. The information available, though, was indicating that the observers' perceptions hardly changed: the population was still experiencing hardships but their morale was high and they supported the Stalin regime that sat firm in the saddle. Some observers also noted that this stability would continue after the war.[12] But the progress of the war effort also had some disadvantages with regard to the discipline of the population according to some. In October the OSS reported that there had been a slackening of labour discipline due to the fact that the enemy had now been driven from Russian soil. The authorities were trying to remedy the problem.[13]

In their January 1945 report the US JIC considered the regime as stable and its political power assured. The prestige of Stalin, the party and the government had increased. In fact, the experience of war was something that had broadened the regime's popular support. The official propaganda apparatus was very effective. The JIC pointed to the strengthening of nationalism in the USSR, and did not expect any serious threats to Soviet power from any ethnical minorities. Nevertheless, some problems were identified that might shake the stability of the regime in the future (e.g. the desire among the population for a higher living standard). The morale of the Red Army and the population in general was regarded as high. This situation was expected to continue, underpinned by pride in their achievements during the war, more relaxed and improved living conditions, in combination with the efforts of the secret police. But a failure to raise the standards of living could, in the long run, mean a lowering of morale.[14]

20.2 The economy and reconstruction

Several US and British reports from many institutions and observers during this period were about the industrial economy and its raw material supply. They estimated that the output of the basic industry was increasing but also that some raw material deficiencies still existed, which was made up with imports. The war destruction and the post-war reconstruction process were also mentioned in several reports, although opinions varied as to how many years the process would take. Some noted the weaknesses of the economy already described earlier, but also that continued economic build-up would remedy this situation. The British JIC, for example, estimated in August that in five to ten years, industry and transport would be stronger than in June 1941. No real hindrance for a continued war effort, or a post-war reconstruction was believed to exist.[15]

Both the OSS and the British JIC (in September and October 1944, respectively) believed that the USSR, in the long run, would be more or less self-sufficient after the war. The OSS assumed that the 1940 national income level could be achieved in 1948 (with the war ending in 1945). A possible participation in the war against Japan was not expected to retard the reconstruction significantly. Furthermore, this pace of reconstruction could be achieved with domestic resources. If the standing army were to be about 4 million men (erroneously assumed to be the 1938 level) pre-war living standards could be reached within one year. With higher military expenditure it would take longer. The importance of foreign loans for reconstruction was played down.[16] This was probably the most optimistic report of the period concerning post-war reconstruction.

The idea that the exhaustion caused by the war and the destruction would affect Soviet foreign policy to some extent was repeated. An OSS report from January 1945 described the economy as battered by the war, to such an extent that the Soviet leadership would think twice before embarking on any adventurous foreign policy after the war. The report (or possibly a revised version) was commented on in May by John Balfour of the British embassy in Washington, who agreed with the view expressed concerning Soviet foreign policy.[17] In January 1945 the US JIC analysed Soviet post-war capabilities and intentions in one of the most comprehensive JIC reports on the USSR during the war.[18] This US JIC report was the first in a long series of reports stretching into the Cold War period that portrayed the USSR as a potential threat.[19] The war in Europe was expected to end in early 1945, and the Soviet Union's economic and military potential would possibly be higher than at present by then. The estimated size of the armed forces, and military expenditures, would be equal to the 1938 level within a year to eighteen months after the end of the war, and a possible participation in the war against Japan would be limited and therefore permit demobilization. They did recognize the war destruction and the assumed fact that the USSR would be industrially weaker after the war then before it.[20]

During earlier periods much attention was paid to the inefficient production conditions in Soviet factories. Not much was made said about this anymore, some observes even noted the contrary. When a few high-ranking members of the US military mission in Moscow visited an aircraft factory during August, they saw some modern features being used in the production process. The machine tool shop was praised and the conveyor belt system was observed.[21] Even though some of the later reports, described the Soviet industrial economy as rather efficient when it came to supporting the war effort, at least in comparison to pre-war assessments, not every Anglo-American observer believed the economy to be efficient in a comparative perspective. Deane's impression of Soviet engineering during the war was nothing short of incompetence. In his war memoirs he described how the Soviets handled the assembly of a whole tyre plant, with an accompanying power station, transferred to the USSR from the US as Lend-Lease. First it took the Soviets very long time to erect the plant – the transfer was 90 per cent complete in November 1943, completed in November 1944, and despite this the total assembly was still not completed by the end of the war with Japan (September 1945) – and then the estimated efficiency of the plant was not more than 70 per cent of its designed capacity, due to changes made by the Soviets during the installation.[22]

On 18 April the Department of Research at the US Army Industrial College held a seminar called "Principles of Russian Mobilisation for War", to which they had invited many prominent US officials. Colonel Michela was one of those invited, now the chief of the Russian specialists at the MIS. In a discussion Michela revealed much about what he thought of Soviet economic efficiency: "[Answering to a question about the bureaucracy's efficiency] there is nothing in the Soviet Union that is efficient. It is extremely effective, which is something else entirely, because they have quantity. Mr. Johnson, for instance, commented in his review with respect to a brickyard. I think he said that with the process that the Soviets go through, production takes about ten times longer than it would take in the United States."[23] It is unknown if the rest of the participants believed in this statement, but it indicates that there still was some observers which believed that the Soviet economy was extremely inefficient even as late as the spring of 1945.

The British Moscow embassy official Mr. Roberts had the opportunity to read a report written by George Kennan, the US chargé d'affaires in Moscow,[24] based on his visit to Siberia undertaken in June. Roberts's comment on Kennan's experiences became another report, which he sent to Warner of the FO in August.[25] Kennan was described as having "great experience" of the USSR and the "general conditions of life" there. The "general impression left" from Kennan's report was that "important" industrial facilities were highly efficient and could compare to similar foreign plants. However, there was also information in the report that pointed in the opposite direction. According to US roller-bearing producers, trying to sell products to the Soviets, there was no risk in selling the latest US technology in this field to them, since technical development was very rapid and Soviet technical skills "so far behind" American, that when the Soviets had learned the technical processes, the Americans would be using even later processes.[26]

Roberts stated that the US embassy in Moscow had noticed that the Soviets were still concentrating on building up their industrial and military strength after the end of the war. Improvements in civilian living conditions were ranked as a second priority. He wrote: "No-one here doubts the Soviet Union's ability to restore and increase her pre-war industrial strength and to develop her military resources by her own unaided efforts, if this is absolutely necessary." However, the existing plans for industrial recovery and expansion were based on the import of foreign machinery and equipment. The supplies were to come from the United States and Germany. The stripping of industrial equipment from the occupied countries in Central and Eastern Europe was an indication that the Soviets were desperate for such supplies. Rapid internal development was a major policy aim. The Americans held the key to this development through their ability to supply aid, which was a basis for the Soviets conforming to certain US terms. But the situation was not so simple, since the Soviets could use the fear of post-war economic problems in the United States as a bargaining argument.[27]

Despite Roberts's assertions it seems that the British eventually noted that military expenditure was decreasing. Clark-Kerr sent a despatch to the FO in August concerning the Soviet 1945 state budget. It was noted in the report that the expenditure on armaments was higher in 1945 than in 1944, but only in absolute figures. Relatively speaking, Soviet expenditure would be shrinking.[28]

The "Stocktaking after VE-day" report by Sargent contained an appendix written by Bruce Lockhart in April. Bruce Lockhart admitted that Soviet military strength had been underestimated in June 1941 and now warned for exaggerating it. He believed that the USSR was among the last nations in Europe that could afford another war, and that she would be unable to solve her "great problems of reconstruction" without US and British aid. Therefore, in his view, it was time for "bolder diplomacy" towards the Soviets.[29]

In their May report the British JIC tried to estimate Soviet war potential as of 1 July 1945, and predicted that the economic war potential would have increased during the first half of 1945. This was due to the territories overrun by the Red Army, especially Upper Silesia, and captured equipment taken from the Germans. However, since the newly conquered territories required a long period of reconstruction and re-organization, the Western Allied supplies, if stopped, could not be replaced immediately. The JIC calculated that the USSR was heavily dependent on Allied supplies in order to maintain her war effort. However, even if these supplies should be lost the JIC could not be sure that the Soviets would be unable to continue a full-scale war effort with full efficiency. Assuming an efficiency loss would occur, it would most probably felt within military transport, aircraft performance and in explosives. If, however, the JIC argued, it was possible that these deficiencies were only temporary, "considerable time would elapse" before the conquered territories could replace the need for machinery currently supplied through Lend-Lease. Foreign help was stressed, to enable the USSR to restore and increase industrial capacity in the liberated regions and elsewhere. The Western Allies were the most obvious suppliers of industrial equipment, but otherwise it was expected that the USSR would strip Germany for what she would need.[30]

The continuation of warfare in the West after 1 July would put a considerable strain on the already impaired Soviet transport situation, since the supply lines were now extended. Considering the overall situation, this assessment could in practical terms only refer to a possible war with the Western Allies. According to the JIC, one of the most important factors in the Soviet capacity to wage war, was whether it would be possible to continue to divert resources from the civilian sector in the same proportion as during the past four years. But all in all the whole analysis of the JIC report was about the short-term position. In the long-term forecast the industrial and raw material position was adequate.[31]

Soviet economic strength was analysed in the late May Operation *Unthinkable* plan report. Not surprisingly the analysis had a close resemblance to the analysis presented in the JIC paper, regarding the loss of Allied aid, captured German equipment and communication problems. But the report also revealed that the Soviets would be able to fight the Western Allies without suffering too much because of economic problems. Nevertheless, since the war was to commence soon (1 July) Soviet communications would be in an even worse shape after the start of Anglo-American air attacks. A shortage of manpower was not a problem, since the Soviets would benefit from the return of former prisoners (from Germany), and they could of course use labour from the occupied territories. The dependence upon Western Allied aviation fuel (about 50 per cent) was a big problem, since the former German plants would be unable to deliver fuel for about six months.[32]

Some observers still perceived what probably can be referred to as a relative shortage in the USSR. A FO Economic Intelligence Department report from June described the economic conditions during the first three months of 1945. The report referred a great deal to shortages in the economy, concerning labour as well as raw materials and transport resources.[33] In a G-2 report from July it was expected that the USSR would strive to reconstruct her economy in order to maintain a high state of national preparedness, and to raise the standard of living. The G-2 expected the Soviet Union to integrate the economies of her neighbouring countries in an attempt to increase her war potential.[34]

In one of the most comprehensive reports on Soviet industry prepared by the US authorities during World War II, the OSS analysed the pre-war, wartime and post-war prospects for basic and heavy industries in July. Although the reduction of industrial capital due to the war was stressed, it was also pointed out that in many branches of heavy industry the present level of output was about the same as in 1940.[35] A substantial post-war output increase was expected in most branches, but the demand for industrial goods was expected to exceed output, and therefore an import need was foreseen, primarily for machines and equipment of all kinds.[36]

20.3 The population, the labour force, food supply and civilian life

By this time most of the USSR had been liberated from Axis troops. The areas that had been under German occupation, especially within the Soviet pre-1939 borders, were by now to large extent a wasteland, and partly depopulated. Several factors had contributed to the depopulation: the 1941 mobilization, civilians fleeing eastwards, the Germans conscripting workers, civilian casualties due to conventional and partisan warfare, and German genocidal policies.

The OSS noted in June 1944 that the liberated areas had been depopulated. The local labour force had to be reinforced by workers transferred from the never-occupied areas. It seems that the R & A branch believed that the authorities organized their labour in a way that made this possible. Although the morale of the workers was high their efficiency was not. The reason for this was in many ways obvious, since the local inhabitants were the nucleus of the labour force, and the more able bodied workers were employed in the war effort. The local population had suffered hardships during the occupation and they comprised mainly of women and young people, who either performed tasks beyond their strength or lacked sufficient training. Ex-servicemen were also employed but they suffered from physical and mental disabilities.[37]

Judging by a July report the OSS was still worried about the food situation, which would not improve markedly in the short run.[38] Clark-Kerr informed the FO about a somewhat improved food and harvest situation in two telegrams during September. The FO answered him and was somewhat more pessimistic.[39] In October the OSS assumed that the nutritional level was inadequate, but also pointed out that the authorities had managed successfully to supply the population essential for the war effort with food. The system of differential food rationing, the use of pre-war food stocks, and access to substantial Lend-Lease deliveries, were the only factors that had made possible an adequate food supply for people engaged in "war-essential occupations". Population groups that had not been directly involved in the war effort had not been adequately fed (e.g. many miscellaneous wage earners and adult dependents). This had resulted in cumulative malnutrition and reduced efficiency. It was expected that the food position would improve somewhat in the future.[40]

The same month they estimated that the population as of 1 January 1945 would be just over 171 million (within the pre-1939 borders), and if the war had not been the population would instead have been 189 million.[41] In November they estimated the labour force to circa 62 million by January 1945 (within the pre-1939 borders). Assuming repatriation of prisoners and demobilization (to the assumed 1938 level of the armed forces – 4 million men) the labour force was expected to be about 68 million by the end of the war. They expected the workforce to be larger than the pre-war workforce, due to the contribution of people from the "large cohorts of young persons attaining working age during the war". Had it not been for the war the estimated labour force would have been 72.5 million by 1 January 1945. Even though the post-war labour force would be larger than the pre-war, it would not be as efficient. The 1944 situation would be about as good as the pre-war, with respect to the efficiency of industrial production and hourly labour productivity, despite food shortages and civilian hardships. But post-war productivity would decline, at least for a while, for several reasons: "the shift from war production to the relatively inefficient consumer goods industries, the geographic relocation of labor, the cessation of wartime incentive drives, and the relaxation of labor discipline. Moreover, working hours undoubtedly will be reduced from the present level of 60 or 66 hours per week."[42] In December the OSS investigated the system of technical training, considered as being something of a success, and partly responsible for the wartime labour mobilization through the "State Labor Reserve".[43]

The OSS assessment can be compared to the ones made by the US and the British JIC. In the January 1945 US JIC report they estimated the war time population loss due to eight million, within the pre-1939 borders, and 10 million within the June 1941 borders. The population decline had not affected the size of the work force (75 million people aged 17 to 64), assuming demobilization and the repatriation of labour and prisoners of war from Germany – the number of children would instead be smaller. But the efficiency of the work force was expected to be lower because of relatively more women and older workers, in combination with a residual malnutrition effect. It was expected that German labourers, participating in the reconstruction, would augment the workforce.[44]

According to the May British JIC report the population had decreased from 202 million on June 1941, within the 1941 frontiers, to 190 million on 1 July 1945. However, they saw no major problems with the decrease. The labour force would soon rise substantially above its reduced level since military personnel would return from service, and labour from the newly conquered territories was and would be even more utilized in the economy. Efficiency in the factories had been improved since the early days of the war. The main reasons for this development were technical improvements, by experience gained at work and by trainee schemes. This improvement was an asset in the post-war economy.[45]

In July the OSS issued a report that can be regarded as the OSS conclusion on military and civilian losses during the war. Civilian dead from 22 June 1941 to 9 May 1945 were nearly 4 million (1941 boundaries), due to executions by the Germans and the fact that people had died in German captivity.[46]

In January 1945 the OSS commented on the development of industrial productivity during the war. The average annual increase in the productivity per industrial worker during 1928–1941 was estimated to about 10 per cent. From the beginning of the Third Five Year Plan (1937) to the outbreak of the war (1941) the annual increase was somewhat lower, about 8 per cent. During the first year of the war the OSS considered that overall productivity declined, but that the productivity of certain munitions-related segments of industry increased. Labour productivity in the aircraft and tank industry had increased by about 30 per cent and 38 per cent respectively, from June 1941 to June 1944. Several other industries – machine building, electrical goods, building construction and light industry – had, according to the OSS, achieved "substantial increases in productivity per worker during 1942–44", even though there was no possibility to compare with pre-war performance.[47]

Several reasons were identified for the productivity increase in these industries. The single most important factor was the introduction of the "Flow" method, particularly in the aircraft industry. This method was described, "in its more advanced form [... it is] essentially what is known as the conveyor-belt system in the United States". Another important reason was competition, both on an individual and group basis. Propaganda, accomplishment reports, and awards were used within industry to raise productivity. Other devices used were what the OSS referred to as "workers suggestions" and "labor inspections". The suggestions from workers helped improve efficiency and the inspections improved the utilization of labour and the diffusion of technical innovations. The very substantial increases in daily working hours during the war were described as another factor affecting productivity. Apart from the increase in working hours instituted in 1940[48] the OSS described the increase during June 1941, when compulsory overtime was introduced, with up to three hours a day for adults and two hours a day for children under 16.[49]

The OSS also evaluated civilian health conditions in three reports (from October, February and May): material conditions had deteriorated during the war, and in turn caused a worsening of the general health situation.[50]

In February the OSS issued three reports, all related to the food situation. As compared to 1 January 1941 it was estimated that livestock numbers had been reduced considerably. It would take until 1949 or 1950 to restore the livestock numbers to pre-war levels; the livestock situation was a weakness in economic capability compared to the 1941 situation.[51] The per capita consumption of meat, fish, fats, oils and sugar had fallen substantially from the pre-war situation (1938) to the year 1943/1944. The situation for 1944/1945 was not expected to improve in general. Lend-Lease was crucial for the government's effort to supply its population with these foodstuffs. The relative importance of Lend-Lease in 1943/1944 as a percentage of domestic output was 15.3 per cent regarding meat, 61.6 per cent regarding sugar, and 67.1 per cent regarding fats and oils. The Lend-Lease of these foodstuffs was "one of the key factors" in permitting the war effort to be waged at such a high level as it had during the last three years. Without these deliveries the OSS imagined that the USSR would have been faced with disaster and starvation in the long run.[52] In the last report he benefits of differential rationing were stressed once again. But even the best-fed categories, even though faring well, would benefit from better and more diversified food. Malnutrition was widespread among adult dependants, less essential white-collar workers and a small group of other categories. These three categories were estimated to constitute about 40 per cent of the total urban population.[53]

In their January 1945 report the US JIC still described the food situation as difficult, even though it was slightly improved since early 1944. They estimated that the USSR would need to import large quantities of some foodstuffs (meats, fats, and oils) several years after the war, even in order to sustain the very low wartime standards for these products. The situation with regards to the most vital consumer goods (e.g. clothing and footwear) and housing was even worse than the food situation.[54]

According to the British JIC report from May, on the war potential as of 1 July, the food situation would not be affected by the cessation of Western Allied supplies, even though it would put a higher demand on reparation claims from eastern Germany. The situation in the countryside was affected by the lack of machinery, tractors and workers, which had lowered agricultural productivity. But despite this the prospects for the 1945 harvest were as good, with an anticipated increase in grain production of 5–10 per cent over 1944. Other improvements in the nutritional standard were also foreseen. Nevertheless, the food consumption for 1945/1946 was expected to stay lower than the pre-war level. It was thought possible that deliveries from Eastern- and Central Europe might alleviate the situation somewhat.[55]

The US Moscow embassy produced a few reports on Soviet agricultural conditions during this period of the war. In reports from December 1944, February, March and August 1945 they described several problems in agriculture but also expressed a belief in a slightly and gradually improving food situation.[56]

20.4 The production and efficiency of munitions and military equipment

In a MI3(c) report dated 6 July 1944, the evacuation of war industries, and the expansion of munitions production in the Urals, Siberia and Central Asia during 1941–1942, was regarded as probably being the single most important factor in the Soviet recovery and later victories. The emphasis on simplicity in production was a recipe for success. A concentration on adequate models rather than the best possible design was regarded as a factor that facilitated "simplicity in operations and production" and a concentration on mass-production. Nevertheless, a tank like the T-34 was an "excellent" medium tank. According to the report, and one of the many FO officials that commented on the report, the higher rate of equipment wastage in comparison with Western Allied standards was compensated for by the organization of production on a large scale. One the other hand Western Allied supplies, especially of trucks and aircraft, had played a great part in the Soviet ability to maintain "the momentum of their recent offensive". Wilson of the FO commented on the report in September and he revealed his views on the comparative efficiency of Soviet and German munitions production: "If Russian resources in equipment were so far Greater [...] they must have had to divert a larger proportion of their population to industrial production than the Germans."[57]

In August the British JIC regarded the main technical limitation of the Soviet Army to be the relative lack of motor transport and the poor maintenance of motor vehicles. This condition was partly explained by the extremely bad road conditions in the East. Even though the quality of most fighting equipment was high (particularly small arms, guns and tanks), it was merely almost as good as German equipment. The Soviets were keen on new technical ideas and had the ability to apply new technology very rapidly, even though their detailed design was not of the same standard as their general design. Some equipment was so good that the Germans had copied it.[58] Aircraft were technically simpler than Western planes, even though the innovation of firing rockets from aircraft was proof of a capacity for further technical development and innovation. Given time, the Soviets were fully capable of developing a large and even efficient strategic bomber force.[59] The ability to build small warships was not questioned, but the ability to construct larger vessels such as battleships and aircraft carriers was doubted.[60]

The crushing superiority in numbers of Soviet arms was an indication of a formidable productive capacity. The JIC described the practical effects of this capacity, and the technical innovations, by referring to the Red Army's increasing number of arms: more and better tanks, more and heavier anti-tank guns, more mortars and automatic weapons, and an increasing number of self-propelled guns. It is obvious that the JIC by now had a considerable respect for the Soviet ability to produce efficient war materials, and for industrial capacity in general, since the report stated: "Russia has made swift strides in technical development and has shown amazing capacity to master technical problems and make good early shortages and handicaps. Her relatively modern and concentrated industry is well adapted to mass production and a quick change-over from one type of equipment to another."[61]

In January 1945 the OSS estimated the monthly output of combat planes, tanks, artillery pieces (37 mm and above in calibre) and mortars to 2350, 1400 (mid-1944), 3000 (minimum) and 10,000 units, respectively. It is interesting to note that the monthly June 1941 tank output was estimated to 2000. It seems that this figure referred to lighter models, but it shows at any rate that the 1941 output had been revised upwards drastically, compared to early war assessments, and that the OSS really did not believe that output had increased during the war.[62] The same month the US JIC estimated monthly combat aircraft output to a minimum of 2500, in addition to 350 Lend-Lease planes. The monthly output of tanks and self-propelled artillery was 1800 (at least 900 T-34s and 400 heavy tanks), in addition to 200–250 Lend-Lease units. The monthly output of field and anti-aircraft artillery was 2100 pieces, mostly 45 mm anti-tank guns and 76.2 mm field guns, and mortar output to 13,000 pieces. Ammunition output was a minimum of two million tonnes per annum, a figure that was expected to rise as the steel position improved. The naval shipbuilding capacity in June 1945 was expected to be below the June 1941 level.[63]

A booklet distributed to military personnel by the WD from April described the result of Soviet weapons design in the 1930s and early 1940s as "remarkable". In the words of the WD, "these weapons stress not only performance, but also rugged simplicity for ease of production and field maintenance." The T-34 and the Stalin tank were the "star weapons" of the Soviet arsenal.[64]

In May the British JIC commented on military equipment, which they considered to be good and not inferior to the equipment of other great powers. The fact that the Germans had copied some features of Soviet armament design was repeated, as was the "formidable output in all armaments on mass production lines", despite the loss of productive capacity due to enemy occupation. This was possible due to "improved production methods, simplicity of design and concentration on a few types". Soviet claims of increased output during the last two or three years were "possibly somewhat exaggerated", even though these claims could not be "lightly dismissed". In addition, the "very small requests" that the Soviets had made for Western Allied supplies during the war, was interpreted as a sign of a large armament production.[65]

No specific figure was given for the output of armoured fighting vehicles, due to lack of information, but it was "considerable in excess of the peak German production of about 1500 per month". They believed that the Soviets had an ample supply of artillery, mortars, small arms or ammunition for current operations. Allied supplies stood for about one fourth of the total needs of explosives. Monthly aircraft output was estimated to at least 3000; mainly single-engine planes. If Western Allied supplies of aluminium (40 per cent of the total supply) were to be cut, it would be impossible to continue production on that scale, without drastically affecting other consumption needs. Most aircraft were described as simple, but nevertheless modern and highly efficient. The fighters were regarded as only "slightly inferior" to British and American fighters.[66] The equipment of the navy was regarded as outdated.[67]

In the Operation *Unthinkable* paper the following was stated about military equipment: "Equipment has improved rapidly throughout the war and is now good. Enough is known of its development to say that it is certainly not inferior to that of other great Powers." Aircraft were modern and adequate, but inferior in general to Western types. The notion that the Soviets produced 3000 aircraft per month was repeated.[68]

The August Clark-Kerr report, concerning the state budget for 1945, stated that expenditure on armaments during the war had increased by much more than the official figures in the budget revealed. This was due to the fact that the costs of production in the armaments industries had been falling continuously during the war.[69]

20.5 The size of the armed forces, losses and military efficiency

The character of the assessments during this period was in line with the preceding period. The losses of manpower and military equipment were regarded as very large. However, the observers still underestimated them in comparison to actual losses. The OSS made several estimates on the military manpower position during late 1944 and 1945, and the US JIC made one, but they still significantly underestimated permanent/irrecoverable causalities. It seems, though that the British WO and MI, were close to the real permanent casualties in two assessments from January, as was the British JIC in May, and information in the Operation *Unthinkable* report. In July the OSS still underestimated permanent losses, calculating them to nearly 5.5 million dead. Actual military deaths was nearly 8.7 million. Generally, the Anglo-Americans made a better job of estimating the manpower size of the armed forces, but it seems that they still underestimated the amount of military equipment in the armed force's possession.[70]

The US JIC, for example, estimated that the SAF had a total of 28,000 aircraft (some of which was transport types) in active units and in reserve on 1 January, but the actual figure in the Red Army alone, and only counting combat aircraft, was 43,300 and all available aircraft (total inventory plus all received during the war (22 June 1941 to 1 January 1945) minus losses) was 59,900. Total tank and artillery strength was also underestimated, although the frontline tank strength was overestimated, but on the other hand frontline artillery strength seems to have been underestimated.[71] The British JIC and the authors of the *Unthinkable* report was probably closest to the truth, at least regarding aircraft, when they estimated the first line operational strength to around 16,500.[72] The actual figure was probably over 20,000.[73]

According to a July US intelligence estimate, based on information from the chief of the Soviet General Staff, General Antonneov, the size of the Red Army by V-E Day was 10–11 million men, 35,000 aircraft, and 75,000 tanks (including 25,000 self-propelled guns). No comment was made regarding the truth value of Antonneov's figures, but remarks concerning the aircraft and tank strength set them "at present" at 15,000 combat aircraft and 20,000 tanks in "excellent condition".[74] According to later research Antonneov's figures was wrong, especially regarding the overestimated tank strength, but the American assessment was still an underestimation, at least if the total strength available to the Red Army at that date is used as a benchmark. The actual figures were 47,500 (combat aircraft) and 35,200 tanks.[75]

The Soviets won great victories over the Germans during this period; the most spectacular being the Operation *Bagration*. Not surprisingly the morale and efficiency of the Red Army was held in relatively high esteem during the period, represented by several reports from many observers. Some observers, which had visited the Soviet frontline, presented descriptions of and several explanations of as to why the Red Army was winning.[76]

According to one official the senior commanders were "practical, confident, bold, and ruthless" and the soldiers were considered to be simple, tough, and possessing a "physical endurance". Soviet superiority in numbers was also mentioned, along with the "superior quality [...] of artillery". He also stressed that Allied material aid and the increasing Anglo-American air offensive in the West greatly had facilitated Soviet success.[77] Another official stated that the Soviet victories was due to "simplified organisation, tactics and technique", adapted to the abilities of its personnel – a "concentration on essentials". The soldiers' high "endurance", "familiarity with terrain and climate", "natural cunning and patriotism" had been utilized to the full extent. The employment of "deception and stratagem" in combination with a "high degree of security" was also important factors. All of the above, in combination with numerical superiority, had "enabled an army with an initially low standard of military efficiency and technique to defeat an army of the very highest professional standard". The Red Army made the most of specialization in the sense that they had "excellent" artillery and tank units and "infantry shock formations of first rate quality". Partisan activity and the earlier scorched earth policies were seen as a deliberate government strategy.[78]

A FO observer commented and stressed the Red Army's material superiority, vis-à-vis the Germans, even more, but did nevertheless think that the Soviets had been quick to learn from their earlier mistakes, and their ability to "sustain the momentum" in their attacks was "one of the wonders of the war". The next day Wilson minuted on the report and played down the importance of the alleged numerical superiority somewhat, thereby indirectly upgrading the quality of Soviet troops.[79]

According to another observer's summer experiences with the Red Army the Russian was "a natural improviser", with "a natural aptitude for getting across country and taking cover" and "a natural cunning which serves him in good stead in warfare". The two last characteristics made him a "fighting man" without the need for "much training". He regarded military training as very simple and thought that many of the soldiers that went into battle could "do little more than fire their weapons". It seems like the observer was a little confused, or perhaps he had visited a rather unrepresentative part of the front, since he argued that the (Russian) ability to improvise came in handy due to the fact that it made it possible for the Red Army to keep things going until they could get their hands on enemy material: "It is on enemy material of all types that a great deal of the Red Army progress is based." This statement is remarkable, especially since it was made by the (new) head of the British 30 Mission, Lieutenant-General M. B. Burrows (an old friend of Eden). Fortunately for the British perceptions like this was not representative (despite the fact that his report later was printed as a COS memorandum). Burrows continued: it did not matter that the soldiers' superiors handled them badly, since this only tended to harden them and their ability at "living on ʼthe smell of an oiled ragʼ and of having some animal instinct of knowing what is the right thing to do" in matters "of life and death". He referred to them as "rabble" that were unaffected by "climate, lack of food and even death". Burrows believed, at least in part and based on his experiences of the front visit, that the Soviet General Staff were unwilling to let foreigners visit Red Army units due to their low "standards of civilization", compared to Western European standards.[80]

He did, however, also deliver some relatively more flattering comments: "Any body of Soviet troops [...] compare unfavourably with a similar body of another Army but the fact remains that the Soviet body of troops gets there and fights." Western armies could learn from Soviet "simplicity", and the "complete ruthlessness and disregard" for human life worked to the Soviets' military advantage. He was less impressed with the officers, but noted the skills of the "technical troops" and the ability to use these troops ruthlessly and rapidly. Once again he was at least partly revealing his confusion, when stating that the (government controlled) partisans and "saboteurs" "probably" were "the most important factor in the recent victories", due to their ability to supply the General Staff with information about enemy movements and the effect they had on German morale. The Soviets had built their war doctrine successfully on what he called the Russian "rabble" of troops.[81]

When Deane visited the areas liberated by the Red Army in Byelorussia during the summer, the Soviets informed him that at least the conquest of the city of Vilna had been achieved by superior mobility. His explanation for this was in part reduced German mobility (due to a German oil shortage caused by the Western Allied bomber offensive) but also the fact that the Soviets had a "preponderance of motorized and mechanized equipment". Deane noted the results of US assistance in the form of delivered trucks and tanks. Advance planning and liaison between units was crude and the Red Army relied on sheer force of numbers.[82]

In August the British JIC described the SAF's ground organization as large and efficient. Its operational efficiency was seen as a "rough and ready affair", compared with Anglo-American standards. The SAF's organization was loose, but its capacity for improvisation was great and despite the "many defects it works". Soviet naval forces were not perceived as a major threat, and doubts were expressed as to the ability to operate large surface ships owing to lack of experience and of cadres of training personnel.[83] From the late autumn onwards relatively little was reported concerning military efficiency. In December the OSS stressed the importance of pre-conscription military training as a complement to ordinary military training, thereby positively affecting the mobilization capacity.[84]

In May 1945 the British JIC praised the High Command's abilities and experience. The army was considered to be "exceedingly tough, lives and moves on a lighter scale of maintenance than any Western Army and employs bold tactics based largely on disregard for losses in attaining a set objective. Security and deception are of a high quality at all levels." Engineering training was described as being "of a high standard", and the JIC identified improvements during the war in wireless communications, in the technique of river crossings, recovery of armoured fighting vehicles and restoration of rail communications. But training and tactics were still regarded as inferior to that of the German Army. It was believed that there were great differences in standards between different corps in the army, since many of the best infantry troops had been drafted into specialist formations. The army was described as suffering from "over-centralization", as a result of the lack of capable staff officers and intermediate commanders. There was evidence that the Soviet command was unable to maintain discipline among their troops abroad.[85]

The SAF was a formidable support arm to the army, but it had several weaknesses. It was "outclassed" by the Anglo-Americans with respect to organization, training, control, and equipment. Furthermore, the SAF was inferior to the German Air Force, even though individual pilots were regarded as capable and reasonably competent in individual operations. The Germans had better training and discipline. The superiority and supremacy of Soviet air power was explained "by sheer weight of numbers". But its "tremendous" experience of tactical support nevertheless made it a very dangerous adversary. In addition, its morale was high, and its ground organization was capable of supporting the forces in the air in difficult conditions. The navy was regarded as neither modern nor effective in any way.[86]

In the *Unthinkable* report the British Joint Planners praised and criticized the armed forces in the same manner. But they also added that the war weariness, and the fact that the Red Army would have to fight outside the USSR, would affect its morale and discipline negatively.

The SAF's morale and efficiency were good, but they also believed that it had less training, discipline and organization than Western air forces, and very inferior radar technology. They regarded it as very doubtful whether the Western Allies could achieve its goal in a speedy manner, since, despite their supposed superior handling of forces and air superiority, the war would be fought on land and the Red Army had a very large numerical superiority.[87] The air superiority was more a question of Anglo-American efficiency since the Red Army would have more tactical aircraft.[88]

In the final July report of the 30 Mission Lieutenant-General J.H. Gammell stated that "The power and efficiency of the Red Army" was one principal reason why the USSR had won the war. Although he was not specific he believed "that the Red Army will be far the most powerful military machine in the [...] land [...] from the Atlantic to the Pacific".[89]

In July the G-2 still identified several military weaknesses. The Red Army lacked adequate transportation and mechanical equipment, such as bulldozers and construction machinery. The infantry was regarded as poor and leadership at lower levels was not as good as the higher command. The G-2 cited the Germans when they concluded that leadership in the higher grades was "superb". The SAF's quality was not comparable to that of the air forces of other major powers. The G-2 concluded: "In measuring Soviet capabilities [...] it must be kept in mind that while the Soviets may be inefficient, they have proved to be effective. This had been accomplished through the mass use of human and material elements."[90]

After the German surrender the Anglo-Americans interrogated many high-ranking German officers who had fought against the Soviets. Apparently, by the end of August the British had just begun to scratch the surface regarding German intelligence on the USSR, since the FO's O. L. Lawrence stated at the JIC's 58 meeting (28 August) that: "Russia was one of the areas about which we lacked information and now much material was available in captured German documents".[91] G-2 conducted several interrogations with German commanders, resulting in reports issued as early as May and June. Some (or maybe all) of these were shared with the British, who also issued their own reports. From the few reports available, within the stipulated time period, the interviews showed that the Red Army's efficiency had improved during 1944–1945, and specialist troops such as armour and artillery formations received much praise. The Soviets were capable and sometimes ingenious adversaries, although some weaknesses also were stressed.[92]

20.6 Why the USSR won the war (according to the 30 Military Mission's final report)

In July Gammell wrote some notes on the USSR in the final report of the 30 Mission, seen by many British officials. Churchill appointed Gammell as head of the 30 Mission just three days before VE Day, in an attempt to raise British status and prestige with the Soviets.[93] Gammell mentioned in the report that the West now had to face a Soviet "iron curtain" drawn across Eastern Europe.[94] He tried to assess the principal reasons for the USSR's success in the war against Germany, and to "estimate how far these reasons will continue to apply after the conclusion of peace in Europe and the Far East". Most of the reasons presented were based largely on the internal stability and morale of the population: Russian patriotism, "Universal admiration for and devotion to" Stalin, "intense hatred for the Germans", "a general belief among the bulk of the people […] that in Communism […] Russia has […] a better future", "The ruthless and centralised control by the Communist party of a huge country with vast man-power and tremendous natural resources", "The all-powerful and ubiquitous N.K.V.D.", "The discipline, training and efficiency of the Red Army, equipped on an ever-increasing scale by an expanding industry", and "the tremendous pre-war expansion and re-distribution of industry achieved by the first and second Five Year Plans". He did not state which of these factors he considered the most important, but just the fact that so many of them were related to the discipline, morale, feelings and political beliefs of the people seems to indicate that he emphasized reasons for victory not directly related to purely economic and military factors. Of course, he did not discount the economic and military factors, and, as stated in other sections of this study regarding assessments of military-economic strength, he did not believe that the USSR would have been able to keep such great military forces in the field during 1941–1945 if it had not been for the expansion of industry since 1928.[95]

Notes

1 Gaddis (1972), 114–115.
2 27-11-1944, JIC(44)479(0)(Final), CAB121/464.
3 Harriman & Abel (1976), 378–379.
4 Ibid, 393–394.

5 Keegan (ed.) (1989), 182–183, 186–187.
6 Harriman & Abel (1976), 435.
7 8–5-1945, JIC(45)148(0)(Final)(Limited Circulation), CAB81/128.
8 22–5-1945, "Operation `Unthinkable'", CAB120/691; 8–6-1945, CAB120/691; 10–6-1945, "General Ismay", CAB120/691; 11–7-1945, "Operation `Unthinkable'", CAB120/691.
9 29–6-1945, PHP(45)29(0)(Final), CAB121/064.
10 23–6-1945, "CIGB/PM/642", CAB121/464.
11 27–6-1945, JIC(45)210(0)(Final), CAB81/129.
12 13–8-1944, "Memorandum [...]", WO208/1844; 22–9-1944, N5774/42/38, FO371/43316; 8–10-1944, N6447/1667/38, FO371/43395; 27-11-1944, N7943/1667/38, FO371/43395.
13 9–10–1944, R&A No. 2524.1, Report #13, Reel-3, UPA1977.
14 31–1-1945, JIC250/1, ABC336Russia(22–8-43)Sec 1-a, Box-250, Entry-421, RG165.
15 11–7-1944, R&A No. 1355.4, Report #6, Reel-3, UPA1977; 26–6-1944, R&A No. 1739.6, M1221, RG59; 2–12–1944, N7945/106/38, FO371/43329; 28–7-1944, N5018/189/38, FO371/43341; 22–8-1944, JIC(44)366(0)Final(Limited circulation), CAB81/124; 18-10-1944, JIC(44)442(0)(Draft), CAB81/125; 9–9-1944, R&A No. 2060, Report #11, Reel-3, UPA1977; 21-11-1944, "Economic [...]", Box-3100, Entry-77, RG165; 5–1-1945 (handwritten), R&A No. 2669, Report No. 5, Reel-4, UPA1977; 31–1-1945, JIC250/1, ABC336Russia(22–8-43)Sec 1-a, Box-250, Entry-421, RG165; 18–1-1945, JIC250, ABC336Russia(22–8-43)Sec 1-a, Box-250, Entry-421, RG165; 2–2-1945, Box-206, RG218; 5–2-1945, "Memorandum [...]", ABC092USSR(14–11–44), Box-96, Entry-421, RG165; 30–4-1945, R&A No. 2516, M1221, RG59; 8–5-1945, JIC(45)148(0)(Final)(Limited Circulation), CAB81/128.
16 18-10-1944, JIC(44)442(0)(Draft), CAB81/125; 9–9-1944, R&A No. 2060, Report #11, Reel-3, UPA1977.
17 5–1-1945 (handwritten), R&A No. 2669, Report No. 5, Reel-4, UPA1977; 31–5-1945, N8125/165/G, FO371/47883.
18 31–1-1945, JIC250/1, ABC336Russia(22–8-43)Sec 1-a, Box-250, Entry-421, RG165.
19 Valero (2000).
20 31–1-1945, JIC250/1, ABC336Russia(22–8-43)Sec 1-a, Box-250, Entry-421, RG165. A summarized version of the report was issued by 18 January 1945, and later a somewhat amended version of that version was in turn issued on 2 February. The later report was presented before the JCS on 5 February as a memorandum for information. 18–1-1945, JIC250, ABC336Russia(22–8-43)Sec 1-a, Box-250, Entry-421, RG165; 2–2-1945, Box-206, RG218; 5–2-1945, "Memorandum [...]", ABC092USSR(14–11–44), Box-96, Entry-421, RG165.
21 The report was regarded as having the highest degree of reliability (A-1) by the MID. 21–8-1944, Report No. 2597, Box-1, Entry-309, RG334.
22 Deane also used the story about the Lend-Lease tyre plant as a metaphor for how long it would take for the USSR to construct an atomic bomb, i.e. probably very long. Deane (1947), 100–102.
23 18–4-1945, Box-2049, Entry-79, RG165.
24 Nadeau (1990), 212.
25 1–8-1945, N10346/928/38, FO371/47933; Smith (1996), 247.
26 1–8-1945, N10346/928/38, FO371/47933.
27 Ibid.
28 10–8-1945, N11067/88/38, FO371/47873.
29 11–7-1945, "Stocktaking after VE-day", Annex I, FO800/880.
30 8–5-1945, JIC(45)148(0)(Final)(Limited Circulation), CAB81/128.
31 Ibid.

32 22–5-1945, "Operation `Unthinkable'", CAB120/691.

33 18–6-1945, N4594/624/G38, FO371/47923.

34 6–7-1945, "Soviet intentions", ABC092USSR(15–11–44), Box-96, Entry-421, RG165.

35 6–7-1945, R&A No. 2060.2, Report #19, Reel-4, UPA1977. The OSS estimate for crude oil output, 40.3 million tonnes, differed from a July MID report. The figure for oil was not substantiated by a July MID report; based on information from the US embassy and Military Mission in Moscow. According to the report, oil output was 21.5 million tonnes on an annual basis. The problems caused by the war were blamed for the output fall since 1940 (estimated at 31.1 million tonnes). 18–7-1945, ID 187 883, Box-1225, Entry-85, RG319.

36 6–7-1945, R&A No. 2060.2, Report #19, Reel-4, UPA1977.

37 28–6-1944, R&A No. 2094.2, M1221, RG59.

38 20–7-1944, R&A No. 2321, Report #7, Reel-3, UPA1977.

39 2–10–1944, N6248/106/38, FO371/43329.

40 19-10-1944, R&A No. 1355.5, M1221, RG59.

41 11-10-1944, R&A No. 2520, Report #14, Reel-3, UPA1977.

42 15-11-1944, R&A No. 2548, Report #19, Reel-3, UPA1977.

43 11-12-1944, R&A No. 2525, Report #21, Reel-3, UPA1977.

44 31–1-1945, JIC250/1, ABC336Russia(22–8-43)Sec 1-a, Box-250, Entry-421, RG165.

45 8–5-1945, JIC(45)148(0)(Final)(Limited Circulation), CAB81/128.

46 16–7-1945, R&A no. 2524.5, Report #20, Reel-4, UPA1977.

47 4–1-1945, R&A No. 2524.3, Report #4, Reel-4, UPA1977.

48 From seven to eight hours and from six to seven hours in certain industries, plus the change from five to six working days in a week. Ibid.

49 Ibid.

50 31-10-1944, R&A no. 1688, Report #17, Reel-3, UPA1977; 10–2-1945, R&A No. 1688.1, Report #7, Reel-4, UPA1977; 1–5-1945, R&A No. 1688.2, Report #12, Reel-4, UPA1977.

51 8–2-1945, R& ANo. 1355.6, M1221, RG59.

52 14–2-1944, R&A No. 1355.7, M1221, RG59.

53 24–2-1945, R&A No. 1355.8, M1221, RG59.

54 31–1-1945, JIC250/1, ABC336Russia(22–8-43)Sec 1-a, Box-250, Entry-421, RG165.

55 8–5-1945, JIC(45)148(0)(Final)(Limited Circulation), CAB81/128.

56 23-12-1944, No. 79, 861-Agriculture, Box-51, MECF1944: 850.4–861.35. RG84; 23–2-1945, "Subject: [...]", 861.1 Foods, Box-90, Entry-59A 543 Pt.6, RG84; 27–2-1945, RA-359, Reel-29, LM176, RG59; 31–3-1945, M-23575, #2 Agriculture, Box-1, Entry-58A 5159, RG84; 20–8-1945, No. 2969, 861-Agriculture, Box-88, Entry-59A 543 Pt.6, RG84; 24–8-1945, No. 3040, #2 Agriculture, Box-1, Entry-58A 5159, RG84.

57 6–7-1944, N5288/1607/38, FO371/43391.

58 For example the T-34 tank was described as a basis for the German Panther and the self-propelled gun SU-85 had influenced other German designs. 22–8-1944, JIC (44)366(0)Final(Limited Circulation), CAB81/124.

59 The JIC believed that: "The only probable limiting factor governing the potential technical efficiency of her air force lies in whatever limitation there may be upon technical education and any further limitation which may be inherent in the Russian character consistently to apply that education." Ibid.

60 Ibid.

61 Ibid.

62 5–1-1944, (handwritten), R&A No. 2669, Report No. 5, Reel-4, UPA1977.

63 31–1-1945, JIC250/1, ABC336Russia(22–8-43)Sec 1-a, Box-250, Entry-421, RG165.

64 31–5-1945, (Intelligence Library), "Our [...]", Project #1846, Box-2857, Document Library Branch, RG319.
65 8–5-1945, JIC(45)148(0)(Final)(Limited Circulation), CAB81/128.
66 But despite this the JIC believed that the Soviet Air Force was "neither organised nor equipped to oppose" a modern air force. Ibid.
67 Ibid.
68 22–5-1945, "Operation `Unthinkable'", CAB120/691.
69 10–8-1945, N11067/88/38, FO371/47873.
70 6–7-1944, N5288/1607/38, FO371/43391; 22–8-1944, JIC(44)366(0)Final(Limited Circulation), CAB81/124; 20-10-1944, D. of Policy (G) 362 and Appendix "A", AIR9/177; 11-10-1944, R&A No. 2520, Report #14, Reel-3, UPA1977; 7–11–1944, R&A No. 2524.2, Report #18, Reel-3, UPA1977; 15-11-1945, R&A No. 2548, Report #19, Reel-3, UPA1977; 4–1-1945, R&A No. 2524.3, Report #4, Reel-4, UPA1977; 5–1-1945, (handwritten), R&A No. 2669, Report No. 5, Reel-4, UPA1977; 27–1-1945, "MI3C/Col/11/45.", MI3(c), WO208/1857; 27–1-1945, ID 109884, Box-671, Entry-85, RG319; 31–1-1945, JIC250/1, ABC336Russia(22 Aug 43)Sec 1-a, Box-250, Entry-421, RG165; 8–5-1945, JIC(45)148(0)(Final)(Limited Circulation), CAB81/128; 22–5-1945, "Operation `Unthinkable'", CAB120/691; 16–7-1945, R&A No. 2524.5, Report #20, Reel-4, UPA1977. See also the literature (regarding the reality) in the note below.
71 31–1-1945, JIC250/1, ABC336Russia(22 Aug 43)Sec 1-a, Box-250, Entry-421, RG165, compared to Zaloga & Ness (2003), 181; Hardesty & Grinberg (2012), 341, 409; and Krivosheev (1997), 85, 245–255.
72 8–5-1945, JIC(45)148(0)(Final)(Limited Circulation), CAB81/128; 22–5-1945, "Operation `Unthinkable'", CAB120/691.
73 Hardesty & Grinberg (2012), 341, 409; compared to Krivosheev (1997), 245–255.
74 July 1945, ID 370 050, Entry-85, RG319.
75 Krivosheev (1997), 245.
76 30–7-1944, "Situation [...]", MI14, WO208/1849; 13–8-1944, "Memorandum [...]", WO208/1844.
77 28–6-1944, N3983/477/38, FO371/43362/38.
78 6–7-1944, N5288/1607/38, FO371/43391.
79 6–7-1944, N5288/1607/38, FO371/43391.
80 August 1944, N5283/96/38, FO371/43390; August 1944, COS(44)690(0), CAB121/464; Smith (1996), 180.
81 Ibid.
82 Deane (1947), 207–208, 210–211.
83 22–8-1944, JIC(44)366(0)Final(Limited Circulation), CAB81/124.
84 11-12-1944, R&A No. 2525, Report #21, Reel-3, UPA1977.
85 The JIC gave the following description in connection with the disciplinary status of the Soviet Army: "Looting and drunkenness are prevalent and are symptoms of a war-weary army in contact with higher material standards than obtain at home." 8–5-1945, JIC(45)148(0)(Final)(Limited Circulation), CAB81/128.
86 Ibid.
87 The Soviet superiority was believed to be four to one in infantry and two to one in armour. 22–5-1945, "Operation `Unthinkable'", CAB120/691.
88 Ibid.
89 July 1945, "Final [...]", ADM223/252.
90 6–7-1945, "Soviet intentions", ABC092USSR(15–11–44), Box-96, Entry-421, RG165.
91 28–8-1945, JIC(45), 58thMtg.(0), CAB81/93(Part II).
92 21–5-1945, "The [...]", G-2, WO208/1861; 8–6-1945 (5–6-1945 (1A)), "Summary [...]", WO208/1802; 9–6-1945, "U.S. [...]", "Report, Reports A-K USSR, Vol. C", Box-3181, Entry-77, RG165; 27–5-1945, "The [...]", G-2, WO208/1861; 26–

6-1945, "Comments [...]", Seventh (US) Army Interrogation Centre, WO208/1861.
93 19–7-1945, N8935/2/G38, FO371/47850.
94 July 1945, "Final [...]", ADM223/252; Smith (1996), 243, 245.
95 July 1945, "Final [...]", ADM223/252.

21 Assessments compared to reality during the last period of the war

A glance at the main Soviet economic indicators during the war reveals that the year 1942 was the low point of economic activity, expressed in national income. There were some exceptions. For trade and catering 1943 was the low point. If consideration is taken to specific branches of industry the picture remains the same in general, although construction materials and the food industry reached a low point in 1943.[1] If instead focusing on the heavy industry quarterly output rates, it is apparent that the turnaround came in the first quarter of 1943 for most branches.[2] The British first seriously noted the fact that the economy was recuperating during the latter part of 1943, even though some improvements were highlighted even earlier in the year. But the British JIC still held to their estimate that industrial output only was 60–70 per cent of the pre-war level in March 1943; a figure that was repeated by G-2 in September. Actual industrial output had surpassed this level even by 1942 as we have seen, and during 1943 it was somewhat larger than the 1940 level.[3] The Americans were more sceptical during 1943 and believed in a long-term exhaustion of economic strength. The British were therefore more correct in their assessments of economic strength during this period of the war.

As the war drew to a close the need for post-war reconstruction of the economy was noted in several reports. The assessments varied as to how rapidly the USSR could reach the pre-war level of economic development. In reality 1950 Soviet GNP had surpassed the 1940 level by 21 per cent and by 28 per cent on a per capita basis.[4] Most observers believed that it would take five years for the Soviet economy to reach the pre-war level regarding output. Therefore, it seems that most observers underestimated the recuperative power of the economy. Material destruction was estimated at one fifth or one fourth of all pre-war material assets in the USSR by the OSS in different reports. Actual losses of physical assets were one fourth.[5]

Estimates of basic industry output during these years were in line with or even greater than actual output in most cases.[6] Most observers therefore actually overestimated the output of steel, oil, non-ferrous metals, and other basic industry products. On the other hand, not many estimates existed which dealt with the manufacturing of finished products, with the notable exception of munitions. In January 1945 the US JIC believed that industrial production would be about 15 per cent below the pre-war level during the first year after the end of hostilities. In 1945 Soviet industry converted from war production to civilian production, which resulted in a fall in industrial production. But despite this, total industrial production (according to Harrison) was still 96 per cent of the 1940 level in 1945.[7]

It has already been proposed that a possible explanation for the Anglo-American underestimate of industrial production might depend on the underestimate of munitions output. This underestimate was evident even in 1942, although some British estimates closed in on the actual production figures. During the last period of the war most estimates approached reality. US military intelligence lagged behind in their estimates, but apart from this, during 1943–1944 most observers estimated monthly output to about 2000 tanks and between 2000–2500 combat aircraft. Since actual annual output of tanks (and other armoured vehicles with a main armament) was in excess of 24,000 in 1942–1943, and nearly 29,000 in 1944, and the output of combat aircraft was nearly 30,000 in 1943 and above 33,000 in 1944, most estimates were correct (with only a slight underestimate).[8] During 1944 the tank production was underestimated in some OSS reports (around 1500 per month). During 1945 both the US and the British JIC upgraded their estimates of aircraft output, and claimed it to be at least 2500 combat aircraft and 3000 aircraft per month. Actual monthly output during the first six months of 1945 was in excess of 2700 combat aircraft and 3300 military aircraft all in all. Tank production during the first six months of 1945 was at least as high as it had been during 1944 on a monthly basis.[9] So it seems that most observers underestimated tanks and aircraft output somewhat during 1943–1945.

But when it came to artillery it was a different matter, since most observers seriously underestimated output. As late as January 1945 the OSS and the US JIC believed estimated monthly artillery output to about 3000 and 2100 pieces, respectively. During late 1944 and the first half of 1945, actual monthly production of medium and large calibre pieces ran at about 4700 per month, and total production (including pieces below 76 mm in calibre) was about 10,000 per month.[10] On the other hand, mortar output was grossly overestimated at the time and stated to be 10,000 and 13,000 units per months, respectively. Mortar output had already reached its peak in the first six months of 1942, with about 20,500 units per month. During the last quarter of 1944 monthly output were only about 600 units, since the Soviets gradually scaled down output from 1942 to 1945.[11] But, as already stated, the cost of producing a mortar was considerably less than producing an artillery piece, only about one tenth for corresponding calibres,[12] which is why the underestimate of artillery output was much more important.

Despite the upgrading of the capacity to produce munitions it seems that this capacity was underestimated in yet another way. Instead of realizing that output had increased swiftly after the outbreak of war, some important observers chose to upgrade the pre-war production of munitions, thereby indirectly concluding that the Soviets were unable to increase their wartime production. This implies that Soviet contingency capacity was underestimated. Furthermore, although many observers noted considerable improvement in the ability to increase factory efficiency, and some even thought that the Soviets produced more munitions than Germany, it does not seem that they were aware of the full extent of Soviet efficiency in this respect. In spite of the fact that most observers actually overestimated the capacity of basic industry the production of munitions were still underestimated. From a resource base that was only slightly larger than Britain's (measured as total GDP 1943–1945), and somewhat less than Germany's, the USSR produced considerably more munitions than either of these two powers during 1943–1945.[13]

As for the quality of munitions most observers changed their mind to a considerable extent during the last period of the war. Many observers believed Soviet munitions, and especially tanks, to be of high quality. A cautious revaluation of the quality of munitions was already apparent during late 1942, and we have also seen that the quality of munitions actually improved after the outbreak of war. Most combat aircraft produced during the latter part of the war were not significantly inferior to the models produced by the Germans.[14] During 1943–1945 the production of the successful T-34 medium tank continued in upgraded versions. This tank constituted about two-thirds of all Soviet tanks produced during the war. The Germans began producing new models in 1943 which were more powerful than the T-34, but only in relatively limited and expensive series. In 1944 the Soviets produced new heavier models, which in turn could match the new German designs.[15] Not many observers specifically commented on the quality of Soviet artillery, but the technical performance of artillery pieces in general was at least as good (or even better) than German artillery for corresponding calibres. But German anti-tank capabilities were, in general, better for those guns that had that ability.[16]

As we have seen most observers still identified many general problems in the Soviet economy. But during 1943 fewer and fewer reports took notice of the problems in the transport sector. In reality the main sector of transports, the railways, was affected by many problems during the entire war but "for the most part the railways met the demands placed upon them".[17] The agricultural situation was still perceived as being inadequate for feeding the population, and the food problem was still the subject of reports as late as 1945. But most observers believed that conditions were gradually improving. As we have seen above, the real food situation was very problematic, affecting the war effort in some ways. During 1944–1945 conditions improved somewhat, but not much, and in 1945 food consumption and general living standards were still below the 1940 level.[18]

From 1943 onwards many observers commented on the shortage of manpower. A shortage of skilled labour was identified, and the British considered the heavy manpower losses as a problem for the labour situation after the war. In 1944 the OSS believed that the USSR would have as much labour after the war as before, and in 1945 they also pointed to the increased productivity in munitions production and some other industrial branches. In reality the workforce had reached full mobilization in 1942, and thereafter there was a bottleneck. There was a lack of labour in engineering, metallurgy and the defence industry that amounted to 0.5 million in 1942. The loss of population due to the invasion and war casualties numbered tens of millions. The working population shrank from 86.8 to 55.7 million during 1940–1942. Recruits to the Armed Forces were to a considerable extent made up from agricultural labour, and women were very widely employed in industry and agriculture. Children and the elderly were also used in the workforce. Barber and Harrison claim that: "Taking the war years as a whole, therefore, the shortage of skilled labour was acute but could not be decisive. Ultimately, what constrained the Soviet productive effort was the shortage of working hands." But in absolute numbers the work force increased from the low point in 1942, and 1942–1943 were the years of acute labour shortage.[19]

The increase in labour productivity, noted by the OSS, although also being commented on more indirectly by other observers, was indeed considerable. When the OSS stated that labour productivity in the aircraft and tank industry had increased by about 30 and 38 per cent, respectively, from June 1941 to June 1944, they were wrong. Labour productivity in the defence industry increased by 103 per cent from 1941 to 1944, while productivity in civilian industry decreased by about 15 per cent during the same period. The corresponding figure for all industry was a 44 per cent increase. Considering the considerable relative value of tank and aircraft industry production as compared to total munitions production – between 55–60 per cent in 1941–1944 (not counting the ammunition made for these arms) – it can safely be said that the OSS underestimated the productivity increase in munitions production during the war.[20] Several other industries – machine technology, electrical goods, building construction and light industry – had, according to the OSS, achieved "substantial increases in productivity per worker during 1942–44". This statement was, on the other hand, to a certain extent an overestimate, since productivity in civilian industry actually decreased. The productivity decline was especially marked in light industry but was also a reality in basic industry. But the underestimate of the productivity increase in the defence industry is perhaps more serious than the overestimate of civilian industry production, since the value of defence industry output constituted about 52 per cent of total industrial production during 1941–1944 (or 62 per cent if only the years 1942–1944 are counted).[21]

The notion that the Soviets were unable to achieve a really high productivity increase in the production of munitions was also substantiated by the already-mentioned belief – harboured by both US and British observers – that munitions output already was very high by June 1941. As we have seen, this was definitively not their estimate in June 1941, but an upward revision made later in the war. This implies that instead of believing in a productivity and output increase for the munitions industry, they chose to believe that it already had a large output when the war started. Another indication that the great productivity increase in munitions production was underestimated is the statement made by Wilson of the FO in September 1944: "If Russian resources in equipment were so far Greater than the Germans, they must have had to divert a larger proportion of their population to industrial production than the Germans did." The fact is that the total Soviet labour force in industry was smaller than the total German industrial labour force in 1944 by about 10 per cent, and it was even smaller during 1942 and 1943.[22]

When the OSS claimed that the work force at the end of the war would be as large as when it started they were wrong. The total actual work force in 1940 was nearly 87 million, while it was close to 76 million in 1945.[23] They did not underestimate the total amount of labour available in the USSR in 1945 – quite the contrary. Most, if not all, observers underestimated civilian losses. While many observers, in the end, made a pretty accurate estimate of permanent military losses, civilian dead were estimated at a few million. Actual civilian losses within the 1945 borders were about 18 million (possibly more).[24] There were many estimates concerning the total population of the USSR during the last year of the war, most of them were overestimates. This is not surprising considering the underestimate of the total population loss in the war. The actual Soviet population at the end of 1945 was 170.5 million.[25]

The economy's dependence on foreign supplies was repeated in many US and British reports. As we have seen, this dependence was also stressed during 1941–1942, but in practice the economy received much more material assistance during the 1943–1945 period of the war than before. While assistance from the Western Allies amounted to about 5 per cent of GNP in 1942 (and was close to 0 per cent in 1941), it increased to 10 per cent per year in 1943 and 1944.[26] Deliveries continued on a large scale in 1945. These deliveries were of great importance for the economy since they provided much material that was in short supply. In this way aid also mitigated the suffering of the civilian population and filled important gaps in the economy that in turn allowed it to function better and produce more. Even though the German Army was essentially stopped in its tracks by 1943, the Red Army's great strategic offensive to the West in 1943–1945 depended to a significant extent on resources delivered by the Western Allies.[27] However, since the observers underestimated munitions output and industrial output during the early part of the war, and even later to some extent, they also by implication overestimated the importance of Western aid.

Appreciation of military efficiency was growing during the latter years of the war. As we already have seen above the Red Army was learning and became gradually more effective, but their main adversary, the German Army and the *Luftwaffe*, were still better fighting forces, relatively speaking, almost until the very end of the war. Due to the relative efficiency superiority of Germany's armed forces the Red Army suffered larger losses.[28] It seems that although most observers considered the Red Army to be effective during the latter part of the war, almost no one seemed to believe that it were more efficient than the Germans or the Western Allies' troops. The OSS grossly miscalculated the relation between Soviet and Axis losses in 1945, in favour of the Soviets. Estimates of material losses were scarce during the war but judging by the one done by the MI3 in July 1944 the Soviets had suffered losses of 49,000 tanks, 30,128 aircraft and 48,000 guns during the three first years of war. Actual losses just during 1941–1943 (not counting the first six months of 1944) were 59,100 tanks, 52,500 aircraft and 158,700 guns and mortars (in excess of 50 mm in calibre).[29] This, of course, implies that actual losses were far greater during the first three years of the war than MI3 believed.

The efforts of the Soviet partisans were noticed by some observers even before Stalingrad, but possibly more so afterwards. The fact that the partisans were to a large extent controlled by the Red Army was noticed. The partisans contributed a great deal to the Soviet war effort,[30] even though it is hard to exactly estimate their contribution, and they were a relatively small force compared to the regular Red Army, and mostly lacked heavy armaments.

As we already have seen, the Soviet regime's popular support grew during the war, as well as hatred for the German invader.[31] The stability of the regime was never in jeopardy during 1943–1945, nor was this believed to be the case by any Anglo-American observer. The fear of separate peace never materialized, and was never seriously contemplated by the observers after 1943.

So although most observers came much closer to reality during this latter period of the war, there was still a considerable gap in some respects between reality and assessments. Even though some aspects of Soviet capacity were somewhat overestimated, such as the capacity of basic industry, manufacturing output and industrial efficiency were still underestimated to some extent. Civilian population losses were underestimated, but the output of munitions and productivity of the defence industry were still underestimated.

Notes

1 Harrison (1996), 71, 93.
2 Harrison (1985), 254.
3 Harrison (1996), 59.
4 Ibid, 297.
5 Ibid, 162.
6 Chapters 9 and 10 compared to Harrison (1996), 68–69 and Harrison (1985), 253.
7 Harrison (1996), 59.
8 Harrison (1996), 68; Harrison (1985), 251; Zaloga & Ness (2003), 180.
9 Harrison (1996), 180; Harrison (1985), 251.
10 And these figures did not even include the production of naval artillery. Harrison (1985), 251.
11 Ibid, 251.
12 Harrison (1996), 181–182.
13 Harrison (1996), 124; Harrison (1998a), 15–16; Harrison (1994), 242.
14 Overy (1996), 214, 218–220; Ellis (1993), 285–286, 288, 290, 292; Harrison (1998a), 29.
15 Mayer (ed.) (1977), 177, 180, 186–187; Ellis (1993), 277, 303–306.
16 Ellis (1993), 304–306; Salmaggi & Pallavisini (1997), 14.
17 Westwood (1994), 168.
18 Barber & Harrison (1991), 78–79.
19 Barber & Harrison (1991), 144–150, 170, 219; Harrison (2002), Table 5–4.
20 Harrison (1996), 88, 188.

21 Ibid, 81, 85.
22 Abelshauser (1998), 160–161 compared to Wagenführ (1963), 139–142; Harrison (1996), 268–269, 272.
23 Harrison (1996), 272.
24 Harrison (1996), 160 compared to Erickson (1994), 259.
25 Harrison (1996), 160.
26 Davies (1998), 61.
27 Harrison (1996), 129–132, 145–146.
28 Kennedy (1989), 349, 352; Johansson (1991), 345; Guderian (1976), 382; Clark (1965), 378–379, 395.
29 Glantz & House (2000), 306.
30 Even by mid-1942 they had succeeded in holding down about 10 per cent of the German Army's overall strength on the Soviet–German front, even though the partisan warfare would reach its climax later in the war. According to German Army figures the partisans engaged 14 German and 14 Axis allies' divisions on 1 October 1943, in addition to a large number of smaller units. However, most of these divisions were so-called security divisions, and not regular army divisions. Grenkevich (1999), 323.
31 Overy (1996), 292–293.

22 The assessments of war potential and material aid to the USSR

How important was the material aid sent to the USSR by the Western Allies during the war? According to Harrison "the economic significance" of economic aid (mainly Lend-Lease) to the USSR was a controversial subject for many years after the war.[1] This study makes it possible to evaluate how the British and the Americans viewed this question at the time. Did the Anglo-American observers believe that Western supplies to the USSR were decisive for the Soviet war effort at the time, and is it possible that Anglo-American intelligence assessments of Soviet military-economic strength had some implications for the delivery of aid to the USSR?

Both Anglo-American Governments decided to aid the USSR. However, US Lend-Lease deliveries were the most important since these supplies constituted about 90 per cent of the total value of all material aid to the USSR.[2] The need for material assistance to the USSR was stressed in many reports from the very start of the war. In some of the earlier reports it was considered crucial for the survival of the country, or at least for a continuation of its war effort. And this notion was repeated during the whole period, from the start of *Barbarossa* up to the German defeat at Stalingrad. It is very difficult to say what significance these assessments had for the decision to aid the USSR in the first place, and it is also hard to say if they had any significance for what specific items the United States and Britain sent to the Soviets, or the further continuation of aid to the Soviets when the Red Army was victorious in 1943–1945.

In order to at least shed some light on the problem, two opposite positions can be taken: either the US assessments of Soviet capabilities had no influence on the decision to send aid to the USSR, or, on the other hand, they had everything to do with it. Arguing for the first position is easy since the US Lend-Lease administration apparently made practically no analysis regarding whether or not the USSR really needed the supplies sent there. And, Roosevelt explicitly forbade any investigation to such ends in 1942. Roosevelt's initial decision to offer aid to the USSR was apparently based less on any specific intelligence report than on personal opinions of such key advisors as Hopkins and Averell Harriman, two of Roosevelt's special envoys to Moscow, both of whom believed that the USSR was military (and economically) viable. When later asked how he had decided that the Soviets was going to withstand the initial German onslaught, Hopkins confessed that he "had a hunch where I wanted to come out and then I looked around to find some reason to justify the hunch".[3]

Furthermore, the USSR was not the only beneficiary, and not even the largest one, since the British Empire, China and the Free French forces also received a great deal of help. The United Kingdom alone received about 2.5 times as much aid from the United States during the war as the USSR.[4] It can therefore be argued that help was given to everyone that fought the Axis, and by this policy the United States probably indirectly saved many American lives. When the Red Army gained ground, and eventually crushed the German Army in 1943–1945, Lend-Lease supplies were still sent to the USSR, up to the last days of the war. In fact, most of the aid was sent during this period and the value of the aid sent in 1944 was higher than in 1943. Even when the war ended in May 1945 aid was still coming into Soviet ports from the United States, and ended only when the war with Japan was over.[5] Consequently, the Soviets received aid whether they were winning or losing.

On the other hand, taking the opposite point of view, it seems fair to argue that the assessments had much to do with how much help the USSR received, at least during the early years. According to Dawson the US decision to aid the USSR in 1941 was spurred both by "the interaction of domestic political forces and considerations of military necessity". Roosevelt wanted to prop up the USSR in order to avoid its collapse, which in turn would have meant Axis domination of Eurasia at a time when the US Armed Forces were not mobilized (i.e. nothing short of a disaster).[6] Therefore, it seems likely that the assessment played some part in the process which resulted in the ultimate decision to aid the Soviets, or at least that the amount of aid shipped was influenced by them. The state of Soviet military-economic strength was under investigation with the intent of evaluation the need of aid, even during the summer of 1941, and some of the assessments was even sent to Roosevelt personally. Since so many reports from this period stressed the importance of foreign help for the Soviet war effort, it seems likely that they had some impact.

We know how much importance Soviet resistance had for the Allied war effort in 1942, since the Red Army at that time was the only force that played a really major part in the war against Germany. A German victory would mean that the lion part of German military strength could be used elsewhere, and in long run also that more economic resources would available to her. The Roosevelt administration wanted to avoid a Soviet collapse at any cost, and even sent equipment to the Soviets that delayed the build-up of US forces. The aid sent to the Soviets created frustration in some Washington circles at the time.[7] Since the Americans believed that the USSR was very weak at the time, a picture gained through their analysis of Soviet war potential, help to her was of course of the utmost importance in order to avoid a collapse. Aid sent to the USSR could be wasted if she really collapsed, as many officials feared in 1941–1942.[8] It hardly needs to be repeated what it would have meant not only to the German, but also to the Japanese strategic position if the USSR had been defeated. Therefore, considering the lingering insecurity concerning Soviet staying power, material aid was of the utmost importance from the Allied perspective. If they Soviets had been perceived as stronger, which they actually were, this could have affected the willingness to give aid

Even though there was much resistance in some quarters regarding sending aid to the Soviets many military officials, the WD and the Joint US Strategy Committee were willing to do it.[9] Since these US agencies were involved in the assessment of the USSR, and also stressed the need for foreign aid to the Soviets in their reports, they apparently must have believed that it also was worth taking the risk (since the USSR could collapse and the aid would be wasted) of sending supplies. There were plenty of extensive reports (and some lesser ones) from 1941 right up to the end of the war, which stressed the need for foreign assistance to the Soviet war effort. When the fate of the USSR still hung in the balance (according to the Americans) in 1941–1942, help was not only considered important but as decisive. When the Soviets were winning it was still seen as a major ingredient in the Soviet effort. It must also be remembered that many US observers had a more pessimistic opinion of Soviet prospects than the British, and that the OSS and the US JIC still believed even after Kursk, that the Soviet war effort would lose steam by the summer of 1944 at the latest. We know that Roosevelt and others feared a Soviet–German separate peace, and that some observers calculated on the possibility that the Red Army would halt its advance once they had evicted the Germans from Soviet soil.

In 1944 the US Chief of Staff General Marshal concluded that Lend-Lease was crucial to the Soviet war effort, and that the Germans might still defeat the USSR if it ended.[10] Whether or not Marshal based his opinions on intelligence assessments of Soviet war potential is uncertain, but it is certain that he had access to them and that the US JIC, G-2 and other US institutions made several assessments of Soviet capabilities in 1943 and 1944. General Walsh and Admiral Standley (who was involved in the assessment of Soviet capabilities in his capacity as the US ambassador to Moscow until the fall of 1943) argued independently "that Lend-Lease was essential for the survival of the Red Army".[11] It is therefore not so strange that Lend-Lease increased in 1943–1944, despite the fact that the Americans gradually upgraded Soviet strength. In addition, we have seen that many reports from 1945 continued to stress the importance of foreign aid for the Soviet war effort. All this implies that the American underestimate of Soviet strength contributed to the continuation of Lend-Lease shipments at a high and increasing level.

If the Americans concluded in 1944 and 1945, as they did, that the Soviet war effort was still dependent on foreign supplies, it seems quite natural that they should continue to send those supplies. After June 1944 the Western Allies were in some sense more exposed to German military power than ever, since they had expanded their military commitment with more ground troops after *Overlord*. The Red Army was still engaging the lion's share of all German divisions, even after June 1944, and the German Army was still suffering the larger part of its casualties in the East.[12] The weaker the Soviets the stronger the Germans, and consequently the Western Allies had to sacrifice more to win in the West. van Tuyll and Harrison argue that Lend-Lease made the US and British war effort much easier, and Harrison also considers that supplying material to the USSR, which relative to the Western Allies had plenty of manpower but fewer material resources, was a way to accomplish labour specialization that ultimately contributed to the Allied cause as a whole.[13]

Therefore it seems logical that US assessments of Soviet strength had at least some contribution to Lend-Lease policies. The use of Lend-Lease was reported to the US congress during the war in a way that justified why the USSR needed aid.[14] Kestner's assertion that the documents of the Lend-Lease administration do not contain any valuable information on the Soviet economic situation during the war (see Chapter 2) is probably right, but that does not mean that the intelligence assessments made by other US government institutions had no impact whatsoever upon Lend-Lease policies. According to Beaumont, there was also a purely political dimension involved in the decision to continue delivering aid to the USSR when she was winning. Once the Western Allies, under Roosevelt's direction, had established the policy of giving the Soviets unconditional aid in 1941–1942 – the years of crisis for the Allies – they had to continue until the end of the war. Roosevelt wanted to end the war as quickly as possible and in the process save the Western Allies from heavy losses. Roosevelt would not dare risk alienating the Soviets by reducing aid.[15]

Notes

1 Harrison (1996), 128.
2 Ibid, 132.
3 Kestner (1999), 15.
4 Keegan (ed.) (1989), 203.
5 van Tuyll (1989), 164–167.
6 Dawson (1959), 290.
7 van Tuyll (1989), 141.
8 Ibid.
9 Ibid.
10 Ibid, 139.
11 Ibid.
12 Glantz & House (2000), 283–284.
13 van Tuyll (1989), 140; Harrison (1996), 152. Leshuk considers that there was no real reason for the Americans to deliver aid that would further strengthen the already strong Soviets. In doing so he fails to take full account of this particular aspect of the Allied war effort, and the fact that aid was delivered to all the major allies of the United States, although he seems to be right in his claim that the US underestimate of Soviet strength was a factor in the willingness of the Roosevelt administration to send Lend-Lease to the USSR. Leshuk (2003), 249–251.
14 "Eleventh report to congress on lend-lease operations", 711. Supplies to Soviet Union-reports, Box-40, MECF1944: 711 Poland, RG84.
15 Beaumont (1980), 215–216.

23   A comment on the assessments in the context of the early Cold War

In a sense there has always been a Cold War between the West and Soviet Russia, right from the start of the Bolshevik takeover. As depicted by several authors, mutual suspicion and animosity existed during the whole interwar period. The perceived threat of communism, and the international dislike of the USSR, was, as we have seen, even a factor that made it hard for the Anglo-French to properly coordinate the defence against Nazi Germany. World War II would, of course, alter the situation considerably. The Anglo-American observers was very well aware in 1945 of the great, and decisive, contribution that the Soviet Armed Forces made in the defeat of Germany and other Axis forces. Officially they expressed thanks to the USSR, but already in 1944 many observers, especially British, begun to privately express concerns over Soviet military power and the Red Army's westward advance. That this was the case, even on the very highest level of British government, is supported by many sources. These concerns was expressed even before some of the problems, like the discord over the support to the August 1944 Warsaw uprising, was on the agenda. Generally the Roosevelt administration looked upon the Soviets more favourably than the British, but at the beginning of 1945 the US JIC started to analyse the Soviets from the perspective of being a potential enemy, and even before that some important US officials expressed concerns over the Soviets.

The Cold War can, of course, in the first place be attributed to political and ideological differences between the Western Powers and the USSR. Had, for example, the Soviets accepted that Western style parliamentary democracy (and free markets) should be allowed in Central- and Eastern Europe after the war, and abstained from supporting Communist and potentially anti-Western movements all over the world; there would have been little ground for a Cold War. But the greatest difference between 1939 and 1945 was not the ideological, or even the political aspect. The Americans was not particularly active in European politics before the war, but the British (and the French) seemed to have nurtured the same perceptions in 1939, in principle, regarding Soviet intentions as in 1945. They believed that the Soviets wanted to spread communism over the globe, and most of the government observers regarded the Soviet system as deplorable. The greatest difference – although of course existing – was not about perceived intentions, but rather instead about capabilities.

In 1939–1941 the Soviets were seen as so weak by the Western observers that few believed that the USSR would be able to resist a German invasion for more than a couple of months or so. Already in 1944 many observers were certain that the Red Army would win over the Germans, not primarily due to military action taken by the Western Allies, but first and foremost due to their own capabilities. They still underestimated Soviet strength in some respects, and also overestimated the importance of Western supplies. In 1945, though, their assessments were more or less in tune with reality, even though the productivity of the defence industry still was grossly underestimated, and the amount of munitions in the Red Army inventory was somewhat underestimated. These underestimations were partly, from the perspective of war potential, offset by the underestimation of population losses caused by the war. The point, however, is that they were close to seeing the reality of Soviet war potential, and they believed the USSR to be very powerful. There is no doubt that the Soviet Union was perceived as a major threat by leading military and intelligence authorities in Whitehall both before and after the end of the war. During his last week as prime minister, in July 1945, Churchill stated that the Soviets were all powerful in Europe and "any time that it took their fancy they could march across the rest of Europe and drive us back into our island".[1]

The Soviets were still seen as a potential threat to Western political interests, just as in 1939, but now the USSR had the military strength and capabilities which made such threats the more dangerous. And perhaps even more importantly, she had an economic and political system that was not perceived as ready for collapse. Regardless of how efficient the economic system was, in comparison to the Western economies, and regardless of how the internal support for the Stalin regime was achieved, the economy was effective in supporting the largest Army in history, and the support for the totalitarian regime was there. That the Soviets were strong, and that they had been the principal military actor in the defeat of Nazi Germany, was of course believed by a wider circle than the Anglo-American government observers in 1945. The Soviet economic system, and therefore also indirectly Stalinism, socialism and even "communism", had stood the test of war, in spite of heavy initial odds. This implicitly made the Soviets more of a threat also on a political and an ideological level than before.

On the American side there is indication that Soviet strength was taken even more seriously shortly after the war, despite the fact that the Anglo-Americans more or less correctly identified the great post-war problems that the USSR faced. In October 1945 the US JCS approved a report from the Joint Strategic Survey Committee on US military options in the light of the perceived Soviet threat. The recent attitude of the USSR was described as "aggressive and uncompromising". The committee stated that six months before "the United States was the greatest military power in the history of the world." But despite this it was not believed that the US would have been able to combat "the military power of Russia", with regard to its "vast and efficient armies".[2] Later, in November, the US JIC made the assessment that if the Red

Army should embark on offensive operations it could probably overrun most of Europe and Asia.[3] From a military standpoint this was more than the Axis was able to achieve during the war.

It was, of course, possible for the Anglo-Americans to counter Soviet military action in several ways, if such a dark scenario would become reality. In addition, the Anglo-American block was at the time economically stronger, in terms of industrial output, than the rest of the world combined. But the assessments nevertheless show, regardless of what can be said about Soviet exhaustion, and the need for Soviet post-war reconstruction, that the Anglo-Americans at least believed that they faced a very credible potential threat.

Notes

1 Hennessy (2003), 5, 12; Carlton (2000), 144.
2 16-10-1945 and 9–10–1945, CCS092USSR(3–27–45) Sec. 1, Box-208, Geographic File 1942–1945, RG 218.
3 15-11-1945, JIC 250/5, CCS092USSR(3–27–45) Sec. 1, Box-208, Geographic File 1942–1945, RG 218.

24 Conclusion

As we have seen, most Anglo-American observers believed in June 1941 that the Soviet Union would be a new easy conquest for Hitler's armies. What was, in fact, already by then the largest (in terms of combat troops and armaments) armed force so far in recorded history, the Red Army, would succumb in a few months, or even a few weeks, according to some, to the military might and brilliance of the *Wehrmacht*. The Anglo-Americans did not doubt that the Soviet Armed Forces was large, even though they also substantially underestimated this aspect. It was, however, primarily other factors that convinced them that the end was near for the Red Army and the Soviet regime. They underestimated the Soviets resilience and staying power at the frontline, as well as at the home front. Undoubtedly the initial stunning German victories confirmed that the Red Army was unprepared for war with the skilled *Wehrmacht*, but soon the Anglo-American observers, just as the Germans was forced to do, revaluated the situation.

This revaluation took time and comprised many aspects. The most important specific misconceptions harboured by the observers could be found in the underestimation of the economy and the economic system, coupled with the idea that the Soviets generally lacked the competence to make the economy work. There are, of course, many features of the Stalinist planned economy that rightly can be criticized, not even mentioning the cost of forced industrialization, and some of these weaknesses were identified by the Anglo-Americans in 1939–1941. However, they drew the wrong conclusions from these assumptions, and believed these would mean that the USSR would be even weaker in wartime. The underestimation of the mobilization capacity and munitions output alone, is basically enough to make clear why they were so fast in writing off Soviet military resistance. These two areas were also, on a concrete level, the most conspicuous error in their assessments.

All of these misconceptions can, of course, not be separated from their perceptions of, and as it seems in most cases, dislike of communism, and their sometimes condescending attitudes towards Russians and Slavic people. The weakness of the economy and the system would not only fail to delivers the necessary material support for the war effort, but would also probably result in revolt against the regime. On the whole, these perceptions, with a few important exceptions, were more or less exactly what Hitler seemingly believed, and which partly motivated him to take the fatal step of attacking the USSR.

It is also obvious that Anglo-American perceptions of Soviet capabilities had an impact upon US and British policy in some respects during 1939–1945. That fact that Soviet strength was held in so low esteem probably mattered a great deal, at least before 1944. Is it possible that events in 1939 could have taken another path if more accurate information about Soviet capabilities had been available? Instead of potentially being a "middle sized military power", or even somewhat less than that according to some British observers, the USSR was in fact potentially the second strongest power on Earth (after the United States). With accurate estimates, would the Anglo-French have dared to plan military action against the USSR in 1939–1940, which became known to Stalin, fuelling mutual suspicions. The notion that Britain stood alone against the German menace after the fall of France can in some ways be further strengthened by knowledge of the nature of British assessments, since it seems that not even Churchill really believed that the Soviets would be able to put up any effective resistance against the Germans.

The underestimation did not end with Barbarossa, but continued well into 1942 and in some respects longer. A collapse or at least a German push to the Urals, with all its implications, was not excluded by many observers even in the summer of 1942. The turning point of the war, from the perspective of (especially the American) observers, was not Stalingrad, but rather the Kursk battle and the period immediately after that. For the Americans the late autumn of 1943 was the time when they seemed to have definitively stopped worrying about a decline of Soviet strength. Even though it probably was necessary for several reasons, the decision not to undertake a Western Allied invasion of Western Europe in 1942, and even in 1943, could in a sense be regarded as a gamble, from the perspective of the USSR holding out. It seems that the difference between US and British assessments during this period played a part. It is obvious that the assessments had implications for the size of the US Army. It is less obvious that the assessments had an importance for the US Lend-Lease policy towards the USSR, even though it cannot be excluded. During the latter part of the war the assessments became more realistic, at least approaching reality. In 1945, the Anglo-Americans could therefore correctly conclude that they faced a strong – albeit in the short term by war economically weakened – Cold War enemy.

References

Primary sources

Official documents

National Archives, College Park, Washington

Record Group 18: Records of the Army Air Forces [AAF], 1903–1964
  Entry 300: (NM-53) Formerly Security Classified Correspondence Relating to Foreign Countries, 1942–1944
Record Group 38: Records of the Office of the Chief of Naval Operations [OCNO], 1875–1993
  Entry 98 (A): Intelligence Division Secret Reports of Naval Attachés
Record Group 59: General Records of the Department of State, 1756–1979
  M1221: Intelligence Reports, 1941–1961
  T1249: Records of the Department of State Relating to Internal Affairs of the Soviet Union, 1930–1939
  T1250: Records of the Department of State Relating to Internal Affairs of the Soviet Union, 1940–1944
  LM 176: Confidential U.S. State Department Central Files. The Soviet Union, Internal Affairs, 1945–1949
Record Group 84: Records of the Foreign Service Posts of the Department of State, 1788–1964
  MECF Moscow Embassy Confidential File (1941–1944)
  Entry 58A: Moscow Embassy file
  Entry 59A: Moscow Embassy file
Record Group 165: Records of the War Department General and Special Staffs [WDGS/WDSS], 1860–1952
  Entry 77: MID Regional File 1922–44
  Entry 79: "Security-Classified" Intelligence Reference Publications ("P" File)
  Entry 421: "ABC-file" Entry 3102: Military Intelligence
  M1443: Correspondence of the Military Intelligence Division Relating to General, Political, Economic, and Military Conditions in Russia and the Soviet Union, 1918–1941
Record Group 169: Records of the Foreign Economic Administration [FEA], 1939–1947
  Entry 141A: Economic Intelligence Division, Numbered Subject Files
Record Group 218: Records of the U.S. Joint Chiefs of Staff [JCS], 1941–1978
  Geographic File 1942–1945

Record Group 226: Records of the Office of Strategic Services [OSS], 1919–1948
  M1499: Records of the Research and Analysis Branch ("Regular" Series), 1941–1945
Record Group 263: Records of the Central Intelligence Agency [CIA], 1894–1993
  Center for the Study of Intelligence History Office, OSS Oral History Project Transcripts
Record Group 319: Records of the Army Staff, 1903–1992
  Entry 47: Army Intelligence Project Decimal File, 1941–1945
  Entry 85: Army Intelligence Document File
Record Group 334: Records of Interservice Agencies, 1916–1973
  Entry 309: United States Military Mission to Moscow, Subject File: Oct 1943–Oct 1945

National Archives, Kew, London

Admiralty (ADM):
  ADM 223: Admiralty: Naval Intelligence Division and Operational Intelligence Centre: Intelligence Reports and Papers, 1914–1978
Air Ministry (AIR):
  AIR 8: Air Ministry and Ministry of Defence: Department of the Chief of the Air Staff: Registered Files, 1916–1982
  AIR 9: Air Ministry: Directorate of Operations and Intelligence and Directorate of Plans: Registered Files, 1914–1947
  AIR 19: Air Ministry, and Ministry of Defence, Air Department: Private Office Papers, 1917–1983
  AIR 20: Air Ministry, and Ministry of Defence: Air Historical Branch: Unregistered Papers, 1874–1983
  AIR 40: Air Ministry, Directorate of Intelligence and related bodies: Intelligence Reports and Papers, 1926–1984
  AIR 46: Air Ministry: Royal Air Force Liaison Missions: Papers, 1939–1960
Cabinet Office (CAB):
  CAB 53: Committee of Imperial Defence: Chiefs of Staff Committee: Minutes and Memoranda, 1923–1939
  CAB 56: Committee of Imperial Defence: Joint Intelligence Sub-Committee: Minutes and Memoranda JIC, JIC(S), JIC(A), 1936–1939, 1974
  CAB 66: War Cabinet and Cabinet: Memoranda (WP and CP Series), 1939–1945
  CAB 80: War Cabinet and Cabinet: Chiefs of Staff Committee: Memoranda, 1939–1946
  CAB 81: War Cabinet and Cabinet: Committees and Sub-committees of the Chiefs of Staff Committee: Minutes and Papers, 1939–1947
  CAB 104: Cabinet Office and predecessors: Supplementary Registered Files, 1923–1951
  CAB 119: War Cabinet and Cabinet Office: Joint Planning Staff: Correspondence and Papers, 1939–1948
  CAB 120: Cabinet Office: Minister of Defence Secretariat: Records, 1938–1947
  CAB 121: Cabinet Office: Special Secret Information Centre: Files, 1939–1955
  CAB 122: War Cabinet and Cabinet Office: British Joint Staff Mission and British Joint Services Mission: Washington, 1940–1958
  CAB 163: War Cabinet, Ministry of Defence, and Cabinet Office: Central Intelligence Machinery: Joint Intelligence Sub-Committee, later Committee: Secretariat: Files, 1939–1973

Foreign Office (FO):
> *FO 181: Foreign Office and Foreign and Commonwealth Office: Embassy and Consulates, Union of Soviet Socialist Republics, (1801–1970)*
> *FO 371: Foreign Office: Political Departments: General Correspondence from 1906, 1906–1966*
> *FO 418: Foreign Office: Confidential Print Russia and Soviet Union, 1821–1956*
> *FO 800: Foreign Office, Private Offices: Various Ministers' and Officials' Papers, 1824–1968*
> *FO 837: Ministry of Economic Warfare and successors: Records, 1931–1951*

War Office (WO):
> *WO 106: War Office: Directorate of Military Operations and Military Intelligence, and Predecessors: Correspondence and Papers, 1837–1962*
> *WO 193: War Office: Directorate of Military Operations and Plans, later Directorate of Military Operations: Files concerning Military Planning, Intelligence and Statistics (Collation Files), 1934–1958*
> *WO 208: Directorate of Military Operations and Intelligence, and Directorate of Military Intelligence; Ministry of Defence, Defence Intelligence Staff: Files, 1917–1974*

Published collections and government publications

Foreign Relations of the United States: Diplomatic Papers 1942: (in 7 volumes). Europe, Vol. 3, U.S. Government Printing Office, 1961.

Halder vol. VI & VII: War Journal of Franz Halder (The Private War Journal of Generaloberst Franz Halder), Volume VI. United States: A.G.EUCOM, 1947.

Hansard 1803–2005 (UK Parliament, www.hansard.millbanksystems.com).

UPA 1977: OSS/State Department Intelligence and Research Reports, Part IV: The Soviet Union (Fredrick, Maryland: University Publications of America, 1977).

UPA 1981: Records of the Joint Chiefs of Staff, part I, 1942–1945: the Soviet Union (Fredrick, Maryland: University Publications of America, 1981).

US State Department Official Website (www.history.state.gov).

Bibliography (including autobiographies and PhD dissertations)

Abelshauser, W., 1998: "Germany: butter, guns, and economic miracles". (*The Economics of World War II*. Ed. Harrison, M., 122–176). Cambridge: Cambridge University Press.

Alanbrooke, A.B., 2001: War Diaries, 1939–1945, London, Weidenfeld & Nicolson.

Andrew, C., 1987: "Secret Intelligence and British Foreign Policy". (*Intelligence and International Relations, 1900–1945*. Eds. Andrew C. & Noakes, J, 9–28). Exeter.

Andrew, C. M., 2009: *The Defence of the Realm: The Authorized History of MI5*. London: Allen Lane.

Barber, J. & Harrison, M., 1991: *The Soviet Home Front, 1941–1945: A Social and Economic History of the USSR in the World War II*. New York.

Baykov, A., 1946: *The Development of the Soviet Economic System: An Essay on the Experience of Planning in the U.S.S.R.* London.

Beaumont, J., 1980: *Comrades in Arms: British Aid to Russia 1941–1945*. London.

Bellamy, C., 2007: *Absolute War: Soviet Russia in the Second World War*. New York: Alfred A. Knopf.

Beloff, L., 1983: "Was there a Soviet appeasement policy?" (*The Fascist Challenge and the Policy of Appeasement*. Eds. Mommsen W. J. & Kettenacker L., 284–285). London.

Bennett, E. M., 1990: *Franklin D. Roosevelt and the Search for Victory: American-Soviet Relations, 1939–1945*. Wilmington, Delaware.

Bialer, S. (ed.), 1984: *Stalin and His Generals: Soviet Military Memoirs of World War II*. Boulder, Colorado, and London.

Bishop, C., 2007: *Wehrmachts pansardivisioner 1939–1945* [*German Wehrmacht panzer divisions 1939–1945*]. Dubai: SMB.

Bond, B., 1983: "The continental commitment in British strategy in the 1930s". (*The Fascist Challenge and the Policy of Appeasement*. Ed. Mommsen W.J. & Kettenacker L., 197–206). London.

Butler, E., 1972: *Mason-Mac: the Life of Lieutenant-General Sir Noel Mason-Macfarlane*. London.

Campbell, A. E., 1985: "Franklin Roosevelt and Unconditional Surrender." (*Diplomacy and Intelligence during the Second World War: Essays in Honour of F.H. Hinsley*. Ed. Langhorne, R., 219–241). Cambridge: Cambridge University Press.

Cantwell, J. D., 1993: *The Second World War: A Guide to Documents in the Public Record Office*. London.

Carlton, D., 2000: *Churchill and the Soviet Union*. Glasgow.

Chant, C., 2007: *Artilleri: fler än 300 av världens främsta artilleripjäser från 1914 fram till idag* [*Artillery: More than 300 of the World's Foremost Artillery Pieces from 1914 until Today*]. Hallstavik: Svenskt military historiskt bibliotek.

Clark, A., 1965: *Barbarossa: The Russian-German Conflict 1941–1945*. London.

Clarke, P., 2002: *The Cripps Version: The Life of Sir Stafford Cripps 1889–1952*. London.

Cline, R. S., 1951: *Washington Command Post: The Operations Division*. Washington, DC.

Colville, J., 1981: *Winston Churchill and His Inner Circle*. New York: Wyndham Books.

Colvin, I., 1971: *The Chamberlain Cabinet: How the Meetings in 10 Downing Street 1937–9 Led to the Second World War: Told for the First Time from the Cabinet Papers*. London: Victor Gollancz Ltd.

Coox, A. D., 1985: *Nomonhan: Japan against Russia, 1939. Volume One*. Stanford, California: Stanford University Press.

Coox, A. D., 1990: *Nomonhan: Japan Against Russia, 1939*. Stanford, California: Stanford University Press.

Cradock, P., 2002: *Know Your Enemy: How the Joint Intelligence Committee Saw the World*. London.

Crowson, N. J., 1995: "Conservative Parliamentary Dissent Over Foreign Policy During the Premiership of Neville Chamberlain: Myth or Reality?" (*Parliamentary History*, Vol. 14, No. 3, 1995, 315–336.)

Davies, J. E., 1943: *Mission to Moscow*. New York.

Davies, R. W., 1994: "Industry." (*The Economic Transformation of the Soviet Union, 1913–1945*. Eds. Davies, R. W., Harrison, M., & Wheatcroft, S. G., 131–157). Cambridge: Cambridge University Press.

Davies, R.W., 1998: *Soviet Economic Development from Lenin to Khrushchev*. Cambridge: Cambridge University Press.

Davies, R. W., Harrison, M. & Wheatcroft, S. G. (eds.), 1994: *The Economic Transformation of the Soviet Union 1913–1945*. Cambridge: Cambridge University Press.

Dawson, R. H., 1959: *The Decision to Aid Russia, 1941: Foreign Policy and Domestic Politics*. North Carolina: University of North Carolina Press.

Deane, J. R., 1947: *The Strange Alliance: The Story of Our efforts at Wartime Co-operation with Russia.* New York.

Dear, I. C. B. & Foot, M. R. D., (eds.) 1995: *The Oxford Companion to World War II.* Oxford: Oxford University Press.

Divine, R. A., 1969: *Roosevelt and World War II.* Baltimore.

Douglas, R., 1981: *From War to Cold War, 1942–48.* London.

Dunn Jr., W. S., 1980: *Second Front Now – 1943.* Alabama: University of Alabama Press.

Duroselle, J.-B., 2004: *France and the Nazi Threat: The Collapse of French Diplomacy 1932–1939.* Enigma Books.

Dutton, D., 1997: *Anthony Eden: A Life and Reputation.* Arnold: London.

Ellis, J., 1990: *Brute Force: Allied Strategy and Tactics in the Second World War.* London.

Ellis, J., 1993: *The World War II Databook: The Essential Facts and Figures for all the Combatants.* London: Aurum Press.

Ericson III, E. E., 1999: *Feeding the German Eagle: Soviet Economic Aid to Nazi Germany, 1933–1941.* Westport, Connecticut.

Erickson, J., 1975: *The Road to Stalingrad: Stalin's War with Germany. Volume 1.* London.

Erickson, J., 1984: "Threat identification and strategic appraisal by the Soviet Union, 1930–1941." (*Knowing One's Enemies: Intelligence Assessments before the Two World Wars.* Eds. May, R.E., 375–423) Princeton, New Jersey.

Erickson, J., 1994: "Soviet War Losses: Calculations and Controversies" (*Barbarossa; the Axis and the Allies.* Eds. Erickson, J., & Dilks, D., 255–277) Edinburgh.

Falkehed, E., 1994: "The U.S. Military Attaché's Reporting from the Baltic States, 1939–40". (*Militärhistorisk Tidskrift*, 1994, 82–123). Stockholm.

Falls, C., 1960: *The First World War.* London.

Farago, L., 1961: *Burn After Reading: the Espionage History of World War II.* New York.

Fedotoff-White, D. D., 1944: *The Growth of the Red Army.* Princeton, New Jersey.

Ferris, J. R., 1995: "Indulged in All Too Little?: Vansittart, intelligence and appeasement." (*Diplomacy and Statecraft* Vol. 6, No. 1, March 1995, 122–175).

Fest, J., 2002: *Hitler.* Houghton Mifflin: Harcourt.

FitzGibbon, C., 1976: *Secret Intelligence in the Twentieth Century.* London.

Folly, M., 2000: *Churchill, Whitehall, and the Soviet Union, 1940–45.* Wiltshire.

Folly, M., 2002: *The United States and World War II: The Awakening Giant.* Edinburgh.

Ford, H. P., 1996: "The US Government's Experience with Intelligence Analysis: Pluses and Minuses." (*Intelligence Analysis and Assessments.* Eds. Charters, D.A., Farson S., & Hastedt G.P., 34–53). London: Routledge.

Frankson, A., 1996: "Lär av det förflutna: Röda armén under andra världskriget." (*Krigsvetenskapsakademins Handlingar och Tidskrift*, 1996, häfte 3, 83–93). Stockholm.

Frieser, K.-H., 2005: *The Blitzkrieg Legend.* Naval Institute Press.

Gaddis, J. L., 1972: *The United States and the Cold War 1941–1947.* New York.

Gander, T. & Chamberlain, P., 1979: *Weapons of the Third Reich: An Encyclopedic Survey of All Small Arms, Artillery and Special Weapons of the German Land Forces 1939–1945.* Garden City, New York.

Gillard, D., 2007: *Appeasement in Crisis: From Munich to Prague, October 1938 – March 1939.* Basingstoke: Palgrave Macmillan.

Glantz, D. M., 1998: *Stumbling Colossus: The Red Army on the Eve of World War.* Kansas: University Press of Kansas.

Glantz, D. M., 2001: *Barbarossa: Hitler's Invasion of Russia 1941.* Stroud.

Glantz, D., 2010: *Barbarossa Derailed: The Battle for Smolensk, Volume 1.* Helion & Company.

Glantz, D. M. & House, J. M., 2000: *When Titans Clashed: How the Red Army Stopped Hitler.* Kansas: University Press of Kansas.

Goldman, S. D., 2012: *Nomonhan, 1939; The Red Army's Victory That Shaped World War II.* Naval Institute Press.

Gorst, A., 1990: "British Military Planning for Postwar Defence, 1943–45". (*Britain and the First Cold War.* Ed. Deighton, A., 91–108). London.

Greenfield, K. R., 1963: *American Strategy in World War II: A Reconsideration.* Baltimore.

Grenkevich, L. D., 1999: *The Soviet Partisan Movement, 1941–1944: A Critical Historiographical Analysis.* London.

Guderian, H., 1976: *Panzer Leader.* London.

Habeck, M. R., 2002: "Dress Rehearsals, 1937–1941". (*The Military History of the Soviet Union.* Eds. Higham, R., & Kagan, F.W., 93–108). New York.

Hara, A., 1998: "Japan: guns before rice". (*The Economics of World War II: Six Great Powers in International Comparison.* Ed. Harrison, M., 224–267). Cambridge: Cambridge University Press.

Hardesty, V., Grinberg, I., 2012: *Red Phoenix Rising: The Soviet Air Force in World War II.* Kansas: University Press of Kansas.

Harriman, W. A. & Abel, E., 1976: *Special Envoy to Churchill and Stalin 1941–1946.* London.

Harrison, G. A., 1951: *The European Theater of Operations: Cross-Channel Attack.* Washington, DC.

Harrison, M., 1985: *Soviet Planning in Peace and War 1938–1945.* Cambridge: Cambridge University Press.

Harrison, M., 1988: "Resource mobilization for World War II: the USA, UK, USSR, and Germany, 1938–45". (*Economic History Review,* 2nd ser., XLI, 2, 1988), 171–192.

Harrison, M., 1990: "The Volume of Soviet Munitions Output, 1937–1945: a reevaluation". (*The Journal of Economic History, Vol. L. No. 3 (Sept. 1990)*, 569–589). Atlanta.

Harrison, M., 1994: "The second world war". (*The Economic Transformation of the Soviet Union 1913–45.* Eds. Davies R. W., Harrison, M. & Wheatcroft, S., 238–267). Cambridge: Cambridge University Press.

Harrison, M., 1996: *Accounting for War: Soviet Production, Employment, and the Defence Burden, 1940–1945.* Cambridge: Cambridge University Press.

Harrison, M., 1998a: "The economics of World War II: an overview". (*The Economics of World War II: Six Great Powers in International Comparison.* Ed. Harrison, M., 1–42). Cambridge: Cambridge University Press.

Harrison, M., 1998b: "The Soviet Union: the Defeated Victor". (*The Economics of World War II: Six Great Powers in International Comparison.* Ed. Harrison, M., 268–301). Cambridge: Cambridge University Press.

Haslam, J., 1984: *The Soviet Union and the Struggle for Collective Security in Europe, 1933–39.* Hong Kong.

Herman, M., 1996: *Intelligence Power in Peace and War.* Cambridge: Cambridge University Press.

Herndon, J. S., 1983: "British perceptions of Soviet military capability, 1935–9." (*The Fascist Challenge and the Policy of Appeasement*. Eds. Mommsen, W.J. & Kettenacker, L., 297–319). London.

Herndon, J. S. & Baylen, J. O., 1975: "Col. Philip R. Faymonville and the Red Army, 1934–43." (*Slavic Review, American quarterly of Soviet and East European studies*, Volume 34, Number 3, September 1975, 483–505).

Haythornthwaite, P. J., 1992: *The World War One Source Book*. London.

Hennessy, P., 2003: *The Secret State: Whitehall and the Cold War*. Suffolk.

Hinsley, F. H., 1987: "British intelligence in the Second World War." (*Intelligence and International Relations 1900–1945*. Eds. Andrew, C., & Noakes, J., 209–218). Exeter.

Hinsley, F. H. et al, 1979: *British Intelligence in the Second World War (Vol. 1): Its Influence on Strategy and Operations*. London.

Hinsley, F. H. et al, 1981: *British Intelligence in the Second World War (Vol. 2): Its Influence on Strategy and Operations*. London.

Hinsley, F. H. et al, 1984: *British Intelligence in the Second World War (Vol. 3, part 1): Its Influence on Strategy and Operations*. London.

Hoffschmidt, E. J. & Tantum, W. H., 1968: *Second World War Combat Weapons*. Old Greenwich, Connecticut.

Hucker, D., 2008: "The Unending Debate: Appeasement, Chamberlain and the Origins of the Second World War". (*Intelligence and National Security*, Vol. 23, No. 4, August 2008, 536–551).

Hymoff, E., 1972: *The OSS in World War II*. New York.

Imlay T., 2003: *Facing the Second World War: Strategy, Politics, and Economics in Britain and France, 1938–1940*. Oxford: Oxford University Press.

Jabara Carley, M., 2016: *Silent Conflict: A Hidden History of Early Soviet-Western Relations*. New York: Rowman & Littlefield Publishers.

Jackson, P., 2000: *France and the Nazi Menace: Intelligence and Policy Making, 1933–1939*. Oxford: Oxford University Press.

Jackson, P., 2008: "Introduction: Enquiries into the Secret State". (*Exploring Intelligence Archives: Enquiries into the Secret State*. Eds. Hughes, G., Jackson, P., & Scott, L.V., 1–12). London: Routledge.

Jakobson, M., 1961: *The Diplomacy of the Winter War: an Account of the Russo-Finnish War, 1939–1940*. Cambridge, Massachusetts: Cambridge University Press.

Johansson, A.W., 1991: *Europas Krig*. Kristianstad.

Jones, M., 2010: *The Retreat: Hitler's First Defeat*. Thomas Dunne Books.

Jones, R.H., 1969: *The Roads to Russia: United States Lend-Lease to the Soviet Union*. Oklahoma: University of Oklahoma Press.

Kahn, D., 1978: *Hitler's Spies: German Military Intelligence in World War II*. London.

Kahn, D., 1984: "The United States views Germany and Japan in 1941". (*Knowing One's Enemies: Intelligence Assessments Before the Two World Wars*. Ed. May, R. E., 476–501) Princeton, New Jersey.

Kahn, M., 2009: *Sovjetekonomin med svenska ögon: svenska statens bild av Sovjetunionens ekonomi 1917–56*. Sekel Bokförlag/Isell & Jinert.

Kahn, M., 2012: "Russia Will Assuredly Be Defeated: Anglo-American Government Assessments of Soviet War Potential before Operation Barbarossa". (*The Journal of Slavic Military Studies*, vol. 25, No. 2, 2012, 220–240).

Kahn, M., 2013: "British Intelligence on Soviet War Potential in 1939: A Revised Picture and Some Implications (a Contribution to the 'Unending Debate')". (*Intelligence and National Security*, Vol. 28, No. 5, 2013, 717–747).

Katz, B. M., 1989: *Foreign Intelligence. Research and Analysis in the Office of Strategic Services 1942–1945.* Boston, Massachusetts: Harvard University Press.

Keeble, C., 1990: *Britain and the Soviet Union, 1917–1989.* London.

Keegan, J., (ed.) 1989: *The Times Atlas of the Second World War.* London.

Kenez, P., 1999: *A History of the Soviet Union from the Beginning to the End.* Cambridge: Cambridge University Press.

Kennedy, P., 1989: *The Rise and Fall of the Great Powers: Economic Change and Military Conflict From 1500 to 2000.* New York.

Kennedy-Pipe, C., 1995: *Stalin's Cold War: Soviet Strategies in Europe, 1943 to 1956.* New York.

Kent, J., 1990: "The British Empire and the Origins of the Cold War, 1944–49". (*Britain and the First Cold War.* Ed. Deighton, A., 165–183) London.

Kershaw, R., 2000: *War Without Garlands: Operation Barbarossa 1941/42.* Shepperton.

Kestner, J. W., 1999: *Through the Looking Glass: American Perceptions of the Soviet Economy, 1941–1964.* Madison, Wisconsin: University of Wisconsin Press.

Klein, B. H., 1959: *Germany's Economic Preparations for War.* Cambridge: Cambridge University Press.

Knorr, K., 1979: *The War Potential of Nations.* Westport, Connecticut.

Koenig, W. & Scofield, P., 1983: *Soviet Military Power.* London.

Krivosheev, G. F., (ed.) 1997: *Soviet Casualties and Combat Losses in the Twentieth Century.* Greenhill Books.

Krivosheyev, G.F., 1993: *Soviet Armed Forces Losses in Wars, Combat Operations and Military Conflicts.* Moscow.

Laqueur, W., 1985: *A World of Secrets: the Uses and Limits of Intelligence.* New York.

Lee, S.L., 2008: *European Dictatorships, 1918–1945.* Routledge.

Leshuk, L., 2003: *US Intelligence Perceptions of Soviet Power 1921–1946.* London.

Levin, M. B., 1971: *Political Hysteria in America: The Democratic Capacity for Repression.* London: Basic Books.

Lewis, R., 1994: "Technology and the transformation of the Soviet economy." (*The Economic Transformation of the Soviet Union 1913–45.* Eds. Davies R.W., Harrison, M. & Wheatcroft, S., 182–197). Cambridge: Cambridge University Press.

Liddell Hart, B. H., 1983: *Andra Världskrigets Historia. 1.* Stockholm. [English edn: *History of the Second World War.* London, 1970].

Lockhart, Bruce R.H., 2011[1934]: *Memoirs of a British Agent.* London: Frontline Books.

Lord, P., 2001: "Blitzkreig – ett utvecklat koncept eller slumpens skördar." (*Militärhistorisk Tidskrift,* 2001, 47–69). Stockholm.

Lukas, R. C., 1970: *Eagles East: The Army Air Force and the Soviet Union, 1941–1945.* Tallahassee.

Lunde, H. O., 2011: *Finland's War of Choice: The Troubled German-Finnish Coalition in World War II.* Casemate: Philadelphia & Newbury.

Luraghi, R., 2001: "The origins of total war – from the French Revolution to the American Civil War". (*The Total War: The Total Defence, 1789–2000.* Editorial Board: Iko P., Ericson L. & Åselius, G., 62–67). Stockholm.

MacDonald, C., 1998: *The Killing of Reinhard Heydrich: The SS "Butcher of Prague".* Da Capo Press.

Maiolo, J.A., 2008: "Anglo-Soviet Naval Armaments Diplomacy before the Second World War". (*English Historical Review,* Vol. CXXIII, No. 2, April 2008, 351–378),

Manne, R., 1981: "The Foreign Office and the Failure of the Anglo-Soviet Rapprochement". (*Journal of Contemporary History*, Vol. 16, No. 4, Oct., 1981, 725–755).

Mark, E., 1998: "Venona's Source 19 and the `Trident´ Conference of 1943: Diplomacy or Espionage?" (*Intelligence and National Security*, Volume 13, Summer 1998, Number 2, 1–31).

Martel, Lieutenant-General Sir G., 1949: *An Outspoken Soldier: His Views and Memoirs.* London.

Mastny, V., 1979: *Russia's Road to the Cold War: Diplomacy, Warfare, and the Politics of Communism, 1941–1945.* New York.

Matloff, M., 1959: *Strategic Planning for Coalition Warfare, 1943–1944.* Washington, DC.

Matloff, M., 1960: "The 90-Division Gamble". (*Command Decisions*, Gen. Ed. Greenfield, K.R., 365–381.) Washington.

Matloff, M., 2003: *United States Army in World War II, The War Department, Strategic Planning for Coalition Warfare 1943–1944.* Washington, DC.

Matloff, M., & Snell, E. M., 1953: *Strategic Planning for Coalition Warfare, 1941–1942.* Washington, DC.

Mayer, S. L., (ed.) 1977: *The Russian War Machine 1917–1945.* London.

McCarthy, P. & Syron, M., 2002: *Panzerkrieg: the rise and fall of Hitler's Tank Division.* London: Constable.

McKercher, B. J. C., 2008: "National Security and Imperial Defence: British Grand Strategy and Appeasement, 1930–1939". (*Diplomacy and Statecraft* 3/4, Sep 2008, 391–442).

McNeill, W. H., 1982/1983: *The Pursuit of Power: Technology, Armed Force, and Society Since A.D. 1000.* Oxford: Oxford University Press.

Miller, N., 1989: *Spying for America: the Hidden History of U.S. Intelligence.* New York.

Milward, A. S., 1965: *The German Economy at War.* London.

Merritt Miner, S., 2014: *Stalin's Holy War: Religion, Nationalism, and Alliance Politics, 1941–1945.* North Carolina: University of North Carolina Press.

Mommsen, W. J. & Kettenacker, L., (eds.), 1983: *The Fascist Challenge and the Policy of Appeasement.* Suffolk.

Murphy, D., 2005: *What Stalin Knew: The Enigma of Barbarossa.* New Haven, Connecticut: Yale University Press.

Müller, R.-D., & Ueberschär, G. R., 1997: *Hitler's War in the East 1941–45: A Critical Assessment.* Oxford: Oxford University Press.

Nadeau, R., 1990: *Stalin, Churchill, and Roosevelt Divide Europe.* New York.

Neilson, K., 1993: "`Pursued by a Bear´: British Estimates of Soviet Military Strength and Anglo-Soviet Relations, 1922–1939". (*Canadian Journal of History*, Volume XXVIII, August 1943, 189–221).

Neilson, K., 2006: *Britain, Soviet Russia and the Collapse of the Versailles Order, 1919–1939.* Cambridge, UK: Cambridge University Press.

Neilson, K. & Otte T. G., 2009: *The Permanent Under-Secretary for Foreign Affairs, 1854–1946.* London and New York: Routledge.

Nekrich, A. M., 1993: *Pariahs, Partners, Predators: German-Soviet Relations, 1922–1941.* New York: Columbia University Press.

Niedhart, G., 1983: "British attitudes and policies towards the Soviet Union and international communism, 1933–9". (*The Fascist Challenge and the Policy of Appeasement.* Eds. Mommsen, W. J. & Kettenacker, L., 286–296). London.

Nove, A., 1992: *An Economic History of the USSR 1917–1991*. London.

Osborn, P. R., 2000: *Operation Pike: Britain versus the Soviet Union, 1939–1941*. Westport, Connecticut.

Overy, R. J., 1994: *War and Economy in the Third Reich*. Oxford: Oxford University Press.

Overy, R. J., 1996: *Why the Allies Won*. London.

Overy, R., 2004: *The Dictators: Hitler's Germany and Stalin's Russia*. London: Allen Lane.

Parker, R. A. C., 1993: *Chamberlain and Appeasement: British Policy and the Coming of the SecondWorld War*. Basingstoke: Macmillan Press Ltd.

Persico, J. E., 2001: *Roosevelt's Secret War: FDR and World War II Espionage*. New York.

Pogue, F. C., 1966: *George C. Marshall: Ordeal and Hope 1939–1942*. New York.

Pogue, F. C., 1973: *George C. Marshall: Organizer of Victory 1943–1945*. New York.

Pollard, S., 1992: *Peaceful Conquest: the Industrialization of Europe 1760–1970*. Oxford: Oxford University Press.

Poulsen, H., 1982: *Bra Böckers Världshistoria: Band 13, Från Krig till Krig, 1914–1945*. Höganäs.

Raack, R. C., 1995: *Stalin's Drive to the West, 1938–1945*. Stanford, California.

Ragsdale, H., 2006: *The Soviets, the Munich Crisis, and the Coming of World War II*. Cambridge: Cambridge University Press.

Ranki, G., 1993: *The Economics of the Second World War*. Wien.

Reese, R. R., 1996: *Stalin's Reluctant Soldiers: A Social History of the Red Army, 1925–1941*. Lawrence: University Press of Kansas.

Reese, R. R., 2000: *The Soviet Military Experience: A History of the Red Army, 1917–1991*. London.

Reese, R. R., 2008: "Lessons of the Winter War: A Study in the Military Effectiveness of the Red Army, 1939–1940". (*The Journal of Military History*, Vol. 72, No. 3, July 2008, 825–852).

Reese, R. R., 2011: *Why Stalin's Soldiers Fought: The Red Army's Military Effectiveness in World War II*. Kansas: University Press of Kansas.

Robbins, K., 1984: *The First World War: The Outbreak, Events, and Aftermath*. Oxford: Oxford University Press.

Roberts, G., 1995: *The Soviet Union and the Origins of the Second World War: Russo-German Relations and the Road to War, 1933–1941*. Hampshire and London.

Rottman, G. L., 2007: *Soviet Rifleman 1941–45*. Osprey Publishing.

Rohwer, J. & Monakov, M. S., 2001: *Stalin's Ocean-Going Fleet: Soviet Naval Strategy and Shipbuilding Programmes, 1935–1953*. Routledge.

Salisbury, H. E., 1980: *Östfronten 1941–45*. Värnamo. [English edn: *The Unknown War*. New York, 1978].

Salmaggi, C. & Pallavisini, A., 1997: *Andra Världskriget Dag för Dag på Alla Fronter*. Stockholm.

Samuelson, L., 1996: *Soviet Defence Industry Planning: Tukhachevskii and Military-industrial Mobilisation 1926–1937*. Stockholm.

Samuelson, L., 1999: *Röd Koloss på Larvfötter: Rysslands Ekonomi i Skuggan av 1900-talskrigen*. Stockholm: SNS förlag.

Scott, L. & Jackson P., 2004: "The Study of Intelligence in Theory and Practice", (*Intelligence and National Security*, Vol. 19 No. 2, 2004, 139–169.)

Seaton, A., 1971: *The Russo-German War 1941–45*. London.

Self, R., (ed.), 2006: *The Neville Chamberlain Diary Letters, Volume 4: The Downing Street Years 1934–1940*. London: Ashgate.

Shirer, W. L., 1984: *Det Tredje Rikets Uppgång och Fall: det Nazistiska Tysklands Historia*. Bungay. [English edn: *The Rise and Fall of the Third Reich*. New York, 1960].

Siddiqi, A. A., 2010: *The Red Rockets' Glare: Spaceflight and the Russian Imagination, 1857–1957*. Cambridge: Cambridge University Press.

Smith, B. F., 1983: *The Shadow Warriors: O.S.S. and the Origins of the C.I.A.*. New York.

Smith, B. F., 1992: "Anglo-Soviet intelligence co-operation and the roads to the Cold War". (*British Intelligence, Strategy and the Cold War, 1945–51*. Ed. Aldrich, R.J., 50–64). London.

Smith, B. F., 1996: *Sharing Secrets with Stalin: How the Allies Traded Intelligence, 1941–45*. Kansas: University of Kansas Press.

Smith, W. B., 1950: *My Three Years in Moscow*. Philadelphia and New York.

Steiner, Z. S., 2003: "British Power and Stability: The Historical Record". (*Diplomacy & Statecraft*, Volume 14, Issue 2, 2003, 23–44.)

Steiner, Z. S., 2011: *The Triumph of the Dark: European International History 1933–1939*. Oxford: Oxford University Press.

Strang, G.B., 2006: "John Bull in Search of a Suitable Russia: British Foreign Policy and the

Failure of the Anglo-French–Soviet Alliance Negotiations, 1939". (*Canadian Journal of History* vol. 41, No. 1, 2006, 47–84.)

Strong, Major-General Sir K., 1968: *Intelligence at the Top: The Recollections of an Intelligence Officer*. London.

Taylor, A. J. P., 1974: *History of World War I*. London.

USSBS 1945a: *The United States Strategic Bombing Survey, Overall Report (European War), September 30 1945*. Washington.

USSBS 1945b: *The United States Strategic Bombing Survey: The Effects of Strategic Bombing on the German War Economy, Overall Economic Effects Dvision, October 31 1945*. Washington, DC.

Wagenführ, R., 1963: *Die Deutsche Industrie im Kriege 1939–1945*. Berlin.

Vagts, A., 1967: *The Military Attaché*. Princeton, New Jersey.

Valero, L.A., 2000: "An Impressive Record: The American Joint Intelligence Committee and Estimates of the Soviet Union, 1945–1947". (*Studies in Intelligence*, Summer 2000, No. 9, Unclassified Edition).

Van Evera, S., 2001: *Causes of War: Power and the Roots of Conflict*. Ithaca, NY: Cornell University Press.

Van Dyke, C., 1997: *The Soviet Invasion of Finland, 1939–40*. London.

Van Tuyll, H. P., 1989: *Feeding the Bear: American Aid to the Soviet Union, 1941–1945*. Westport, Connecticut.

Wark, W. K., 1985: *The Ultimate Enemy: British Intelligence and Nazi Germany, 1933–1939*. London.

Watson, D., 2002: "Molotov, the Making of the Grand Alliance and the Second Front 1939–1942". (*Europe-Asia Studies*, Vol. 54, No.1, 2002, 51–85).

Watt, D. C., 1984: "British intelligence and the coming of the Second World War in Europe". (*Knowing One's Enemies: Intelligence Assessment Before the Two World Wars*. Ed. May, E. R., 237–270). New Jersey.

Wegner, B., 1987: "The tottering giant: German perceptions of Soviet military and economic strength in preparation for 'Operation Blau' (1942)". (*Intelligence and International Relations 1900–1945*. Ed. Andrew, C., & Noakes, J., 293–311). Exeter.

Werner, M., 1939: *Military Strength of the Powers*. New York.

Westwood, J. N., 1994: "Transport." (*The Economic Transformation of the Soviet Union 1913–1945*. Davies, R.W., Harrison, M. & Wheatcroft, S.G. (eds.), 158–181). Cambridge: Cambridge University Press.

Wheatcroft, S. G. & Davies, R. W., 1994: "Agriculture". (*The Economic Transformation of the Soviet Union 1913–1945*. Davies, R. W., Harrison, M. & Wheatcroft, S. G. (eds.), 106–130). Cambridge: Cambridge University Press.

White, B. T., 1979: *Tanks and Other A.F.V.s of the Blitzkrieg Era 1939 to 1941*. London.

Whiting, K. R., 1978: "Soviet Aviation and Air Power under Stalin." (*Soviet Aviation and Air Power: A Historical View*. Higham, R. & Kipp, J.W. (ed.), London: Brassey's.

Willmott, H. P., 1992: *The Great Crusade: A New Complete History of the Second World War*. London.

Woodward, L., 1970: *British Foreign Policy in the Second World War. Volume I*. London.

Woodward, L., 1971: *British Foreign Policy in the Second World War. Volume II*. London.

Worley, M., (ed.), 2004: *In Search of Revolution: International Communist Parties in the Third Period*. New York: I. B. Tauris.

Yeaton, I. D., 1976: *Memoirs of Ivan D. Yeaton, USA (Ret.) 1919–1953*. Stanford, California: Hoover Institution on War, Revolution and Peace.

Zabecki, D. T., (ed.), 1999: World War II in Europe: An Encyclopedia. London: Routledge.

Zaloga, S. J. & Grandsen, J., 1984: *Soviet Tanks and Combat Vehicles of World War Two*. London: Arms and Armour Press.

Zaloga, S. J. & Ness, L. S., 2003: *Red Army Handbook, 1939–1945*. Sparkford.

Ziegler, C. E., 2014: "Russian–American relations: From Tsarism to Putin". (*International Politics*, Vol. 51, No. 6, 2014, 671–692.)

Ziemke, E. F., 1968: *Stalingrad to Berlin: the German Defeat in the East*. Washington, DC.

Index

White House (US) 7
White-Russian 57
Whiting, K. R. 107n14
Wilson (of the FO) 239, 293,
  297, 308
Winterton, P. 235, 245, 247n26,
  247n32
womens labour 62–3, 155, 210, 212,
  236–38, 262, 266, 290–1, 308
Woodward, L. 99n98, 109, 114
working class 20

world revolution 21, 59
World War I 2, 13–14, 19–20, 23, 25, 29,
  37, 80, 82, 96n10, 101, 107, 111,
  142n22, 143, 187, 206

Yeaton, I.D. 76, 83–5, 87–9, 93–6, 113,
  118, 121, 134n63, 144, 167, 170, 210–1
Yugoslavia 57, 111

Zhukov, Marshal 107n15
Ziegler, C. E. 20

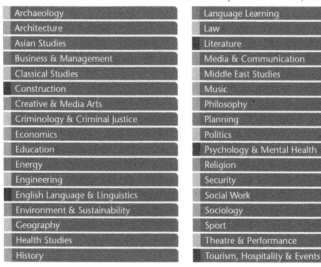

For Product Safety Concerns and Information please contact our EU
representative GPSR@taylorandfrancis.com
Taylor & Francis Verlag GmbH, Kaufingerstraße 24, 80331 München, Germany

www.ingramcontent.com/pod-product-compliance
Ingram Content Group UK Ltd.
Pitfield, Milton Keynes, MK11 3LW, UK
UKHW021020180425
457613UK00020B/1000